Thinking and writing about the past has always been of critical importance to the way that any culture or civilization views itself and its role in the world. In a work which surveys an entire tradition of historical thought and writing across a span of eight hundred years, Tarif Khalidi examines how Arabic-Islamic culture of the pre-modern period viewed the past, how it recorded it, and how it sought to answer the many complex questions associated with the discipline of history. Arguing that this tradition underwent the successive influence of four epistemic 'domes' – *hadith, adab, hikma,* and *siyasa* – the author combines a topical with a chronological method, thus placing the tradition within its broader intellectual context and socio-political environment. In a selection of quotations from historians and scholars, the reader is introduced to some of the principal intellectual texts of Arabic-Islamic culture.

Cambridge Studies in Islamic Civilization

Arabic historical thought
in the classical period

Cambridge Studies in Islamic Civilization

Editorial board
DAVID MORGAN (general editor)
MICHAEL COOK   JOSEF VAN ESS   BARBARA FLEMMING
TARIF KHALIDI   METIN KUNT   W. F. MADELUNG
ROY MOTTAHEDEH   BASIM MUSALLAM

Titles in the series

Arabic historical thought in the classical period

TARIF KHALIDI

American University of Beirut

CAMBRIDGE
UNIVERSITY PRESS

Published by the Press Syndicate of the University of Cambridge
The Pitt Building, Trumpington Street, Cambridge CB2 1RP
40 West 20th Street, New York, NY 10011–4211, USA
10 Stamford Road, Oakleigh, Melbourne 3166, Australia

First published 1994
Reprinted 1995,1996

Printed in Great Britain by Redwood Books, Trowbridge, Wiltshire

A catalogue record for this book is available from the British Library

Library of Congress cataloguing in publication data
Khalidi, Tarif, 1938–
Arabic historical thought in the classical period / Tarif Khalidi.
    p.   cm. – (Cambridge studies in Islamic civilization)
Includes bibliographical references (p.) and index.
ISBN 0 521 46554 0
1. Islamic Empire – Historiography.   2. Historiography – Islamic
Empire.   I. Title.   II. Series.
DS38.16.K445   1994
909′.097671′0072–dc20   93-51021 CIP

ISBN 0 521 46554 0 hardback

For Hani and Raja

But I did not get my picture of the world by satisfying myself of its correctness; nor do I have it because I am satisfied of its correctness. No: it is the inherited background against which I distinguish between true and false.

Ludwig Wittgenstein, *On Certainty*

Contents

Preface

Historians may be informative in either of two very different ways: for what they may or may not tell us about the past or for what they tell us about *thinking* about the past. My own interests have for some years now been centred on this latter aspect of historiography – one which, where Arabic-Islamic culture is concerned, has clearly not received the attention it merits. It also seemed to me, when I began to investigate the historiographic corpus, that historians in general do not concern themselves too much with the theoretical dimensions of their work and that the epistemic canopy under which a historian normally shelters is furnished, generally speaking, by the neighbouring social sciences. The 'data' or 'events' or 'archive' which historians for the most part examine come to them already refracted, most often by other historians. That process of refraction dooms most historical writing to be second-hand but is also of course compounded by the fact that historians are themselves conditioned in their manner of receiving, filtering or transmitting the past.

Accordingly, in attempting to trace the development of historical thought in the Arabic-Islamic tradition, it quickly became apparent that the net must be cast wide, to include not only the historians themselves but the various conceptual frameworks within which they operated. Once these epistemic canopies were determined, it was also important to show how these were, in turn, implanted in social and political developments. But even when all these problems became less obscure, there still remained the daunting obstacle of the size of the historiographic corpus. When the full range of historical writing in classical Arabic-Islamic culture, that is to say from the eighth to the fifteenth centuries – the approximate temporal boundaries of this work – is spread before us, one is confronted with a body of writings in the order of several hundred thousand volumes. Inevitably, one has to select and to hope that such selection will be a 'fair' sample of both the majority of bread-and-butter historians who did not systematically reflect upon the epistemic implications of their work as well as the small minority of historians who did.

Books, once begun, often take on a life of their own, as many novelists at least would confirm. This work, too, tended as it progressed to organize itself a little too neatly for my liking. It is therefore necessary to point out that this division into four dominant epistemic canopies or modes should be qualified in four important respects. In the first place, the succession of these canopies broadly reflects the order of their appearance in time. Thus, *Hadith* cast its shadow over historical writing approximately from the 1st–4th/7th–10th centuries, *Adab* from the 3rd–5th/9th–11th centuries, *Hikma* during the 4th–5th/10th–11th centuries and *Siyasa* from the 6th–9th/12th–15th centuries. But this division does not mean that these canopies were entirely separate from one another. In point of fact, they overlap but with some difference in time of first appearance. Still less can one classify historians rigidly in accordance with this division for it is clear that many historians shelter under more than one canopy. I do not seek to impose such a division artificially upon all historians. Rather, I attempt to determine the epistemic framework within which they operated in order to understand the full range of their diverse historical styles and methods.

In the second place, the dates suggested for the ends of each of these epistemic divisors do not of course mean that the influence of this or that canopy ended in this or that century. They are meant only to delimit the period during which such influence reached its furthest theoretical extent. My ultimate purpose is to show how historical writing evolved in step with the expanding horizons of Arabic-Islamic culture through the attempt to understand the nature and causes of the evolutionary process itself.

In the third place, the historiography of any culture or age is subject not only to dominant currents of thought and belief but also to the dictates of political life in the widest sense of the term. In choosing purely epistemic divisors, it was not at all my intention to ignore or downplay the manner in which the configuration of political structures and events affects the nature and purpose of historical writing. I have therefore attempted throughout this study to show how the sphere of politics helped to shape the historical outlook, the last chapter being the most explicit attempt in this direction. I have also attempted to understand the social background of the historians examined and the development of history as a craft practised by succeeding generations. It was Ibn Khaldun who first recognized that the arts and sciences were not abstract entities but crafts produced by diverse periods of an ever-developing human culture (*'umran*). This connection between the arts and sciences on the one hand and the marketplace on the other is an insight which intellectual history can ignore only at its peril.

In the fourth place, it seemed to me that one important way in which a particular historian or group of historians could be distinguished from another lay in the manner in which their 'inherited background' determined their attitude to truth and falsehood. In suggesting a scheme of four major epistemic canopies or divisors, I hoped to clarify the nature of that background and hence to exemplify the theoretical range of speculation on the meaning and method of history. I have little doubt that other, equally suitable, canopies might be proffered, and do not claim for mine any methodological finality. If mine have any merit, it lies in whatever capacity they may possess to provoke further inquiry into the history of Arabic historical thought.

Accordingly, this study is constructed in two tiers: in each chapter I first examine the epistemic canopy and then turn to the historians who may be said to represent its most obvious indwellers. In my choice of figures to represent both tiers of the analysis, I was guided by no particular principle of selection other than my own estimate of their influence or typicality. However, I was determined to include more quotations from the sources than is perhaps the norm in such studies, partly because I wanted to lend the work an anthological semblance but also because the works of Arabic historians are still very largely inaccessible to non-Arabists.

This work was begun in Oxford and finished in Cambridge. As a Senior Research Associate at St Antony's and with a very generous grant from the Muhammad Salam Educational Fund, I spent an initial year of reading and planning. In Cambridge, I was elected to an Overseas Visiting Scholarship at St John's, which made it possible for me to finish the bulk of the writing. To all these institutions my gratitude is profound. Three people in particular read portions of this work or discussed its basic assumptions: Muhammad Ali Khalidi, Tamima Beyhum Daou and Basim Musallam. The first read chapter 4 and suggested basic changes in structure and argument. The second read chapter 2 and helped to clarify many of its obscurities. The friendship of the third was constantly abused to test out pet arguments or theories. No author could wish for more perspicacious critics. To all three my debt is enormous and my thanks are whole-hearted.

CHAPTER 1

The birth of a tradition

For historians, literary traditions are the most complex of subjects. They do not possess the familiar contours of events. They do not lend themselves easily to classification as to their beginning, middle or end. When speaking of them, historians often use metaphors of transparency like 'atmospheres' or 'climates'. How they come into existence and how they relate to their environment are notoriously difficult problems. The normal tools of the historical trade, all the way from a dictionary to a pair of strong boots, do not seem to work so well when traditions are investigated. Traditions are untidy and the elements that enter into their make-up themselves belong to the debris of earlier traditions. Unlike an event, a tradition is not 'born' but emanates by slow stages from a cultural background. In the case of historical writing, the most relevant part of an environment is frequently an axial text, e.g. Homer for Greek, the Bible for Christian and the Qur'an for Islamic historiography. But these axial texts which inspire and control traditions are in their turn products of a particular consciousness, a particular way of viewing and representing the past.

The tradition of Islamic historical writing emerged from the environment of *jahili* ('lawless' or 'savage') Arabia. This epithet was given to the pre-Islamic period by the Qur'an. It is in itself an important historical judgement on Arabia's past and will be considered in its proper place. However, some two to three centuries before the coming of Islam (*c.* third to sixth centuries AD) *jahili* Arabia had achieved linguistic unity, an impressive and lasting legacy. This unity coincided with the emergence, after centuries of southern domination, of the North as Arabia's centre of political, economic and religious gravity. The North was an arc of commercial and religious towns joining north-western to north-eastern Arabia and curving through southern Syria and southern Iraq. It was in this arc that the North Arabic script and dialect developed and then dominated the Peninsula. This was in effect a reformulation of a very ancient language with deep affinities to the languages of the ancient Near East. The entire Peninsula was turning its face northwards while the civilization of the South became a distant, dimly perceived memory and cherished most of all by tribes claiming southern descent. The South, *Arabia Felix*, well known to the classical world of Greece and Rome, was being superseded in pre-eminence by a northern *Arabia Ferox*, which was to develop its own traditions in a new cultural zone. The devastation of the imperial wars of the Near East reverberated throughout the Peninsula, especially during the sixth century. Cities of the northern arc like Mecca, Yathrib (later Medina) and Hira and regions like Bahrayn and Yamama in the north east benefited commercially from nearby wars, while an intensification of missionary activity by Christianity and Judaism first brought turmoil to the moribund South and then began to disturb the traditional modes of thought and life throughout the Peninsula.

But the new *Arabia Ferox* of the northern arc was an altogether more turbulent, more militant and tribal region than the South had been. The gap between nomadism and settled life was narrow and easily bridgeable. The towns were relatively new and fragile foundations with few urban institutions and populations that probably did not exceed 10–15,000 inhabitants. Powerful nomadic and semi-nomadic tribal confederacies controlled the major trade routes and had to be appeased or subdued by ambitious towns. The tribes, nomadic or settled, were fiercely independent entities claiming the total allegiance of individual members. The towns were not only emporia of trade but often claimed for their territory a sanctity in the name of a local idol. *Arabia Ferox* was a region whose cultural traditions were largely of local inspiration. In this kind of environment great honour was paid to the arts of war. Eloquence, on the other hand, was a gift of the gods, a cause of wonder and dread.

It was in poetry that this eloquence was most typically manifested. From the last three centuries before Islam a substantial corpus of poetry has survived containing a genuine core as well as forgeries dating from early Islamic times. Later Muslim scholars called this poetry the *diwan* of the Arabs, the register of their achievements, their heritage. This is what Ya'qubi (d. c. 284/897), the first historian of world culture in Islam, says about *jahili* poetry:

For the Arabs, poetry took the place of philosophy and most of the sciences. If a tribe produced a skilful poet with striking imagery and the right choice of words, they would bring him to the annual markets and the seasons of pilgrimage. The tribes and clans would gather around listening to his poetry. For the tribe concerned, this was regarded as cause for pride and self-esteem. In fact, the Arabs had nothing to refer to for their opinions or actions except poetry. It was with poetry that they fought; it was poetry they quoted; in it they vied in virtue, through it they exchanged oaths and with it they exerted themselves against each other; in it they were praised or blamed.[1]

[1] Ya'qubi, *Tarikh*, 1:262. There is an important discussion of *jahili* culture as seen in the Byzantine sources in Irfan Shahid, *Byzantium and the Arabs in the Fourth Century* (Washington: Dumbarton Oaks, 1984), pp. 418–62; see especially pp. 444 ff. for the earliest

Jahili poetry, often embedded in stories relating to the lives of the poets, was collated and provided with commentaries in literary anthologies of the 3rd–4th/9th–10th centuries. For the student of the Islamic view of history, this poetic corpus is of tantalizing interest. There is no history here in any formal sense of the term. Nonetheless, the past is recreated or evoked in a manner which the Qur'an was later to brand as *jahili*, even while it shared with this poetry certain terms to describe and situate that past. This poetry speaks to us in many moods: epic or lyrical, tragic, ironic or nostalgic. Where the past is concerned, two terms, *Dahr* ('Time') and *al-Manaya* ('the Dooms') are especially relevant to historical sensibility:

> They defeated us but one day, without escape
> The *Dahr* will overturn this, ever-changing.

> They cared not what *Dahr* would bring thereafter
> Nor what evil things catch men unawares.

> I saw the *Manaya* strike blindly, whom they hit
> They slay, whom they miss lives on to weak old age.
> He who dreads the ropes of *Manaya*, they snare him
> Even were he to ascend the ropes of heaven on a ladder.
> And he who does not defend his fort with his weapons
> His fort will be destroyed; and he who does not oppress
> Will himself be oppressed.

> But when the arrows of the *Manaya* are aimed at a man
> Neither medicine nor magic avails him.[2]

The *Dahr*, endless, ever-changing Time, brings both good and bad fortune to men. It is an abstract, faceless power against which there is no appeal. To each man the *Dahr* allots a fate, but this fate remains forever obscure:

> I know what today brings and, before it, yesterday
> But I am blind in my knowledge of tomorrow.[3]

One instrument of *Dahr* is the *Manaya*. Like the *Moirai* of ancient Greece, the *Manaya* are feminine plural, armed with arrows or ropes and lying in wait to trap or strike down the unwary. Railing against them is a legitimate, indeed laudable gesture of manliness but fruitless all the same. Where future time is unknowable, past time holds no moral lessons. Only the vivid present is significant: the pleasures and glories of life and nature to which so much *jahili* poetry is devoted:

references to *jahili* 'odes'. On the rise of historiographic traditions in general, see the stimulating remarks of Paul Veyne, *Writing History* (Middletown, Conn.: Wesleyan University Press, 1984), chapter 5.

[2] M. A. Jad al-Mawla *et al.*, *Ayyam al-'Arab fi'l Jahiliyya* (Cairo, 1942), pp. 164, 227, 276, 317.

[3] *Ayyam al-'Arab*, p. 276.

> Roast flesh, the glow of fiery wine
> to speed on camel fleet and sure
> As thy soul lists to urge her on
> through all the hollow's breadth and length;
> White women statue-like that trail
> rich robes of price with golden hem,
> Wealth, easy lot, no dread of ill
> to hear the lute's complaining string –
> These are Life's joys. For man is set
> the prey of Time, and Time is change.[4]

A past recollected in grief and a future anticipated with dread is a common symmetry in *jahili* poetry. Youth is always recalled in sorrow: this is the judgement of the early Islamic grammarian Abu 'Amr ibn al-'Ala' (d. *c.* 154/770): 'The Arabs mourned nothing so much as youth – and they did not do it justice!'[5] Thus, in an environment without code of law or ethical system, *jahili* poetry supplied much of the wisdom and the practical moral standards handed down from one generation to the next. The function of history was often served by the model lives of the poets themselves: the wandering prince in search of his kingdom, the low-born rebel defying his tribe, the noble warrior preferring death to dishonour, the stern avenger of murdered kinsmen, the old sage reflecting on a turbulent life, the brigand, the libertine, the unwavering friend and so forth. Where the poet glorifies his tribe rather than himself his boasting verses are frequently an explicit or veiled reminder to his enemies of the historical prowess of the tribe, a recounting of its battle-days of glory expressed not so much in all their Homeric details but in allusions to victories presumed to be well-known to the audience. Strewn among the verses are lines of proverbial wisdom meant to drive home the moral of the poem: the unforeseen change from prosperity to wretchedness, the fleeting character of life and friendships, the exhilaration of love and wine, pride in lordly generosity or even-handed revenge. In *jahili* poetry, narration defers to moralizing, an attitude not without relevance to the later Qur'anic conception of history.

But the influence exerted by *jahili* poetry was not solely confined to the way in which the past was recollected or expressed. In structure and manner of transmission also, *jahili* poetry was to exercise an important influence on the earliest modes of Islamic historical writing. A typical *jahili* ode (*qasida*) was structurally a collection of single lines, each being of two hemistichs and constituting an autonomous unit within a larger whole, more or less coherent in theme or mood. The first hemistich, the *sadr* of a line, was completed by the second, the *'ajuz*. The similarity between

---

[4] C. J. Lyall, *Translations of Ancient Arabian Poetry* (London, 1930), p. 64.
[5] Ibn Qutayba, *'Uyun al-Akhbar*, 4:50.

the individual line of verse and the individual report (*khabar*) of early historiography as well as the analogy between the *sadr/'ajuz* of each line and the *isnad/matn* (transmission chain/substance) of each report is significant when one is examining early historiographic forms.[6] Where transmission is concerned, the early poets usually had their own transmitters (*rawiya*) who acted as the guarantors of the authenticity of the poetry. In this area too the poem with its *rawiya* is similar to the historical report with its transmitter. The *jahili rawiya* is in reality the ancestor of the Muslim historian. Later Muslim literature was to spin out the lives of some of these *rawiya*s and story tellers (*qussas*) into hundreds of years, as if to bridge the gap between the cradle of the culture and its vigorous youth, the *jahili riwaya* and the Islamic *khabar*.

In addition to poetry, there was the well-known Arabian tribal preoccupation with genealogy (*nasab*) which was to flourish as an independent science especially in Arab Islam. Where the tribe was the basic social and political unit, genealogy was essential to the determination of individual or collective status. Which tribe is related to which was for centuries before and after Islam the very fabric of political life. Paraphrasing Aristotle, one might say that an Arabian without *nasab* was either above humanity or below it. Although the Qur'an and the preaching of Muhammad called for the strict equality of the believers and certain prophetic sayings restricting inquiry into genealogies gained wide currency, *nasab* was too deeply ingrained not only in a certain way of life but also in a certain delineation of reality. Abu Bakr, we are told, was the Prophet's genealogist, advising him on the structure of tribal alliances. We may infer that Abu Bakr was in this respect simply a representative of a long line of *jahili* genealogists who believed that their heroic traditions preserved the memory of real heroes and actual events. These genealogies were sometimes incompatible especially when they sprang from different parts of Arabia and detailed the *nasab* of various eponymous founders of tribes, clans or dynasties. The 'correction' of confusion in these genealogies was to be one of the primary tasks of early-Islamic genealogy. Nevertheless, genealogy betrayed a consciousness of common origins among the tribes of the Peninsula as well as an attempt to link these origins to those of nearby nations.

Strictly speaking, however, prose is the normal vehicle of history. When we come to pre-Islamic prose, the problems we face are intricate and very old. Here, once again, is the opinion of Abu 'Amr ibn al-'Ala':

What has come down to you from the sayings of the Arabs is only the smallest portion. Had it survived in bulk, much knowledge and poetry would have reached you.[7]

---

[6] Josef Horovitz, 'The Earliest Biographies of the Prophet and Their Authors', *Islamic Culture*, 2 (1928), p. 24, note 3. This is a subject which deserves further investigation.

[7] Ibn al-Anbari, *Nuzhat al-Alibba'*, p. 17.

Or the more explicit view of ʿAbd al-Samad ibn al-Fadl al-Raqashi, a poet of the mid-second/eighth century:

> The Arabs produced more good prose than good verse. But hardly a tenth of the prose has been preserved and hardly a tenth of the verse has been lost.[8]

In other words, the loss of what was believed to have been the bulk of *jahili* prose was bemoaned before Islam was two centuries old. In the Qur'an, there are numerous references to books, writing, tomes, writing tablets, records, codices and so forth, but the context suggests their association either with divine ordinances and revelations or with formal documents, and not with literature in the broad sense of the term. In what, then, is this prose supposed to have consisted?

The views of second/eighth century Muslim men of letters are in point of fact all we have on this subject. There are the wise sayings of various sages, fragments of rhymed prose from the mouths of soothsayers, the tribal lore in which *jahili* poetry is embedded and a corpus of Biblical, Mesopotamian and Yemeni antiquities. Taken together, this material provided the bulk of information on the pre-Islamic period in early-Islamic historical and literary works. Although Islamic scholars undoubtedly recast this material, much of it must have been the common and undifferentiated property of the *rawiyas* and *qussas* of Arabia who continued to supply this lore for centuries after the coming of Islam:

> You ordered me [writes the famous philologist al-Asmaʿi (d. 213/828) to his patron] to collect what has reached me of the reports of ancient Arab kings . . . I found it a difficult task to accomplish fully because of the paucity of information . . . I travelled widely among the tribes, searching out the transmitters of reports and keepers of ancient histories until I extracted all the stories of the genealogists and learnt the tales related by old men regarding their ancestors.[9]

The Arabian tribal lore, the so-called Battle-days of the Arabs (*Ayyam al-ʿArab*) and the Biblical and Near-Eastern antiquities (*Isra'iliyyat*) are the two largest collections of prose narratives reputedly dating from pre-Islamic times. The *Ayyam*, as transmitted for example by Abu ʿUbayda Maʿmar ibn al-Muthanna (d. 209/824), bear clear signs of the editorial activity of their transmitter. A typical Battle-day begins with a raid by a single hero or a small band who carry away camels or horses. Rape is often committed and women frequently reveal the identity of the raiders. An angry confrontation follows which then leads to the battle itself. The confrontations often include proverbial sayings while the battles are preceded or followed by verses full of blood and threats and generally inferior in merit to the *jahili* odes. Neither date nor duration is ever specified. A stylized, deliberately archaic mood is created and then enhanced by the

---

[8] Jahiz, *Bayan*, 1:287; cf. Ibn Rashiq, *ʿUmda*, 1:8.
[9] Asmaʿi, *Tarikh al-ʿArab Qabl al-Islam*, p. 3.

transmitter's commentary on the verses which is normally confined to short linguistic glosses.[10]

The *Isra'iliyyat* and Yemeni antiquities are commonly associated with the name of Wahb ibn Munabbih (d. 114/732), a Yemenite of Persian descent and usually regarded as the most influential propagator of this material. Biblical, quasi-biblical and apocryphal tales together with Yemenite historical lore here also betray the art of their Islamic editor to the point where it is impossible to arrive at any meaningful judgement on the form or substance of pre-Islamic prose.[11]

What are we to conclude, then, from this summary of the *jahili* Arabian environment in which the Qur'anic view of history was to emerge? One may speak of an environment in which there is a sharpening in the perception of a common identity, probably as a reaction to increased political, religious and cultural penetration of the Peninsula by its neighbours. A string of new northern towns was becoming proudly aware of its place in the affairs of a much larger world and a roving band of poets was of crucial importance in spreading a common language and ethos among the tribes. Their poetry, in which narrative defers to moralizing and the lines of verse are neatly bisected, bears a significant resemblance to Qur'anic narrative and early-Islamic historiographic forms. But there is little in this epic scene framed by the causality of the *Dahr* which prepares us for the arrival of the Qur'an. Later Islamic scholars were to return repeatedly to the history and culture of *jahili* Arabia, and some would make of it the natural recipient of revelation, citing such things as the purity of its desert air or the rarefied souls of its inhabitants. *Jahili* culture, however, was essentially pre-literate. Written texts were almost exclusively religious or legal in nature. Although a common memory was slowly crystallizing, this is not by itself a sufficient precondition for the appearance of historical thought and writing. The Arabs learnt a new history when they acquired a new religion.

An axial text is an end and a beginning, a *summa* and a programme for thought and action, a theory and its paradigms. The Qur'an is a source of ideas on history as well as a repository of historical examples offered for contemplation. It proclaims its own appearance *as a book* as an event of seismic proportions:

If We sent down this Qur'an upon a mountain, you would see it humbled, shattered by the fear of God (Qur'an 59:21).

[10] The *Ayyam* of Abu 'Ubayda are conveniently assembled in 'Adil J. al-Bayati, *Kitab Ayyam al-'Arab Qabl al-Islam* (Beirut: 'Alam al-Kutub, 1987).
[11] On Wahb, see A. A. Duri, *The Rise of Historical Writing Among the Arabs*, ed. and trans. Lawrence I. Conrad (Princeton: Princeton University Press, 1983), chapter 3, with updated bibliography on Wahb by the editor-translator. See also R. G. Khoury, *Wahb b. Munabbih* (Wiesbaden: Otto Harrassowitz, 1972).

A document of its own time and place but also from, and of eternity, the Qur'an repeatedly contrasts human affairs with divine providence, calling itself 'the Distinguisher' and 'the Reminder'. Two time-scales with two corresponding orders of existence are set forth side by side, the one earthly and illusory, the other divine and real. The Qur'an's 'descent' (*nuzul*) into the world is an occurrence which intersects the earthly order, creating a new historical era where truth (*al-haqq*) can finally and manifestly be distinguished from falsehood (*al-batil*). To explore these issues in more detail, three principal Qur'anic themes may be singled out: the vision of history, the narratives of prophets and kings and views of man and his place in the order of things.

1. *The vision of history*
The Qur'anic vision of history rests upon a certain conception of time and space and a certain style to express that conception. Islam and history are coeval: 'It was God who called you Muslims from days of old'. (22:78) A community, or *umma*, of God has from time immemorial been the 'witnesses' of God on earth, 'calling to virtue and forbidding evil'. It is a 'community of the centre' (*ummatan wasatan*) which came into being with Adam. Thereafter, the Qur'an pans over a landscape where time is less a chronology than a continuum, where Abraham, Moses, Jesus and Muhammad are all described in a grammatical tense which one is tempted to call the eternal present. The whole of history is present at once to God. Within this design, events are arranged in clusters, repetitive in form. This means that a Qur'anic *qissa*, or tale, is closer in function and meaning to a 'case in point', an 'affair' or even a 'parable' than it is to a story or narrative. 'As when [*idh*] Joseph . . .' or 'as when Moses . . .' is a common introductory phrase to the Qur'anic *qasas* (variant of *qissa*), suggesting an extended moral example or paradigm which is often repeated with only minor changes to suit the moral (*'ibra*) at hand. To know God is, among other things, to recognize the overwhelming evidence of His presence in the past:

Have they not journeyed in the land and seen how those before them met their end? They were stronger than them in might, they cultivated the land and built upon it more than they did. (30:9)

Qasas is contrasted with *asatir*, which are mere fables or legends, false or devoid of moral. 'We relate to you the best of *qasas*' implies a choice, a divinely selected anthology of history based upon the factual accuracy and didactic value of each *qissa*. Where there is doubt or dispute concerning historical figures, the Qur'an corrects the record:

Such was Jesus, son of Mary; this is the truth of the matter concerning which they are in doubt. (29:34)

To warn, to remind, to authenticate the past: these are the primary functions of the *qasas*. They record and illustrate history as seen from the divine point of view, a history moreover whose three modes of past, present and future are run together. History is an on-going plot where God is the ultimate 'schemer':

They scheme and God schemes, and God is the best of schemers. (8:30)

The inscrutable, impersonal *Dahr* of *jahili* Arabia is a mere delusion:

They say: there is nothing but our earthly life. We die, we are born and only the *Dahr* destroys us. But they have no knowledge of this for they are only guessing . . . Say: It is God who gives you life, then makes you die, then restores you to life upon the Day of Resurrection, of which there is no doubt. But most of mankind is ignorant. (45:24–6)

Events acquire their moral significance from their *'aqiba*, or outcome, and this *'aqiba* is at the same time the *'ibra*, or moral, of the narrative, a key-word in later Islamic historiography. To think an event through is to perceive that this is a universe full of God's signs (*ayat*). That other universe of the poets, with its *Dahr* and *Manaya*, is peopled by the ignorant or self-deceived, is indeed the *jahili* universe of doubt and despair.

Of time past, the basic units in the Qur'an are generations (*qurun*) and peoples (*umam*). The time-scale is vast: a day with God is a 'thousand years' or even 'fifty thousand years' by human reckoning (32:5; 70:4). All time is intense, equidistant from God. The *qurun* and *umam* are summoned to mind to show how mankind is repeatedly seduced into paganism, dictatorial kingship and corrupting luxury and the outcome in each case is divine punishment. By sheer dint of repetition, fact becomes parable. Hence all events are ethically charged, all are at once real and allegorical.

2. *Narratives of prophets and kings*

The Qur'anic view of prophecy is an extension of its view of time's eternal presentness. The prophets of the Qur'an are types of moral life. They reveal essentially the same message and their lives follow closely similar patterns. Theirs is the story of the lonely voice crying out against the injustice or indifference of his community and undergoing similar social, political and spiritual crises. Their credibility is always at stake, and turmoil seems to be an inescapable consequence of their mission. The following passages set forth the broad outlines of the history of prophecy:

Mankind was one nation; then God sent the prophets, bearing good tidings and forewarning. With them He sent down Scripture with the truth to judge mankind concerning their differences. And only those to whom Scripture was sent differed concerning it, and this after clear signs had come to them, because of their transgression. And God, by His leave, guided those who believed to the truth concerning which they had differed. (2:213)

Every Nation resolved to seize their prophet and disputed with falsehood in order to refute the truth. Then I seized them, and what a punishment it was! (40:5)

Then We sent Our messengers, one after another. Whenever its messenger came to a nation, they called him a liar. So We caused them to follow one another and made them parables. Away with a people who do not believe! (23:44)

Now that all nations have received prophets, the Qur'an announces the end of the cycle. Prophecy, so to speak, has run its course. The lessons of the past have been amply vindicated. The 'book with the truth' is a summary of God's repeated interference in history, which thereby gains the coherence of a pattern made decisively clear. It is Abraham who first demonstrates the naturalness of belief in God: the stars, the moon and the sun are examined by him and in turn rejected as objects of worship in favour of Him Who created them. (6:75-9) Muhammad 'seals' this belief by revealing the book of God. Between these two epochal figures countless messengers are sent to mankind:

Messengers We have told you of and messengers We have not . . . messengers bearing good tidings and warning, so that mankind might have no argument against God. (4:164-5)

When examined closely, the stories of these messengers are found to be variations on a single theme which, when repeated, often with the same phrases from one prophet to another, creates an impression of one divine revelation frustrated by pride or ignorance, opposed by powerful kings or corrupted by the wilful distortions of disputing schismatics. The obviousness of religious truth as demonstrated by Abraham needs to be reaffirmed over and over: in the Qur'an the messengers argue the case for God in debates with opponents punctuated by the 'he said . . . they said' of polemic and the 'O you who' of rhetoric. The message is distinct and clear (*mubin*) and yet the majority of mankind 'do not understand'. This is what gives the prophetic *qasas* a grim sense of missions unfulfilled and of human insolence rising to challenge the divine call. Hence prophets are always followed by cataclysms in which entire *qurun* and *umam* suddenly vanish, leaving behind the magnificent ruins that are the silent reminders of past grandeur:

There stand their dwellings, empty ruins because of the evil they committed. Here indeed is a sign for a people who understand. (27:52)

The most prominent enemies of the Prophets are the kings, who typify human pride at its peak. At their head stands Fir'awn (Pharaoh), a major Qur'anic figure. His struggle against Moses prefigures the entire history of the relationship between prophets and kings, a theme of recurring importance in Islamic historical thought and writing. Fir'awn is tyrannical, blasphemes before the 'signs of God', fights divine truth with magic and sows discord among the people. He commits the ultimate blasphemy by declaring:

Council, I know of no other god of yours but me. (28:38)

Fir'awn is the Anti-Prophet. His transgressions, writ large, are those of all men of power or wealth who fight the divine mission of unity in submission to God:

When kings enter a city, they ruin it. By them the high are brought low. (27:34)

3. *Views of man*
Qur'anic man is forgetful, inconstant, impatient, fickle, frivolous:

Those who believe and then disbelieve and then believe and then disbelieve and then increase in unbelief – God is not ready to forgive them nor to guide them to the true way (4:137)

Man needs God not only for salvation but also for psychological harmony and social peace. Without belief, man is unstable, a prey to all the violence and barbarism of the *Jahiliyya*, which is as much a historical era as it is a warped state of mind, the 'original sin' of Qur'anic man. Disasters in history are caused by man abandoning God to run after personal whim and amusement, shadows that are soon dissipated by God's reality. Where man succeeds, it is because of patience and constancy of vision, of loyalty to the divinely rational order of the world and of forsaking the chaotic desires of the self. Man is, as it were, poised between the rationality of the divine dispensation and the haphazard activity of the soul. God is called upon only in misery:

And if We show favour to man, he turns away and withdraws; but if evil touches him, he is loud in prayer. (41:51)

The Qur'an echoes the bustle and din of human society, of mankind buying and selling, arguing, divided into factions, easily swayed by Satan into luxury and vice:

And if We wish to destroy a city, We order the affluent and they transgress therein and the verdict is justly passed against it and We destroy it utterly. (17:16)

Man's life has its seasons:

It is God who created you out of weakness, then appointed after weakness strength and then, after strength, appointed weakness and grey hairs. (30:54)

His progress from conception in the womb to senile old age ends with:

And you see the earth barren but when We send down water upon it, it quivers and swells and puts forth plants from every lovely pair. (22:5)

This serves to link the human cycle with that of nature and to entrench the dense image of all creation eventually 'coming home' to God, the Qur'anic expression for the end of history. Man is both the 'deputy' (*khalifa*) and the 'slave' (*'abd*) of God. The wide chasm between these two attributes creates an extensive range of psychological moods and experiences, with examples drawn from the era of Adam to that of Muhammad. This spectrum of moods is displayed in the existence of a large number of pairs of opposites scattered all over the surface of the Qur'anic text: heavens/earth, male/female, wealth/poverty, brightness/shadow, first/last, right/left, guidance/going astray, certainty/conjecture, believers/hypocrites, ease/difficulty, laughter/weeping and so forth. Human nature seems to be attracted to opposite moral poles, opposite states of understanding, opposite spiritual stations:

God strikes a similitude: a man in whom quarrelling partners share and a man belonging wholly to one man. Are the two equal in likeness? (39:29)

Pulled in various directions and torn between competing desires, mankind is argumentative, prone to factionalism and consists in its majority of ignorant creatures of habit and conformity. Especially in the Medinese chapters of the Qur'an, hypocrisy is singled out for censure, the 'political' sin of the man ostensibly within the *umma* of Muhammad but who is less than wholehearted in his loyalty to its ideals. Compared to such hypocrites, even otherwise erring Jews and Christians are to be preferred since among them also this same mixture of belief and unbelief appears to obtain:

They are not all alike. Some of the People of the Book are a nation upstanding . . . believing in God and the Last Day, bidding to good works and forbidding evil . . . these are of the righteous. (3: 112–14)

To the steadfast believer, a vision of future bliss is repeatedly promised and minutely described. But above all, man is ordered to remember. It is in remembering that faith is acquired and morality is fortified through repeated historical examples. In the Qur'an the relationship between man and God is based on a historical record, a register of deeds and misdeeds which need to be impressed upon memory: 'And remind them of the days of God.' (14:5) These 'days of God', perhaps an echo of the 'days' of *jahili* Arabia, remind mankind of the vicissitudes of life (cf. 3:140), but more pointedly perhaps, of the fact that God *is* time, that the cycle of birth and death, faith and unbelief, glory and decline is circumscribed by God's knowledge and displayed for all to see in His book. Forgetfulness, in contrast, is the beginning of sin:

Our Lord, take us not to task if we forget or go astray. (2:286)

It is a peculiarly Satanic activity to seduce man from the recollection of God into spiritual blindness and oblivion, as if the cosmic struggle between good and evil is fought over man's memory.

'A providential scheme of history had thus been formulated in an environment where no *textual* tradition prepares us for its arrival. While other Mediterranean world views can easily be paired off, with Roman emanating from Greek and Christian from Jewish, the Qur'anic view cannot as easily be so paired. The Qur'anic conception of Islam as a 'community of the centre' places it of course in the midst of the Judeo-Christian tradition. With that tradition, the Qur'an shares a world historical view which European scholarship has thoroughly investigated. With the *jahili* Arabian tradition, it shares less.[12] However, the Qur'anic view of history, while inspired by both traditions, cannot be said to have *emanated* from either. It is, rather, a view which breaks in upon its environment, seeking a *reductio ad unum verbum* (cf. 3:64), a canopy of meanings with which to envelop the significance of history. All cultural and ethnic differences between peoples are submerged in historical abstraction. All unbelievers are *kuffar* just as all believers are *muslimun*. There are no glad tidings of a new man about to be born nor yet the awful tidings of a catastrophe about to engulf the earth but an ever-presentness which infuses past and future at once, obliterating historical signposts. True, the early Meccan verses of the Qur'an are densely apocalyptic, but even these verses are less pronouncements about what is to come soon and more like moral images of the end of the world. If history is the science of particulars, there are hardly any particulars in the Qur'an.

In summary, one might argue that Qur'anic history partakes of two elements. It is both orderly and accidental, rational and chaotic, wholly under the care of God but subject also to the blind violence of the human will. This view of history had a profound effect on the Islamic historical tradition. But, with the possible exception of the apocalyptic material, the Qur'an's impact on historiography was not immediately felt among the early historians, for it was only one among several other, more pressing stimuli to historical thought and writing. We have to wait until the third/ ninth century before we meet historians who grasp fully the historiographical challenge of the Qur'an. Meanwhile other factors, other circumstances were initially more decisive in the formation of this tradition.

The remainder of this chapter will examine briefly the major experiences of the early *umma* and their bearing upon the rise of the tradition of Islamic historical writing in the first fifty years or so of Islamic history.

---

[12] On the Biblical influence see Franz Rosenthal, 'The Influence of the Biblical Tradition on Muslim Historiography' in B. Lewis and P. M. Holt, eds. *Historians of the Middle East* (London: Oxford University Press, 1962) pp. 35–45. P. Crone and M. Cook, *Hagarism* (Cambridge: Cambridge University Press, 1977) and J. Wansbrough, *The Sectarian Milieu* (Oxford: Oxford University Press, 1978) both emphasize the Judaic influence. M. M. Bravmann, *The Spiritual Background of Early Islam* (Leiden: Brill, 1972), stresses the continuities with pre-Islamic Arabia.

When Islamic Arabic scholarship begins in earnest in the early years following the death of the Prophet, it has as baggage, so to speak, both a *jahili* and a Qur'anic manner of interpreting nature, man and time. What the earliest scholars shared in common was an Arabian or Near-Eastern heritage, now overlaid by the Qur'anic text, and all of this accompanied by a radical change in political fortunes. To begin with, many thousands who had accompanied, met or otherwise seen or heard Muhammad were now plunged into a world conquest. Men of humble Arabian origins found themselves ruling the richest provinces of Persia or Byzantium, rapidly becoming the successors of the great emperors of antiquity. The shadow of the Prophet fell across these events and proceeded to lengthen in the eyes of his followers. The earliest social hierarchy among Muslims began to emerge. It was based upon seniority in embracing Islam (*sabiqa*), the determination of which was an open invitation to historical inquiry.

Side by side with the escalating image of the Prophet, there are the escalating fortunes of the Islamic empire. Here, however, great conquests and empire building were mixed with calamitous civil wars. *The painful birth of the early empire was the single most important motive for the emergence of Islamic historiography*. There was plenty of drama and pathos here, of military conquests and religious setbacks. The pious scholars of the early-Islamic communities in Syria, Iraq and Hijaz had many historical examples to hand and strong motives to record them, not least of which was the increased demand for guidance, public and private, historical and normative. Within fifty years or so, these examples could be drawn from across a wide expanse of lands and regions, once parts of inimical empires and now united and allowed to mingle regularly and freely. To these scholars, the life of Muhammad was a total triumph, but the triumph of his *umma* was clearly less than total. There are echoes here of the Qur'anic view, audible 'to anyone who cares to listen and understand'. One might add that this *ambiguity* of significance is a powerful stimulant in the rise of any historiographical tradition.

The tempo of change, and one cannot overemphasize this point, was very rapid. Many fast and radical changes must have been squeezed into the life time of someone, say, like Mu'awiya ibn Abi Sufyan (d. 60/680). Given his crowded life, the reports which make him out to be the first systematic patron of Islamic historiography seem credible. To the fast tempo of dramatic change one must add the very early adoption of a dating system, the *Hijri*, an event of considerable scholarly as well as administrative importance. Among the so-called Abrahamic religions, Islam was the fastest to provide itself with a chronology. With this chronology, the temporal scaffolding of Islamic culture was now in place.

The society in which this first half century of scholarship began was not of course monolithic. In different regions, different relations obtained between conquerors and conquered. In Syria, stability was soon achieved and the two settled down to coexistence, dialogue, occasional worship together and polemics. The conquering group was small and on the whole a mild lot, tending to blur into the background. Prosperity reports from Arabic sources are confirmed by European pilgrims. The rump of the Byzantine bureaucracy was kept on since the early conquerors had practically no state apparatus of their own to impose. A mystique of semi-nomadism surrounded these conquerors: in their own eyes and in the eyes of their beholders they were a people who seemed to belong to two habitats, two worlds. In addition to the mixture of conqueror and conquered there was a mixture of Arab tribes in Syria where there were many small tribal fragments. The pre-Islamic Arab tribes of the periphery of Syria, Ghassan and Lakhm, had no difficulty at all in playing a major role in the politics of the new empire.

In Iraq, on the other hand, society was more easily recognizable as subservient to a conquering caste. The tribes arrived in Iraq in bulk and settled down in their own camp cities as Muslim neighbours but also as Arabian rivals. The bureaucratic structure was rigid and tended to stiffen tribal identity. Riches were made quickly. The large Iraqi craft sector was indigenous and strong, while investment in the rich soil of Babylon brought enormous profits. Large-scale booty and vigorous trade with the East completed the picture. The register of tribes on a war-footing (*diwan*) soon became a kind of who's who of privileged clans deemed worthy of receiving state subsidy (*'ata'*). Here there were more palpable distinctions between conquerors and conquered and among the conquerors themselves. Cities were recent foundations and thus richer and more turbulent than the cities of Syria.

In Hijaz, the twin cities of Mecca and Medina were soon overtaken in importance by their northern sisters, Damascus, Kufa and Basra. After an initial and short period of prosperity, they tended to be watched carefully and perhaps kept deliberately underdeveloped. These two cities became a home of lost causes for the many pretenders to supreme power. Defeated politically and militarily, Mecca and Medina reared their aristocratic heads, becoming at once frivolous (e.g. the singers of Mecca) and austere (the Medinese scholar-notables).

These differences undoubtedly affected the colouring, structure and preoccupations of early-Islamic scholarship, including historical writing. Early-Iraqi literature paid much attention to tribal lore, Hijazi to aristocratic and religious tradition, Syrian to ancient histories. Tribal history, sacred history and 'world' history were in all likelihood the three initial shades of interest that evolved from the preoccupations of the ruling elites of these three societies. There is a slight danger in overrating regional factors since scholarship was undertaken by mobile scholars who cannot often be identified with only one region.[13] In Prophetic and Qur'anic studies especially a pan-Islamic interest is in evidence from the outset and eventually these regional distinctions were no longer valid even for historical writing. In a search for origins, however, these initial differences of nuance should be kept in mind because they illustrate the extent to which early historiography received different stimuli from differing environments. These three areas of historical curiosity came into being under the shadow of *Hadith*, to which we now turn.

[13] Duri's distinction between a *hadith*-oriented Medinese school of historians and a tribal-oriented Iraqi school (see *The Rise of Historical Writing*, chapter 4) has been criticized in Albrecht Noth, *Quellenkritische Studien zu Themen, Formen und Tendenzen fruhislamischer Geschichtsüberlieferung* vol. I (Bonn: Bonner Orientalistische Studien 25, 1973). I argue above that while regional *specialization* may be untenable, the different environments provided different *stimuli* to early-Islamic scholarship.

Noth's work has been translated into English and revised under the title *The Early Arabic Historical Tradition: A Source-Critical Study* (Princeton: Darwin Press, 1993). The work, very influential in other respects, suffers from the lack of any analysis of the larger theoretical issues within which one can assess historical sources, e.g. the definition of historical 'truth' in various periods: this has recently been done for Greek and Roman historiography by A. J. Woodman, *Rhetoric in Classical Historiography* (London: Croom Helm, 1988); see also Ernst Breisach, ed., *Classical Rhetoric and Medieval Historiography* (Kalamazoo: Western Michigan University, 1985), especially the essay by Nancy F. Partner. Noth also makes liberal, even arbitrary, use of the concept of 'topos' but without placing it in any larger theoretical framework, or explaining why a concept originally developed by Erich Auerbach and E. R. Curtius for the aesthetic appraisal of medieval Latin literature is also relevant to the assessment of the facticity of early-Islamic historiography. Belonging to the Noth 'school' but less clear in methodology is Stefan Leder, 'The Literary Use of the *Khabar*: A Basic Form of Historical Writing', in Averil Cameron and Lawrence I. Conrad, eds., *The Byzantine and Early Islamic Near East, I, Problems in the Literary Source Material* (Princeton: Darwin Press, 1992), 277–315.

CHAPTER 2

History and *Hadith*

It was under the general rubric of *Hadith* that the basic religious sciences of Islam, including historical writing, were to develop. In Europe, sustained academic study of *Hadith* began in the middle of the nineteenth century. In the Muslim world, the study of *Hadith* has been continuous and, in the last fifty years or so, has begun to take stock of western scholarship on the subject. Its *origins, mode of transmission* and *authenticity* have all absorbed a long tradition of commentary. The critical examination of these three aspects of *Hadith* carries us into the heart of one of the most intricate problems that a historian can face in connection with a textual source. The *Hadith* for one thing is vast. Its apparent simplicity of structure is deceptive. It has its own ancient critical apparatus in the form of the chain of transmitters (*isnad*) of each individual *hadith* and its own technical vocabulary of transmission (*tahammul al-ʿilm*). Almost from its inception, the *Hadith* literature has carried within itself its own 'antibodies': a streak of scepticism regarding its validity and authenticity as well as many *hadith*s which flatly contradict one another, to the point where many Islamic reformers or leaders have advocated its partial or complete abandonment as a pillar of the *Shariʿa*, the Islamic law of life. Moreover, and within the last half century or so, a lot of early *Hadith* texts have come to light, often necessitating modification or rejection of existing theories or views.

In the long history of *Hadith* and of the various sciences which evolved from it, including historical writing, two ages of intensity may be distinguished: the first in the 3rd–5th/9th–11th centuries, when *Hadith* was classified and edited, and the second in the 8th–9th/14th–15th centuries, when the great Mamluk biographical dictionaries of *Hadith* transmitters and related topics were completed. Only the first age will be discussed here for it was during this period that history and *Hadith* were most intimately connected. But something must first be said about origins.

The word *hadith* is one of a number of Qurʾanic terms which came to constitute the common vocabulary associated with reporting and representing the past. *Hadith* is to be found in the company of such other terms as *khabar, nabaʾ* and *ʿilm*. In the Qurʾan, *hadith* has two basic meanings.

In Meccan verses especially, the *hadith* of Moses or of Pharaoh, for instance, means 'story' or, better still, 'parable'. In Medinese verses, *hadith* tends to mean 'speech' or 'report'. This is already, if correct, an indication of a shift in the function of *hadith* from a private to a more public role of guidance. A *muhaddith* (21:2) is a preacher or reciter. Again, *khabar* and *naba'* occupy approximately the same area of meaning; *khabar* is perhaps closer to *hadith* in its meaning of parable while *naba'* is more often a piece of information, of neutral moral content. The word *'ilm* is still more problematic. In Qur'anic, and particularly Medinese usage, it connotes knowledge or wisdom, especially such as is derived from sacred scriptures, and is therefore often contrasted with *zann*, or guessing, an attribute of the unbelievers. It is a term which serves to highlight the kind of wisdom acquired through reflection upon the moral of Qur'anic narratives: real history as opposed to legend or illusion.[1]

A set of terms was thus provided through which to report and unveil the past. The vocabulary now made available, e.g. *hadith*, *khabar*, *naba'*, *qissa* and so forth, could refer to a variety of events, secular as well as sacred. Early *Hadith* was like a ball of many coloured threads. The material relating to the life and sayings of the Prophet and his Companions was an undifferentiated mass of individual reports of widely differing import and religious gravity. Legal injunctions, ritual, the virtues of individuals or tribes, eschatology, ethical conduct, biographical fragments, the Prophet's expeditions, correct manners, admonitions and homilies were all intertwined.[2] This tallies well with what we know about the loose and interchangeable manner in which many early technical terms were used and indeed with the lack of specialization in public functions throughout the Rashidun and early-Umayyad periods.[3]

But an awareness of history-in-the-making was probably the primary and dominant urge among Islam's earliest scholars:

[Yazid ibn Abi Habib (d. 128/746)] was the *mufti* (jurisconsult) of the people of Egypt of his days. He was a moderate and wise man, the first to establish the primacy of religious knowledge in Egypt and to expound on the licit and the illicit. It is reported that *before this* [my italics] the people of Egypt used to relate *hadith*

---

[1] On *'ilm*, the standard classical treatise is Ibn 'Abd al-Barr (d. 463/1070), *Jami' Bayan al-'Ilm wa Fadlihi*. F. Rosenthal, *Knowledge Triumphant* (Leiden: Brill, 1970) is a recent and exhaustive treatment.

[2] The reader would get a good idea about the contents of early *Hadith* by examining the earliest collections to be found in works like the *Musnad* of Ibn Hanbal or the *Muwatta'* of Malik. On the genesis of *Hadith*, the reader should consult both books as well as the detailed studies of Schacht, Abbott, Sezgin, Azmi, Wansbrough and Juynboll, to name only a few of the more significant modern treatments of this topic.

[3] Such terms as *jizya* and *kharaj* in the sphere of taxation or *sunna*, *sira* and *maghazi* in religious scholarship were used with considerable latitude up to the mid-Umayyad period. Likewise, the early governors had very wide executive, judicial and even legislative powers.

about the incitement to virtue (*targhib*), times of trouble (*fitan*) and cataclysms (*malahim*).[4]

Hadith, the earliest vehicle of Islamic scholarship, came into being and reached maturity very much under the impact of political events and conflicting expectations. The early conquests, the first civil war between ʿAli and Muʿawiya (36/656–40/661) and the second between ʿAbd al-Malik and Ibn al-Zubayr (65/685–73/692) – all these events had a devastating effect on the loyalties and beliefs of early-Islamic society and the *Hadith* echoes the resultant social and economic upheaval:

Time was [says ʿUtba ibn Ghazwan (d. 17/638)] when, as the seventh of seven followers of the Prophet of God, I and my companions had no food but the leaves of trees, to the point where our mouths became ulcerous. I would pick up a garment, tear it in half and share it between me and Saʿd ibn Malik. But today, lo and behold, there is not one of us who has not become governor of some city or another. God forbid that I should be great in my own eyes but small in the sight of God. But then, there has never been a prophecy which time has not in the end transformed into a kingdom. You will indeed experience what governors are really like when we are gone.[5]

The *Hadith* began hesitantly, almost shyly. It had to overcome the reluctance of many early Muslims to tolerate *any* text that seemed to them to threaten the textual finality of the Qur'an or the sense of awe which this inspired. Recorded in both memory and writing from the earliest decades after the death of the Prophet, the *Hadith* rapidly asserted its authority as a repository of the community's early religious and historical experiences. The periods it traversed in its first hundred and fifty years of existence may roughly be described as moving from an initial stage of *collectanea*, simple jottings recorded as heard or remembered, to a second stage when these were put together in a book, to a final stage when the various items were classified according to subject. This corresponds with the transition from a *sahifa*, one or more pages of parchment, to a *kitab* (or *diwan*, an official archive, a significant synonym derived from early bureaucracy) to a *musannaf*, or specialized monograph. At every stage in this evolution,

---

[4] Dhahabi, *Tarajim*, p. 83; cf. the early popularity of the Book of Daniel in Baghdadi, *Taqyid*, pp. 51, 57. See also the report that knowledge of the licit and the illicit reached North Africa only in the days of ʿUmar II, as cited in Ibn ʿIdhari, *Bayan*, 1:48. On the apocalyptic literature, see Lawrence Conrad, 'Apocalyptic Tradition and Early Islamic History', paper presented at the Seminar on Early Islamic Historiography, School of Oriental and African Studies, University of London, 28 January 1985. Conrad argues that much of this literature is as old as the mid-Umayyad period. I would say it is as old as anything else in *Hadith*.

[5] Muslim, *Sahih*, 8:215; cf. also 8:220 for the exchange between ʿAbdullah ibn ʿUmar and a supposedly poor Meccan Emigrant. Quite apart from the historicity of such *hadith*s, they nevertheless typify conditions and states of mind that are very widely documented in the biographies of Companions and Successors (*Sahaba* and *Tabiʿun*).

social and administrative factors and political partisanship were of paramount importance in determining both content and structure. And at every stage also, tension may be noted between the 'writers' and the 'memorizers'. When the evidence is carefully weighed, little doubt remains that a substantial corpus of written *Hadith* existed by at least as early as the first half of the first century AH, while the stage of classified works was in all likelihood reached by the first half of the second century.[6]

When we turn to the mode of transmission of the *Hadith* literature, we encounter even greater complexities than those associated with its origins. We might begin by asking why it took the form it did, that is to say the form of what were predominantly short, i.e. one- to ten-line reports, and what significance this had for their mode of transmission. At issue, to begin with, is a cluster of reasons which may have dictated the concise and fragmentary character of earliest *Hadith* such as the scarcity of writing materials and early suspicion of any non-Qur'anic texts. But there are more complex reasons for the form that *Hadith* took, reasons which have to do with the evolution of religious knowledge in general and which need to be examined in some detail.

In early days, the possession of only a few *hadith*s afforded their possessor a nucleus of early Islamic *'ilm*, that is to say a body of knowledge emanating from Muhammad or his pious Companions to complement the Qur'anic text, particularly in absorbing and digesting the drama of the first fifty years of Islamic history.[7] The transition from this early *sahifa* stage to a stage of greater *control* and *legalization* of the material was

---

[6] To substantiate the arguments of this paragraph would require lengthy documentation. The standard classical treatise on the subject of the origins of recorded *Hadith* is Baghdadi (d. 463/1071), *Taqyid al-'Ilm*, with a valuable introduction by the editor, Yusuf al-'Ishsh. The arguments of N. Abbott, *Studies in Arabic Literary Papyri*, Vol. 2 (Chicago: The University of Chicago Press, 1967) and F. Sezgin, *Geschichte des Arabischen Schrifttums*, Vol. 1 (Leiden: Brill, 1967) regarding the historicity of early *Hadith* are fortified by M. M. Azmi, *Studies in Early Hadith Literature* (Indianapolis: American Trust Publications, 1978). All three address themselves to the scepticism of Schacht in his *The Origins of Muhammadan Jurisprudence* (Oxford: Clarendon Press, 1953) and *An Introduction to Islamic Law* (Oxford: Clarendon Press, 1964). The return to scepticism regarding early origins in the works of J. Wansbrough, especially his *Quranic Studies* (London: Oxford University Press, 1977), seems to run directly counter to the researches of J. Burton, *The Collection of the Qur'an* (Cambridge: Cambridge University Press, 1977). G. H. A. Juynboll, *Muslim Tradition* (Cambridge: Cambridge University Press, 1983) is prepared to grant authenticity to 'at least part of the prophetic traditions'. The debate within the Islamic tradition is partly reflected in M. A. al-Khatib, *Al-Sunna qabl al-Tadwin*, 2nd edn (Beirut: Dar al-Fikr, 1971) as well as in the works of al-'Ishsh and Azmi, cited above. R. S. Humphreys, *Islamic History: A Framework for Inquiry* (Minneapolis: Bibliotheca Islamica, 1986), pp. 68 ff. reviews the literature on the subject of the early historical tradition but his own views are, in many places, questionable. See also the interesting article by Gregor Schoeler, 'Die Frage der schriftlichen oder mündlichen überlieferung der Wissenschaften im frühen Islam', *Der Islam*, 62/2, (1985), 201–30, who argues that the controversy over written versus oral transmission hinges upon an exact definition of the terms 'written' and 'oral'.

[7] Ibn 'Abd al-Barr, *Jami'*, 2:120–33, cites and comments upon numerous reports warning against excess in *Hadith* collection. See also al-Khatib, *Al-Sunna*, pp. 110–11.

accomplished by the end of the first century at the hands of specialists, many of whom were in the service of political causes. The first serious and systematic challenge to the Umayyad caliphate by the Zubayrid counter-caliphate (64/683–73/692) probably coincided with the appearance of the more manageable and more easily disseminated *kitab* which carried more clearly the stamp of its scholarly transmitter:

> We used [says Abu 'Imran al-Jawni (d. 128/746)] to hear about a *sahifa* which contained religious knowledge (*'ilm*) and would visit it repeatedly as a man visits a legal scholar (*faqih*) until the Zubayrids came to us in Basra and had with them a group of *faqih*s.[8]

To meet this challenge, the Umayyads, beginning with 'Abd al-Malik (reigned 65/685–86/705), made a serious and sustained effort to garner as much *Hadith* as possible and then to mobilize their own party of *faqih*s charged with its diffusion. Regarding two of these *faqih*s in particular several oft-quoted reports survive, e.g.,

> We used [says al-Zuhri (d. 124/742)] to dislike the writing down of *'ilm* until forced to do so by these rulers and thus we came to believe that it should not be withheld from any Muslim.
> They were not [says Ibn Sirin (d. 110/728)] in the habit of asking about the *isnad* but when civil war broke out they said 'Mention to us your transmitters'. The people of the community (*ahl al-sunna*) were investigated and their *hadith* was accepted while the heretics (*ahl al-bida'*) were investigated and their *hadith* was rejected.[9]

From this battle of the *faqih*s, not a single *faqih* of the first century can be said to have escaped unscathed. Each and every one of them, *including the masters*, is tainted by an imputation of ignorance or political partisanship or of some moral turpitude, as if they were all dabbling in a commerce of dubious religious validity.[10] In fact the term 'money-changers' (*sayarifa*) came to designate those masters who considered themselves or were held by their disciples to be adept at distinguishing true from false *hadiths*:

---

[8] Baghdadi, *Kifaya*, p. 355 and see also Baladhuri, *Ansab*, 4/1:402 and 407 for early-Zubayrid *fuqaha'*; cf. footnote 4 above for the transition from *hadith* on *fitan* to *hadith* on licit and illicit.

[9] For Zuhri, see Ibn Sa'd, *Tabaqat*, 2:389; see also Ibn 'Abd al-Barr, *Jami'*, 1:76, as well as the reports about Zuhri assembled in H. 'Atwan, *Al-Riwaya al-Tarikhiyya fi Bilad al-Sham fi al-'Asr al-Umawi* (Beirut: Dar al-Jil, 1986), pp. 105–8, and cf. the similar and revealing comments of Ayyub [al-Sakhtiyani, d. 131/748] in Baghdadi, *Kifaya*, p. 240. For Ibn Sirin, see Muslim, *Sahih*, 1:11 and Azmi, *Studies*, pp. 213, 217. Confirmation of growing rigour in *isnad* usage is found in, e.g., Ibn Sa'd, *Tabaqat*, 7:231.

[10] See, e.g., the remark by Yahya ibn Sa'id al-Qattan (d. 198/814) reported in Muslim, *Sahih*, 1:13–14: 'We have not witnessed pious men to be more untruthful in anything than they are in *Hadith*.' Muslim adds the comment that they do so unintentionally. See also the report about the ignorance displayed by the great Malik in Abu Zur'a, *Tarikh*, 1:422, para. 1018, and, further, A. Fischer, 'Neue Auszuge aus ad-Dhahabi und Ibn an-Naggar', *ZDMG* 44 (1890), 418, on Nakha'i's opinion of Sha'bi and Sha'bi's opinion of 'Ikrima.

Al-A'mash [d. 147/764] said: Ibrahim al-Nakha'i [d. 96/715] was a money-changer (*sayrafi*) in *Hadith*. I would hear *hadith*s from some men and then make my way to him and submit what I had heard. I used to visit Zayd ibn Wahb and others like him in *Hadith* once or twice a month, but the man I visited almost daily was Ibrahim.[11]

It was during this same period also, that is, the second half of the first century, that these state- or faction-sponsored lawyers began to introduce new rules into the manner of transmission and then into *isnad* itself. Hitherto, one must assume that in the first, or *sahifa* period, the importance of direct oral transmission was highly prized, and this continued to be so for a slowly decreasing band of purists:

This *'ilm* [says al-Awza'i (d. 157/774)] was a noble thing when it was received and memorized from the mouths of men. But when it came to be in books, it lost its glow and passed on to people who are unworthy of it.[12]

But the propagation of religious knowledge in a manner which would make it available to state or faction use was soon to lead to a situation where the transmission of *texts* without direct oral authorization was more practicable. To compensate for the loss of personal authority in transmission, i.e. the value of having heard or recorded *Hadith* 'from the mouths of men', the *isnad* was applied with increasing rigour. The *isnad* was in reality a chain of *authorities* appended to each *hadith*. It was to become an instrument of control in the hands of master traditionists as they prepared to battle each other's claims or interpretations. The more intense the polemic the more rival masters strove to outwit one another in assembling or authenticating their own, and in casting doubts upon the *isnad* of their opponents. At about the same period when the caliph 'Abd al-Malik ibn Marwan (d. 86/705) was standardizing the imperial coinage, *Hadith* was becoming the basic 'coinage' of Islamic scholarship and the *isnad* an essential aspect of its 'circulation'.

The *isnad*, at least in the highly developed form which it reached in the second Islamic century, was a unique product of Islamic culture.[13] With

---

[11] Ibn Abi Hatim, *Jarh*, 1:17; cf. Ibn Abi Hatim, *Taqdima*, pp. 349–51. There is an interesting antecedent usage of the term 'expert banker' in Origen, in connection with the establishment of the New Testament canon: see E. Hennecke, *New Testament Apocrypha* (London: Lutterworth Press, 1963), 1:54, and the Jesus *agraphon* at 1:88.

[12] Baghdadi, *Taqyid*, p. 64. Important parallels in Jewish and early-Christian literary traditions are found in B. Gerhardsson, *Memory and Manuscript: Oral Tradition and Written Transmission in Rabbinic Judaism and Early Christianity* (Copenhagen: Munksgaard, 1964), especially pp. 123 ff., 196 ff. See also J. Pedersen, *The Arabic Book* (Princeton: Princeton University Press, 1984), chapter 3.

[13] The classical literature on the *isnad* is vast. A modern Muslim view is forcefully set forth in Azmi, *Studies*, chapter 6, who among other things re-examines the theories of Schacht and Robson. The works of Abbott, Sezgin and Juynboll cited above should also be consulted. Oddly enough, only twelve lines are devoted to *isnad* in the new edition of the *Encyclopaedia of Islam*.

time, the *isnad*s came to resemble pyramids of authority, the apex being the substance (*matn*) of the *hadith* in question and the sides and base a slowly increasing company of narrators. Among other effects of this enormous growth in *isnad* was the impulse it gave to the production of books:

The *isnad* has grown long [says Marwan ibn Muhammad (d. 210/825)] and people will have to consult books.[14]

The *isnad* was thus a network of scholarly relationships which came into being, in all likelihood, in the heat of early polemic, its equivalent in the social realm being the principle of *sabiqa* or seniority in embracing Islam, according to which a Muslim found his proper place in the hierarchy of the early community. But other and competing sources of privilege, e.g. tribal aristocracy, were also advanced, and the struggle between these varying concepts of political authority intensified the need for a tightly regulated transmission of authoritative religious knowledge. The *isnad* was particularly suited to both controversy and documentation: to controversy because it forced consideration of what constitutes a man's reputation (e.g. trustworthy/untrustworthy) and to documentation because *isnad* created discrete, self-contained units of knowledge, easily memorized if needed and easily classifiable under separate headings if books or monographs are required. Hence the form that *Hadith* took was bound up with the development of the *isnad* and with the emerging class of scholars who sought to regulate the production of religious scholarship.

As may be expected, the new *isnad* expert was a different type of scholar from the earlier *rawiya* or *qass*, who was, or came to be perceived as, a relic from the days of *jahiliyya*. More often than not, these experts were in government service.[15] They were increasingly called upon by rulers or governors to supply information or deliver learned opinions on specific issues relevant to public policy and this fact contributed both to the appearance of specialized monographs as well as to a new sense of poise and self-confidence among them:

Al-Mahdi said, 'O Abu 'Abdallah, [i.e. Sufyan al-Thawri (d. 161/778)] relate something to the Commander of the Believers which God Almighty might cause him to benefit therefrom.' Sufyan replied, 'If you were to ask me about something of which I have knowledge ['*ilm*], I will inform you.' When al-Mahdi persisted in his request, Sufyan answered, 'I am not a *qass*.'[16]

---

[14] Baghdadi, *Kifaya*, p. 230.
[15] See, e.g., the biographies of some of these early experts in Dhahabi, *Tarajim*, and in Abu Zur'a, *Tarikh*, 1:198 ff.
[16] Ibn Abi Hatim, *Taqdima*, p. 112. Sufyan's antipathy towards *qussas* is confirmed in Ibn Sa'd, *Tabaqat*, 7:281. See also a similar sentiment expressed much earlier by Abu 'Abd al-Rahman al-Sulami (d. 74/693) in Muslim, *Sahih*, 1:15, as well as other reports collected in M. A. al-Khatib, *al-Sunna*, pp. 210–13, and in Juynboll, *Muslim Tradition*, p. 11, note

Much of their expertise was transmitted by correspondence, with each other or with officialdom. The fact that the word *kitab* came to mean both book and letter in the course of the first century underlines the role played by scholarly epistles in the formation of the earliest monographs. A letter writer is more clearly an author than an anthologist, a narrator or an editor. A case in point is a sizeable body of letters from the celebrated jurist al-Awza'i (d. 157/774) to caliphs, high officials and colleagues which is preserved and appears authentic.[17] These letters indicate how a *Hadith* expert was induced through correspondence to focus his materials upon a certain topic in order to make them yield legal or ethical rulings, thus contributing to the growth of specialized authorship. This was the stage of the *musannaf*, or specialized monograph, which, as we have seen above, was reached by the first half of the second Islamic century.

Much, too, has been written about the 'journey in quest of knowledge' (*rihla fi talab al-'ilm*) and about debates between scholars as important aspects of the transmission of early *Hadith*. By establishing a civil service drawn from multi-tribal roots and by rotating its members from one province to another, the Umayyads undoubtedly contributed to the mobility of a class to which religious scholars also belonged. Debates between scholars, on the other hand, were a reflection of the growing polemical skills and diverse political loyalties of *Hadith* scholars in the first century. The sharpening of differences tended to the creation of scholarly factions led by masters the integrity of whose teaching was controlled by a 'licensing act' (*ijaza*) through which the material was transmitted and a 'following' (*ashab*) of the master established:

I heard Sa'id ibn 'Abd al-'Aziz [d. 167/783] reproving the followers of al-Awza'i and saying, 'Why do you not meet together? Why do you not review [your religious knowledge] together?'[18]

In general, these *Hadith* scholars of the first hundred and fifty years did not believe that they were creating a new science but simply preserving

7 (where Sulami's remarks need to be considered) and p. 162. See also the comments on *qussas* in R. G. Khoury, 'Un écrit inédit attribué à Wahb b. Munabbih', *Al-Machriq*, 64 (1970), 600–4; G. H. A. Juynboll, 'On the Origins of Arabic Prose' in G. H. A. Juynboll, ed., *Studies on the First Century of Islamic Society* (Carbondale: Southern Illinois University Press, 1982), pp. 165–7 and Khalil 'Athamina, 'Al-Qasas: Its Emergence, Religious Origin and its Socio-political Impact on Early Muslim Society', *Studia Islamica*, 76 (1992), 53–74. The Umayyad 'Abd al-Malik seems to have separated the office of judge (*qadi*) from that of preacher (*qass*): see Abu Zur'a, *Tarikh*, 1:200, paras 146–8.
17 See Ibn Abi Hatim, *Taqdima*, pp. 187–202, and Fazari, *Siyar*, pp. 125–30. Baghdadi, *Kifaya*, pp. 342–5, details the importance of correspondence between scholars, a subject which merits further investigation.
18 Abu Zur'a, *Tarikh*, 1:361, para. 775. On the evolution of the *ijaza*, the best treatment is still in Sezgin, *GAS*, 1:58 ff. The first few pages of Ibn Qutayba, *Ta'wil Mukhtalif al-Hadith* preserves a vivid record of scholarly debates and the polemical uses of early *Hadith*. On Umayyad bureaucrats in Syria, see Salih Ahmad al-'Ali, 'Muwazzafu Bilad al-Sham fi al-'Ahd al-Umawi', *Al-Abhath*, 19 (1966), 44–79, and, in Iraq, by the same author, *Al-*

for the community a record, normative, didactic or homiletic, of Muhammad and the drama of the early years of the community's history. They
were animated by an essentially conservative spirit which tended to view
the past as a process of steady decline and their own days as inferior in
morality and knowledge to the days of Muhammad and of his four 'rightly
guided' successors. Among the great *Hadith* masters of the mid-second
century, the belief that real scholars are few in number is very common,
as is the apprehension that religious scholarship is being perverted or put
to worldly use by opportunists:

[Sufyan al-Thawri] said, 'We have become a mere merchandise to the people of
this world . . . A man becomes our disciple until, when he is known as such and
transmits our knowledge, he is appointed governor or chamberlain, steward or
tax-collector and says, "Al-Thawri related to me." '[19]

In passing on the wisdom of ancestors these scholars believed that they
were transmitters rather than creators. But the process of transmission
became, as so often in the history of cultures, creation through transmission. Succeeding generations of scholars spoke for their own day and age
for which the pious wisdom of the ancestors had to be newly interpreted.
In the process, the *Hadith* made its own distinctive contribution to Islamic
culture, was indeed the first Islamic science.

The last aspect of *Hadith* that needs to be examined here is the laby-
rinthine problem of its authenticity. At issue is not merely the truth or
falsity of reports about the Prophet and his followers but the history of
Islam itself as recorded and transmitted up to the second or third centuries.
In the last decade or so, some western Islamicists have subjected early-
Islamic tradition to a withering critique, attempting to show that no trust
can be placed in the authenticity of any *Hadith* or *Hadith*-like material
before the third century, all such materials being essentially an imaginative
reconstruction by later generations. The force of this attack has been
blunted somewhat, if only because the advocates of this radical view do
not seem to have won many adherents. More telling is the fact that this
critique seems so far not to have inspired alternative strategies of interpretation as to the origins and evolution of Islamic history or scholarship
in these first two or three, allegedly dark centuries. There are on the other
hand western scholars who, while admitting the authenticity of much of
the early materials, despair of ever being able to devise reliable criteria
which can distinguish genuine from spurious.

There is value of course in advancing hypotheses to explain how the
Hadith was put together by succeeding generations or to classify *Hadith*
into literary types, especially when one is faced by seemingly insurmount-

---

Tanzimat al-Ijtima'iyya wa'l Iqtisadiyya fi'l Basra fi'l Qarn al-Awwal al-Hijri, 2nd edn
(Beirut: Dar al-Tali'a, 1969), p. 122, and *passim*.
[19] Ibn 'Abbad al-Rundi, *Al-Rasa'il al-Sughra*, p. 41.

able internal contradictions. There is value also in employing a control mechanism in the form of other comparable traditions, e.g. Greek or Syriac, to test the veracity of the *Hadith* materials. When one learns to recognize the mythopoeic activity of third-century scholars and to understand that much of this material is meant to edify or to propagate a sectarian viewpoint rather than to inform, one might begin to see the material in a new light. This said, however, the proponents of the view that this material basically came into being two to three centuries after the 'events' reported in it and contains little if any facticity would still need to explain how and why something that must have resembled a massive conspiracy produced not only *Hadith* but also the Qur'anic text itself.

One central issue in this controversy about the authenticity of the *Hadith* materials is the theory that Islamic scholarship passed through two phases, the first oral and the second written. Despite the very detailed arguments advanced against this theory, its supporters still cling manfully to its tatters. If one argues that this scholarship began by being oral in nature and transmission, then one can more easily posit the view that little trust can be placed in its authenticity, although even this view is debatable as we learn more about the oral traditions of various peoples. In point of fact,

[20] We arrive here at the heart of the problem of authenticity. It is a problem which will certainly occupy Islamicists for decades to come, if only because new material is being constantly added to the debate with the publication of several important *Hadith* collections every year. It will not be necessary to substantiate all the arguments advanced in the three paragraphs above: the *Hadith* specialist will be familiar with the issues while the student of the subject would hopefully find the references cited to be of use.

The latest phase in Western orientalist scepticism regarding the authenticity of *Hadith* began some forty years ago with Joseph Schacht, whose works are cited in footnote 6, above. Schacht's scepticism was itself attacked by Abbott and later by Azmi; see also footnote 6. Scepticism was renewed and resupplied with arguments in the works of Wansbrough, Crone and Cook. A view which comes close to despair at ever arriving at a meaningful solution is found, e.g., in Juynboll, *Muslim Tradition*, p. 71. In recent years the non-Muslim scholar who has explored *Hadith* collections most thoroughly is M. J. Kister. His attitude may be characterized as one of cautious acceptance: see, e.g., his 'On "Concessions" and Conduct, A Study in Early Hadith' in G. H. A. Juynboll, ed., *Studies on the First Century of Islamic Society*, pp. 89–107, where he discusses certain first-century customs whose historicity is reflected in *Hadith*.

In his *The Sectarian Milieu: Content and Composition of Islamic Salvation History* (Oxford: Oxford University Press, 1978) John Wansbrough is not directly concerned with the question of authenticity, unlike his earlier *Quranic Studies* which is very sceptical about early-Islamic traditions. His attention is focused rather on what he calls 'morphological constants' derived, via Structuralism, from the Judaeo-Christian tradition. He nowhere explains why he chose to ignore the 'morphological constants' spawned by the vast *Hadith* literature itself, and seems to regard most *Hadith* as the product of recasting by later generations. But scepticism also assumes other forms. In his *Muhammad*, Past Masters Series (Oxford: Oxford University Press, 1983), Michael Cook devotes pages 61–76 to a discussion of sources. Cook not only clings to the old view that postulates an oral first century, despite considerable evidence to the contrary, but seeks also to question the authenticity of reports about the literary activity of early historians, e.g. al-Zuhri. These reports depict Zuhri as being at once a writer and a non-writer of traditions. Therefore, the sources are 'bewilderingly inconsistent', p. 66. An illuminating parallel, however, may be found in the practice of the early Church Fathers, e.g. Origen as recorded in Eusebius,

however, a close reading of the *Hadith* literature would unearth evidence in plenty that written materials existed alongside oral transmission from the very beginning and that respect for prodigies of memory did not necessarily exclude resort to writing. It was argued above that the Umayyad state was probably the major sponsor of the written tradition but this does not mean that the Umayyads ushered in the age of writing. The dilemma that the Umayyads, and indeed the drama of events, created for some scholars was not that they forced them to write down their oral learning but rather that they encouraged, perhaps even pressured, them to make their materials available in written form *to a wider public*. If this situation is kept in mind and close attention is paid to the vocabulary of transmission, many apparently contradictory reports about the same scholar which depict him at one time as a memorizer, at another as a writer would be resolved. A prodigious memory was always a highly prized gift and part of the scholarly image, but this could and did coexist with a willingness to dispense knowledge in written form as private and public need for this increased.[20]

Then again, if these first century materials were doctored *in toto* by later ages, all one can say is that it was a pretty bad doctoring job. The frag-

Historia Ecclesiastica, VI, 35, where Origen consented at last to have his lectures recorded in writing though he had never before agreed to this. In the case of both men, consent to writing was the result of a new and vigorous phase in the propagation of the religious message.

But what do we really need to do before we can tackle the problem of the authenticity of *Hadith*? We must first of all recognize the fact that we are dealing with a scripto-oral tradition. Therefore the question of authenticity cannot be brushed aside, nor need we despair of ever finding the needles of historicity in a haystack of religious lore. Then again, modern anthropological studies of oral tradition, e.g. Jan Vansina, *Oral Tradition as History* (Madison: The University of Wisconsin Press, 1985) stress the importance of studying traditions in their context, not as they relate to some other tradition which they supposedly 'ape' (e.g. the Judaic in the case of Wansbrough). We have much to learn from such accounts of how traditions originate and spread, and how and why they eventually become specialized. More general studies of tradition also contain material that is of much help to the overall study of *Hadith*, for instance Edward Shils, *Tradition* (Chicago: The University of Chicago Press, 1981) and Jaroslav Pelikan, *The Vindication of Tradition* (New Haven: Yale University Press, 1984). Much may also be learnt from current folklore theory as regards the historicity of orally transmitted narrative, e.g. Richard M. Dorson, *Folklore, Selected Essays* (Bloomington: Indiana University Press, 1972), especially pp. 208–13, and from studies in mythology, e.g. Mircea Eliade, *Myth and Reality* (New York: Harper Colophon Books, 1975), especially chapters 7 and 9. When comparative material is being sought, the net should be cast wide. Thus, the genesis and evolution of attitudes towards a heroic past in the classical Chinese and Greek traditions, both of which were scripto-oral, can illuminate certain aspects of *Hadith*, e.g. the creation or preservation of an ethical ideal couched in historical terms for purposes of unification or central state building; see M. I. Finley, 'Myth, Memory and History', *History and Theory*, 4 (1965), 281–302 and Jean Gates, 'Model Emperors of the Golden Age in Chinese Lore', *Journal of the American Oriental Society*, 56 (1936), 51–76.

In my view, one of the most urgent tasks for researchers in this field is the exhaustive examination of the rise and development of the critical methodologies employed by the *Hadith* scholars themselves. This would certainly throw light on the question of authenticity, where a great deal of modern argument still reflects subjective standards of credibility.

mented, often contradictory state in which these materials are found is perhaps the best proof that they were transmitted with only haphazard and generally recognizable doctoring, of the type and quantity that one may well expect in any similar body of traditions transmitted in both written and oral form. After having allowed for this doctoring (admittedly with the numerous problems raised therein) we still possess a body of materials, daunting in volume and constantly increasing, which needs careful and laborious examination. To determine its authenticity, one ought to apply to it the usual rules of evidence and, especially where *Hadith* is concerned, the juxtaposition of text and historical context, despite the dilemma created by the fact that the context itself is furnished by *Hadith*. One must also bear in mind that one is dealing with material which is remarkably self-critical. Thus, for example, one of the most prestigious collections of early *Hadith*, the *sahifa* called *Al-Sadiqa* (the truthful), ascribed to 'Abdullah ibn 'Amr ibn al-'As (d. 65/684), was challenged as early as the first century by certain scholars:

Al-Mughira [ibn Miqsam (d. 136/753)] attached no value to the *hadith* of Salim ibn Abi al-Ja'd (d. 98/716), the *hadith* of Khilas (d. end of first century) or the *sahifa* of 'Abdullah ibn 'Amr. Al-Mughira said, "Abdullah ibn 'Amr had a *sahifa* called *Al-Sadiqa* and I would not want to possess it even if it cost two *fils*."[21]

Lastly, and in seeking to classify *Hadith* by genre, topos, trope or any other model derived from literary theory prior to determining authenticity, one must remember that the *Hadith* has its *own* thematic classification scheme, e.g. into *sunna, sira, targhib, tarhib* and so forth, which should form the basis for any other classificatory model one may care to adopt. The exploration of these terms and the delineation of their respective areas of meaning in various periods of the history of *Hadith* is a task which, if properly fulfilled, would greatly enhance our understanding of the conceptual structure of the diverse materials from which the *Hadith* was composed.

From *Hadith* to history

Somewhat like Molière's M. Jourdain, cultures often practise history before they are conscious of its parameters as a special discipline or craft. The incubation period may be either long or short, depending largely upon how quickly a society acquires distinct social and political parameters. Concurrently, the past as image-building frequently precedes the past as 'neutral' information; it becomes easier for specialists to wield and more interpretable as it becomes more charged ideologically. Built into *Hadith* from the start, as we have seen above, was the urge to put a certain image into a certain kind of record. We have also argued that this urge, this

---

[21] Ibn Qutayba, *Ta'wil Mukhtalif al-Hadith*, pp. 53–4.

proto-historical consciousness was at first less impressed by the over-arching historical lessons of the Qur'an, and more by the drama of events, especially the early conquests and civil wars – what Ibn Khaldun would later call the 'amazement' (*dhuhul*) of early Muslims. As the Umayyads in their middle period (*c.* 685–724) acquired the stability needed to settle down to serious state formation, specialization on a wide spectrum of activities became more evident. In large measure, specialization was the result of two processes: greater differentiation of social and economic functions associated with new or rejuvenated cities reasserting mastery over their hinterlands, and greater institutionalization of power by both the Umayyad state and its internal rivals.[22]

Accordingly, as the *Hadith* moved into this new middle Umayyad period, important structural changes began to occur in its content and form. Hitherto, *fitan* and *malahim*, i.e. the apocalyptic mood, was in all likelihood the prevailing manner in which the early Muslims interpreted their present, that is to say the present in terms of an onrushing future.[23] But a state which has just suppressed its enemies and consolidated its vast international dominions seeks the vision of a legitimizing past rather than that of an apocalyptic future. The elaboration of this vision had become the specialty of jurists. The apocalyptic literature of earlier days together with its chief purveyors, the *qussas*, became suspect:

'Asim [ibn Bahdala, d. 127/744] said, 'We used when young to visit Abu 'Abd al-Rahman al-Sulami [d. 74/693] who would say to us, "Do not keep the company of the *qussas* except for Abu al-Ahwas".'[24]

The *fitan* and *malahim* were not to disappear. They were to provide a powerful stimulus to the rise of 'world' historiography, and especially when *Adab* (Belles-Lettres) began to affect historical writing in the third/ninth century. The jurists, meanwhile, turned their attention to the life of Muhammad and his military exploits, the *Sira* and *Maghazi* genre. *Here*, so to speak, was the historical parallel, and not the Book of Daniel.

The new historical mood was characterized by the systematic collection of reports of the Prophet and his age, at first with minimal linguistic or

---

[22] Instructive parallels drawn from African societies as regards the relationship between political centralization (including a system of clientship) and historiography are to be found in Jan Vansina, *Oral Tradition: A Study in Historical Methodology* (London: RKP, 1965), pp. 166–9.

[23] See footnote 4 above. The *fitan* and *malahim* genre may well have been encouraged in the early-Islamic milieu by Jews and Christians who saw in the Islamic conquests a fulfilment of their own millenarian expectations. *Their* Hour had come – or at least they had had a taste of it. In this regard, see S. P. Brock, 'Syriac Views of Emergent Islam' in G. H. A. Juynboll, ed., *Studies*, pp. 9–21.

[24] Muslim, *Sahih*, 1:15; see also the attitude adopted by jurists to Wahb ibn Munabbih in R. G. Khoury, *Wahb b. Munabbih* (Wiesbaden: Otto Harrassowitz, 1972), p. 311, and A. Fischer, 'Neue Auszuge . . .' *ZDMG*, 44 (1890), 419 for the hostile view of *malahim* expressed by Ahmad ibn Hanbal.

historical commentary and later with more obvious signs of editorial activity. It may therefore be appropriate at this juncture to recall and elaborate the three-fold division of themes or historiographical shades of interest suggested at the end of the last chapter, namely, sacred history, tribal history and 'world' history. Each was to spawn its own sub-divisions: the *Sira* and *Maghazi* of sacred history, the *Ayyam* (battle-days) and *Ansab* (genealogies) of tribal history and the *Qisas al-Anbiya'* (tales of the prophets) of 'world' history. In turn, these sub-divisions also radiated their own branches, for example the *Futuh* (conquests) reports were a natural extension of the *Maghazi* literature, the *Ansab* applied rigour in the delineation of the new Islamic aristocracy while the *Qisas al-Anbiya'* supplied pre-Islamic materials with chronology and system. How all these themes unfolded in detail is a problem which one may not be able to answer but it is clear that what we have is a mass of interlocking materials which is becoming progressively more circumscribed and less tangled as we move into Islam's second century. Each theme will now be examined in turn.

Sacred history

The formalization of sacred history, i.e. the *Sira* and *Maghazi* of the Prophet, may be examined in the work of 'Urwa ibn al-Zubayr (d. 94/712) and his student al-Zuhri (d. 124/742). They were both from Quraysh and thus aristocrats in the new Umayyad state for which both men represented the type of scholar best suited to bring order and authoritative interpretation to prophetic and early-Islamic materials. Neither can be described as a propagandist for the Umayyads but both had certainly made their peace with the new regime, as many other influential Qurayshites were to do in the course of the first century. Both men possessed in their own lifetime a widely recognized authority which derived at least in part from their being regarded as experts in law by the imperial family. They are both vivid personalities, single-minded in their pursuit of historical reports and vehement in expressing their opinions on points of juristic or historical dispute. Most important of all, they are *authors* who speak with the historian's voice, and not mere collectors or editors. It is this aspect perhaps which more than any other entitles this teacher-student pair to special attention as we investigate the transition from *Hadith* to history.

Piecing together the fragments of their works found in later writers, the modern scholar can nowadays arrive at fairly reasonable conclusions regarding the scope and nature of their achievement. 'Urwa seems to have attached himself closely to his maternal aunt, 'A'isha (d. 58/678), the Prophet's favourité and most important wife, and after her death gained enormously in stature from being the expert on her *hadith*. 'Urwa must first of all be regarded as the founder of the Zubayrid school of jurists who as we saw above displaced the earlier solitary masters with their unsystematic collections.[25] He is frequently depicted in our sources as an interrogator, a man who questioned his informants closely in search of accuracy and then passed authoritative judgements based on wide-ranging knowledge of Qur'anic *tafsir* (exegesis), prophetic lore, poetry and juristic skill.[26] His reports tend to be somewhat short and are often legal in their implications. A widely known body of his writings is his correspondence with the Umayyad caliph 'Abd al-Malik ibn Marwan.[27] It is a good example of the influence of the epistle on the rise of specialized historical monographs.

This correspondence shows 'Urwa as a careful composer of historical narrative. A detailed examination of his letter to the caliph regarding the caravan of Abu Sufyan and the Battle of Badr (2/624), which is one of the longest fragments of his work, reveals the following features:

1 The report is transmitted on 'Urwa's own authority, i.e. it is without *isnad* and suggests that it is based upon a composite account made by 'Urwa. At least half of all surviving fragments from 'Urwa are without *isnad*, hinting at his authority.

2 The narrative is made up of short segments tightly woven together with conjunctions and causal phrases, and furnished with numbers, routes of advance and three references to the verses of the Qur'an that relate to this incident.

3 The dramatic climax of the narrative is the capture of an enemy slave and a comic scene ensues when he reveals to his Muslim captors whatever they wish to hear, being genuinely ignorant of the whereabouts of the caravan. The Prophet intervenes and skilfully extracts the truth, that the man is part of a relieving force, and not of the caravan. The Prophet also gives an accurate estimate of enemy numbers.

4 The conclusion is a precise answer to the caliph's inquiry. The focus is on Abu Sufyan and his group and the battle itself together with its outcome is mentioned in one concluding sentence.

It is not difficult to gauge from this account something of 'Urwa's concern for precision as well as some features of his historical method. With 'Urwa we detect the hand of the legal expert moulding his materials into fairly short and manageable units that allow him to assign precise dates

[25] See footnote 8 above. The starting point for the investigation of this school, which lasted well into the third Islamic century, is Zubayr ibn Bakkar, *Jamharat Nasab Quraysh wa Akhbariha*, 1:32–350, where many members of this family are said to have been either scholars or generous patrons of scholarship and poetry.

[26] 'Urwa's habit of interrogating his informants may be found in Ibn Ishaq, *Sira*, p. 77, para. 96 and p. 212, para. 308; see also Abu Zur'a, *Tarikh*, 1:647, para. 1914.

[27] Tabari, *Tarikh*, 1:1284–8. 'Urwa's correspondence as well as other aspects of his life and work are discussed in Duri, *The Rise of Historical Writing*, pp. 76–95, with updated bibliography on 'Urwa by the editor-translator of this work. M. M. A'zami has collected 'Urwa's *Maghazi* and provided them with an introduction under the title *Maghazi Rasul Allah li 'Urwa ibn al-Zubayr* (Riyad: Maktab al-Tarbiya al-'Arabi, 1401/1981).

and exact Qur'anic parallels to the events reported. His precision may
also be seen in his lists of names of participants in various incidents in the
life of the Prophet. Such lists had political as well as fiscal importance in
the new Umayyad state as it strove to create uniformity in governmental
routine. His own critical comments or glosses on the material he transmits
are very few in number but the sources preserve occasional reports in
which 'Urwa expresses forthright opinions on such things as the dating of
various incidents in the Prophet's life and shows himself to be something
of a poet.[28] The material dealing with the early caliphs does not seem to
possess the same structure or authority and may even be spurious. It serves
in any case to underline the fact that 'Urwa was a specialist primarily in
the life of the Prophet, to which he devoted his juristic and historical skills.

'Urwa's student, Zuhri, seems from early times to have been intimately
associated with his master. There are even suspiciously similar incidents
in their lives: both, for example, are insulted in the presence of caliphs
and both are reprimanded for alleged anti-Alid remarks. But the scope
and content of Zuhri's work, more voluminous and more recoverable than
that of 'Urwa, reveals the same authoritative voice of a historian not
merely transmitting but also judging his materials.[29] Here is a more than
usually detailed example of Zuhri's authorial activity:

Zuhri said, 'I was informed by (*akhbarani*) Sa'id ibn al-Musayyab, 'Urwa ibn
al-Zubayr, 'Alqama ibn Waqqas and 'Ubaydullah ibn 'Abdullah ibn 'Utba ibn
Mas'ud about the *hadith* of 'A'isha, wife of the Prophet, when the liars said what
they said about her and God declared her innocent. All of them related to me
part of this *hadith*, some of them being more mindful of it than others and more
sound in preserving a record of it. I myself took care to preserve from each inform-

[28] Ibn Ishaq, *Sira*, p. 197, para. 283: 'Urwa elucidates to Zuhri an incident connected with
the emigration to Abyssinia. Ibn Sa'd, *Tabaqat*, 2:180: 'Urwa specifies that he was present
when a report was transmitted about the Prophet's last pilgrimage. Baladhuri, *Ansab*,
3:17: 'Urwa comments on a report from the Meccan period by saying that Islam was then
still preached in secret. Abu Zur'a, *Tarikh*, 1:144–6, paras. 4–5: 'Urwa corrects a date in
the Prophet's life by tracing the error to a poet. Tabari, *Tarikh*, 1:1243: 'Urwa suspends
judgement on the Prophet's early living quarters in Medina by stating that he had heard
two different versions. Tabari, *Tarikh*, 1:1654: 'Urwa states emphatically that the Prophet
remained no longer than half a month in Mecca after its conquest. For his lists, see A'zami,
Maghazi Rasul Allah, pp. 121–2, 126, 127–60 and *passim*. For Umayyad attempts to create
uniformity in governmental practice, see the interesting reports in Abu Zur'a, *Tarikh*,
1:202, para. 156 and 1:351, para. 723.
[29] Similar incidents in the lives of 'Urwa and Zuhri may be found in Abu Hilal al-'Askari,
Sina'atayn, p. 17, and in Dhahabi, *Tarajim*, pp. 72–3 and cf. Baladhuri, *Ansab*, 5:370–1.
Zuhri studies are likely to expand in the future as more early texts come to light containing
his materials, most recently in al-San'ani, *Musannaf* and Abu Zur'a, *Tarikh*. Modern
scholarship on Zuhri began with the works of Duri and Abbott, often cited above. Most
recently, H. 'Atwan, *al-Riwaya al-Tarikhiyya*, pp. 105–202 has collected and classified
many Zuhri reports, performing a valuable service to any scholar who wishes to analyse
these reports.

ant the *hadith* he related to me, with some parts of their *hadith* confirming other parts. This is what they related.'[30]

It is in this and similar comments that one begins to glimpse the critical editorializing of Islam's earliest historians. Zuhri is of course still the *Hadith* scholar. But in creating composite accounts out of discrete narrative and in exercising upon them certain formal norms of testing their accuracy, i.e. norms that had to do essentially with his opinion of the memory and methodical competence of his informants, Zuhri was preparing the ground for the emergence of a new style of historical narrative.

Like his teacher, 'Urwa, Zuhri was known for his interrogatory style and his assiduous cultivation of informants. He seems to have acquired his scholarly reputation in his early youth and with it a self-confidence that remained with him for the rest of his life:

I have been travelling from Hijaz to Syria and from Syria to Hijaz for forty-five years and have not come across a single *hadith* that was new to me.[31]

His relations with the Umayyad court were more intimate than those of 'Urwa. He was advisor to several caliphs and governors and was a tutor to Umayyad princes. This elevated position may well explain the authority that his historical materials carry since approximately one-third of these materials have no *isnad* even though he is said by some later scholars to have been the first to lay down the rules of *isnad*. We possess a considerable body of reports relating to his life and his views on various topics but the materials he transmitted do not carry many more critical comments or glosses than those found in 'Urwa. It is clear however that the attempt to transform scattered information into connected and organized narrative was now being achieved.

Zuhri's historical reports have a polished structure. They have distinct beginnings and endings. A final comment frequently 'wraps up' the report, either bringing it up to date or drawing its moral or giving it a literary ending or deducing its legal significance or quoting a Qur'anic verse as a conclusion. The speeches he reproduces are stylized and well-structured polemics. His terse judgements on historical points of dispute are accepted without question by later writers who incorporate his materials into their works.[32] But perhaps most indicative of Zuhri's historical interests is his concern to establish 'firsts': the first person to do this or that or the 'great-

---

[30] Ibn Hanbal, *Musnad*, 6:194.

[31] Abu Zur'a, *Tarikh*, 1:409, para. 948. For Zuhri as interrogator, see Ibn Sa'd, *Tabaqat*, 2:389 and Dhahabi, *Tarajim*, p. 69.

[32] The Zuhri materials preserved in Ibn Sa'd are the easiest to consult for structure and style: see references in 'Atwan, *Riwaya*, p. 123, note 10 and Duri, *Bahth*, pp. 143–51. See also the precious fragment from a formal report by Zuhri on taxation in Abu 'Ubayd, *Amwal*, p. 231.

est' event up to a particular time. This interest in historical signposts has its parallels in other historiographical traditions, e.g. the Greek.[33] In both cases it indicates a growing awareness of progress in both moral and political life. In Zuhri's case one might add that this interest coincided with the many 'firsts' that the Umayyad empire itself was experiencing, momentous events which carried it from under the shadow of the timeless Qur'anic vision of history and into the more time-bound realities of empire building. Thus the Qur'anic verses most often commented upon by Zuhri are those that allude to the Prophet's political activities rather than to the abstract *umam* and *qurun* of the larger Qur'anic scheme of world history.

Therefore, in selecting 'Urwa and Zuhri as two prominent examples of the transition from *Hadith* to history, one might argue that their importance lies not so much in their selection or choice of materials but in the consciousness displayed in their works of a history being made by a community and arranged in accurate sequence to serve as moral and legal precedents. The transition from *Hadith* to history is the transition from providential to communal history, from the overwhelming and monumental Qur'anic time to the sequential listing, dating and recording of individual actions performed by members of a community that was beginning to realize the merit of its progress in time. Who performed what action and when were not points of pedantic dispute but signs of the coming into being of a time scheme which strove to historicize early Islam and to use it to establish hierarchies of moral or social seniority or prestige.

Muhammad ibn Ishaq (d. 151/761)

The work of 'Urwa and Zuhri and of other less renowned contemporaries was consummated by Muhammad ibn Ishaq, a figure styled 'Prince of *muhaddiths*' or even 'Commander of the Believers in *Hadith*' by men of his own generation.[34] He is of pivotal importance in the transition from *Hadith* to history and his life and achievements have been scrutinized for a millennium or more by Muslims and for about a century by western orientalists. In more recent years, Muslim scholars have unearthed and edited portions of the Ibn Ishaq materials which approximate more closely than ever to his original work, thus facilitating the examination of the work's basic structure.[35]

---

[33] For Zuhri's interest in 'firsts' see, e.g., Ibn Sa'd, *Tabaqat*, 1:241, 251, 381, 430; Abu Zur'a, *Tarikh*, 1:575, para. 1604; Waqidi, *Maghazi*, p. 358; Baladhuri, *Ansab*, 1:455, 458, 470, 471, 528, 543; Abu 'Ubayd, *Amwal*, p. 19; Duri, *Bahth*, p. 148. For parallels with Greek historiography, see Arnaldo Momigliano, *Essays in Ancient and Modern Historiography* (Oxford: Basil Blackwell, 1977), p. 194.

[34] Baghdadi, *Tarikh*, 1:214–33, *passim*.

[35] I am referring primarily to the two *Siras* published by Suhayl Zakkar (Beirut: Dar al-Fikr, 1978) and Muhammad Hamidullah (Rabat: Ma'had al-Dirasat wa'l Abhath li'l

Ibn Ishaq's major work goes by many titles. It has been known as the Book of the Genesis of Creation (*Bad' al-khalq*; also *al-Mubtada'*) and of the Life of Muhammad (*Sira*) and his Military Exploits (*Maghazi*). It is often called simply the *Maghazi* or else the *Sira*. There is no doubt, however, that we are dealing here with one work originally structured in two, possibly three divisions. In the earlier part, one finds material that aims to organize prophetic history in a historical continuum within the non-historical (or perhaps meta-historical) framework provided by the Qur'an. In the other two divisions, the same continuum is imposed upon the life of Muhammad. Within half a century of its appearance, the work was edited, or perhaps bowdlerized, by Ibn Hisham (d. 208/834) but the numerous passages or phrases excised can now be more fully recovered than hitherto, thanks to recent discoveries of manuscripts of the original work.

What made this work possible and what is its originality? To answer the first question, one must recreate the transitional period between the Umayyads and the Abbasids as it related to Ibn Ishaq's work. One notes, to begin with, a certain hardening of attitudes during the late-Umayyad caliphate. An 'official' party of scholars had made their peace with the ruling dynasty, helping to confer legitimacy and orthodoxy upon the Umayyad system. This in turn had bred, as we have seen above, pockets of counter-orthodoxy. As Umayyad power declined, scholarly polemics became more deeply charged with political undertones.[36] 'Urwa and Zuhri had each in his own way contributed to the formation of the official orthodoxy of the community by providing the necessary historical scaffolding for the life of Muhammad. Ibn Ishaq was a major beneficiary of their work but his age was more revolutionary than theirs, as the enemies of the Umayyads began to sharpen their ideological weapons.

One way of countering the prevailing orthodoxy was for disgruntled scholars like Ibn Ishaq to challenge its view of history by appealing to a wider, and specifically prophetic, vision of legitimacy. To show how the world began and then to place the life and deeds of Muhammad within that larger perspective was to measure power and legitimacy against prophetic standards as opposed to their being founded upon communal consensus. This may also be related to the fact that the Abbasid revolution failed to satisfy general expectations; hence the emphasis on the role of Muhammad in prophetic history as the fulfilment of God's promises to mankind. With Ibn Ishaq we have reached the stage where the Qur'anic view of history in its larger, moral sense begins to be examined, following an earlier period

Ta'rib, 1976) and of the *Tarikh* of Abu Zur'a, often quoted above. The preface by Hamid-ullah to his edition of the *Sira* has a useful introduction to the life and works of Ibn Ishaq.

[36] A good example of such political undertones in the field of theology is analysed in J. van Ess, 'Early Development of *Kalam*' in G. H. A. Juynboll, ed., *Studies on the First Century of Islamic Society*, pp. 109–23.

when, as argued in Chapter One above, attention had been focused on Muhammad's immediate period as it related to state and community building. Ibn Ishaq's emigration from Medina to the more ancient world of Iraq, Egypt and the East symbolizes the move from Muhammadan *Hadith* to prophetic history.

Wherein lies his originality? Like most scholars of his day and age, Ibn Ishaq was a controversial figure, even more so than 'Urwa and Zuhri.[37] His mastery of his subject was widely acknowledged even if the charge of transmitting *hadith*s with defective *isnad*s (*tadlis*) was also made against him. He had received materials directly from Zuhri and indirectly from 'Urwa and his own work is made up of essentially the same discrete units of individual *hadith*s, varying in length, although they tend to be more substantial in size. Like them, too, there is in Ibn Ishaq a large corpus of *hadith*s related only by him, a display of the authority he commanded. And, finally, like them also, Ibn Ishaq helped to suppress the messianic-apocalyptic mood through which events had often been filtered in earlier periods.

The reader of Ibn Ishaq detects the voice of the historian beginning to speak and not merely that of the transmitter, however authoritative. Personal comments and reflections come to the fore and the *hadith*s, in the traditional sense of reports with their *isnad*, are now used as evidence to support such reflections. Typical is the following:

When the time came for revelation to descend upon the Prophet of God, he was already a believer in God and in what was to be revealed to him. He was, moreover, fully prepared to act accordingly and to suffer for his faith what God had imposed upon him, both the pleasure and displeasure of mankind. Prophecy imposes heavy burdens and responsibilities which can only be shouldered by prophets of authority and courage, with the aid and blessing of God. This is because of what prophets meet with from people and what God-ordained events may befall them.

These are of course Ibn Ishaq's own reflections on the history of prophecy. But right next to these reflections, Ibn Ishaq appends a *hadith* transmitted from Wahb ibn Munabbih:

I heard Ibn Munabbih in the mosque of Mina when he was asked about the Prophet Jonah. Wahb said, 'Jonah was a pious servant of God but he was an impatient man. When the burdens of prophecy – and prophecy is burdensome – were imposed upon him he cracked under the heavy strain. Jonah threw off this burden and fled.'

In these and similar passages,[38] Ibn Ishaq handles *hadith*s not as ends in themselves but as illustrations. The main building-blocks of his narrative are made up of these reflective passages which help to tie the work

[37] Ibn Ishaq was accused of being a Qadarite as well as a pro-Shi'i. What exactly these terms meant at the turn of the first century AH is a difficult question. But they certainly imply an attitude of opposition on the part of Ibn Ishaq towards the ruling Umayyads.
[38] Ibn Ishaq, *Sira*, p. 111, paras. 153–4. For other examples, see *Sira*, p. 57, paras. 54–5.

together, making it more decidedly a *book*, a work of individual authorship rather than a body of transmitted materials.

Characteristic also of Ibn Ishaq's style and pronounced literary interests
is a large body of verse which he uses to dramatize events. Audiences of
his day were accustomed to accounts of men both acting and reciting
poetry. Although the authenticity of this verse has been questioned by
Muslim scholars since very early days, the role it plays in Ibn Ishaq's work
is a sign of his attention to the literary polish of his narrative. In tandem
with this is a much broader concern, as exemplified by the first part of
the work, with Yemenite, Biblical and legendary materials. Among other
things, this enables Ibn Ishaq to project an image of Muhammad as sharing
many of the miraculous or supernatural attributes of earlier prophets,
including, for instance, miracles of loaves or of gold multiplying, and temptation stories like the following, related from ʿAli ibn Abi Talib:

> I heard the Prophet of God say, 'I never desired women as the people of the
> *Jahiliyya* used to do except on two nights, on both of which God Almighty granted
> me chastity. One night I was with some Meccan youths herding our families' sheep
> and said to my companion, 'Will you look after my sheep while I enter Mecca and
> spend the night there as youths are in the habit of doing?' He agreed so I went
> into Mecca and in the very first house I came to I heard the music of drums and
> pipes. I asked what the occasion was and was told that a wedding was taking place.
> So I sat and waited. God made me deaf to the music and I awoke when the sunlight
> touched me and returned to my companion. He asked, 'What did you do?' 'I did
> nothing,' I replied, and related what I had experienced. [Exactly the same experi-
> ence takes place on another night and the Prophet continues:] 'I never desired or
> returned to the same sort of act thereafter and then God Almighty dignified me
> with His prophecy.'[39]

If in such stories Ibn Ishaq touched upon the sensitivities or credulity of
his audience, he was not prepared to excise, like his piety-minded editor
Ibn Hisham, many stories whose bold, embarrassing character lend the
life of Muhammad an earthier and thus perhaps more credible aspect.
The following account relates to the period when 'signs' of the coming of
Muhammad began to appear:

> A certain clan of the Ansar would relate what they heard from the Jews regarding
> the mention of the Prophet of God. They relate that the first such sign to occur
> in Medina before the mission of Muhammad began was that a woman called Fatima
> . . . a prostitute of the *Jahiliyya*, had a companion. She would relate that whenever
> he entered her house, he would break in upon her and whoever was with her.
> One day he came in and fell against the wall, not acting in his usual manner. When
> she asked him what the matter was he replied, 'A prophet has been sent forbidding
> fornication.'[40]

---

[39] Ibn Ishaq, *Sira*, p. 58, para. 57. For miracles of gold or loaves multiplying, see *Sira*, p.
71, para. 70 and p. 126, para. 189, some of them being echoes of the miracles of Jesus.
[40] Ibn Ishaq, *Sira*, p. 92, para. 122. Other accounts of the same nature, omitted of course
by Ibn Hisham, may be found in *Sira*, p. 21, para. 26 and p. 217, para. 319.

Such stories must have scandalized men of the following century like Ibn Hisham or Ahmad ibn Hanbal. But so also did some of Ibn Ishaq's methods of collecting information. He was criticized, for example, for having Jewish informants and for his cavalier use of *isnad*. In both cases Ibn Ishaq was in fact helping to move *Hadith* in the direction of wider historical perspectives and of connected, more interpretative historical narrative. The range of his scholarly interests may be gauged from his frequent lexical, exegetical, geographical and anthropological comments, as in the following passages:

> The name of the Abyssinian Negus was Mashama which in Arabic is 'Atiyya. The Negus is in fact the title of their kings as you might say Kisra or Herakles.
>
> At that time [i.e. the period of the Prophet's grandfather] the land between al-Sham and al-Hijaz was desert.
>
> Quraysh and other Arabs of the *Jahiliyya* would, when in earnest prayer, break into *saj'* and recite poetry.
>
> The Arabs of the *Jahiliyya* were illiterate, having no books to study, knowing nothing of prophetic covenants and ignorant of paradise, hell or resurrection except for what they heard from the People of the Book. But they preserved nothing of this in their hearts and it had no effect on their behaviour.[41]

Numerous also are his explications of the historical circumstances attending various passages in the Qur'an, these glosses eventually becoming a major source for later Qur'anic exegetes. This branch of knowledge, later called 'circumstances of revelation' (*asbab al-nuzul*) had already come to constitute an important segment of the work of *muhaddith*-historians like 'Urwa and Zuhri. In Ibn Ishaq, however, such explications tend to be fuller, but also more guarded where doubt seems necessary, and more ready to challenge the old masters:

> They allege that 'Umar ibn al-Khattab recited the following verses after his conversion . . . Others say that the verses were recited by Abu Talib. God knows best who recited them.
>
> It is said that these Christians were from Najran, but God knows best. It is also said that the Qur'anic verses . . . were revealed on their account, but God knows best.
>
> 'Urwa said, 'It was 'Uthman ibn 'Affan who addressed the Abyssinian Negus' . . . Ibn Ishaq said, 'This is not so but it was Ja'far ibn Abi Talib who addressed him.'[42]

Ibn Ishaq's use of the *isnad* and other issues having to do with his informants have been the object of attention of Muslim and western orientalist scholars. One must first recall that Ibn Ishaq antedated the great debate about the *isnad*, to be discussed below, which was to flare up in the half century after his death. No strict rules of *isnad* usage had evolved

---

[41] Ibn Ishaq, *Sira*, p. 201, paras. 292–3; p. 4, para. 6; p. 6, para. 12; p. 62, para. 61.
[42] Ibn Ishaq, *Sira*, p. 193, para. 278; p. 199, para. 287; p. 199, paras. 284–5.

in his days. Ibn Ishaq quoted *isnad*s in full, and also used collective *isnad*. But he also often quoted 'a trustworthy informant', 'a man of good memory', 'an old man in Mecca some forty or more years ago', 'some scholars', 'one of my companions', 'I asked Zuhri'. Alongside this inconsistence in *isnad* usage there is Ibn Ishaq's frequent interest in specifying dates and years authoritatively. This, together with the careful chronological structure of his narrative, suggests that Ibn Ishaq was prepared to accept other criteria of veracity besides that of personal witness, the backbone of *isnad*. The inclusion of non-Muslim informants, mainly Christian and Jewish, is of course tacit acknowledgment of the expertise of these communities in pre-Islamic history in general and in Biblical history in particular. This was to become a source of great enrichment for later Muslim historiography.[43]

Ibn Ishaq's ultimate achievement rests upon the degree to which he was able to integrate Muhammad's life into the history and hagiography of Near-Eastern prophecy and to arrange that life sequentially by subordinating *Hadith* to interpretation and chronology. But the image of Muhammad which passes through his filter is still one which retains credibility and humanity. We are not yet in the days when Muhammad is cast in an infallible or supernatural mould:

> The Prophet of God was frequently subject, when in Mecca, to the evil eye, before revelation descended upon him. Khadija his wife would use the services of an old Meccan woman who would employ the necessary magical spells to protect him. When the Qur'an descended upon him and he still suffered from the evil eye, Khadija asked him, 'Prophet of God, shall I send for that old woman to perform her spells?' He replied, 'It is no longer necessary.'
>
> Every day the Prophet received from Sa'd ibn 'Ubada a bowl of food which followed him wherever he went. Whenever the Prophet asked for the hand of a woman, he would offer her the bridal money he wished and add, 'And Sa'd ibn 'Ubada's bowl of food will come to you every morning.'[44]

The *isnad* debate of the third/ninth century

In the period that followed the death of Ibn Ishaq, the *Hadith*, or more specifically its principal criterion of veracity, the *isnad*, became the object of an intense debate. This debate had far-reaching results for the science of *Hadith*, a matter which does not concern us directly here. What does concern us are the implications of the debate for historical writing, especially for the manner in which this debate helped to create for historiography a more sharply focused territory and method.

When the Abbasids came to power as a result of some thirty years of

---

[43] For Ibn Ishaq's use of the *isnad* and related matters, see the bibliography in the Hamidullah edition of the *Sira*.

[44] Ibn Ishaq, *Sira*, p. 104, para. 143; p. 243, para. 376.

intense revolutionary propaganda, they posed as the champions of a restored legitimacy. They were to rule as the guardians of the prophetic heritage, claiming spiritual as well as political authority. But far from rallying the *Umma* around the Prophetic 'House' their first century in power witnessed an intensification of the intellectual ferment of the late-Umayyad period. *Hadith* was deeply, indeed irretrievably embroiled in political–religious polemic. And much of this polemic was historical in nature: Did Muhammad establish clear guidelines regarding the question of political succession? Did Muhammad specifically delegate authority to 'Ali? Were the Umayyads legitimate? These and similar questions entailed historical research. In the course of such research many questions were also raised regarding the criteria of trustworthiness among transmitters, that is to say the criteria of *isnad*. The *isnad* tended to be divided into series and groups and various parties or sects arrogated to themselves those chains of transmission which seemed most unassailable and to attack or otherwise disparage rival chains. Certain chains, for instance, would be labelled 'Shi'i' by opponents and if such chains recurred in the works of someone, he would be liable to the charge of Shi'ism. The case for Shi'ism rested ultimately on the historical determination of a delegation of authority of some sort from Muhammad to 'Ali and/or his uncle 'Abbas, and a large proportion of the historians of the second/eighth and third/ninth centuries who were sympathetic to the Alid cause were indiscriminately called Shi'i. In any event, the case for or against Shi'i claims was a most powerful stimulus of historical *Hadith* and of historical writing in general. The influence of sectarian polemics on the evolution of *isnad* and of historical thought cannot be overemphasized.

One place in which this debate about the *isnad* can best be examined is the introduction to the *Sahih* of Muslim (d. 261/875), one of the most authoritative collections of *Hadith*. The discussion of *isnad* methodology in this introduction is almost certainly the earliest comprehensive analysis of a problem which had become, by Muslim's days, a source of considerable controversy among *Hadith* scholars. By examining Muslim's introduction, one gains insight into the divergent opinions relating to *isnad* among the various Islamic sects, and Muslim himself is writing from a committed standpoint, best described perhaps as proto-Sunni.[45] But one can also detect in this debate changes in the conception of *isnad* which relate directly to the question of the status and style of historical narrative.

Muslim begins by arguing that,

---

[45] Muslim's views on *isnad*, from which the quotations in this section are taken, appear in *Sahih*, 1:2–28. By criticizing the views of Alid, Mu'tazilite and Hanbalite scholars, Muslim was preparing the ground for the consolidation of Sunni *Hadith* and thus of Sunni jurisprudence, or *fiqh*.

The correct delimitation (*dabt*) of a small number of reports and doing so well (*itqan*) is easier for a person to undertake than to deal with too many, especially when done by the ignorant masses (*'awamm*) who lack discrimination . . . Hence, to seek to attain knowledge of a small number of authoritative (*sahih*) reports is more proper than to increase the number of flawed (*saqim*) reports . . . As for the ignorant masses, who are to be distinguished from the select few, men of perception and knowledge, there is no point in them seeking to collect many reports when they are unable to master a few.

He proceeds to explain his own method of selection:

*Hadith*s will not be repeated except in cases where it is necessary to repeat a *hadith* which contains some significant addition or an *isnad* standing next to another for some reason, in which case the significant addition acts like a complete *hadith*. In such cases, it is necessary to repeat in full the *hadith* containing that addition, or else the addition itself may be explained in brief in the body of the *hadith* . . . But we do not intend to repeat *hadith*s in full where there is no need to do so.

He then divides reports (*akhbar*) into three categories and transmitters likewise into three groups. The first category consists of

reports which are more free from blemish and more genuine than others, their transmitters being men of uprightness in *Hadith* and of skilled knowledge . . . while their reports are free from any serious contradictions or grave misrepresentation (*ikhtilaf shadid*; *takhlit fahish*) as may be found among a great number of *Hadith* transmitters.

The second category consists of reports transmitted by men of lesser knowledge although upright in character. The third consists of reports which Muslim calls 'suspect' (*munkar*) because of fabrication or error. For Muslim, a suspect *hadith* is one which,

when compared with other *hadith*s transmitted by upright men is found to be totally or almost totally divergent. If most *hadith*s of a certain transmitter are of this type, his *hadith* is considered unacceptable and unusable . . . For it is the judgement of men of learning and of what we know of their method regarding the status of uniquely transmitted *hadith*s that the man who does so needs to share with trustworthy scholars some of what they have transmitted and to share also their opinions. If he then adds something not to be found in the works of his colleagues, such addition becomes acceptable. As for the man who resorts to relating *Hadith* from such venerable authorities as Zuhri or Hisham ibn 'Urwa whose multitude of scholarly disciples and corpus of well-known writings are all acceptable by common consent, and then dares to relate from them a number of *hadith*s that are unfamiliar to these disciples and does not, moreover, share with them authoritative *Hadith*, then such a man's *Hadith* cannot be accepted.

Suspect *hadith*s circulate because their greatest appeal is to the stupid (*aghbiya'*) and vulgar (*'awamm*) for these people cannot tell sound from unsound *isnad* nor recognize the weaknesses of substance or transmission, nor are they able to shun reports transmitted by the suspect, the renegade or the heretical. Muslim then adds:

Although a report (*khabar*) differs in some respects in its meaning from legal witness (*shahada*), in most other respects they have a common connotation. For the report transmitted by a sinful man (*fasiq*) is unacceptable to scholars just as his witness is inadmissible to all. In this respect, the manner in which Prophetic tradition (*Sunna*) rejects suspect reports is similar to the manner in which the Qur'an rejects the reports of sinners as occurs in the famous tradition from the Prophet: 'He who relates from me a *hadith* that he knows to be a lie is himself a liar.'

But not all suspect *Hadith* is necessarily fabricated. Many *hadith*s according to Muslim circulate through perfectly good intentions as in cases where the transmitter is truthful but not discriminating, like the man who 'receives reports from every comer and goer or the one who unconsciously improves the *isnad* the longer he transmits *Hadith*.' To illustrate his point, Muslim relates at some length stories of early transmitters, most of which sound credible. In general, they reflect the intense heat of *Hadith* and related controversies. Through them we glimpse the scholarly contempt for story-tellers, for extreme Shi'ites, for Mu'tazilites, for simpletons, for well-intentioned people who expatiate upon *hadith*s when carried away by their imagination.

Summing up his argument thus far, Muslim affirms that there is enough authentic *Hadith* around, making it unnecessary to transmit from untrustworthy or non-credible sources, except where a transmitter wishes to show off his extensive knowledge before the ignorant masses.

His final critical comments are reserved for what one might call the rigorists, that is, those who argued that oral transmission (*sama'*) was a prerequisite of sound *Hadith*. Muslim rejects this view. Since the issue cannot often be positively established but remains possible (*'ala al-imkan*), the report is to be accepted if it is known in general (*'ala al-jumla*) that any two parts of the *isnad* chain lived in the same period, even if direct contact between them is unattested. For Muslim, it is only when fabrication is suspected that one must ask for evidence of *sama'* as one means of establishing veracity. Since Muslim does not mention by name any of those who held this rigorist view, one must assume that he is referring to Hanbalite circles whose basic method in *Hadith* arrangement was one by transmitters rather than by topics, thus overemphasizing personal authority.

In sum, the views of Muslim were probably typical of an emerging consensus among scholars as regards the function and methodology of *Hadith* in an age when the mantle of the just state was being claimed by the scholars, judges, notaries-public, witnesses and other legal officials now well structured and well organized in hierarchies. This class was closing its ranks against heretics on the one hand and conservatives on the other. They were beginning to construct an image of an enduring traditional orthodoxy, regarding themselves as the true heirs of Islam's earliest saints and scholars. For them, the *Hadith* was a major purveyor of this image behind which lay a particular and slowly congealing interpretation of the history of Islam and the Muslim community. An intimate knowledge of the orthodox scholars in this field was essential, whence the importance of biographical lists and of biographical literature as a whole. So also was a knowledge of a fixed corpus of *hadith*s, now sufficient in number to constitute the basic mass from which legal and historical expositions could be derived. Significantly, this mass is often called 'reports' (*akhbar*) by Muslim, a term wider in connotation than *Hadith* because it now included not only the prophetic materials *per se* but the historical reports, i.e. the image, in which these materials were embedded. The *isnad* was becoming a science, mastered only by a long-trained elite. It was also acquiring distinct literary conventions: useless repetition was discarded and latitude was allowed in merging reports which dealt with similar subjects. Rigorism was attacked as unnecessary and literalist and, in accepting reports, the criterion of possibility was advanced as a rational alternative to insistence upon direct oral transmission. The arrangement of these reports by topic, e.g. Prayer, Faith, Fasting and so forth, laid down a clear structure, emphasizing the practical use for which such *Hadith* was intended.

In delimiting the scope and criteria of *Hadith*, Muslim and his generation were in fact helping to emancipate historical writing. *Hadith* had reached its quantitative limit and spelled out its method. In the process, however, a field of knowledge broader than *Hadith* had evolved, that of *akhbar* or historical reports in a general sense. A new principle of regulation had also been introduced, the principle of historical possibility. This principle would clearly become of relevance in reports where *isnad* was either unavailable or unnecessary, e.g. in areas such as ancient or Biblical history. In other words, over a wide spectrum of 'reports' the status of *isnad* was not as clearly defined as it had now become for Prophetic *Hadith*. Furthermore, veracity had been linked to consensus to the point where one might speak of a consensual theory of truth to be employed by *Hadith* scholars and historians, as will be discussed below.

For Muslim and his generation of *Hadith* scholars and *Akhbari*s (transmitters of *akhbar*), the lines were being more tightly drawn around their respective territories of interest. The *Hadith* scholars were surrendering the open spaces around them to looser, more ambiguous standards of evidence and to greater latitude in literary form and expression. *Hadith* was removing itself from history: it was becoming a fixed, almost theophanic subject. But all around it the flow of history would continue and need to be written and understood in new ways.

Sacred history continued: the scholarly consensus of Waqidi and Ibn Sa'd

Waqidi (d. 207/823) and Ibn Sa'd (d. 230/845) are a pair, like 'Urwa and Zuhri. But they are distinctly more like historians in the sense that the didactic and homiletic elements in the work of Ibn Ishaq and even more of 'Urwa and Zuhri, are now less explicit and secondary to the establishment of well-attested, consensually accepted facts. The historical record is now to be set straight: the story is still of course sacred at its core but the spirit is less ideological. They have no visible axe to grind. With Waqidi in particular, one now meets a historian whose personality and method are for the first time fully apparent. He is a historian who regards himself as a member of a community of scholars engaged in a common pursuit. That scholarly community is then detailed in the biographical 'generations' of Ibn Sa'd, among the earliest in what was to become a long and distinguished genre of Islamic historiography.

In the year 144/761, a great-grandson of 'Ali ibn abi Talib, a man named 'Abdullah ibn al-Hasan, was implicated in a plot against the Abbasid caliph al-Mansur (d. 158/775). He and his family were carried off to prison in Medina, but two of his sons escaped. The caliph now appeared in Medina on pilgrimage and demanded the surrender of the two sons. Failing to do so, the family was transferred to Kufa and most of its members met a violent death. In the following year, Muhammad ibn 'Abdullah, one of the two sons, appeared in Medina to lead an open rebellion which was eventually crushed and Muhammad's head was carried off to be paraded in the cities of Iraq.

Waqidi gives two eye-witness accounts of these momentous events, merged here into one,

I saw 'Abdullah ibn al-Hasan and his family being taken out of the house of Marwan following the evening prayer in irons and carried away on mounts with no covering beneath them. I was then a youth approaching puberty and capable of remembering what I saw . . . Muhammad ibn 'Abdullah became master of Medina. News of this reached us so we the young men came out. I was then fifteen years old. We reached him and found a crowd had gathered to stare at him. No one was being turned away. I came nearer and saw him at close range. He was mounted on a horse and wearing a stuffed white shirt and white headdress. He had a mutilated nose and his face was pock-marked. He sent a force to Mecca which surrendered to him and raised white banners and sent his brother Ibrahim to Basra which he captured and whose people also raised white banners.[46]

This is a rare glimpse of a historian in the making, of one whose eagerness to check names, places and events for himself and whose attentiveness to

---

[46] Tabari, *Tarikh*, 3:187 and 223. Lengthy passages of Waqidi's autobiography are translated and discussed by J. Horovitz, 'The Earliest Biographies of the Prophet and their Authors' cited above, chapter 1, footnote 6.

detail were qualities that remained with him for the rest of his working life. The corpus of Waqidi's writings, made up of one fully preserved work, the *Maghazi*, and of numerous quotations in the works of others, notably Ibn Sa'd and Tabari, show him to have been more specialized in his historical range than Ibn Ishaq. He was essentially a historian of Muhammad and the first century or so of the Muslim era; but as a historian of the early *jama'a*, or community, his works teem with names and dates as if an entire community, both the high and the low, now finds itself enshrined in his pages. Waqidi then subjects so many of these names and events to scrutiny and comparative analysis that the community and its history come alive. Two main features of his method need to be highlighted: the first is his use of the principle of consensus (*ijma'*) in confirming the truth of events and the second is his preoccupation with dating and chronology in what appears to be an attempt to make his history more systematic and accessible to official and scholarly use.

To understand the genesis of consensus, one must bear in mind the attempts of both the later Umayyads and the early Abbasids to bring uniformity into legal judgements, perhaps as an instrument of state coercion but also to help centralize governmental routine. It is therefore likely that the initiative in the direction of evolving the concept of a consensus of scholars came from the ruling circles. As we saw above, groups of *fuqaha'* had already been marshalled into service in the second civil war, to begin with by the Zubayrid party. Thereafter, 'Abd al-Malik's attentions to the scholars of Medina had as their object a consensus of support for his policies. These scholars were the spiritual constituency of the empire. Under 'Umar II (d. 101/720) the policy of Islamization clearly required uniformity of judicial practice at least, if not of legal theory. Finally, the urgency with which the early Abbasids curried the favour of Iraqi jurists in particular must also have inclined them to push for a consensus which they could then control. It is in the early manuals of jurists like Abu Yusuf (d. 182/798) and Yahya ibn Adam (d. 203/818) that we find the development of a concept of consensus which is not so much a spontaneous growth of like-minded groups of jurists as much as a government-inspired imposition of uniformity on a mass of often contradictory views and practices in vital areas of the economy such as the land-tax.[47]

---

[47] See Abu Zur'a, *Tarikh*, 1:351, para. 723; 1:202, para. 156 and 1:439, para. 1081 for three reports relating to Walid I, Umar II and al-Mansur. Ibn al-Muqaffa' in his *Risala fi'l Sahaba* also advances similar ideas: see M. Kurd 'Ali, *Umara' al-Bayan* (Cairo: Lajnat al-Ta'lif, 1937) 1:155. The suggestion that the *ijma'* was a 'contrary process' to state centralization advanced by F. Gabrieli in 'Ibn al-Muqaffa'' *EI2* seems puzzling. The article '*idjma*'' in *EI2* by M. Bernand does not deal adequately with its historical genesis. If I have overemphasized the role of government in inspiring *ijma'* this is because that role is generally overlooked in modern research. It seems clear for instance that the activity of scholars like Abu Yusuf and Yahya Ibn Adam was in large part at least called forth by government request. Their frequent references to the consensus of their 'colleagues' (e.g.

But the concept of consensus was not solely a method of verification. To Waqidi and Ibn Saʿd consensus was essentially the agreement of scholars whose views and judgements from one age to the next under-pinned the history of the whole community:

I have set down in writing in the *Maghazi* all the names of the Prophet's companions that reached me, all the Arabs who visited him and all who related *hadith* from him. As far as possible, I elucidated this information as it reached me or was narrated to me even though I did not absorb all this knowledge. The companions of the Prophet were followed by the successors, children of the Emigrants and Helpers as well as others, among whom were lawyers and scholars proficient in the transmission of *Hadith*, history, jurisprudence and legal judgements. These passed away, to be succeeded by another generation (*tabaqa*) and then by other generations until this our present age.[48]

The term *tabaq* in the Qur'an signifies a level or stage. In Waqidi and Ibn Saʿd the term *tabaqa* denotes a human generation and becomes one of the earliest time divisions in Islamic historiography. These generations provide the continuity between the then and the now and confer structure and meaning upon the material assembled. Structurally, the *tabaqat* of Ibn Saʿd, whose nucleus are the *tabaqat* of Waqidi, are built upon a plan which lists distinguished companions and successors in order of seniority in Islam. Their descendants are also listed down to approximately the year 230/844. Each entry is provided with a biography commensurate with the import-ance of the figure. The *tabaqat* then move to the various major urban centres of Islam, first of Arabia then of Iraq and further east and finally of Syria, following for each city a similar listing scheme in order of senior-ity. At the very end is a most valuable section devoted to the *tabaqat* of women. Inevitably, repetition ensues since many companions and their families appear in both the chronological as well as the topographical section. But why this duality of classification? What may have been at issue is a kind of apostolic truth theory whereby the Prophet's companions and their descendants act as guarantors of the true faith in the cities where they settled. As these generations radiate in time and space they are not only an unimpeachable chain of witnesses to the truth but also carry the certainty of the faith to the major cities of the *umma*. Here are the believers, arranged in ranks and with their women praying behind them.

But this structure is also tied together by the very obvious interest in 'updating' terms, events and customs displayed by the two historians:

qala ashabuna and *ajmaʿa ashabuna*) are often references to *conflicting* legal opinions eman-ating from different cities or regions which they then feel free to settle by expressing their *own* opinions: a good example may be found in Abu Yusuf, *Kitab al-Kharaj*, p. 105. Waqidi was doing something similar in the field of history.
[48] Ibn Saʿd, *Tabaqat*, 2:377–8.

In the early days in Medina two people would be conversing and one of them would tell the other, 'You are more bankrupt than a *qadi*.' Today *qadi*s have become governors, tyrants or princes, with income from estates, commerce or wealth.[49]

The past is linked to the present in numerous ways, suggesting its continuing relevance. For instance, current sites of momentous events of the past are identified for the benefit, one assumes, of pilgrims or scholars: 'it is on your left as you enter Mecca', 'it is now a graveyard', 'it is today in ruins'. There is also a clear interest in the persistence of certain customs or rites: 'even now, the Ansar women begin by weeping for Hamza before they weep for their own dead', 'and this is what imams in Medina still do', 'and so people became used to carrying their dead to that place and praying over them until the present day'. Genealogical and religious concerns lie behind the attempt to trace the descendants of the Prophet's companions still living in various cities. Hijazi terms that are clearly unfamiliar to contemporary, probably Iraqi, audiences are given modern equivalents. In these and other ways, Waqidi and Ibn Sa'd stress the abiding importance of tradition. But it is also this sensitivity to persistence which makes Waqidi, and to a lesser degree Ibn Sa'd, systematically critical historians, since it enables them to spot anachronisms or express doubt.[50]

In examining their critical method it becomes necessary now to separate this pair, so far treated together. For it is clear that Waqidi is in fact the senior partner. Ibn Sa'd, known of course as 'katib al-Waqidi' was a secretary-editor of his master and of the materials he had assembled and then amplified. But the division into *tabaqat* and the critical, investigative spirit which permeates the *Tabaqat* of Ibn Sa'd belongs primarily to Waqidi.[51] A great deal is known about his life, thanks to large autobiographical fragments. But more pertinent are the frequent references to Waqidi at work, so to speak, interrogating informants, seeing for himself,

---

[49] Ibn Sa'd, *Tabaqat*, 5:280.

[50] On sites of events, see, e.g., Ibn Sa'd, *Tabaqat*, 1:99; 2:57; 3:266, 550; 7:397; Tabari, *Tarikh*, 2:1467. On persistence of customs, see, e.g., Waqidi, *Maghazi*, pp. 65, 207, 312, 1032, 1033; Ibn Sa'd, *Tabaqat*, 1:249, 257; 2:44; 5:322. Tracing descendants of companions in the various cities is found in almost every biographical entry, especially from vol. 3 onwards of Ibn Sa'd, *Tabaqat*. Linguistic equivalents are found in profusion in the *Tabaqat* and often preceded by the word *ya'ni* ('which means'). On spotting anachronisms, *Tabaqat*, 2:29 and 106 are typical. On doubt, *Tabaqat*, 2:173 is typical: 'There are several versions of each report but God knows best.' But Waqidi is rarely in doubt.

[51] I do not mean to disparage the achievement of Ibn Sa'd: see, e.g., the following references to his critical activity in *Tabaqat*, 1:117 (correcting a site), 2:21 and 287 (settling a date), 2:309–10 (clinching an argument with a massive *isnad*), 3:266 (geographical curiosity), 3:454, 577; 4:47 (critique of copyists), 3:462; 4:371 (research into genealogies), 3:503; 8:320, 336 (correcting Waqidi's information – rare instances). There is a useful introduction to Ibn Sa'd in the Dar Sadir, Beirut, edition of the *Tabaqat*, 1:5–17 (by Ihsan 'Abbas). Ibn Sa'd accumulated a great deal of information independently of Waqidi. But his critical *method* does not represent an advance on that of his master.

answering Ibn Saʿd's questions, curtly dismissing weak reports, correcting details, consulting archives and written records, pinning exact dates to events, untangling history from popular imagination or errors of copyists, and explicitly distancing himself from the work of Ibn Ishaq. This image of a historian in his 'laboratory' is more vivid and biographically complete than that of any other Muslim historian, with the possible exception of Ibn Khaldun. Waqidi is an historical *expert* and his reader is not allowed to forget it.[52]

In one sense, the work of Waqidi represents a retreat from the universal horizons of Ibn Ishaq. The pre-Islamic panorama of the latter is abandoned, as is his tendency to highlight the sacred and miraculous, even the bizarre elements in the life of Muhammad. In the *Maghazi* of Waqidi, Muhammad is primarily a political-military leader and only secondarily a prophet-lawgiver. But in so doing, Waqidi was helping to move history in the direction of factual accuracy and specialization within a single theme, that of Muhammad and his community. As a vision of history, it is less grand perhaps than the vision of Ibn Ishaq. But it is also a more rigorous, more practicable vision and one which Waqidi in all probability hoped would be of use to the growing corps of state secretaries, jurists and scholars of the early-Abbasid state. The historical record is pruned of its fantastic elements, made normative, given a graspable structure, dated, arranged in generations, and made to stretch in one unbroken chain of legitimacy and social custom, fortified by consensus. The *isnad* is used by Waqidi at two levels: detailed and explicit for controversy, collective and impersonal for more mundane events. Like Ibn Ishaq, Waqidi was attacked for loose *isnad* usage by strict practitioners of *Hadith*, who were now distinguishing themselves more sharply than ever from their scholarly colleagues. Stricter specialization was in the air. Waqidi's *Maghazi* and *Tabaqat* commemorate a prophet *and* his community. The result is a view of history as a usable political record. With Waqidi, the break between *Hadith* and historiography is now more or less complete.[53]

---

[52]   Only partial references will be cited, since other references have already been cited in the footnotes above. For interrogation of informants, see, e.g., Waqidi, *Maghazi*, pp. 344–5; Tabari, *Tarikh*, 1:1283, 1812 and 4:2357. For conversations with Ibn Saʿd, see *Tabaqat*, 1:191; 2:100; 4:17; 5:221. For consulting archives see, e.g., *Maghazi*, p. 1032 and *Tabaqat*, 1:290 and further *Maghazi*, pp. 441, 572 for his own reliance upon writing. For correction of popular error due to poetry, see *Tabaqat*, 2:81. For his relationship with Ibn Ishaq, see footnote 53, below.

[53]   Neither Horovitz (footnote 46 above) nor Marsden Jones (see below) seem to have noticed the many instances in the *Tabaqat* of Ibn Saʿd where Waqidi not only refers to Ibn Ishaq but consistently calls his data into question. Ibn Saʿd himself is clearly aware of the antagonism between the two masters: see, e.g., *Tabaqat*, 3:52, 53, 168, 169–70, 234, 245, 386, 391, 418, 459, 487; 4:225. Waqidi mentions Ibn Ishaq by name and declares him wrong in several places: see *Tabaqat*, 3:470, 503, 555, 568, 584; 4:35 and possibly at 3:493 and 498. For the views of Marsden Jones on Waqidi see his 'The Chronology of the Maghazi – A Textual Survey', *BSOAS* 19, part 2 (1957), 245–80, and 'Ibn Ishaq and al-Waqidi: The Dream of ʿAtika and the Raid to Nakhla in Relation to the Charge of

Tribal history: genealogy

Attention to genealogy (*nasab*) appears to have been prevalent among the Arabs since very early times. Genealogies, for example, account for a large number of Safaitic graffiti dating from approximately the first century BC and found in northern Jordan. Typical of these genealogies is the following:

By Hani' b. Zann'el b. Ahlam b. Mann'el b. Shimiq b. Rabban b. Himyat b. Sabb b. Dahmal b. Gamil b. Taharat b. ha-Yasir b. Buhaish b. Daif.[54]

Such genealogies must have been cherished and handed down with care from one generation to the next. They belong to the same world which produced, not much later, such genealogies as the one found right at the beginning of the Gospel according to St Matthew, and they echo without doubt a very ancient Near-Eastern preoccupation. But *nasab* was not simply a tribal or communal concern since it extended also to horses, suggesting the chivalrous connotations of the subject. In general, *nasab* must be thought of first as an organizing principle, an epistemic instrument which relates history by arranging it in a family-tree structure. Secondly, *nasab* emphasizes the *fuhul* among both men and horses, which among other things meant 'producers of progeny'. Hence *nasab* as an organizing principle is not very far from *tabaqat* except that (1) *tabaqat* are entirely Muslim and human whereas *nasab* is not, and (2) *tabaqat* have a religious and topical structure, by *sabiqa* and region, whereas *nasab* is a forest of family trees aligned by tribe.

Qur'an 23:101 offers the following image of the terrors of the Day of Resurrection:

And when the trumpet shall be blown, no kinships shall there be on that Day, nor shall they question each other about them.

There could hardly have been a more telling image to impress upon an Arab tribal audience the idea of a total breakdown in social relationships. These kinships (*ansab*) were of vital importance in tribal politics and loss

---

Plagiarism', *BSOAS* 22 (1959), 41–51, as well as his introduction to his edition of the *Maghazi* (London: Oxford University Press, 1966), in all of which places Waqidi is basically assessed as a historical source. The critique of Ibn Ishaq by Waqidi, despite the words of praise for him in Tabari, *Tarikh*, 3:2512, cited by Horovitz, reflects a very different concept of the scope and value of prophetic history and possibly also the different positions occupied by the two historians inside their respective political societies. Waqidi was far more closely associated with the Abbasid programme than Ibn Ishaq. On Waqidi's use of *isnad*, the valuable biography of him in Baghdadi, *Tarikh*, 3:3–21, contains an interesting account (at 3:7) of Waqidi's preference for collective *isnad* because the citing of each individual transmitter and his report would unnecessarily lengthen the material. If genuine, this account may be one of the earliest references to the methodological parting of ways between historians and *Hadith* scholars.

[54] F. V. Winnett, *Safaitic Inscriptions from Jordan* (Toronto: University of Toronto Press, 1957), p. 28, inscription no. 130.

of interest in genealogy would mean an end to political life and all social interaction. This image of the disappearance of all kinship ties and of all interest in them complements other images of the Last Day ('wherein no buying or selling') which are meant to evoke a cessation of all activity. Whether or not Muhammad himself was against the excessive pursuit of *nasab*, and his career would suggest an antipathy towards tribal pride, genealogy did not occupy a comfortable place inside the historical sciences of Islam. For one thing, this science would not be meaningful to non-Arab *mawali*, or clients, nor perhaps to an increasingly urban environment. For another, the Arab tribal aristocracy, who were the main heroes and patrons of *nasab*, lost most of their political and military influence in the early Abbasid period. It was in this period in fact that genealogy as an historical science achieved a high degree of development as if it were an assertion of Arab identity in an increasingly multinational empire. And yet the Prophet was an Arab of purest stock. Eventually, a compromise formula was reached: some knowledge of *nasab* was necessary in order to know the *nasab* of Muhammad and for marriage and inheritance purposes. But the great *nasab* works appeared precisely when the Islamic empire was no longer ruled by an Arab aristocracy. They may be thought of as a kind of epitaph to the Arabs of both the *Jahiliyya* and Islam.[55]

The earliest systematization of *nasab* was in all probability the work of a father-son team, the al-Kalbis of Kufa, whose own aristocratic family spanned the *Jahiliyya* and Islam. It is the son, Hisham ibn Muhammad (d. 204 or 206/819 or 821), known simply as Ibn al-Kalbi, who seems to have set down, in a prolific but disorganized fashion, the mass of materials he had received from his father and other teachers. For someone who quickly became *the* authority on Arab genealogy, and is so often quoted in the sources, little is known about the life of Hisham. The *Hadith* scholars tended to dismiss him as a mere 'entertainer' or worse. His alleged Shi'i leanings may conceivably have been responsible for his neglect by the increasingly formidable Sunni *Hadith* establishment. It is as likely however that Kufa in early Abbasid days preserved a genealogical tradition of pride in Arab descent considered frivolous or even subversive by the new pan-Islamic state. Kufa became the home of lost causes, with Alid Shi'ism and Arab *nasab* heading the list.[56]

---

[55] For the evolution of the science of genealogy, see Ignaz Goldziher, *Muslim Studies*, ed. S. M. Stern (London: George Allen and Unwin, 1967), 1:164–90; S. D. F. Goitein's Introduction to his edition of Vol. 5 of Baladhuri, *Ansab al-Ashraf* (Jerusalem: Jerusalem University Press, 1936) pp. 14–24; A. A. Duri, *The Rise of Historical Writing*, index, but especially pp. 146–7; Werner Caskel, *Gamharat an-Nasab: das genealogische Werk des Hisam ibn Muhammad al-Kalbi* (Leiden: Brill, 1966), Vol. 1; M. J. Kister and M. Plessner, 'Notes on Caskel's *Gamharat an-Nasab*', *Oriens*, 25–6 (1976), 48–68.

[56] On the Kalbis, father and son, see 'Al-Kalbi', *EI2*. On Kufan politics, see Martin Hinds, 'Kufan Political Alignments and their Background in the Mid-seventh Century A.D.',

Historians of the *Sira*, such as Ibn Ishaq, a contemporary of Ibn al-Kalbi *père*, had paid scant attention to genealogies. Ibn Ishaq begins his *Sira* with the genealogy of Muhammad, probably in conscious imitation of the genealogy of Jesus in Matthew. Thereafter, however, extensive genealogies are rare. Two women who occupy a central place in the Muhammadan *Sira*, Halima, foster-mother of the Prophet, and Khadija, his first wife, merit a long genealogy. But lengthy descent is cited only rarely and only when an individual is singled out for special honour. In Waqidi, genealogy is not a central concern and long-spun descent is cited mostly in connection with lists of names of participants in momentous events. And yet we know from our sources that experts in genealogy, many of them Kufan, maintained this tradition unbroken well into the Islamic period. The kind of attitude that a genealogist like Hisham ibn al-Kalbi had to face is best captured in the contemptuous remark of the great *Hadith* scholar Ibn Hanbal:

Hisham ibn Muhammad al-Kalbi? Who would relate [sc. *Hadith*] from him? I never imagined anyone would relate from him.[57]

Other historians of the *Sira*, such as Ibn Saʿd, quoted Hisham at some length on the subject of genealogy, especially the controversial link between Maʿadd ibn ʿAdnan and Ismaʿil, the two great ancestors of the Arabs. But having detailed the different lines of descent between these two figures, Ibn Saʿd adds:

I found no difference among them [sc. genealogists] that Maʿadd was a descendant of Qaidhar ibn Ismaʿil. But this difference in lines of descent indicates that the true lineage was not preserved but was taken over from the People of the Book who translated it for them. Differences therefore arose. If this line had been correctly established, the Prophet would have been the most cognizant of it. Therefore, our common view is to stop at Maʿadd ibn ʿAdnan and to suspend discussion of any lineage beyond him back to Ismaʿil.[58]

Such comments were of course a veiled criticism of the kind of traditions that Hisham dealt with and of their connections with dubious non-Muslim lore. They show that scholars of *Sira* and *Hadith* were determined to circumscribe the folkloric elements which might intrude upon their specialized pursuit of sacred historiography.

Hisham tells us that his father taught him 'while still a mere youth' the genealogy of the Prophet. There was much that he transmitted from his

IJMES 2 (1971), 346–67. On Kufa as home of the Arab tribal aristocracy, see, e.g., Ibn Saʿd, *Tabaqat*, 6:5 ff. There is much information on the religious and literary life in Kufa in Yusuf Khulayf, *Hayat al-Shiʿr fiʾl Kufa ila Nihayat al-Qarn al-Thani liʾl Hijra* (Cairo: Dar al-Katib al-ʿArabi, 1968).
[57] Baghdadi, *Tarikh*, 14:46.
[58] Ibn Saʿd, *Tabaqat*, 1: 57–8.

father, especially on the history of prophets and on pre-Islamic antiquities and genealogies. But there was also much that he learnt on his own:

I used to extract (*astakhriju*) the histories of the Arabs and the genealogies of the tribe of Nasr ibn Rabi'a together with the ages of those among them who worked for the family of Kisra from the monasteries of Hira which contain records of their kingdom and of all their affairs.[59]

From citations in Ibn Sa'd, we learn that he had a wide network of inform-ants among the Arab tribes represented in Kufa. From citations in Tabari, we find that Hisham transmitted bulky historical reports from the Kufan Abu Mikhnaf and his fellow Kalbite historian 'Awana ibn al-Hakam. When this literary activity is spread before us, we detect a range of curios-ity which took in pre- and post-Islamic history and Biblical as well as Persian antiquities. There is however a distinct interest in genealogies, 'firsts' (*awa'il*), time spans, ages at death, regnal periods and other chrono-logical pinpointers. It was in this area that Hisham was most heavily cited by later historians and where he eventually acquired his wide but shaky reputation.[60]

The *Jamaharat al-Nasab*, the principal but incomplete genealogical work of Hisham, is a roster of Arab tribes, which commences with Quraysh and goes on to detail the kinship structure of the major tribes, clans and famil-ies, providing brief biographical information on prominent personalities. The work has neither the sacred significance nor even the literary interest of, say, Ibn Ishaq or Waqidi. Nor is it a purely authored work since it includes glosses, comments and additions by many hands. There are few if any methodological reflections, some brief sceptical comments, a few corrections of names, some comments on the authenticity of the verses cited and a few admissions of ignorance. It was intended as a work of reference and if Hisham's *Genealogies of Horses* is any guide, may have been provided with a kind of index at the end to facilitate reference.[61]

But it is also a work which must have had a considerable impact on its own and later ages. We get a sense of this impact from the way in which the work documents the diffusion of Arab tribes in the Middle East and

---

[59] Tabari, *Tarikh*, 1:770. On Hisham's early training, see Ibn Sa'd, *Tabaqat*, 1: 55.

[60] For tribal informants, see Ibn Sa'd, *Tabaqat*, 1: 300, 301, 309, 325, 333, 334, 340, 342, 346. With post-Muhammadan history, Hisham *apud* Tabari is little more than a transmitter of Abu Mikhnaf and 'Awana. Much is heard of Kufa: see, e.g., Tabari, *Tarikh*, 1: 2805 and 2: 185. For Hisham's interest in 'firsts', see his *Jamhara*, pp. 135, 186, 312, 381, 434, 468, 563 and Tabari, *Tarikh*, 1: 204, 226, 347. There is a recent spirited but unduly laudatory defence of Hisham as a source for pre-Islamic history in Irfan Shahid, *Byzantium and the Arabs in the Fourth Century* (Washington: Dumbarton Oaks Research Library and Collection, 1984), pp. 349–66.

[61] For some examples of Hisham's comments, see *Jamhara*, pp. 19, 22 (corrections of names), 20 (etymologies), 326 (critique of authenticity of verse, and cf. Tabari, *Tarikh*, 1: 751), 340 (a very rare expression of doubt), 472–3, 488 (critique of al-Sharqi ibn al-Qutami, a fellow genealogist).

their transformation from Arabian communities into imperial political parties. It is not therefore an exercise in antiquarian reconstruction but seeks on almost every page to show where a tribe, clan or family has settled and to update the history of tribal notables. The present status of each clan is as important as its pedigree. In order to construct this living genealogy, Hisham employed a set of terms which became the technical vocabulary of his science. The word *daraja* for instance is employed to indicate that a particular line of descent has passed away, leaving no progeny; the phrase *wa ilayhi al-bayt wa'l 'adad* means that a particular clan is currently the most prominent and numerous within its tribal group. Other terms are more problematic, for instance the frequently used trio *sharif, ra's* and *sayyid*.[62] Do they indicate moral qualities or are they also used of political leadership? They denote in any case the aristocratic classes of the empire, the judges, governors, military leaders and tribal notables whose lineage stretches back, for good or ill, into the days of the *Jahiliyya*. Built into the very structure of Hisham's work is a certain heroic, perhaps even *jahili* dimension since it is only the outstanding few in any one clan who are worthy of mention and celebrated in verse. This must be contrasted with the community-minded histories of Waqidi or Ibn Sa'd if we are to understand both the pan-Arab appeal of this work as well as the suspicion with which it was regarded in pan-Islamic circles.

An added perspective of Hisham's achievement is gained if one examines the numerous citations from him found in the universal history of Tabari. Here the full range of Hisham's historical interests is revealed and is seen to extend all the way from Adam to the Abbasids. Hisham is the authority for a large mass of reports on *awa'il* many of which might be called myths of origins. These reports include such 'firsts' as the first Persian King, the first king to impose taxes or mint coinage, the first doctor and astronomer, the first man to have grey hair and become bald, the first to entertain guests and so forth as well as the origin of wild animals and similar stories of origin.[63] Here also Hisham is a genealogist, not only of Arabs but of other nations, especially the Persian. But his lack of expertise in this area is highlighted by Tabari, who often takes him to task for failing to take account of the 'experts' in this field.[64] Like Ibn Sa'd before him, Tabari largely neglects Hisham when he arrives at the history of the Prophet and picks him up again in the post-Prophetic period only as a transmitter of Abu Mikhnaf and 'Awana.

A story is told in Tabari, on the authority of Waqidi, about Hisham

[62] There is only a brief discussion of this important problem in Caskel, *Gamharat an-Nasab*, 1:37. A thorough investigation of these terms would throw considerable light on the formation of early Islamic elites. The following are especially significant references: *Jamhara*, pp. 126, 228, 268, 556, 561 (*sharif*); 175, 293 (*ra's*); 194, note 1 and 199 (*sayyid*).
[63] For references, see footnote 60 above.
[64] Tabari, *Tarikh*, 1:154-5.

which even if untrue reveals something of his image among contemporaries and in later scholarship. Hisham was apparently a poor man who went about in rags. One day, says the narrator, he finds him mounted splendidly and dressed in the finest clothes. When asked about this change, Hisham asks the narrator to keep the matter private and proceeds to tell him how he has been summoned by the Abbasid caliph al-Mahdi who shows him a letter so vile in its abuse of the Abbasids that Hisham is only with difficulty induced by the caliph to continue reading. Upon inquiring who the author is, Hisham is told that it is the ruler of Andalusia. Hisham is incensed and proceeds to abuse that ruler and his ancestors to the delight of the caliph. A scribe is promptly summoned and Hisham dictates a treatise of defamation which pleases the caliph hugely, is appended to a reply by the caliph and dispatched post-haste to Andalusia. For this, Hisham is richly rewarded by the grateful caliph.[65]

Hisham ibn al-Kalbi was a polymath the spirit of whose scholarship had more to do with the *jahili* past than with the Islamic present. It was the kind of scholarship which was being rapidly overtaken by events and by a shift in mood and models. His particular specialty, genealogy, was closely linked with social snobbery and could easily be turned into slander. As the various Islamic sciences were beginning to sharpen their tools and delineate their fields, the activity of Hisham must have appeared anachronistic, dangerous and diffuse. Before it could be brought into line with these emerging sciences it had to be restructured in subject and method. This task was accomplished by a new generation of genealogists.

Tribal history continued: genealogy reformulated

A slightly older contemporary of Hisham, al-Mu'arrij ibn 'Amr al-Sadusi (d. 195/811), is the author, according to his modern editor, of the earliest surviving work on genealogy, entitled *Kitab Hadhf min Nasab Quraysh* ('A Concise Genealogy of Quraysh'). This is indeed a short treatise of some ninety-five pages but it is conceived in a spirit quite alien to that of Hisham. This spirit is proclaimed in the very opening sentence of the work:

This is a concise book of genealogy. Had I chosen to write an exhaustive work, the life history of the Prophet and of the Abbasid family would have occupied me time without end.[66]

This is a genealogy conceived and formulated in accordance with a structure which outwardly resembles Hisham's but where content and ideological thrust are new. To call it a piece of Abbasid propaganda would not

---

[65] Tabari, *Tarikh*, 3:528.
[66] Mu'arrij, *Hadhf*, p. 2.

be entirely false but it would not do justice to the significance of the work within a genealogy now recast to serve a new age. This new age, the age of the 'Blessed Call to Truth' (*al-Da'wa al-Mubaraka*) ushers in the rule of the Prophetic family, a vatocracy where the pious community once more can offer legitimate obedience to a 'blessed' ruler. Quraysh now occupies centre stage, but it is a Quraysh divided morally into two camps: the virtuous Abbasids 'second to none in their labour on the Prophet's behalf' and the sinful Umayyads, 'all of whom were destined to be killed'.[67] The confrontation is Qur'anic in its theological finality, pitting good against evil and very far removed from the epic *Ayyam* of the *Jahiliyya*. Genealogy was being taken under a new wing, a process that eventually enriched the genre by intensifying its historiographic polemicity, especially when other parties and individuals also came to practise that genre.

The work is in essence a specialized monograph detailing the family structures of Quraysh and arranged in a kind of sacred priority where the House of 'Abbas is the political and religious dome of that structure. To that extent it typifies the vast volume of literature produced by the new Abbasid state to justify the ambivalent historical role of its eponym. But it also seeks to deploy a consensual system of verification which accents the role of ascetics and scholars.[68] In other words, this new and pious scholarly elite is not only the ornament of the genealogical tree; it also determines truth, moral and historical. Hence the purpose of this kind of genealogy is not, like Hisham's, primarily referential. Rather, it is programmed by a view of history designed to highlight the arrival of a 'blessed' dynasty through which all values are to be redirected.

It follows that this genealogy is more clearly historical in its layout than Hisham's precisely because it is more polemical:

His son 'Abd al-Malik ibn Marwan rose up and killed Ibn al-Zubayr and assumed the caliphate for himself and his descendants. It was to remain with them until God removed it from their hands through this Blessed Call to Truth . . . Marwan ibn Muhammad rose to power and his sedition (*fitna*) lasted long until God removed power from his hands and delivered it to the House of 'Abbas.[69]

The entries are frequently provided with short biographies and extensive verse, lending the work a literary and historical dimension, not unlike the *Tabaqat* genre of a somewhat later generation of historians. Both the Qur'an and Prophetic *Hadith* are quoted where they bear upon individuals or incidents. From time to time the author will also append some lexical comments. But he is specially concerned to point out who died as an unbeliever and who died a Muslim, inscribing a moral roster of the com-

---

[67] Mu'arrij, *Hadhf*, pp. 7, 33, 36.
[68] See, e.g., *Hadhf*, p. 51 and *passim* for lawyers and ascetics (*faqih*, *'abid*).
[69] *Hadhf*, p. 33.

munity in line with the author's intention to recast genealogy as a hierarchy of piety.[70]

The genealogical work of Mu'arrij is thus a genealogy of homage towards pious Muslim ancestors rather than one of pride in a heroic Arab past. It seeks to redirect communal reverence, to regroup the Arab 'forest' around the Abbasid 'tree', to establish a priority of righteousness such as would turn genealogy into an auxiliary of sacred history. It is in this same direction that two scholars of the Zubayrid family, the uncle and nephew team of Mus'ab and al-Zubayr ibn Bakkar, carried on their genealogical pursuits.

Mus'ab (d. 236/851), the uncle, and al-Zubayr (d. 256/870), the nephew, are the products of a first-century Zubayrid literary tradition briefly discussed above.[71] This tradition was in turn an outgrowth of a dynasty whose leader, 'Abdullah ibn al-Zubayr, had been recognized as a caliph for a number of years in the late first century. The Zubayrids soon lost power but not before they had marshalled a body of scholars to bolster their claim to be champions of a pristine Islam, focused upon reverence to the *Sahaba*, or Companions, of Muhammad. Unlike the Alids, who were often to rise in rebellion against both Umayyads and Abbasids, the Zubayrid clan was quietist, channelling its talents into religious scholarship and literature. Over the years, the clan produced poets and legal scholars, judges and ascetics, commemorated especially in the genealogical work of al-Zubayr.

Both uncle and nephew centred their attention, like Mu'arrij, on Quraysh. Unlike Mu'arrij, they were of course insiders, that is to say they were themselves from Quraysh, descendants of Zubayr, Muhammad's cousin, a man who came to be known as the *hawariyy* or apostle of the Prophet. The first century or so of the Abbasid period, the century in which both these men lived and worked, was one of ideological experimentation. The early Abbasids, having shed the extremism of their revolutionary days, swung pendulum-like between various political postures. In exploring each option (e.g. the narrowly Abbasid, the Alid, even the Umayyad), the caliphs were of course encouraging scholars to explore the roots of these conflicting bases of political authority. Genealogies were particularly suited for such exploration since they illustrated the range of contributions of these ruling families to Islamic history. The two Zubayrid genealogists, especially al-Zubayr ibn Bakkar, highlighted their own family's role even as they reconstructed the aristocratic 'houses' of Quraysh.

Mus'ab was the beneficiary of a long line of genealogists, many of whom he names as *nassaba* before him.[72] The consensus of these genealogists is

---

[70] Typical would be *Hadhf*, p. 35: 'Abu Uhayha had ten sons . . . five died as unbelievers, five died as Muslims.'
[71] See above, footnotes 8 and 25.
[72] Mus'ab, *Nasab Quraysh*, pp. 201, 203, 262, 273.

for Mus'ab, as it was for Waqidi, what confirms truth: 'All genealogists agree, there being no difference among them.'[73] But genealogy is now beginning to fill out into narrative, into what is in reality a history in lineage form of the early-Islamic community with occasional updating to his own days. Each 'house' in Quraysh is traced through episodic biographies, long or short, of its prominent members. Verse is used to illustrate and corroborate although Mus'ab is occasionally critical of its authenticity. But more to the point is the attempt to consecrate the senior Companions, to elevate them above party politics and controversy:

Abu Hurayra related that the Prophet was seated upon a rock in Hira' when the rock moved. 'Be still,' said the Prophet, 'For upon you sit none but a prophet, a man of truth or a martyr.' Abu Hurayra added: there sat upon it the Prophet, Abu Bakr, 'Umar, 'Uthman, 'Ali, Talha and Zubayr.[74]

The nephew, al-Zubayr, seems to have greatly expanded the materials he received from his uncle in the direction of what some of his own contemporaries at least no longer regarded to be, strictly speaking, a work of genealogy but of 'narratives' (akhbar).[75] Al-Zubayr was a typical 'alim of his period, a trustworthy muhaddith and an expert in poetry and language. These diverse interests were reflected in a work whose dimensions are anthological. Almost half the work is verse, much of which is quoted for literary merit alone and not for any corroborative value. The Zubayrid family are prominently displayed and verses in praise of various family members are cited at great length. Both uncle and nephew pay special attention to maternal lineage, naming the mothers of mothers through several generations, especially the mothers of their own family members, as if in further celebration of their Arab-Quraysh pedigree. As one Zubayrid succeeds another the impression is of a muster of heroes of the spirit: noble, generous, brave, God-fearing, eloquent, ascetic and scholarly, spanning the gamut of Islamic virtues. Their sharaf, or distinction, is beyond dispute.

In Zubayr's genealogies the stories are fuller and more vibrant than in those of Mus'ab. Where Mus'ab is primarily concerned with listing parents and progeny, Zubayr brings characters and events alive with verse, wise sayings and anecdotes and is somewhat less reverent to ancestors. Many of Zubayr's stories illuminate character and strike a more didactic tone:

'Abd al-Wahid [ibn Hamza ibn 'Abdullah ibn al-Zubayr] was an ill-tempered man. He would say: 'I have two opinions, one humane and one savage. I have never benefited except from the savage.' 'Abbad ibn Hamza [his brother] was the lord of Hamza's children and the eldest. He would often visit 'Abd al-Wahid and say, 'I swore I would not dine today except in your house.' In reply 'Abd al-Wahid

[73] Mus'ab, Nasab, p. 4.
[74] Mus'ab, Nasab, p. 104.
[75] Baghdadi, Tarikh, 8:469.

would curse him and say 'You took our money and did such and such with it, and now you come to jest with me! May God do such and such to you!' 'Abbad would then say to himself, 'Taste this [bitterness].' 'Abd al-Wahid would continue, 'I know that you did not come because you are fond of me but only to punish your soul through me. Luxury has spoilt it so you have come to discipline it. By God I shall cure you of it and make it hear what will displease it! But we shall not deny you food.' 'Abbad would add, 'By God I would not leave until he had cured the corruption of my soul and my soul would say: Never again.'[76]

There is less of the heroic element here than one finds in Hisham al-Kalbi. The *awa'il* genre is gone, that mythical genre of 'firsts' who dot the days of the ancients. In fact the genealogies of uncle and nephew are relatively free of the pious reverence to ancestors which a century or more of rigorous *isnad*-criticism and party strife had helped to dilute. The only 'hero' here is Quraysh itself, the last survivor of both Arab and Islamic aristocracy, surviving in the genealogies of the two Zubayrids but only as an aristocracy of religion or the spirit:

When the caliph 'Umar ibn al-Khattab decided to assign the *'ata'* [pension] he consulted the Muhajirun [Meccan Emigrants] who concurred with his view. He then consulted the Ansar [Medinese] who also agreed with their Muhajirun brethren. He next consulted the Muslims who embraced Islam at the time of Mecca's conquest and they too agreed with the Muhajirun and the Ansar, all except Hakim ibn Hizam who said to 'Umar, 'The people of Quraysh are merchants. If you assign *'ata'* to them, I fear that they would come to depend upon it and abandon trade. Someone coming after you might withdraw the *'ata'* from them and trade would have departed from them.' It turned out as he had foretold.[77]

The genealogies of al-Baladhuri

The genealogies of Mu'arrij, Mus'ab and Zubayr had reformulated genealogy in terms of the new piety dominant at the time of the early Abbasids. Their focus, as we have seen, was on Quraysh as the fulcrum of the community, its true aristocracy, its guiding spirit. But the genealogies of Baladhuri (d. c. 279/892) were conceived on a much vaster scale. The scale in fact is so vast that the *Ansab al-Ashraf* ('Genealogies of the Nobility') of Baladhuri is more like a comprehensive history loosely arranged around prominent families than a work of strict genealogy. There is also a corresponding shift in mood. Where earlier genealogies might be described as epic in either the heroic or religious sense, the genealogies of Baladhuri are distinctly more 'romantic',[78] less deferential towards Quraysh, more

[76] Zubayr, *Jamharat*, 1:60.
[77] Zubayr, *Jamharat*, 1:373.
[78] The terms 'epic' and 'romantic' are used in the sense first defined by M. M. Bakhtin, *The Dialogic Imagination*, ed. Michael Holquist (Austin: University of Texas Press, 1981).

consciously jocular and more directly aimed at the secretarial class to which the author himself belonged.

By the time of Baladhuri, the Abbasid state, which he seems to have served as a middle-ranking bureaucrat for most of his professional life, was more than a century old. During that first century the Abbasid caliphs pursued a bewildering variety of policies and religious options. Shifts were often very rapid and dramatic. And while these policy shifts were instrumental in destabilizing the political-military elite of the empire, they must also have contributed to the cultural vitality of the great Abbasid cities. This third/ninth century might be called the age of debate and recapitulation in Arab Islamic intellectual history. The proliferation of parties, sects and intellectual circles with their sharp dialectic skills are caricatured in the tergiversations of the great Jahiz (d. 255/868), as he switches from one intellectual position to its opposite in the same essay. At the same time, and perhaps because of this ideological instability at the top, a mood is detected which seeks to encompass, to restate, to reformulate the salient features of the community's traditions. If it was the century of mavericks like Jahiz it was also the century of 'Master Traditionists'[79] like Bukhari and Muslim who gave definitive shape to *Hadith*. As for the middle echelons of the bureaucracy, they seem not to have shared the unstable careers of their seniors and to have continued the imperial bureaucratic routine. This latter had by now reached a high degree of sophistication and complexity. It was destined to become the major institutional legacy of the Abbasid empire, to be inherited and further developed by successor states.

Baladhuri's *Ansab* range over all the major provinces of the empire, wherever the *Ashraf* had made their influence felt. The work begins with a lengthy biography of the Prophet whose principal documentary value is that it relies extensively on a fellow genealogist, Hisham al-Kalbi, an authority normally shunned by consensus-minded biographers like Waqidi. The result is a more vivid and literary account with plentiful verse and smoother-flowing narrative. At the end of the Prophetic period the work assumes a genealogical mode in detailing the extended family of Muhammad, followed by a long 'catalogue' of information relating to various aspects of his personal life. Once this Prophetic introduction is completed, the vast work itself begins to unfold. The great Quraysh families come first, to be followed in succession by lesser known families of the northern Arab, or Nizari stock. The work seems to have been left unfinished.

In broad perspective, Baladhuri's *Ansab* resemble a series of pyramids, with the leading figures of each family forming the apex. Overlapping in time and *dramatis personae* is inevitable but is skilfully kept under control.

[79] The phrase is Nabia Abbott's.

Major themes weave their way between these pyramids, one of these being the great oppositional movement of the first three centuries of Islam, the Khawarij. The juxtaposition of nobleman and rebel lends a sense of irony to the work, an irony further enhanced by the author's apparent freedom from all ideological attachment. Leading figures are introduced through a sequence of stories which often seem polished, even doctored, in order to provide a lesson or a piece of wisdom, wit or aphorism. On occasion, Baladhuri resorts to the literary *topos*, e.g. of the caliph or the governor asking a wise man a series of questions (what is courage? what is generosity? what is reason? and so forth) and drawing from him short and didactic answers. On the whole, however, the portraiture betrays a conscious attempt at realistic balance. Stories about the Umayyad caliph Mu'awiya, for instance, reveal him in both a favourable and unfavourable light, while other stories poke fun at the hypocrisy of revered party leaders. In the following story, Ibn 'Idah, the Meccan governor of the Umayyad caliph Yazid, is attempting to force the reluctant 'Abdullah ibn al-Zubayr to pay allegiance to his master:

Ibn al-Zubayr said to Ibn 'Idah: 'I am but a pigeon among the other pigeons of this mosque. Can you find it in yourself to kill a mosque pigeon?' 'Soldier,' said Ibn 'Idah, 'fetch me my bow and arrows.' The soldier fetched them and Ibn 'Idah pulled out an arrow, centred it in his bow, took aim at a mosque pigeon and said, 'Pigeon, does Yazid drink wine? Say yes and I swear to God I'll kill you. Pigeon, do you refuse allegiance to Yazid the Commander of the Faithful and abandon the community taking refuge in the sanctuary so that your life may be spared? Say yes and I swear to God I'll kill you.' 'Woe to you, Ibn 'Idah,' said Ibn al-Zubayr, 'Do birds speak?' 'No,' answered Ibn 'Idah, 'But you do, and I swear to God you will either pay allegiance willingly or unwillingly or you will be killed. If we are ordered to kill you and you take refuge in the Ka'ba we will destroy it or burn it down on your head . . .' Ibn al-Zubayr said, 'You would violate the Sanctuary and the Ka'ba?' 'He violates it who commits unbelief therein,' replied Ibn 'Idah.[80]

The critical tools of the historian's trade as employed by Baladhuri in the *Ansab* are fairly simple. By far the most frequent phrase used by him to settle arguments about the veracity of a report, a date or an event is: *wa hadha al-thabat* ('and this is the firm, or established, truth'). The phrase is significant when contrasted with the consensual formula preferred by Waqidi and his school: *wa hadha al-mujtama' 'alayhi* ('and this is the agreed-upon truth'). Where this last appeals to a community of like-minded scholars, Baladhuri's formula seems to be derived from bureaucratic practice, from the curt and dismissive tone often adopted by bureaucrats towards lesser mortals.[81] It seems in any case to emanate from a historian who, in the later, post-Prophetic portion of his work, frequently

---

[80] Baladhuri, *Ansab*, 4/1:309.
[81] Jahiz launches a scathing attack on the morals and supercilious attitude of state secretaries in the epistle entitled 'Dhamm Akhlaq al-Kuttab' in *Rasa'il al-Jahiz*, ed. Harun, 2:187–209, especially at 191–2.

resorts to collective *isnad*, expressed in phrases like *qalu* ('they say') or *yuqal* ('it is said'). It is worthy of note that this switch from strict citation of *isnad* for Prophetic history to a more narrative style for non-Prophetic materials in the *same* work shows how the historians of that third century were prepared to adopt a different attitude to *akhbar*, a word now more strictly employed to denote historical reports in general.

But glimpses of the historian at work are very rare indeed in Baladhuri's *Ansab*. There are no comments on the criteria adopted to test reports, no indications as to why one authority was preferred to another, no 'asides' to the reader (or listener) in the form of remarks or reflections. His own brusque assertions of the truth must suffice.[82] But a lot of reading and research must have accompanied this massive collection of genealogy and biography, as witnessed by such extremely rare comments as:

Mus'ab ibn 'Abdallah al-Zubayri said to me: 'Narrators are in the habit of wrongly inserting historical reports from the first siege [of Mecca] into the second, and *vice versa*.'[83]

But if the work as a whole has any ulterior argument or purpose, this might well lie in an in-built political moral of the spectacle of powerful dynasties rising and falling, of founding fathers laboriously creating the edifice which less-talented or less-fortunate progeny then proceed to destroy:

News reached the caliph 'Abd al-Malik that the Kalb tribe was mobilizing in preparation for an attack upon the Qays and the Fazara in particular. He wrote to them swearing by God that if they killed a single man of Fazara he would exact retaliation for him. They desisted. He then wrote to Hajjaj ibn Yusuf, his governor of the Hijaz, ordering him to send Sa'id ibn 'Uyayna and Halhala ibn Qays, both men of Fazara. When they were sent to him he imprisoned them. A delegation from the Kalb arrived to see 'Abd al-Malik. He offered them blood-money but they refused. 'But only old men and young boys among you were killed,' said the caliph. In reply, al-Nu'man ibn Furayya said, 'There was killed among us such as, had they been your brother, would have been chosen instead of you.' 'Abd al-Malik was furious and wanted to strike his head off but was told he was old and senile, so desisted. Thereupon, the royal princes, sons of Qaysi women like Walid and Sulayman and Aban ibn Marwan said to 'Abd al-Malik, 'Do not accede to their demands except for the blood-money.' Khalid ibn Yazid and the sons of Kalbite women argued for retaliation. An argument broke out . . . their voices rose in anger and mischief was imminent.[84]

From his bureaucratic vantage point Baladhuri was uniquely qualified to offer ironic though reticent testimony to the lives of the political elite.

---

[82] See, e.g., Baladhuri, *Ansab*, 1:226 (*athbat 'indi*: an unusual phrase) and 228; 4/1:413 (severe criticism of Abu 'Ubayda).
[83] *Ansab*, 4/1:339.
[84] *Ansab*, 5:311.

Tribal history continued: the conquests

The most common superscription on the earliest Islamic coins was the Qur'anic verse: 'It was He Who sent His Apostle with right guidance and the religion of truth to make it triumph over all other religions, despite the hatred of polytheists.' The conquests of the first Islamic century unfolded in great waves, interrupted by periods of recuperation, devastating civil wars, epidemics or official policies of retrenchment or consolidation. Each wave was characterized by the same combination of zeal for this world and zeal for the next. In each wave, the Companions of Muhammad or their Successors were there, in fact or according to later tradition, to mediate the necessary apostolic assurance of divine aid. After every victory, the truth of the message glowed more brightly in pious minds and hearts. And yet, the *Umma* was inflicting lasting wounds not only on the 'polytheists' but also upon itself. There was a great deal to be learnt from this alternation of triumph over the enemy and tragic civil war. A historian in particular would have found much to muse upon in such startling reversals of fortune.

To add to it all, and as is often the case in human history, the impact of the conquests on the conquerors was more profound than it was on the conquered. Within the space of a hundred years or less, a radical transformation had come over the political, social and economic structure of Arab tribes. Not only had many of them left their ancestral Arabian homelands for ever, but the vast majority had to relocate and to readapt to very different social, geographical and cultural environments. This process was no doubt smoother in areas relatively nearer to Arabia, but in many other areas the encounter with foreignness must have been fascinating as well as traumatic. Within the ranks of the conquerors, the new regional ties were becoming as powerful as the earlier tribal ones. All this meant that the conquerors underwent a total change in their way of life within the span of one or two generations. This too must have led the thoughtful or the pious to re-examine belief and action and to try to relate the present to the past.

Conquest, or *Futuh*, historiography has received considerable attention from students of the early Arab conquests. It has long been recognized, for instance, that these accounts are marred by the heroics and sentimentalities of later generations who may have wanted to portray these conquests in terms which conformed to the religious and political requirements of their *own* times.[85] But the genre itself seems to have had a considerable body of eye-witness transmitters, either individuals who took part in certain battles or else collective traditions that came to be known by

---

[85] For an influential critique of these accounts, see Albrecht Noth, 'Isfahan-Nihawand: eine quellenkritische Studie zur frühislamischen Historiographie', *ZDMG*, 118 (1968), 274–96.

the name of the tribal group which transmitted them, e.g. the Bahiliyyun. Perhaps the most convenient place to examine the genesis of this historiographic corpus is the history of Tabari, which preserves most of the corpus in its pristine condition. By comparing the reports of the first and second great waves of conquests, some notion may be gained of the rise and development of the genre.

The first great wave of conquests, approximately in the caliphate of 'Umar and the early caliphate of 'Uthman (c. 13–32/634–652), is described in accounts which vary enormously in style, mood, accuracy and sources. These accounts form a sort of collage where different, sometimes contradictory, versions are left to stand side by side. One central node in this web is Sayf ibn 'Umar (d. 180/796), by far the most important source for this first wave of conquests in Tabari. Sayf brought together a large array of source information, weaving it together into a style which can quite easily be recognized. It is, on the one hand, well crafted, full of drama and moral dialogue, neat and polished in both its facts and figures, often heroic, often contrived, as for instance in 'set pieces' where characters become actors playing roles in a melodrama, as in the following account of the arrival of an Arab envoy at the Persian war camp:

He had his hair tied in four braids on his head, erect like the horns of a mountain she-goat. They said, 'Lay down your weapons.' 'It was not I who came to you so that I might do your bidding but you who invited me. If you refuse to allow me to come as I please, I shall go back.' They told Rustam who said, 'Allow him in. He is after all only a single man.' So he advanced, leaning on his spear . . . slashing their cushions and carpets as he walked so that no cushion or carpet was left unslashed . . . They asked, 'What made you do this?' 'We do not like to sit on these ornaments of yours.' 'What brought you here?' asked Rustam. He replied, 'It was God who called us forth and it was He who sent us to bring out whom He wills from the worship of creatures to the worship of God . . .'[86]

Dreams, omens and portents, great feats of heroism, strange voices and marvels, heroes with names like al-Qa'qa', al-Hammal, and al-Ribbil, verse in the *rajaz* metre reminiscent of the 'battle-days' of pre-Islamic Arabia, set debates between conquerors and conquered and the even more stereotyped debates among the enemy commanders just before battle is joined – these are some of the hallmarks of the Sayf ibn 'Umar style.

On the other hand, Sayf had a wide network of informants many of whom are identified as eyewitnesses. Variant accounts are often preserved,[87] and the lore of Syrian and Iraqi tribes is transmitted, seemingly with care and concern for reliability. But perhaps the most striking aspect of Sayf's activity as a historian is his attempt at reconciliation. In his days,

---

[86] Tabari, *Tarikh*, 1:2271.
[87] See, e.g., Tabari, *Tarikh*, 1:2551–60, for divergent accounts of the encounters between 'Umar and al-Hurmuzan.

the picture of early Islam had already acquired its heroes and its villains for sizeable segments of the community. History was clearly one area where such images could be refocused and where wounds could be healed. His account of the conquests was obviously well suited to this task of rehabilitation. But it is in the earliest *fitan*, or civil wars, that Sayf's ultimate purpose is revealed:

'A'isha said, 'I wish to God I had died twenty years before this battle' . . . 'Ali said, 'I wish to God I had died twenty years before this battle.' Thus their words were the same . . . 'A'isha said, 'My sons, we blamed each other because we considered that things moved too slowly or too much. Let none of you do harm to the other because of what they may have heard of this matter. I swear that in former days there was nothing between me and 'Ali except what may exist between a woman and her in-laws. In my view, 'Ali remains, despite my chagrin, a man of high virtue.' 'Ali said, 'O people, by God she has spoken truly and virtuously. There was nothing between us except that which she has mentioned. She is indeed the wife of your Prophet, in this world and the next.'[88]

When we examine the next great wave of conquests in Tabari, that is the conquests under the caliph al-Walid (86–96/705–715), Sayf vanishes as a source and is largely replaced by 'Ali ibn Muhammad al-Mada'ini (d. 225/ 839). The hero here is one man, Qutayba ibn Muslim al-Bahili, conqueror of Transoxania. As we follow the rise to glory of this proud, rash but brilliant commander, the mood is no longer epic but tragic when, forced into rebellion by an unfriendly caliph, this leader of great armies is finally left to his fate with hardly anyone to defend him. There is little of Sayf's 'romance' here, no miracles or omens. The military campaigns are detailed with detachment and obvious expertise, the localities are specified with care, credible figures are cited and the tone is sombre and restrained. Even the verse is of superior literary merit and often modelled on early-Arabian odes. Mada'ini clearly owes more to the *Hadith* scholars than does Sayf and from time to time spells out his method of arrangement:

Mada'ini said, 'Abu al-Dhayyal mentioned from al-Muhallab ibn Iyas, and al-Mufaddal al-Dabbi from his father, and 'Ali ibn Mujahid and Kulayb ibn Khalaf al-'Ammi – each mentioned one part which I then harmonized, and the Bahiliyyun also mentioned one part which I appended to the former account and then harmonized.'[89]

The contrast with Sayf in style and tone is distinct and due to the much less obvious interference in, and reformulation of the original sources by

---

[88] Sayf ibn 'Umar, *al-Fitnah wa Waq'at al-Jamal*, pp. 177, 183. Sayf has recently been studied by E. Landau-Tasseron, 'Sayf ibn 'Umar in Medieval and Modern Scholarship', *Der Islam*, 67/1 (1990), 1–26, a valiant but logically contorted defence of Sayf which only touches the tip of the problems associated with this historian.

[89] Tabari, *Tarikh*, 2:1204–5. See also Gernot Rotter, 'Zur überlieferung einiger historischer Werke Mada'inis in Tabaris Annalen', *Oriens*, 23–4 (1974), 103–33.

Mada'ini. Regular attention to the dating of the various campaigns lends the work a sense of precision and seriality. Mada'ini generally leads off with his named informants, giving the Bahiliyyun, i.e. the colourful lore of the tribe to which Qutayba himself belonged, the second and clearly less important place in his 'harmonized' narrative.[90]

Hence, in reviewing the beginnings of this particular strand of historical writing, produced in an atmosphere of combative missionary zeal on the one hand and a deep disturbance of spirit because of communal divisions on the other, and later to be recapitulated by skilled historical compilers, at least two main intentions can be traced. The first is the desire to edify, and more specifically to show how the conquests followed naturally from the promise given by God to His prophet. Thus the conquests were the extension of the prophetic *Maghazi* onto the world stage. The second was the desire to narrate the exploits of various tribes, the style well suited for dramatic public recitation. But neither intention necessarily precluded a desire to create an image of a community which, despite its deep divisions, needed to remain united. In the third/eighth century, a third intention is detected, namely the desire to establish an accurate record of the conquests for reasons that may broadly be described as bureaucratic. These intentions will be further explored in the works of three influential historians.

The conquests: three representative histories

The first of them, the *Futuh Misr* ('Conquests of Egypt') by Ibn 'Abd al-Hakam (d. 257/870), is justly renowned for its wealth of detail and its important historiographic lineage, the father of our author having also been a distinguished transmitter of historical reports on early-Islamic Egypt. As a province of the early Arab empire, Egypt was prosperous but politically less significant than Syria, Iraq or Khurasan. It was the gateway to North Africa and Spain, and European travellers were awed and amazed by the wealth of Alexandria. But it was only in the mid-third/ mid-ninth century that Egypt was able once again to reassert its ancient polity under powerful hereditary and semi-autonomous governors. Since time immemorial, the Egypt–Syria axis had been a salient feature of Near-Eastern political life. In the lifetime of Ibn 'Abd al-Hakam, the strategic weight of this axis was to be felt again as the governors of Egypt began to struggle with Iraqi caliphs and strongmen for control of the central Syrian lands and the holy cities of western Arabia. It was a struggle fought with words as well as swords and it pitted the enfeebled Abbasids against vigorous, wealthy and vocal Egyptian governors. Feelings of regional sep-

[90] See Tabari, *Tarikh*, 2:1223, 1230, 1246.

arateness must also have been involved or encouraged as scholars were brought in by both sides to attack or defend the Egyptian 'usurpers'.

The title of the work is a misnomer. Ibn 'Abd al-Hakam arrives at the conquest of Egypt only after a lengthy introduction devoted to Egypt's Biblical and Islamic antiquities. It is an introduction made up almost entirely of *hadith*s of the Prophet, the Companions and early-Egyptian transmitters on the virtues and the antiquities of Egypt, so that when the author finally comes to the conquest itself this appears to be within the divine scheme of things and part of what God intended for this ancient nation. Past and present are frequently conjoined in the manner made popular by Zuhri and his school, namely updating, so that occasional landmarks or social customs are said to have continued 'until today'. The work also ends in *hadith*s arranged in *musnad* form, where the Companion-conquerors and other distinguished personalities who settled in Egypt are listed in approximate order of merit and to each is ascribed the *hadith*s related by or about him. In between these two typical *Hadith* formats come not only the conquests of Egypt itself, together with those of North Africa and Spain, but a compendium of information on the historical topography of Egypt, its taxes and fiefs, the official correspondence of its early conquerors and governors, its judges and so forth. The hero of this middle section is undoubtedly 'Amr ibn al-'As, Egypt's conqueror and a major personality of early Islam. Both 'Amr and the other Companion-conquerors are treated with utmost deference by the author. They are elevated into what may be termed the patron saints of early Egypt, especially at the end of the work where, as pious *muhaddith*s, they impart to Egypt a venerable religious heritage.

There can be little doubt of Ibn 'Abd al-Hakam's broad intention: to place Egypt firmly on the religious map of Islam. Conquered by distinguished Companions of the Prophet, the country still retained many of the mosques, palaces and the other public works that are their memorial. But like the mainstream historians of the *Hadith* school, Ibn 'Abd al-Hakam says little or nothing about his conceptual framework. However, it is conceivable that a frequent motif in *Futuh* historiography, the enemy ambassadors reporting their first impressions of the conquerors, does have contemporary relevance in Ibn 'Abd al-Hakam's version:

We encountered a people for whom death is more welcome than life and humility more than grandeur. None of them has any desire or greed for living . . . Their leader is like one of them, the high cannot be distinguished from the low, nor the master from the slave. When prayer time comes, none is absent.[91]

Given the overall *Hadith*-like structure of the work, such reports may have been meant as a silent reminder of the contrast between pious and

---

[91] Ibn 'Abd al-Hakam, *Futuh Misr wa Akhbaruha*, p. 65.

egalitarian conquerors and the new luxury and magnificence of the Tulunid governors of Egypt.

The second of these works, the *Futuh al-Sham* ('Conquests of Syria') of al-Azdi (d. third/ninth century), is more problematic, since serious doubts exist regarding its dating and authorship.[92] If it is an early work, it is an unusual blend of epic modelled on the ancient tribal battle-days of Arabia, with the southern or Yamani tribes very much to the forefront, and of Qur'anic verses interwoven in the speech, correspondence and sermons of the chief actors. The *isnad* is also somewhat unusual since it comes only at the beginning of long narratives. Azdi's conquests are cast entirely in the heroic mode but his heroes speak as much as they act. In fact, the work begins with a long debate in Medina with speeches by Abu Bakr and other senior Companions about the conquests and then proceeds through sermons, letters, conversations and connected narrative to construct an account where arguments and counter-arguments are as common as the clash of weapons. It is clear that the conquests are a victory not only of Muslim arms but of reason and truth:

> Khalid ibn al-Walid said, 'If I am endowed with reason, it is God who must be thanked for this . . . Keeping faith can only come from reason and a man of no reason cannot keep faith while a man of no faith has no reason.' Bahan replied, 'You are the most rational of men.'[93]

The third of these works, the *Futuh al-Buldan*, ('Conquests of the Lands') of al-Baladhuri, is by far the most famous of the works in this genre. Its fame rests on several grounds. To begin with, it is a work which is not confined to one region but deals with all the conquests both eastern and western. Secondly, it uses a wide spectrum of oral, written and archival sources. Thirdly, it pays close attention to administrative and economic affairs like early local government, fiefs, revenue and taxation. Fourthly, it follows a fairly strict chronological order which facilitates reference and consultation. Finally, it relies quite heavily on the inhabitants of each conquered region for information concerning that region.

The *Futuh* of Baladhuri emanate from the *Maghazi* of the Prophet, as if in fulfilment of this latter. It proceeds to the conquests of the various regions with particular attention to the manner in which these conquests were consolidated, i.e. with or without a treaty, and the resultant taxation in each case. The bureaucratic character of the work is accentuated in its final part, where five seemingly independent sections are devoted to the

---

[92] See Lawrence Conrad, 'Al-Azdi's History of the Arab Conquests in Bilad al-Sham: Some Historiographical Observations' in M. A. Bakhit, ed., *Proceedings of the Second Symposium on the History of Bilad al-Sham*, vol. 1 (Amman: University of Jordan, 1987). Conrad reviews the evidence and proposes, a shade too forcefully, an early date for the work.

[93] Azdi, *Futuh al-Sham*, p. 200.

land tax, the caliph 'Umar's distribution of booty and brief histories of official seals, currency and writing. It is not impossible that what we have here is an abbreviated version of a larger work, a not infrequent practice of the period when handy manuals were becoming more popular with the expanding corps of Abbasid state secretaries. And yet the work exudes an authority which one quickly learns to associate with Baladhuri. As in his *Genealogies*, so also in his *Conquests*, there is the same brusqueness in judging one version 'more firmly established' (*athbat*) than another and the same contrast between reports that carry important legal implications where the *isnad* is very detailed and general historical accounts where the *isnad* is less so. The aim is to construct from the most trustworthy authorities one definitive version of the conquests whose accuracy would help to establish uniformity in legal and administrative precedents.

But in his *Conquests*, Baladhuri reveals more of his strategy as an historian than he does in his *Genealogies*. Having selected his informants from the regions directly involved, often it seems through correspondence,[94] and from a very wide range of sources, including a caliph, state secretaries and scholars, in addition to the works of specialists like Waqidi and Mada'ini, Baladhuri shuns the prodigies and romances of tribal lore. Sayf is cited in only two places and the subsequent contrast between the two historians of the conquests is perhaps intentional. Where Sayf's battles are stirring narratives of feats of individual prowess, the battles of Baladhuri are more controlled accounts where the administration of the conquered regions is the primary concern. The taxes, topography and later administrative history of a province is described with the precision of a trained bureaucrat. Updating is very frequent, and is especially evident in the care taken by Baladhuri to list in detail what the Abbasids ('the blessed state') did by way of building, fortification and land development in each province since its conquest.

The *Futuh* of Baladhuri face in several directions: the accuracy of the civil servant, the taste of the man of letters quoting verse that seems genuine and contemporaneous, the scholarly concerns of the *faqih* citing at length the debates of lawyers on issues of land-tax and of war. These leave little room for fantasy or miracle, for the conquests are transfigured into the genesis and development of empire.

The histories of prophets

The historical sections of the Qur'an are largely devoted to the histories of prophets, Biblical and non-Biblical. These histories, as we saw earlier, are basically stories *retold* to fit into a pattern made up of a prophetic mission with basically the same invitation to people to submit to the One

---

[94] Baladhuri, *Futuh al-Buldan*, pp. 193, 198, 201.

God, the rejection of that mission by the high and haughty, and the disaster which finally overtakes the *umma* of each prophet. Prophecy in the Qur'an is thus a cyclical phenomenon, doomed to a failure from which it can only be rescued by a final revelation. The Muhammadan experience is at once the exemplar and the triumphant completion of that futile cycle.

There seems to have been much interest in these prophetic stories in the early-Islamic milieu, a milieu much more porous than it was to become later on when the full weight of legalism began to be exerted. In fact, stories about figures like Moses and Jesus began to circulate very early in pious Muslim circles and many of these stories were inspired neither by the Bible nor by the Qur'an but by the historical evolution of the community and in answer to its own needs.[95] The early Arab-Muslim societies of Iraq, Syria and Egypt were interpenetrated by older Christian and Jewish communities. Relations with these communities varied a great deal from one province to another but generally speaking all lived in close geographic and spiritual proximity. In addition, the Qur'an itself was not entirely consistent in its attitudes to Christianity, for example. Monastic Christianity fares much better than ecclesiastical to the point where some Christians are said to be the closest of believers to Muslims and even more honest than some Muslims in their business ethics. On the other hand, and if first-century official inscriptions are any indicator of governmental mood, that mood may have been somewhat less tolerant and more intent upon emphasizing the theological differences between Islam and Christianity.[96] On the popular level, Christian hagiography and the sayings and stories of the early Church Fathers undoubtedly filtered into Muslim sentiment and had a particularly deep influence on the mood of early asceticism.

Therefore, the historiography of prophecy needed no stimulus, arising as it did from Qur'anic as well as communal incentives. And yet, many of the earliest transmitters of prophetic history, like Ka'b al-Ahbar, 'Abid ibn Shariya and Wahb ibn Munabbih, were themselves to be engulfed in the same legendary mist which engulfs their own materials. There were several reasons for this. A later generation of legal-minded scholars was impatient with the fantastic or miraculous stories which prophetic lore engendered. One way of casting doubt on such lore was to cast doubt on the very existence of the transmitter.[97] In addition, the lore itself was saddled with so much accretion that *Hadith* specialists and lawyers tended to dismiss such lore as *qasas* and *isra'iliyyat*, a free-floating mass of legends

[95] See Tarif Khalidi, 'The Role of Jesus in Intra-Muslim Polemics in the First Two Islamic Centuries', in S. K. Samir and J. Nielsen, eds., *Christian Arabic Apologetics during the Abbasid Period* (Leiden: E. J. Brill, 1994), pp. 146–56.

[96] See, e.g., the discussion of the inscriptions inside the Dome of the Rock in Jerusalem in Oleg Grabar, *The Formation of Islamic Art* (New Haven and London: Yale University Press, 1973), pp. 62 ff.

[97] Wahb has been rehabilitated by R. G. Khoury: see footnote 24, above.

to which any man's fancy could contribute.[98] Finally, stories about the creation of the world and about ancient prophets were bound up with early attempts at Qur'anic exegesis and often raised disturbing theological issues such as sin and responsibility. Neither the state nor community of consensus-minded scholars in the first two Islamic centuries were willing to look kindly upon a corpus of legends which could be used to fuel civil and religious discord. Accordingly, this corpus had to be islamized, 'domesticated', pruned of its outrageous elements and, like genealogy, made to serve more exacting ideological masters.

It appears therefore that the historiography of prophecy passed through a first period of collection and transmission of a mass of materials by 'experts' who probably continued an ancient narrative tradition, and a second period of increasing control and manipulation by Qur'anic exegetes, lawyers and *Hadith*-inspired historians. In the first period, the function of these stories of ancient prophets appears to have been homiletic while their character and mood was manifestly more popular and with a special appeal to pious and ascetic circles. In the second period, these stories are overlaid with moral examples and a more strict Islamic framework with the clear intention of bringing them into closer accord with dominant legalistic and theological positions. In both periods, sectarian polemics are noticeable.

In examining these developments in greater detail, it is best to begin with Wahb ibn Munabbih (d. c. 112/730), the most celebrated transmitter of ancient and prophetic history in early Arabic historiography. The longest extant work ascribed to Wahb is the *Kitab al-Tijan*, edited by the same Ibn Hisham who edited Ibn Ishaq's famous life of Muhammad. But it is clear from the outset that this is a work heavily infiltrated by later accretions and long passages where Wahb disappears from the text completely. It is more likely that what we have in *Kitab al-Tijan* is an anthology of ancient materials made by Ibn Hisham who takes considerable liberties not only with Wahb's work but also with the materials of the even more shadowy figure of ʿAbid ibn Shariya. Can one recover something of the original Wahb from this pastiche?

The early pages on the creation of the world belong not to Wahb's century but to Ibn Hisham's, for they bring in medical theory and the views of theologians and philosophers current in his days. In all likelihood, Wahb's own materials come a little later, when the stories of Biblical figures like Adam, Noah and Abraham are found intermixed with narratives of the ancient kings of the Yemen, commentaries on Qur'anic verses, homilies, lines of verse, proverbs and tribal genealogies – an apparent medley which was to remain the basis of the account of pre-Islamic times

---

[98] The early layers of such *isra'iliyyat* are discussed in M. J. Kister, '"A Booth like the Booth of Moses . . ." A Study of an Early *hadith*', *BSOAS*, 25 (1962), 150–5.

that later historians accepted, rejected or modified. But it is not impossible to make some sense out of this medley. At the base of it is the attempt to synchronize Biblical and Yemeni history under the aegis, so to speak, of Qur'anic prophetology. The Yemeni, and especially the Himyar, kings are the major actors in this drama which reaches its climax with the identification of the Qur'anic Dhu'l Qarnayn, a mysterious world conqueror derived from the Alexander legend, with a king of Himyar. The moral drawn is one of ever-changing fortune where might always meets its match:

> We have seen in the centuries before us and among the nations of our own times how the powerful and savage oppress the weak and forlorn and how the high and mighty tyrannize the humble and lowly . . . but there has never been a mighty man against whom God has not sent another more mighty to rob him of his power . . . nor any people but God has exacted revenge upon them through another people.[99]

Unfairly, perhaps, Wahb has been censured by later generations of scholars for his large stock of fables and wonders. It is not difficult to understand such censure. Wahb's stories are peopled with jinnis, dragons and snakes, with freaks and monsters, with caves and coffins and corpses buried for hundreds of years and then resurrected. They are full of 'firsts', a favourite with myth-makers of all cultures. And yet one might argue that, for Wahb, entertainment was as legitimate a goal for history as truth or example. This is especially so if entertainment took the form of moral fables about the wonders of creation, the genealogies of the nations, the tyranny of kings and the agonies of prophets.

A later generation of historians was to take a different view of prophetic history. *Hadith*-inclined historians began to work upon these materials, arranging and classifying them. Gradually, they discarded the more monstrous or supernatural components, furnished the stories with Islamic terms, customs and regulations, ascribed to Muhammad more *hadiths* about earlier prophets, increased the number of Qur'anic verses about the prophets and the commentaries upon them, decreased the verse allegedly spoken by ancient patriarchs and prophets and increased the references to the coming of Muhammad by earlier prophets. Among this later generation of historians of prophecy, Abu Rifaʿa ʿUmara ibn Wathima al-Farisi (d. 289/902) in his *Kitab Bad' al-Khalq wa Qisas al-Anbiya'* provides an early and conspicuous example of the transformation of this genre at the hands of the *Hadith* historians.

The work is incomplete but fairly well defined in structure and intention. It is organized in sections called either *sha'n* or *qissa* (account; story) and devoted in the main to prophets cited explicitly in the Qur'an or by its exegetes and in accordance with accepted chronological order. The overall intention appears to be to reformulate the Biblical scriptures through three major devices. The first is the very large number of *Hadith Qudsi*, the so-called divine speech, where God speaks directly or through revelations to prophets, most often to announce or prepare for the coming of Muhammad:

Then [the prophet al-Khidr] said, 'Lord, shall I fight him or shall I not?' God revealed to him: Do not fight him for I have not imposed the duty of fighting except on those who come after you and have not decreed this except for these. Among them is a prophet called Musa ibn 'Imran, the first that I send forth with the sword, then Yusha' ibn Nun, then Dawud and then Muhammad.[100]

A second device is to weave into the stories extensive passages of Qur'anic commentary relevant to each prophet. The intention here is to establish the correct Islamic version of the events by making them concordant with the Qur'anic account. A third device is Muhammadan *Hadith*. The tone and form of many tales of the prophets is set or introduced by *hadith*s from Muhammad which are designed to draw the moral of these tales:

They asked, 'Prophet of God, what are the character traits of prophets?' The Prophet replied 'Among them are honesty, loyalty, thanksgiving, praising God, patience, generosity, benevolence, piety and fear of God.' God had implanted all these traits in al-Khidr.[101]

Echoing the terminology of the Qur'an, a large number of Islamic words and phrases are deployed which have the effect of enveloping the tales in a purely Islamic garb: *dinar, kuttab, dawawin, qadi, hajib, sahib al-shurat, sahib al-suq* and so forth. The speech of prophets is, as in the Qur'an, entirely Islamic in its formulation and one of them, Ilyas, is encountered by Muslims and asked about civil discord. Miracles are virtually confined to prophets while the freaks of creation are reduced to a minimum. But the prophets' tales are well suited to advance certain theological views, notably concerning the problem of *Qadar* or predestination.[102] Several prophets question God on this matter and are told by Him not to pry into this *sirr*, or mystery, since their intellects are too weak to comprehend it. On the other hand, prophecy is entirely consonant with reason:

For everything there is a limit, a fixed purpose and an end, but reason has no limit, fixed purpose or end. Men, however, differ in mind and the contrast between them is as far as what separates heaven from earth. Indeed, the Qur'an itself was revealed through reason, the prophets were sent with reason and they were made superior to the nations by virtue of their minds. Sa'id ibn Jubayr said, 'I was informed that reason was divided in a thousand parts and Muhammad was given nine hundred and ninety parts while his nation was given one part. The same holds

---

[100] Abu Rifa'a, *Kitab Bad' al-Khalq*, p. 22.
[101] Abu Rifa'a, *Bad'*, p. 6.
[102] Abu Rifa'a, *Bad'*, p. 292 ff.

true for other prophets before him.' In fact, God chose the prophets for their reason and He did not endow them with knowledge and perspicacity nor were they able to live the ascetic life in this world with the struggle and patience that this involved except by virtue of their reason.[103]

In sum, the tales of the prophets were to acquire a permanent place in historical writing, especially such as was devoted to world history, where the creation of the world and the early history of prophecy formed the inevitable introduction. It was a particularly sensitive genre because it dealt with the scriptures of Jews and Christians but had to do so not on *their* terms but in conformity with the Qur'anic view and with the inescapable theological problems that this entailed.

Tabari, the 'imam' of *Hadith* historiography

It is fitting that this chapter on History and *Hadith* should end with Muhammad ibn Jarir al-Tabari (d. 310/923). His *History of Prophets and Kings* and his Qur'anic *Commentary* were both massive works and brought him an equally massive reputation even in his own lifetime. As a scholar of the law and *Hadith*, he was propelled into public life and embroiled in controversy, probably against his own inclinations, inspiring a legal 'school' or *madhhab* which was named after him and which lasted for a brief while. His immense output spanned much of the third/ninth century and reflected a wide range of that century's scholarly concerns. In his *History of Prophets and Kings*, Tabari combined the history of creation and prophecy with the history of ancient nations, especially the Persians, adding to them a *Sira* of Muhammad, his *Maghazi*, the conquests, and a history of the community up to his own days. In his methodology, it is possible to find echoes of Ibn Ishaq's universalism, of Waqidi's consensualism and accuracy, of Baladhuri's crisp verdicts and of Ibn 'Abd al-Hakam's moral epic. And it was Tabari who composed what was by far the most explicit defence of the *Hadith* method in historical writing, while his annalistic arrangement enshrined a style that lasted until modern times.[104]

In a famous passage near the beginning of his history, Tabari sets forth what he takes to be the only means by which one can arrive at a knowledge of the past:

---

[103] Abu Rifa'a, *Bad'*, p. 128
[104] In classical Arabic literature, the two most important sources for Tabari's life and works are Baghdadi, *Tarikh*, 2:162–9 and Yaqut, *Irshad*, 18:40–94. In English, see E. L. Petersen, *'Ali and Mu'awiya in Early Arabic Tradition* (Copenhagen: Munksgaard, 1964), pp. 149–59 and, especially, Franz Rosenthal, *The History of Tabari*, vol. 1, *General Introduction and From the Creation to the Flood* (Albany: SUNY Press, 1989), pp. 5–134.

Let him who examines this book of mine know that I have relied, as regards everything I mention therein which I stipulate to be described by me, solely upon what has been transmitted to me by way of reports which I cite therein and traditions which I ascribe to their narrators, to the exclusion of what may be apprehended by rational argument or deduced by the human mind, except in very few cases. This is because knowledge of the reports of men of the past and of contemporaneous news of men of the present do not reach the one who has not witnessed them nor lived in their times except through the accounts of reporters and the transmission of transmitters, to the exclusion of rational deduction and mental inference. Hence, if I mention in this book a report about some men of the past which the reader or listener finds objectionable or worthy of censure because he can see no aspect of truth nor any factual substance therein, let him know that this is not to be attributed to us but to those who transmitted it to us and we have merely passed this on as it had been passed on to us.[105]

Knowledge of the past cannot be deduced or inferred; it can only be transmitted. Echoing terms that were becoming current in his days for the division of the sciences into *'aqliyya* (rational) and *naqliyya* (transmitted), Tabari sought to place history squarely in the second category, making it into a branch of *Hadith*.[106] But before we explore his *History*, an overall idea of the nature of the problems he faced and the range of his scholarship can best be obtained from his Qur'anic *Commentary*.

Tabari's *Commentary* is a massive work of erudition, displaying its author's mastery over a wide spectrum of subjects and argumentation. A fairly consistent plan is followed in the exegesis. To begin with, each verse is carefully paraphrased. Then follow *hadith*s from Muhammad or his Companions and the views of distinguished early scholars in support of the paraphrase and amplifying its historical and theological context. If these *hadith*s are in conflict, Tabari concludes with a summary of his own views. In a great many cases, the exegesis of a single verse can extend over several pages and it is here that Tabari is both erudite and polemical. If a grammatical problem is at issue, the views of both Kufan and Basran grammarians are quoted and assessed. Poetic examples are used profusely as illustration. If a historical event is in dispute, the *isnad* deemed most trustworthy is accepted. If a point of law is involved, *qiyas*, or reasoning by analogy, is deployed to settle the argument, the analogy resting upon other Qur'anic texts, Muhammadan *hadith* or the 'consensus of the exegetes' (*ijma' ahl al-ta'wil*). In general, the levels of priority used to establish proof (*hujja*; *shahid*) of correct interpretation may be set out as follows:

[105] Tabari, *Tarikh*, 1:6–7. R. S. Humphreys, *Islamic History: A Framework for Inquiry*, p. 72, discusses this passage briefly, mistranslating it in several places. He ascribes Tabari's reluctance to speak in his own voice to the (otherwise undefined) 'concept of knowledge in early Islamic culture'.
[106] For the division of the sciences in this period, see, e.g., Farabi, *Ihsa' al-'Ulum*.

1 Reports from God or His Prophet through abundant transmission.
2 Consensus of exegetes on points of law, history or doctrine.
3 Analogy, e.g. from accepted grammatical usage or poetry.

Levels 1 and 2 are dependent upon reports (*akhbar*) and are therefore transmitted (*manqul*). Abundant (*mustafid*) transmission is never fully defined but appears to imply a quantitative and qualitative yardstick as in the following terse comment:

> Of the two interpretations that of Hasan is closer to the literal meaning of Revelation . . . but the *akhbar* regarding the second interpretation are greater in number and those who hold it are more knowledgeable in exegesis.[107]

Level 3 is called by Tabari analogy (*qiyas*), inference (*istidlal*) or scholarly judgement (*ijtihad*). He resorts to this when Levels 1 and 2 are lacking or in conflict. His formidable knowledge of grammar is applied in almost every verse he paraphrases in order to establish the correct reading and understanding of the text. This grammatical standpoint is linked to his view of the Qur'anic text as one where literal (*zahir*) interpretation, based upon common Arabic discourse, must be applied.[108] Analogies with other verses of the Qur'an or other *hadith*s from the Prophet are employed to infer meaning where meaning is ambiguous. Where legal issues are involved his view is that commandments must be regarded as applying in an absolute or general sense unless a specific application can be demonstrated.[109] Combining all three levels of proof, Tabari's theology is inimical to many powerful groups of his day such as the Qadariyya, the Jahmiyya, the Khawarij and some Sufis.[110]

The elaborate scheme of interpretation arrayed in the Qur'anic *Commentary* is fairly rigidly demarcated. The paraphrase, the grammatical gloss, the analogies, the *hadith*s quoted and the legal inferences drawn are all centred upon a text of manifest clarity. If one strategy of interpretation fails, another is brought into play but the revelation itself is ultimately accessible through literal interpretation and hence incapable of misrepresentation except by the perverse or stupid. Tabari is rarely in doubt as to his own views on what revelation means or implies.

But in his *History* the landscape is quite different. Here, there is no manifest clarity, no *bayan*, but only *akhbar* which, stretching from the creation of the world to the Last Hour across a span of 14,000 years in Tabari's estimation, vary enormously in import and veracity.[111] Tabari was faced here with 1) a mass of pre-Islamic historical materials transmitted by such authorities as Ibn 'Abbas, Wahb and Ibn Ishaq, 2) a fairly well-

---

[107] Tabari, *Tafsir*, 3:225.
[108] E.g., Tabari, *Tafsir*, 5:109.
[109] Tabari, *Tafsir*, 4:27, 136.
[110] Tabari, *Tafsir*, 3:111–12; 5:20; 7:109; 8:91.
[111] Tabari, *Tarikh*, 1:55.

delineated *Sira* of the Prophet, thanks to the labours of scholars like Ibn
Ishaq and Waqidi and 3) an enormous and expanding body of historical
reports covering the conquests, the Umayyad and the early-Abbasid
periods transmitted by scholars like 'Awana, Abu Mikhnaf, Sayf, the two
Kalbis, Mada'ini, Waqidi and so forth.[112] Unlike the *Commentary*, where
inference and deduction could be employed to wrest meaning out of a text
whose ultimate clarity is, as it were, vouched for by the Almighty Himself,
in the *History* Tabari is at the mercy of his transmitters. The historian's
constricted role may be seen in the following hypothetical objection of
one who legitimately uses Tabari's own reasoning against him:

If someone says, What is your proof that the six days in which God created His
creation amounted each to one thousand years by earthly reckoning . . . since God
Himself tells us in His book 'He Who created the Heavens and earth and what is
between them in six days' . . . and you yourself claim that God's discourse to His
creatures in His revelation is directed to the most obvious, literal and patent
meaning whereas you now seem to interpret God's own words in His book about
the creation of the world in six days in a manner which does not tally with the
usual meaning of a day . . . for it is God's command, if He wills something, to
say to it Be! and it is . . . We answer that we have already asserted in this work
that we rely in most of what we describe in this book of ours on traditions and
reports from our Prophet – upon whom blessings and peace – and from pious
ancestors before us, to the exclusion of rational or mental deduction since most
of it is an account of past events and present happenings, and these cannot be
comprehended by rational inference and deduction.[113]

This passage is a convenient point at which to observe the contrast between
Tabari's *Commentary* and his *History*. For whereas a fairly wide range of
interpretative resources are available to elucidate revelation, history is
made up of *akhbar* which cannot be inferred or deduced but can only be
transmitted. Moreover, if the 'Be! and it is' of the divine command governs
creation, there is no obvious procedure by which one can separate the true
from the false in history since the command must always be admissible. For
Tabari, the category of *ja'iz* (possible; admissible) was always operative
where no divine revelation or prophetic *hadith* declares the contrary. For
instance, in discussing the original site of the Ka'ba, Tabari sets forth the
alternatives:

It is possible (*ja'iz*) that it was a ruby or a pearl made to descend from heaven. It
is also possible that Adam had built it and that it fell into ruin until its foundations
were raised by Abraham and Ishmael. We have no knowledge as to which of these

---

[112] The most exhaustive treatment of Tabari's sources is in Jawad 'Ali, 'Mawarid Ta'rikh
al-Tabari', *Majallat al-Majma' al-'Ilmi al-'Iraqi*, 1 (1950), 143–231; 2 (1951), 135–90; 3
(1954), 16–58; 8 (1961), 425–36. See also Claude Gilliot, 'La formation intellectuelle de
Tabari (224/5–310/839–923)', *Journal Asiatique*, 276 (1988), 203–44, who follows Tabari's
life from place to place and lists his masters in each.

[113] Tabari, *Tarikh*, 1:55–6.

two alternatives it was. For the reality of this can only be arrived at by a report from God or from His prophet by abundant transmission (*naql mustafid*). In this instance there exists no report establishing proof and necessitating acceptance. Nor is this a case which, in the absence of a report such as we described above, can be proven by inference or by analogy as compared with other cases, nor can it be deduced by individual reason.[114]

Given the derivative nature of historical reports, can there be no room at all for internal criticism, even if only the curt verdicts of a Waqidi or a Baladhuri? The surface of Tabari's text, aside from the passages cited above, contains very few comments on method or even on the truth or falsity of the *akhbar* he transmits. But in examining these comments, one or two broad principles of selection may be noted.

The first principle is the one already familiar from the *Commentary* and, earlier on, from Waqidi, namely the appeal to the majority view of early scholars:

The first report is of better derivation (*asahhu makhrajan*) and with greater claim to truth because it is what most predecessors affirm.[115]

A 'better derivation' is of course a better *isnad* while the majority view is supplemented by what Tabari considers to be reports too well known to be in dispute:

The people of the Torah claim that there is no mention of 'Ad, Thamud, Hud or Salih in the Torah. But they are as well known among the Arabs of both the *Jahiliyya* and Islam as Abraham and his people. Had I not been loath to prolong this work . . . I would have quoted verses about 'Ad and Thamud by *jahili* poets . . . enough to convince any who dispute their fame among the Arabs.[116]

Well-known verse becomes an additional channel of verification, as it had been for earlier historians.

The second principle of selection is what may be called the appeal to experts. At their head stands Muhammad, 'most knowledgeable of God's creatures in what has happened in the past and what is yet to happen'.[117] More broadly, the principle is phrased as follows, in the course of a critique of Hisham al-Kalbi:

What Hisham says here with regard to king Hushang is baseless since this king is better known to experts on Persian genealogy than al-Hajjaj ibn Yusuf is to Muslim genealogists. Every people is better acquainted with their own ancestry, genealogy

---

[114] Tabari, *Tafsir*, 1:410; cf. *Tarikh*, 1:85.
[115] Tabari, *Tarikh*, 1:52; cf. 1:252–3.
[116] Tabari, *Tarikh*, 1:252–3. Why did Tabari not consult the Bible directly? Other contemporary historians, e.g. Ya'qubi, had clearly done so. Perhaps, and in line with his view about consulting the experts of each nation regarding their own history (see footnote 118, below), he felt that the Arabs alone could settle the problem of the Arabian prophets.
[117] Tabari, *Tarikh*, 1:416–17.

and achievements than others. In all matters of doubt, recourse must be had to the experts (*ila ahlihi*).[118]

The little that Tabari has to say on the epistemic status and the evaluation of historical reports is to be found in the pre-Islamic portion of his *History*. The reason is largely because it was in that era that Tabari felt most urgently the need to *reshape* history in order to conform with both the form and the substance of the Qur'anic view. He was thus, as we shall see below, one of the earliest of Islam's historians to project a vision of history inspired by the regular rhythms of Qur'anic narrative. For the history of the pre-Islamic era, two great historiographical traditions were recognized by Tabari as authoritative and of particular relevance to Islam: the Biblical and the Persian. The Biblical tradition had of course been incorporated already into Islamic historiography by earlier scholars, notably Ibn Ishaq. But the Persian tradition was one which Tabari was to defend explicitly, preferring it above all others, e.g. the Yemenite, as in the following passage:

Writing the history of the world in times past in accordance with the reigns of their kings is easier to expound and more illuminating than it is with the reigns of kings of other nations. For no nation among those that claim descent from Adam is known to have had a lasting kingdom, a continuous kingship, kings to unite them and chiefs to defend them against enemies . . . in an uninterrupted, constant and regular manner, where the last takes over from the first . . . except them . . . hence, the history written in accordance with the reigns of their kings is the best documented and the clearest.[119]

Later, he adds a further clarification:

As for nations other than the Persian, it is impossible to arrive at a knowledge of their history since they did not have uninterrupted kingship, either in ancient or in modern times, except such as cannot form the subject of a continuous history . . . In the Yemen, there were kings ruling kingdoms but kingship was interrupted. One king would follow another but there were long gaps in between which scholars cannot estimate because little care was taken in this regard or in recording the age of each and of the following king, for there was no continuous succession.[120]

These long historical traditions had the added advantage for Tabari of overlapping and then merging into one another so that the Biblical line of the Israelites was ended by the Persian and the Persian was ended by the *umma* of Muhammad.[121] Tabari therefore set himself the task of bringing these histories into harmony by synchronization of chronologies. This meant that the Biblical line of descent from Adam and his progeny was

---

[118] Tabari, *Tarikh*, 1:155; see also 1:847.
[119] Tabari, *Tarikh*, 1:148.
[120] Tabari, *Tarikh*, 1:353.
[121] ibid.

to be reconciled to the line from Kayumarth, the Persian Adam, and his royal successors. Thus, the stories of such figures as Adam, Noah, Abraham and Moses were taken from the Islamic historical tradition, amended if necessary by reference to the Qur'an and *Hadith*, and then interwoven with their contemporaneous Persian kings.[122] One, continuous and comparative history of the pre-Islamic world was now created. The *umma* was thus shown to be the prophetic heir of Biblical tradition and the temporal heir of Persian dominion.[123]

Accordingly, a fabric had been built by which the Muslim community could situate itself with respect to the past. One might argue that Tabari's intention was to historicize the Qur'an, to transform its timeless, one-dimensional allegories into historical narrative that reflected the scholarly interests and attachment to 'pious ancestors' current among the *Hadith* group to which he belonged. But his *History* also had a more explicit intention:

Our intention in this work is to record what we have indicated to be its content, that is, the history of mighty kings, both those who disobeyed and those who obeyed God, and the times of messengers and prophets . . . Let us now turn to the mention of the first to be given dominion and blessings by God who then showed ingratitude, denied and rebelled against God and waxed proud. God then withdrew His blessings, shamed him and brought him low. We shall follow this with a mention of those who followed in his path . . . and earned God's wrath . . . as well as contemporaneous or later praiseworthy kings who obeyed God.[124]

In this as in another passage on the same theme,[125] Tabari seeks to illustrate what he takes to be the origin, structure and ultimate destiny of world history, as symbolized by the struggle of prophets and kings. It was a vision inspired by the Quranic conflict between prophets and 'pharaohs', a parallel history first set in motion by Adam and Satan and their respective 'party' (*fariq*)[126] and thereafter traceable in the histories of 'every despotic king and every appointed caliph'.[127] The Adamic fate is one of sin, repentance and ultimate reconciliation with God. The Satanic is of unrepentant disobedience. It is a history of moral 'types', and one which might be expected to set the stage for what is to come in the Islamic portion of the work.

But the Islamic portion is far different. It is made up of a *Sira* built mainly from the materials of Ibn Ishaq and Waqidi, a section on the conquests and an annalistic history of the leading figures of the community until the year 302/915. The annals are introduced with the beginning of

---

[122] E.g., Tabari, *Tarikh*, 1:506.
[123] The Persian influence will be discussed in Chapter Three.
[124] Tabari, *Tarikh*, 1:78.
[125] Tabari, *Tarikh*, 1:4–5.
[126] Tabari, *Tarikh*, 1:164.
[127] Tabari, *Tarikh*, 1:5.

the Hijri calendar, approximately half way through the prophetic mission, and strictly adhered to until the end. There is no trace in this whole portion of the *History* of any explicit judgement on men or events nor any speculation on the course or significance of events. Within each year one or more major event is usually introduced as a 'headline' and subsequently its causes, development and outcome are presented by tying together the accounts of several informants, or by keeping these accounts separate, resulting in much repetition and what are often minor variations in detail.

There is much that needs to be explained in this abrupt change of structure and mood. The annalistic scheme was perhaps a natural one to select for the *Hijri* era and the scheme itself had already been adopted by the historians of the third/ninth century.[128] Its year-by-year tempo parallels the verse-by-verse analysis of the *Commentary*. More difficult to explain, however, is the almost total absence of any comments on the veracity of reports or any moral verdict on events of momentous consequences to the Muslim community. It may of course be said that Tabari had already asserted that a historian was only a transmitter, and yet a pattern of conflict was seen to obtain in the pre-Islamic period which was nowhere spelled out in the Islamic. The 'Adams' and the 'Satans' of Islamic history are left largely to the judgement of the reader.

The three centuries or so of Islamic history that Tabari records were dotted with events that had grievous political and theological consequences. Many of the issues engendered were still very hot in Tabari's own days. Several strands of historical writing had arisen which show bald or subtle bias in favour of one party or another. As we saw above, Tabari in his *Commentary* had expressed views inimical to the Qur'anic interpretations of some of these politico-religious groups like the Qadariyya, Jahmiyya, Khawarij and Sufis. But historical reports could not be similarly attacked or dismissed. One must therefore presume that Tabari exercised great care in selecting reports which he held to have been most trustworthy, in line with his avowed reliance on the experts in each field. And yet, the first *Fitna* or civil war in Islamic history, which pitted the third caliph 'Uthman against his enemies, was one event whose disastrous repercussions could still be deeply divisive. Few if any of the Prophet's Companions could be said to have come out of that ordeal unblemished in character or behaviour. In reconstructing that civil war, Tabari relied heavily on Ibn Ishaq, Sayf and Waqidi, all of whom, upon very close examination,

---

[128] No fully satisfactory explanation has yet been given of the origins of annalistic historiography in the Arabic tradition. R. S. Humphreys, *Islamic History*, p. 106, says that the *Tarikh* of Khalifa ibn Khayyat (d. 241/855) 'seems in fact to have been the first general annalistic work to be composed in Arabic'. A more likely candidate for this honour is al-Haytham ibn 'Adi (d. 206/821): see Duri, *Rise*, pp. 53–4, and Noth, *The Early Arabic Historical Tradition*, p. 42. It is not impossible that both Ibn Ishaq and al-Waqidi used an annalistic format in some of their works: see, e.g. Tabari, *Tarikh*, 1:2479–80 and 2516.

reveal some degree of bias in favour of one group or another. How did Tabari handle these terrible events?[129]

In transmitting the materials of his three distinguished predecessors, Tabari was bound to transmit also three divergent and divisive versions of the *Fitna*. There was no way in which he could create, as he tried to do in his *Commentary*, a single or unified interpretation which would exclude 'heresy'. And to identify the 'Adams' and 'Satans' of that particular episode in history would almost certainly have meant the adoption of an extreme sectarian position, a highly unlikely position for him to adopt given his general anti-sectarianism. What he really thought of these events and especially of their implications regarding the moral behaviour of Muhammad's Companions will probably never be known. But there are a few hints as to his process of selection:

As for Waqidi, he records many incidents in connection with the reasons which made the Egyptians march out against 'Uthman and their camping at Dha Khushub. I have related some of them above and refrained from mentioning others owing to my abhorrence at mentioning them due to their repugnant nature (*basha 'atih*).[130]

Later, he adds,

We have mentioned already many of the reasons which those who killed him [sc. 'Uthman] cited as a pretext for killing him but have refrained from mentioning many more for reasons which call for such refraining. We turn now to how he was killed and how this began.[131]

It is fairly clear from these two short passages that while Tabari could not, in conformity with his definition of a historian, edit, rationalize or argue away the trauma of that war, he did attempt to minimize the damage by avoiding any reference to reports he considered 'morally repugnant'. If it was too late to rescue Islamic history from partisanship, it could at least be pruned of its more offensive episodes.

Concluding observations

Hadith had served history well. It had inspired its earliest form and methods. It had provided it with its chief vehicle for the establishment of veracity, the *isnad*. It had instilled into it something of its own dry factuality and attention to detail. By preserving divergent accounts of events, the

---

[129] The late Marshall Hodgson attempted a brilliant analysis of Tabari's handling of the murder of 'Uthman in his 'Two Pre-modern Muslim Historians: Pitfalls and Opportunities in Presenting them to Moderns', in John U. Nef, ed., *Towards World Community* (The Hague: W. Junk, 1968). But perhaps too much is read into Tabari's account as regards his ultimate political and moral position.

[130] Tabari, *Tarikh*, 1:2965.

[131] Tabari, *Tarikh*, 1:2980.

history written under the epistemic umbrella of *Hadith* enables the modern historian to assess the different historiographical traditions and to reconstruct the emergent views of various politico-religious parties and movements.

Nevertheless, a parting of the ways was bound to occur as the territory and interests of each discipline were more rigidly defined. As *Hadith* became more circumscribed by succeeding generations of scholars intent upon greater control and testability of the material, encouraged in this endeavour by governments pursuing greater uniformity of judicial and administrative practice, history was expanding beyond the bounds of such control. Even Tabari, when he approaches his own days, is found to abandon the *isnad* and to resort increasingly to such terms as 'I was told', 'It reached me' or simply, 'It was said'. As the history of the *umma* filled out to catch the winds, it was regarded with ever-increasing fascination by both the ruling elites and the literati as an imperial history on a par with the history of other great nations. It was natural that parallels would be detected, that hopes and fears would be raised.

In order to see history in this broader, more universal perspective, *Hadith* was obviously ill equipped. The *isnad* was largely unobtainable or irrelevant where foreign nations were concerned. But more importantly, the *isnad* was designed not for the expression of personal opinion but for accuracy of transmission. If history was to yield its lessons, the historian would have to sever the 'chain' of *isnad* and draw out the full implications of the narrative by revealing his own intentions and strategy. Other criteria would have to be applied to both the selection of reports as well as their assessment. Other styles would need to be employed to express the new mood. History began to be affected by *Adab*.

CHAPTER 3

History and *Adab*

In the course of the third/ninth century, historical writing began to respond to the increasing influence of *Adab* and, in doing so, to modify its content, form and perspective. A gradual shift in mood carried history into a new and more 'secular' environment. In this environment, the style and horizons of *Hadith* were no longer seen to be adequate carriers of a history now required to be more pragmatic and more sensitive to the challenge of foreign cultures. *Adab* was the chief instrument of this transformation.

In many European histories of Arabic literature the word *Adab* is translated as 'Belles-Lettres'. One could argue that the classical Greek 'Paideia' is a more accurate rendering of the term since *Adab*, like Paideia, refers to a process of moral and intellectual education designed to produce an *adib*, a gentleman-scholar, and is thus intimately connected with the formation of both intellect and character. In its earliest days *Adab* meant education. With time it came to mean a *special* kind of education, a moral and intellectual curriculum aimed at a particular urban class and reflecting the needs and aspirations of that class. To understand its influence on historical writing, one must first explore the environment in which *Adab* grew and attempt to show how and why it came to exercise that influence.

The rise of *Adab*

We saw above how early *Hadith*, by casting its net wide over the lore of the community, pulled in a mixed bag of 'traditions', an undifferentiated mass of reports differing greatly in nature and religious importance. By slow degrees, and largely under state or factional guidance, groups of specialized scholars began to give this mass a more manageable structure so that this structure could function as legal precedent and historical image to a society more intent on separating itself from its environment, more determined to delineate its religious contours. With specialization came rigour and with rigour a 'science' with its distinct principles and method. It was under this 'Science of *Hadith*' that historical writing first found shelter.

But if the history of *Hadith* in its first three centuries is the history of a process which first expanded and then systematically narrowed the content and focus of its subject-matter, creating thereby a core of specialized knowledge and of specialists, the history of *Adab* followed a different, even an opposite trajectory. Perhaps the earliest category of reports to undergo vigorous sifting by the *Hadith* scholars were the reports that had to do with the antiquities of Arabia and of other nations, which these scholars felt to be irrelevant to a strict ordering of the life of Muhammad and his Companions. But as the Umayyad state took shape, it became a large-scale consumer and patron of this body of antiquities and of the auxiliary skills which were needed to comprehend them:

For the first third of the night, Mu'awiya would occupy himself with the history and the *Ayyam* of the Arabs . . . retire to sleep for the second third then rise and settle down, order that the volumes containing the lives and histories of kings and their wars and stratagems be brought to him and have them read to him by servants specially assigned to do so and entrusted to memorize and recite them. Thus, each night, he would listen to a series of reports, life histories, tales of the past and all kinds of political precepts.[1]

Although such reports were perhaps ascribed to Mu'awiya by a later age, they are nevertheless credible and indicate an increasing concern by the Umayyads as a whole with the theory and practice of politics. There is little doubt that Mu'awiya was intent upon dynastic rule as soon as he had consolidated his power after the first civil war. In Syria, Iraq and Egypt, where dynastic government had been the norm for centuries, the Umayyads were surrounded by monuments and memories of imperial predecessors. But to induce the powerful tribes and groups in the Arab empire to accept the dynastic principle required, in addition to force and bribery, a massive campaign of persuasion. Hence the need for a new kind of political rhetoric to be disseminated by the caliph himself and by royal propagandists: poets, state secretaries, learned courtiers and even religious scholars, who could be prevailed upon to shed their suspicion of autocracy (*mulk*) and to defend dynastic rule. The 'lives and histories of kings' of foreign nations were clearly an important part of the process of persuasion since their aim was not only to inspire the caliph himself but also to familiarize his subjects with historical parallels and continuities.

Many later Umayyads, we are told, were as interested in ancient history as Mu'awiya and as intent upon the cultivation of the orator's skills. But perhaps the most important political impulse to the systematic development of interest in the sciences of the Arabic language came from the arabization of the administration, undertaken by the caliph 'Abd al-Malik

---

[1] Mas'udi, *Muruj*, 3:222, para. 1836.

and carried through by his successors.[2] This policy resulted in a gradual and far-reaching transformation of the bureaucratic structure, the creation of new routines of government and the rise of new classes of bureaucrats and a new secretarial 'style'. The new bureaucrats were soon to become skilled professionals who were trained to express the finest shades of mood and meaning in the letters and directives of their masters and frequently passed on their jobs and skills to their descendants. As court procedure came to be imitated in provincial capitals, a corps of state secretaries with a highly developed art began to occupy a distinct and influential position throughout the empire and to be associated in the popular mind with a particular style of literature, to which we shall return below.

But the rise of *Adab* is also linked to a host of other religious, cultural, political and social factors which cannot be as easily outlined as the bureaucratic factor. As the term *'ilm* in the mid- to late-Umayyad period came to refer increasingly to religious knowledge, that is to say primarily *Hadith*, *Tafsir* (Qur'an exegesis) and *Fiqh* (jurisprudence), it is tempting to apply the term *Adab* to secular knowledge, that is to say philology, grammar, poetry, history, the natural sciences and so forth. But this would be too simplistic since linguistic skill has always been considered an essential prerequisite for religious knowledge. And yet it might be possible for us to draw a distinction between two spirits, two intentions, two attitudes to the function and propagation of learning in society. For while the *Hadith* scholar of the second or third centuries of Islam was occupied with the collection, assessment and arrangement of his materials for the sake of incorporating them into a system of belief and action, the *adib* would be more typically occupied in the pursuit of such materials for their own sake and wherever they might lead him. Where a *muhaddith* would be likely to regard Islam as a complete and completed cultural system, an *adib* would be more likely to regard Islam as a cultural beginning, a constant invitation to examine the world of man and nature. Where a *Hadith* scholar might regard knowledge itself as a necessarily circumscribed and even shrinking commodity, an *adib* might be more inclined to view knowledge as progressing endlessly into the future. And finally, where a *muhaddith* might consider certain subjects as irrelevant, uncouth or even harmful to the religious life, an *adib* would be more likely to tolerate all knowledge for its potentially aesthetic appeal.

The spirit of *Adab* fed from many springs. Certain tensions, which in times of trouble could erupt into war, were in stable times a fertile source of literary controversy. The tensions between the cities of Kufa and Basra, between Iraq and the Hijaz, between city man and nomad, between Arab

---

[2] Abbott, *Studies*, 3:4. See also the symbolic anecdote in 'Askari, *Masun*, pp. 169–72, about the caliph 'Abd al-Malik and the rise of *Adab*.

and non-Arab, between northern Arabs and southern Arabs, between the Islamic ethos and the lure of the *Jahiliyya*, between one social class and another in newly established capitals, and between religious scholars (*'ulama'*) and preachers (*qussas*) and *adibs* – all these tensions inspired a great deal of polemic, in verse and prose.[3] *Adab* thrived on the cut and thrust of argument, on the subtleties of rhetoric and on the free use of testimony from all quarters to validate its ideals.

The Qur'an and *jahili* poetry were the two earliest textual inspirations of the kind of activity that was later to be called *Adab*. Orthography and grammar were intimately linked with early Qur'an exegesis while *jahili* poetry called forth a host of linguistic and critical skills intended to explain and assess this poetry.[4] What concerns us most directly here is the way in which these early experts and critics used historical arguments to prove or disprove the authenticity of verse which was always used to corroborate events:

Abu 'Ubayda [d. 211/826] said, 'Al-Nisar are a chain of mountains . . . regarding which we have reports and claims from the Ribab . . . which in my view are false, contradictory and taken from ignorant people. Verse, authentic and undeniable, affirms the opposite . . . The Day of Nisar was after the Day of Jabala, and not as the Ribab maintain . . . the proof being that if Hudhayfa had been alive, he would have led the alliance and not his son Hisn who is mentioned in the following verse . . . further proof is that Hajib would not have led Tamim if Laqit had been alive and Laqit was killed on the Day of Jabala.'[5]

The verses which Ibn Ishaq included in his *Sira* were criticized in the following manner:

Among those who did violence to poetry and corrupted it, transmitting so much worthless verse was Muhammad ibn Ishaq . . . He was a scholar of history (*siyar*) and men transmitted his verse too. He would apologize and say, 'I have no knowledge of poetry. It is passed to me and I transmit it.' But this is no excuse. In his history he included verse by men who never spoke any verse . . . and moreover he ascribed some of it to 'Ad and Thamud. Did he not wonder and ask himself who carried this verse and transmitted it for thousands of years? For God says, 'He it was who destroyed the First 'Ad and Thamud, leaving no trace.'[6]

---

[3] For some examples of these tensions, see, e.g., Ibn Qutayba, *'Uyun*, 1:220 (Basra and Kufa); Ibn 'Abd al-Barr, *Jami'*, 1:153 (Kufa and Mecca); Ibn al-Jarrah, *Waraqa*, pp. 102–3, and Jahiz, *Bayan*, 2:310 (city men and nomads); Jahiz, *Bayan*, 3:12 ff. and Ibn Qutayba, *K. al-'Arab* in Kurd 'Ali, *Rasa'il*, pp. 344 ff. (Arab and non-Arab); Isfahani, *Aghani*, 20:208–9 (North vs. South); Jahiz, *Hayawan*, 2:108 (*Jahiliyya* and Islam); Jahiz, *Hayawan*, 5:105 (class characteristics); Jumahi, *Tabaqat*, p. 18 and chapter 2, footnote 16, above, (*'ulama'* vs. *qussas* and *udaba'*).

[4] The best introduction to this subject is Abbott, *Studies*, 3.

[5] Dabbi, *Mufaddaliyyat*, pp. 363–4.

[6] Jumahi, *Tabaqat*, p. 4.

Early critical texts such as these display a pronounced willingness to speak in the first person singular, to pass severe and explicit verdicts on men and events and to use historical and literary evidence to prove or disprove authenticity. Unlike the transmitters of *Hadith*, who felt themselves constrained by their subject-matter to withdraw into the background and allow their material to speak for itself, the early *adib*s felt no such constraint. The attack on Ibn Ishaq is typical: to an expert on poetry, the verses he transmits are pronounced worthless no matter how renowned he may be as an authority on biography and history. Where the strictly religious sciences aimed increasingly at consensus and uniformity, *Adab* tolerated an ever-widening spectrum of individual taste and critical judgement.

But the greatest achievement of early *Adab* was what may be called the rediscovery of the *Jahiliyya*. If there was one overriding motive for this, it may well have been the restructuring of Arab tribes, the most important political issue of the Umayyad period. Following the waves of conquests, profound changes would occur in the settlement patterns, political alignments and social disposition of the tribes. The Umayyad house was the apex of a tribal pyramid but the relationship between base and apex was a dynamic one, changing in response to political and economic pressures. In this turbulent atmosphere of shifting loyalties, it was perhaps natural to seek to uncover origins, to re-establish the links with pre-Islamic Arabia which the ethos of Islam had attempted to circumscribe and the trauma of conquests had forcibly severed.

In late-Umayyad and early-Abbasid *Adab*, two principles of Arabic philology were widely accepted: the superiority of *jahili* over Islamic poetry as a model of prosody, grammar and usage, and the nomadic Arabs as the arbiters of correct Arabic and of eloquence (*fasaha*).[7] The process by which these two principles were established was essentially an exercise in antiquarian reconstruction in the course of which debate was often fierce. At the end of it, a body of *jahili* prose and poetry had been 'recovered', though its authenticity was an endless subject of dispute which need not detain us here. But the debate itself helped to free the potentialities of *Adab*, to mark out new lines of expertise and to resurrect and develop a 'humanistic' spirit which did not always coexist in peace with the rapidly maturing *Hadith*:

Abu 'Awanah [*muhaddith* of Basra, d. 170/786] said, 'I witnessed 'Amir ibn 'Abd al-Malik asking Qatadah about the *Ayyam* of the Arabs, their genealogies and their tales and delighted in it. I later returned to ask him about these topics and he replied, "It is none of your business. Leave this kind of knowledge to 'Amir and go back to your own work."'[8]

---

[7] See, e.g., Zajjaji, *Majalis*, pp. 141–2, 169–70; Marzubani, *Muwashshah*, pp. 191–2.
[8] Jumahi, *Tabaqat*, p. 18. For further instances of tension between *adib*s and *muhaddith*s, see also Zajjaji, *Majalis*, pp. 121, 177 and especially 237, for an encounter between the

In sum, the *jahili* lore of poetry and prose that early *adib*s reassembled with care and affection rapidly acquired the status of a linguistic model whose value would ultimately be acknowledged by religious scholars, notwithstanding their reservations about the spirit of the *Jahiliyya*. Such luminaries of early literary criticism as al-Asma'i (d. 213/828) would even underline the difference between the two spirits, the *jahili* and the Islamic, in the realm of poetic excellence as follows:

If you were to lead poetry into the path of virtue, you would enfeeble it. Do you not see how Hassan ibn Thabit had attained eminence in the *Jahiliyya* and Islam but when his poetry followed the path of virtue, as in the elegies he composed on the Prophet, Hamza, Ja'far and others, his verse became feeble (*lana*)? The path of poetry is the path of 'studs' (*fuhul*), of poets like Imru'ul Qays, Zuhayr and Nabigha, who sing of encampments and departures, defamation and panegyric, flirtation with women, the wild ass and the horse, war and glory.[9]

In rediscovering the *Jahiliyya*, the early *adib*s were also resurrecting its ethos, its world of manliness and epic glory, its geography, genealogies and history. As the Quranic exegetes and traditionists were embedding their materials in narratives that explained or amplified the sacred tradition, so the *adib*s were now engaged in the pursuit of the antiquities of Arabia, a pursuit that a great jurist like al-Shafi'i (d. 204/820), for example, regarded with grudging admiration.[10] By the third/ninth century, a literary critic like Muhammad ibn Sallam al-Jumahi (d. 231/845) could speak of poetry as a 'craft' (*sina'a*) like other arts and crafts and compare the expert in poetry to the expert money-changer (*jahbadh*) or the master jeweller.[11]

But it was the prose allegedly recovered from the *Jahiliyya* which most clearly manifested the ethics and aesthetics of *Adab*. The pre-Islamic sages were held up for admiration by the literati of the second and third centuries as models of eloquence, generosity, honour, moderation and solicitude towards kinsmen and friends. Their terse, proverb-like utterances, often in rhymed prose, were at their most formal in their 'last testaments' (*wasaya*) which were supposedly addressed to their children:

Qays ibn Ma'dikarib made the following testament to his children, 'In your name, O God. Preserve a memory of my conduct (*adabi*) and it will suffice you. Follow my counsel and you will be among the virtuous of your people and your prestige

---

famous grammarian Abu 'Amr ibn al-'Ala' (d. 154/771) and the renowned jurist Abu Hanifa (d. 150/767).
[9] Marzubani, *Muwashshah*, p. 62. There is much on early literary criticism in Abbott, *Studies*, 3:122–63.
[10] See the remark attributed to him in Abbott, *Studies*, 3:34 and note 119: 'Philologists are the jinns of mankind; they comprehend what others fail to perceive.'
[11] Jumahi, *Tabaqat*, p. 3.

will grow. I refer you to my conduct now that the man in charge of you is departing."[12]

In these and other passages, the term *Adab* is the one used to denote the totality of manners and morals which these pre-Islamic figures epitomize, many of whom were said to have lived incredibly long lives and to have survived into the Islamic period.[13] Such longevity was one way in which ancient wisdom and *Adab* was perceived as having enduring relevance and value to modern times.

But this image of an Arabian past did not go unchallenged. Many *Hadith* scholars correctly detected in it a kind of paganism, even as they were forced to accept its paradigmatic value for linguistic studies. Some scholars of non-Arab origin ridiculed the culture of *jahili* Arabia and pronounced it uncouth and primitive in comparison with older civilizations of the East. Other non-Arab scholars were to take *Adab* into new and foreign fields. In any case, the juncture between the Umayyads and the Abbasids, important historically, was also important for the history of *Adab* and the consolidation of its authority.

The Umayyad state secretaries

The bureaucracy of the Umayyad empire was the last stronghold of the ancient pre-Islamic cultures of western Asia. In Egypt, Syria, Iraq and Iran, non-Arab and non-Muslim bureaucrats continued to serve their new masters long after 'Abd al-Malik arabized the state administration. Indeed, throughout Arab history, a disproportionately large number of non-Muslims were employed in governmental service (e.g. in Fatimid and Mamluk Egypt), a state of affairs which occasionally resulted in tensions. Experts especially in finance and bureaucratic routine, they brought to their work the wisdom passed on by generations of experience.

In the central lands of the Umayyad empire, Greek and Persian bureaucrats helped their masters to adapt to imperial rhythms of government. They were often found to be easier to employ than Arab Muslims whose tribal attachments made them prone to tribal rivalries, a dilemma well expressed by the Umayyad governor of Iraq, 'Ubaydullah ibn Ziyad (d. 67/686):

If I employed an Arab as tax collector and he embezzled the land-tax and I punished him, I risked antagonizing his tribe. If I fined him, deducting the fine from the pension of his clan, I did them harm. If I dropped the matter I would be wasting God's money . . . I found therefore that the *dihqan*s [Persian gentry] were

---

[12] Sijistani, *Mu'ammarin*, p. 125.
[13] Best examined in Sijistani, *Mu'ammarin*.

more knowledgeable about tax collection, more honest with their trust and easier for me to call to account.[14]

Well-trained bureaucrats were in ever greater demand as the Umayyad empire in its middle period tightened its control over society and finance. Non-Arab, non-Muslim bureaucrats seem to have made the transition to arabization without much difficulty and to have dominated the state administration in certain key provinces like Khurasan until the very end of the Umayyad period and beyond.[15] As these state secretaries (*kuttab*) grew more powerful, so did their sense of their own importance. In what is the earliest surviving epistle addressed to these *kuttab*, 'Abd al-Hamid al-Katib (d. 132/750), secretary of the last Umayyad caliph Marwan II, having praised them as the 'eyes and ears of the ruler' and for having attained 'the noblest of stations in life', warns them repeatedly against the dangers of arrogance, ostentation and wasteful extravagance.[16] Nonetheless, and by the middle of the second/eighth century, the *kuttab* had emerged as a distinct social class in Arab Muslim society and were now set to make their own contribution to the evolution of *Adab*.

'Abd al-Hamid's epistle, once again, best illuminates the nature of that contribution:

The *katib* needs himself to be, and is required by his master, who trusts him in important affairs, to be forbearing (*halim*) when appropriate, prudent when opinion is required, daring when need be but ready to retreat if necessary, chaste, just and fair by preference, a keeper of secrets, loyal in times of crisis, capable of predicting calamities, having a sense of the proportion of things. He should have examined every branch of knowledge and mastered it; if he cannot master it, he should acquire of it a measure sufficient for his needs. He should know by rational impulse, good education (*adab*) and a store of experience what will happen to him before it happens and what results his actions will produce before he acts, to the end that he readies for each affair its requisite stores and for each problem its proper form and usage.[17]

This is probably the first full portrait we possess of the *katib* as he came into view at the end of the Umayyad period. There is much in it which would hold true of the Byzantine, Persian or even Chinese bureaucrat, and perhaps a hint of the Stoic prudently 'anticipating' the flux of events. Closer to our concerns, however, is the ideal of learning to be possessed by the *katib* as one which, falling short of a total mastery of knowledge, aims to acquire a broad familiarity with *useful* knowledge. The education

---

[14] Baladhuri, *Ansab*, 4/2:109.
[15] Jahshiyari, *Wuzara'*, p. 67.
[16] 'Abd al-Hamid, *Risala ila al-Kuttab* in Kurd 'Ali, *Rasa'il*, pp. 222–6. The epistles of 'Abd al-Hamid and of Salim Abu al 'Ala' have been edited recently, and with an important introduction, by Ihsan 'Abbas, *'Abd al-Hamid ibn Yahya al-Katib wa ma tabaqqa min rasa'ilihi wa rasa'il Salim Abi al-'Ala'* (Amman: Dar al-Shuruq, 1988).
[17] 'Abd al-Hamid, *Risala*, pp. 222–3.

(*adab*) of the *katib* consists therefore of a certain moral character and of a particular kind of learning. Together they prepare him to function well in a certain kind of job. The novelty of this pragmatic ideal can best be seen when contrasted with the ideal of contemporary *Hadith* scholars to amass the greatest possible body of *'ilm*, i.e. religious knowledge, and the ascetic and other-worldly ideal of the great preachers of the period. Compared to these two types, the state secretary is a well trained 'craftsman', an agent of the state for whom efficiency is the ultimate accomplishment.

What curriculum should the *katib* pursue? 'Abd al-Hamid notes the following:

> Therefore, circle of *kuttab*, vie with one another in the diverse kinds of knowledge (*adab*) and instruct yourselves in religion. Begin by knowing the Book of God Almighty and the religious duties and then the Arabic language, for it sets your speech straight. Master calligraphy for it ornaments your correspondence and recite poetry, learning its obscurities and meanings. Learn about the *Ayyam* of Arabs and non-Arabs, their tales and life-histories, for this will help you to attain your ambitions, and do not neglect arithmetic for it is the mainstay of tax officials.[18]

History makes its appearance in the curriculum in the form of lessons or moral examples which the *katib* needs to comprehend in order to maintain a lofty sense of his mission in life. To that end, it is not just Arab history which is relevant but the history of other nations also. Secretarial *Adab* therefore tended to transcend the Arabian-Islamic horizons of philology and *Hadith* in its quest for a diffuse, 'universal' education, all the more to be expected given the non-Arab and even non-Muslim contribution to the evolution of the imperial bureaucracy.

The typical form of secretarial *Adab* is the epistle, real or contrived, in which caliphal directives or else advice, thanks, congratulations, apologies, condolences and so forth are proffered. The epistle in each case was composed with consummate care and meticulous attention to the choice of words. Pleonasms are frequent, but not, generally speaking, rhymed; clauses are short and often in apposition; construct phrases are used in succession to unfold meaning or demonstrate virtuosity; conditional and conjectural clauses allow for wise and measured response; contrasts between moral choices or predicaments highlight the role of wisdom (*hikma*) as arbiter. As befitted the 'noblest of stations', secretarial *Adab* is grave in tone, didactic, often melancholic and conscious at all times of human frailty and the fickleness of fortune. As he fled from the battlefield with his master, 'Abd al-Hamid wrote to his family:

> God Almighty encircled the world He made with evil and joy; whoever is helped by fortune feels at home therein but whoever is bitten by its fangs rebukes it in

---

[18] 'Abd al-Hamid, *Risala*, p. 225.

his wrath and complains of it, desiring that it offer him more. The world had once made us taste its sweetest milk but has now bolted away with us, throwing us to the ground in its flight. The sweetness has turned to salt, the soft has become coarse . . . I write as the days increase both the distance from you and the longing for you. If this catastrophe reaches its furthest limit, it will be the end for both you and me. If I am to be caught in the talons of the bird of prey who now holds sway over you, I shall return to you in the shame of captivity, and shame is the worst of neighbours.[19]

Both 'Abd al-Hamid and his more famous contemporary Ibn al-Muqaffa' (d. *c.* 139/756) were to meet violent deaths at the hands of political opponents, a clear sign of the power that these *kuttab* had now attained and presaging the later and often stormy careers of their successors. The essays, epistles and animal fables of Ibn al-Muqaffa' have, for more than a millennium, been held up as models of both the style and spirit of *Adab*. But while 'Abd al-Hamid simply shared the fate of his master, the execution of Ibn al-Muqaffa' had much to do with his own brilliant, ironic and original imagination and his barely concealed disdain for narrow religious learning. In Ibn al-Muqaffa' we have the first representative of Hellenistic culture, an *adib* who openly invites his readers to ponder the achievements of foreign wisdom and champions the superiority of ancients over moderns, and all this at a time of violent religious and political revolution. In fact, there is a sense in which Ibn al-Muqaffa' belongs not to his own but to the following century, when the encounter between Arab-Islamic culture on the one hand and alien cultures on the other was in full tumult.

Cities of the Umayyad empire seem from early days to have harboured a rich ethnic mixture of Arab and non-Arab elements. In the days of Ibn al-Muqaffa', Islam was over a century old but its dominant religious culture had so far remained largely non-reactive to foreign influence, inward looking, unconcerned to define its cultural contribution to civilizations contemporaneous with or more ancient than itself, content to elucidate the foundations of its own legal and historical traditions. On the level of popular culture, much more difficult to determine, Islam was in a receptive mode, ready and willing to absorb the customs, folklore and skills of indigenous cultures. But the Arabic language was the only acceptable medium of direct cultural interaction, just as Arabic was, by caliphal fiat, made the only acceptable medium of political administration.

But there were many ways in which the dominant Arab-Islamic elite was forcefully reminded of foreignness. To begin with, the presence of a very large Muslim but non-Arab population, the *Mawali*, posed increasingly acute problems of identity and of social, political and especially economic equality. During the second great wave of conquests under al-Walid, areas of contrasting cultures, and widely regarded as exotic, fell

[19] 'Abd al-Hamid, *Risala*, p. 221.

under Umayyad rule and were rapidly incorporated, enriching the ethnic mixture of the empire. Then again, close to a hundred years of intense and detailed study of the vocabulary of the Qur'an was now beginning to change, perhaps in response to imperial transformations, to a more encompassing interest in the Qur'anic vision of 'nations' and 'eras' of great antiquity and profound historical exemplarity. Finally, a translation movement, consisting most probably at first of epigrammatic 'wisdom literature' of Indian, Persian and Greek sages and soon followed by scientific works, introduced the elite of the empire to the cultures of the world around them. As all this was happening, the great palaces and mosques of the later Umayyads, objects of suspicion in many pious circles, creatively synthesized elements of ancient Near-Eastern art and architecture.

In these circumstances, *Adab* led the way in responding to the challenge of foreign cultures and Ibn al-Muqaffaʿ was a leading figure in the formulation of that response. By temperament and culture, he was no ordinary *katib* but an intellectual of enormous breadth and deeply interested in the theory and practice of politics. He saw himself in the role of advisor to caliphs rather than executor of their will. In almost everything he wrote, one detects an overview, an ascendancy of tone and vision, as if one is being addressed by a sage standing on some natural height and commanding a broader prospect than that of his audience:

The rational man must divide people into two distinct categories and wear two distinct garments for them: for the class of commoners he should wear a garment of dejection, reserve, caution and restraint in every word and every step; with the elite class, he may remove his garment of severity and don the garment of geniality, kindness, generosity and common discourse. Only one in a thousand belongs to that class, all of whom are admirable in judgement, steady in affection, discreet with secrets and loyal in friendship.[20]

The hero of Ibn al-Muqaffaʿ is the 'rational man' (*al-ʿaqil*), defined not only by his intellect but also by the need to 'dispute with his own soul, call it to account, pass judgement upon it, rebuke it and penalize it'.[21] Rational man's most persistent enemy is passion or caprice (*hawa*), which rules the lives of most men and renders them slaves to this world and its illusory attractions. The *ʿaqil* on the other hand must not regret anything that this world has failed to offer him, nor be overjoyed by anything that it does offer him, but should constantly recall death so as to restrain ambition and greed. For man has not been placed in this world to lead a life of riches and ease but one of poverty and toil. But men in their vast majority are greedy, opportunistic, scheming, destructive. Against this, the *ʿaqil* must be armed with patience, humility and the pursuit of learning.

[20] Ibn al-Muqaffaʿ, *al-Adab al-Saghir*, in Kurd ʿAli, *Rasaʾil*, p. 13.
[21] Ibn al-Muqaffaʿ, *al-Adab al-Saghir*, p. 10.

Given this ascetic and intellectualist ethic, it is not surprising that Ibn al-Muqaffa' was critical of the increasingly professional bearing and function of men of religion in his days. Two things troubled him, the hypocrisy inherent in their becoming a social class and the surge in theological controversy:

He who appoints himself a leader of men in religion ought to begin by teaching himself and reforming his character, his way of life, livelihood, opinion, speech and the company he keeps, to the end that his own life becomes a more eloquent teacher than his tongue. For just as words of wisdom please the ears, so acts of wisdom please the eyes and hearts . . . The difference between religion and opinion is that religion is fortified by faith while opinion is fortified by dispute. He who makes his religion a point of dispute has turned religion into opinion while he who makes his opinion a religion becomes a legislator and whoever lays down the law for himself has no religion.[22]

By temperament and conviction, Ibn al-Muqaffa' was a conservative, believing that originality of thought and expression was an unattainable ideal. The wise or eloquent man is like the jeweller who skilfully arranges precious stones in necklaces or bracelets but is not himself their discoverer. Therefore he should not bask in self-esteem but rest content with communicating to others, in word and deed, what he has learnt from learned and pious predecessors. Inaugurating a great debate on the respective merits of 'ancients' and 'moderns' in classical Arabic culture, a theme we shall pursue below, Ibn al-Muqaffa' championed the 'ancients' without reservation. They were superior in physical and mental stature, longer lived, more experienced, more pious, more learned, while their books and their wisdom have spared later generations the trouble of finding things out for themselves:

Such was their concern that if one of them, to whom a branch of knowledge was revealed . . . found himself in an uninhabited land, he would inscribe this wisdom on rocks . . . for fear that this learning might be lost for those who came after him . . . hence, the most that a scholar of our days can hope to attain is to borrow from their wisdom, the most a virtuous man can attain is to emulate their example . . . We find that they have neglected no subject whatever which some eloquent author, wishing to write about, does not find already treated in their works, whether it be in glorifying God and arousing desire for His promise, or in belittling the world and its renunciation or in instituting the branches of knowledge, dividing them into categories, delineating their divisions and elucidating their methods . . . or in any branch of character formation or ethical conduct. In all fundamentals, nothing remains to be said for they have said it all.[23]

[22] Ibn al-Muqaffa', *al-Adab al-saghir*, pp. 14, 21.
[23] Ibn al-Muqaffa', *al-Adab al-Kabir* in Kurd 'Ali, *Rasa'il*, pp. 40–1. Suggestive parallels with early European literatures on the debate between 'Ancients' and 'Moderns' are found in Ernst R. Curtius, *European Literature and the Latin Middle Ages* (Princeton: Princeton University Press (Bollingen Series XXXVI), 1990), pp. 251 ff. Curtius in fact alludes to the debate in Arabic literature.

Ibn al-Muqaffaʿ viewed his own contribution as one of merely expounding some 'obscure details' (*lataʾif*) left over for 'men of small minds' from the weighty wisdom of the ancients. These details were to include his theoretical and practical essays on government, i.e. his general counsel to rulers, governors and courtiers as well as the specific proposals submitted to the new Abbasid regime regarding certain urgent problems of state. In his theoretical observations, Ibn al-Muqaffaʿ mixes psychological insights with moral maxims, extolling virtues like patience, consultation and decisiveness for men of authority, and caution and prudence for courtiers. One piece of advice for the courtier is of particular relevance to history since it deals with the credibility of reports:

> Next, examine reports of marvels (*al-akhbar al-raʾiʿa*) and treat them with caution, for human nature covets tales, especially marvels. Most men narrate what they hear but care not from whom they heard it. This perverts truth and belittles reason. If you can report nothing except what you believe in, and your belief is bolstered with proof, do so. Do not repeat what fools say: I merely report what I heard. For most of what you hear is false and most reporters are fools. If you come to apprehend and transmit reports (*ahadith*), what you apprehend and transmit from common men will exceed by far what any fabricator (*mukhtariʿ*) can fabricate.[24]

In sum, the essays and epistles of Ibn al-Muqaffaʿ breathe a spirit distinctly, self-consciously at variance with the dominant culture of his age. His writings are astonishingly free from any references to Islam or Muslim learning but his critical views of the established religion lurk transparently beneath the measured eloquence, the terse maxim, the calculated barb. For him, *Adab* meant essentially two things: the educational process by which reason is nurtured and the moral character which complements reason. Both senses of *Adab* derive, in his view, from cultural models far more ancient and, by implication, superior to the Islamic models of his days. But while this particular view concerning the superiority of the ancients was challenged by later *adibs*, much of what he propagated was to become typical of the spirit and practice of *Adab*: the need to face the challenge of foreign cultures, the intellectual snobbery, the scepticism of reason, the predilection for terse and brilliant epigram, the attempt to construct a craft of government based upon universal rules of ethics and psychology. In the case of Ibn al-Muqaffaʿ, there was also the distinctive impact of his style with its short, dense sentences, its tendency to categorize and classify, its bold use of comparatives and superlatives, its litigatory and dialectical tone.

The Umayyad secretaries greatly expanded the conception and scope of *Adab*. While the grammarians and philologists may have been indistinguishable from their colleagues, the Qurʾan and *Hadith* scholars, courtly

---

[24] Ibn al-Muqaffaʿ, *al-Adab al-Kabir*, pp. 94–5.

Adab assumed the existence of a new social type, the sophisticated and worldly *adib*. *Adab* was the training in character and intellect which prepared him for leadership. In the transition from Umayyad to Abbasid rule one of the few institutions which did not suffer much change was the secretarial class and the *Adab* ideal which they had cultivated.

From *Adab* to history: the second–fourth centuries AH (eighth–tenth AD)

Between the second and fourth Islamic centuries (eighth to tenth AD) *Adab* was to witness a transformation and expansion of its horizons. The dynastic change from Umayyads to Abbasids was effected through a revolution which, at first, went about methodically eradicating all vestiges of its predecessor, exhuming even the mortal remains of individual Umayyad caliphs and scattering them to the winds. But these very dramatic surface events should not obscure for us a number of deeper sociocultural continuities. In particular, structures of thought, routines of business and government, ways of life – these were to experience a more gradual pace of change. The themes and styles of Umayyad *Adab* were carried into the Abbasid era but the new environment in which *Adab* operated eventually resulted in a wider spectrum of interest and appeal.

With early Abbasid *Adab* one gets the feeling that the audience has expanded, that whereas Umayyad *Adab* was essentially an elite phenomenon, cultivated in the courts of caliphs, princes and powerful governors, Abbasid *Adab* was more diffuse, and also a more educationally structured activity. Renowned masters of lexicography or grammar begin to acquire disciples and 'schools' begin to emerge. Much more is heard of *majalis al-adab*, literary *salons* where a master would hold forth on diverse topics to fellow scholars or students and where vigorous debate was often the most common method of teaching. The new or rejuvenated Iraqi cities, Kufa, Basra and Baghdad, the hub of the Abbasid empire, provided the vitality, prosperity and ethnic variety needed for *Adab* to percolate into wider sectors of society.

In more specific terms, Abbasid *Adab* was much nearer the Persian–Indian–Hellenistic cultural zone and more open to the challenge of foreign cultures than Umayyad *Adab* had been. This meant a more susceptible cultural environment. Then again, the early Abbasids were not ideologically stable but experimented with one sectarian and theological position after another. The result was a wider spectrum of conceptual choice. Furthermore, the replacement of the Arab Umayyad elite by a mixed Arab-Persian Abbasid elite resulted in new political, ethnic and cultural permutations. These, in turn, tended to feed polemic and controversy, for which *Adab* had already been well armed through cultivation of rhetoric. Affecting *Adab* also was the messianic aura with which several early-

Abbasid caliphs attempted to surround their reign. Court-circulated propaganda was centred on the coming of a new era of justice and goodness and the contrast with the earlier era of wickedness. This comparison of eras stimulated literary and historiographic theorizing.

Thus, between the second and fourth centuries AH, *Adab* was the arena in which a number of debates of distinct relevance to history were fought out. Five major controversies may be singled out in this particular field: first, the controversy between 'Ancients' and 'Moderns' and the reflections on time and on progress and decline which this engendered; second, the emergence of a new literary style and of theories of literary criticism; third, the debate between 'specialists' and 'generalists' and its repercussions; fourth, new and more critical attitudes to poetry and to literary anecdotes and, finally, the great cultural debate between Arabs and non-Arabs.

The controversy between 'Ancients' (*qudama'*) and 'Moderns' (*muhdathun*) is associated with the rediscovery of the *Jahiliyya* in late-Umayyad times and of Umayyad times in the mid-Abbasid period. The *Jahiliyya*, as was seen above, was enshrined as a model of linguistic usage by the earliest critics and experts of lexicography and literary taste. Inherent in this was the view that *jahili* Arabic was purer, less corrupt than the Arabic of the *amsar*, or provincial capitals, and that the beduin were the last carriers of the language in its pristine purity. Implied also was a comparison of larger dimensions between past and present. For if language was purer, then presumably life itself, manners and morals, and knowledge were all superior then to what followed later, a view most eloquently defended by Ibn al-Muqaffa'. Thereafter, many were found to uphold and amplify that view but many were also prepared to defend other opinions quite contrary to the above.

Championing the 'Ancients' could take several forms. Certain opinions would be ascribed to venerable early-Islamic figures that implied progressive deterioration of existence:

It is said that 'A'isha, God be pleased with her, said, May God be merciful to Labid, how splendid are the verses in which he says: 'Gone are the men in whose shelter one can live and I remain behind, among posterity that resemble a leper's skin. No use are they, nor can any good be hoped from them; and their orator, even if he speaks no wrong, is faulted.' 'A'isha added, How will it be if Labid saw the posterity of our age! Al-Sha'bi said, How will it be if the Mother of the Faithful saw the posterity of our age![25]

Sentiments that echo the above are ascribed to major literary figures of the early period like Abu 'Amr ibn al-'Ala' (d. 154/771), 'who used to say that in comparison with those who came before us we are like a sprout

---

[25] Abu Zayd al-Qurashi, *Jamhara*, p. 69. On progress and decline, see T. Khalidi, 'The Concept of Progress in Classical Islam', *Journal of Near Eastern Studies*, XL, no. 4 (Oct. 1981).

(*baql*) at the foot of a towering palm-tree (*raql*)'.[26] The renowned
Umayyad poet al-Farazdaq (d. 110/728), when pressed to assess inferior
verse, concocted the following allegory of the history of poetry for the
benefit of the hapless versifier:

> Poetry was once a magnificent camel. Then, one day, it was slaughtered. So
> Imru'ul Qays came and took his head, 'Amr ibn Kulthum took his hump, Zuhayr
> the shoulders, al-A'sha and al-Nabigha the thighs, and Tarafa and Labid the stom-
> ach. There remained only the forearms and offal which we split amongst ourselves.
> The butcher then said, 'Hey you, there remains only the blood and impurities.
> See that I get them.' 'They are yours,' we replied. So he took the stuff, cooked
> it, ate it and excreted it. Your verses are from the excrement of that butcher.[27]

But if the views of such second-century luminaries as Ibn al-Muqaffa',
Abu 'Amr and al-Farazdaq reflected a sentiment common in their own
days, such views were to be changed perceptibly by later generations. In
the third/ninth century, a certain degree of relativity is observed in judgements of this issue. It may be that the growth of professionalism and of
the idea of poetry as a craft practised by specialists gave later scholars a
measure of self-confidence in their skills and of the distance they had
covered in their research:

> Muhammad ibn Sallam [al-Jumahi, d. 231/845] said: I heard a man asking Yunus
> [ibn Habib, d. 182/798] about Ibn Abi Ishaq [d. 127/744] and his knowledge. He
> replied, He and grammar are one and the same – that is, he is the ultimate author-
> ity. The man asked, How is his knowledge to be compared with the knowledge of
> people today? Yunus replied, If there was someone today who knew only what
> he knew, he would be laughed at. But if there was someone today who had his
> mind and perspicacity and had examined what men of today have examined he
> would be the most knowledgeable of men.[28]

In more general terms, the concept of a time in constant decline was
offset by more cautious views, inspired perhaps by the intellectual 'optimism' of natural science, to be discussed in the next chapter, as by the
gradual recognition that good poetry could be found in all ages. To gain
acceptance, such views had to be ascribed to 'venerable ancestors' and
the result was aphorisms such as: 'Abu al-Darda' said, Today's virtue is
yesterday's vice and today's vice is the virtue of days to come.'[29] Similar
sentiments were expressed by poets:

> Abu Ja'far al-Shaybani said, One day, as we sat in a group, we were visited by
> the poet Abu Mayyas who asked us, What are you discussing? We replied, We
> are discussing the present time and its corruption. He answered, No, for time is

[26] Ibn al-Anbari, *Nuzhat al-Alibba'*, p. 16.
[27] Qurashi, *Jamhara*, pp. 54–5. See also *Jamhara*, p. 82, for the verdict of Abu 'Ubayda:
     'Poetry was launched by Imru'ul Qays and ended with Dhu al-Rummah [d. *c.* 117/735].'
[28] Sirafi, *Akhbar*, p. 26. For poetry as a 'craft', see footnote 11, above.
[29] Ibn al-Mu'tazz, *Badi'*, p. 76.

merely a receptacle and the good or evil thrown into it remains constant. Then he recited . . . They say the times are corrupt but it is they who are corrupt and not the times.[30]

By the end of the third and the coming of the fourth centuries, the belief in the progress of poetic invention was winning more adherents among the major arbiters of literary taste. If the 'Moderns' were not actually superior to the 'Ancients' by virtue of their greater experiences and accumulation of wisdom, they were certainly worthy of consideration as their equals or else to be judged on merit alone and without regard to the age in which they lived. This last seems to have been the verdict of, among others, two celebrated authorities, al-Mubarrad (d. 285/898) and Muhammad ibn Yahya al-Suli (d. 335/946).[31] But others, e.g. Ibn 'Abd Rabbihi (d. 328/940) and Ibn Faris (d. 395/1004), were to go further and to assert flatly that the 'Moderns' were superior to the 'Ancients' in all branches of knowledge:

Each age has its own science. The noblest of sciences are the sciences of our present age, for which God be thanked.[32]

These controversies were of course related not only to aesthetics but also to different perceptions of time, originality, progress and historical change. Of importance to historical style was the debate over the use of *isnad* in fields that were not traditionally within the purview of *Hadith*, and the development of new theories of literary criticism. Laxity in the use of *isnad* for the transmission of poetry and literary anecdotes dates probably to the late second/eighth century as evidenced in the sense of novelty detectable in the words of Jumahi regarding transmission from his master, Khalaf al-Ahmar (d. 180/796):

Ibn Sallam [al-Jumahi] said: Our colleagues agree that he [Khalaf] was the most perceptive of men where a line of verse was concerned and the most truthful in speech. When we received a report (*khabar*) from him or he recited poetry to us, we used not to care that we had not heard this from the original source (*sahibihi*).[33]

---

[30] Ibn 'Abd Rabbihi, *'Iqd*, 2:340–1. See also Mubarrad, *Kamil*, 1:29, where the renowned critic delivers the following verdict: 'It is not because he is ancient that an author should be preferred nor because he is modern that the fellow who hits the mark should be censured, but each should be given his proper due.'

[31] See footnote 30, above, and *Kamil*, 1:348. See also Suli, *Akhbar Abi Tammam*, pp. 16–17, 'Their eyes [i.e. the 'Ancients"] have not seen what the "Moderns" have seen . . . nor have the Moderns seen what the Ancients witnessed at first hand . . . each is forever inferior to the other in what was not witnessed.'

[32] Ibn Faris, *Sahibi*, p. 37; see also pp. *ha'* and *waw* of the introduction, which contains an important epistle of Ibn Faris on the comparison between *jahili* and modern poets. For Ibn 'Abd Rabbihi, see *'Iqd*, 1:2. For similar views, see Ibn 'Abd al-Barr, *Jami'*, 1:99; Ibn al-Mu'tazz, *Badi'*, p. 106; Tawhidi, *Imta'*, 1:85. This did not of course prevent the 'optimists' from bewailing the manners of their colleagues: see, e.g., Ibn 'Abd al-Barr, *Jami'*, 1:169–70; Suli, *Akhbar Abi Tammam*, pp. 7–8; Ibn Qutayba, *Adab al-Katib*, pp. 1–4.

[33] Ibn al-Anbari, *Nuzhat al-Alibba'*, p. 37; cf. Jumahi, *Tabaqat*, p. 9.

One generation after Jumahi, a great literary authority like al-Mubarrad came to be known for his indifference towards the use of *isnad* in the literary reports he transmitted.[34] His contemporary, the celebrated Ibn al-Mu'tazz (d. 296/908), decided to omit *isnad* even in the Prophetic *Hadith* cited in his work on *badi'* (figures of speech), because this would be excessive (*min al-takthir*).[35] A little later, al-Suli defended his abandonment of *isnad* in most of his reports on the grounds of convenience and ease of access.[36] But the most explicit discussion of this issue is in the introduction to *al-'Iqd al-Farid*, the massive literary anthology of Ibn 'Abd Rabbihi:

I have deleted the *isnads* from most reports, my purpose being to achieve lightness of touch and conciseness and to avoid being ponderous and prolix. For these are entertaining stories, pieces of wisdom and anecdotes, which benefit not from any *isnad* being attached to them nor are they adversely affected if the *isnad* is deleted. Some men used to delete the *isnad* from customary sunnas and prescribed laws, so why should we not delete it from a humorous anecdote, a common proverb, an unusual story or a tale whose brilliance would be dulled if it is spun out and made too long?[37]

If conciseness was a key factor in the abandonment of *isnad* in literary prose, it was also regarded as the hallmark of eloquence in verse and prose. Several critics of the third and fourth centuries cited conciseness, simplicity, originality, and clarity as the components of the style they most admired.

This sensibility was accompanied by further refinements in the sources, scope and function of *Adab*, especially as seen in the debate between 'generalists' and 'specialists', and the place of history in the evolving curriculum of *Adab*. One might begin with the saying attributed to Ibn Qutayba (d. 276/889):

He who wishes to become a scholar (*'alim*), let him pursue one subject (*fann*). But he who wishes to become an *adib*, let him seek breadth in learning (*yattasi' fi al-'ulum*).[38]

It was also felt that no distinction could come from narrow specialization, from excelling in one area of knowledge only:

Abu Zayd [al-Ansari, d. 214/830] did not go beyond grammar. Khalaf al-Ahmar said to him: You have applied yourself too closely to grammar and have not gone

---

[34] Sirafi, *Akhbar*, p. 102, quoting Niftawayhi. This is confirmed by Mubarrad himself in *Kamil*, 2:574, 628 and *passim*.

[35] Ibn al-Mu'tazz, *Badi'*, p. 17.

[36] Suli, *Adab al-Kuttab*, p. 21.

[37] Ibn 'Abd Rabbihi, *'Iqd*, 1:4.

[38] Ibn 'Abd Rabbihi, *'Iqd*, 2:208; cf. 'Askari, *Masun*, p. 115, for the advice of Yahya al-Barmaki to his children: 'Examine all the sciences for he who is ignorant of anything will make it his enemy and I would hate you to be an enemy of any of the sciences.'

beyond it. Rarely can one gain distinction by being an expert solely in this field. You should study poetry and history (*akhbar*).[39]

In the cultural war between the two cities, Basra had the reputation of being the city of specialists while Kufa was said to be the home of generalists.[40] Further light is thrown on this issue by a passage in Suli who, in the course of chastising the pretensions of contemporary scholars, says that such renowned authorities as al-Mubarrad and Thaʻlab (d. 291/904) never claimed knowledge in areas outside their expertise such as ancient history, the Prophetic period, genealogy, the caliphal period, *Fiqh* and *Hadith* – even though these, according to Suli, are sciences indispensable to true faith.[41] By the third/eighth century, *Adab* was of course the habitat of generalists. Suli, for instance, could quote Yahya the Barmakid, Euclid, the theologian al-Nazzam, Aristotle and a great deal of poetry almost in the same breath. Yet there is also in him and in other authors an admiration for the specialist, for Asmaʻi, for example, who avoided all exegesis of Qur'an or *Hadith* because it lay outside his competence. Hence, the debate between the two spirits was never fully resolved in favour of either, although it remained generally true that the state secretaries of this period cultivated and preached a broadly based *Adab* as being essential to a life in public service, while urban scholars, living and working in close proximity to increasingly specialised urban tradesmen, tended to pursue excellence in one particular field.

The typical literary products of the great *adib*s of this period were the anthologies, which often originated in series of lectures (*amali*) delivered at restricted sessions (*majalis*) held in private homes. One gains the impression that the audience addressed in these works are, increasingly, readers rather than listeners. Thus, a style is developed which moves from subject to subject, from mood to mood, and the author is concerned not to bore his reader but to give him a taste of all branches of *Adab*:

This is a work we composed which brings together diverse kinds of literature: passages of prose, polished verse, common maxims, edifying sermons and excerpts from noble speeches and eloquent epistles.[42]

History, since the days of Ibn al-Muqaffaʻ, had been installed in the curriculum of *Adab*. It was now to fortify this place and to constitute the dominant component of the leading *Adab* anthologies of the third and fourth centuries, most of which were grounded in *akhbar*, stories or anecdotes which illuminated, illustrated or entertained. In manuals written for state

---

[39] ʻAskari, *Masun*, p. 122.
[40] See the anecdote, obviously contrived but nevertheless revealing, of the Kufan governor of Basra and his cross-examination of its scholars in ʻAskari, *Masun*, pp. 123–5.
[41] Suli, *Akhbar Abi Tammam*, pp. 7–8.
[42] Mubarrad, *Kamil*, 1:3. See also two important passages in 2:668 and 708 on entertaining the *reader* and the significance of mood shifts.

secretaries, history and dating became 'the bulwark of truth and dissipater of doubt; through it, rights are established and commitments are kept'.[43]

In general, the *adibs* tended, as explained above, to array a wider range of critical devices towards their materials than the *Hadith* scholars to theirs.[44] A renowned authority like Abu 'Ubayda, with his formidable knowledge of history, could be a devastating critic where literary *akhbar* were concerned:

I asked Abu 'Ubayda about similar reports from the Arab side and he replied: the non-Arabs lie and claim that there once existed a man made of one third copper, one third lead and one third ice. The Arabs counter such claims with similar absurdities.[45]

When literary critics came to examine the poetic heritage of the *jahili* and Umayyad periods – in a process termed above a rediscovery – they often resorted to history to separate the genuine from the forged. A critic like Jumahi, for example, was able to explain how forgeries arose by reconstructing the historical reasons for their production:

When the Arabs began to review the recitation of poetry and the historical record of battle-days and glories, some tribes found that their tribal poets had produced little verse and that their exploits had gone unrecorded. Thus a group of such tribes with few exploits and little verse, wishing to catch up with other tribes with a richer heritage, forged verse and ascribed it to their poets. Then came professional reciters who added to the verse. But experts are not normally deceived by such accretions nor by modern forgeries, although some doubt arises in cases of verse recited by a poet who is a nomad and a descendant of poets. . .The first man to collect the poetry of the Arabs and to transmit their narratives (*ahadith*) was Hammad al-Rawiya. He was unreliable and would ascribe one man's verses to another and add to verses.[46]

The great *Kulturkampf* between Arabs and non-Arabs, known as the *Shu'ubiyya* controversy, was a complex societal crisis which involved both the place of non-Arabs as well as the relevance of non-Arabic culture in the Arab-Islamic empire. It was a crisis which swelled in the second and third centuries and engaged some of the finest minds of that age. Its impact on the understanding of history was to force a reconsideration of the very orientation of the imperial culture and of the place of the Arabs and of

---

[43] Suli, *Adab al-Kuttab*, p. 184.
[44] This was acknowledged even by some *muhaddiths*: see the comments of Yahya ibn Sa'id al-Qattan (d. 198/813) in Qali, *Amali*, 3:106. See also the discussion of this theme in George Makdisi, *The Rise of Humanism in Classical Islam and the Christian West* (Edinburgh: Edinburgh University Press, 1990), pp. 99–105.
[45] Mubarrad, *Kamil*, 2:555; see also 2:560. See footnote 5, above, for another example of Abu 'Ubayda's historical criticism. On his reputation as an historian, see Sirafi, *Akhbar*, p. 68, and see now Wilferd Madelung, 'Abu 'Ubayda Ma'mar ibn al-Muthanna as a Historian', *Journal of Islamic Studies*, 3:1 (1992), 47–56, which assesses his reliability as an historical source.
[46] Jumahi, *Tabaqat*, p. 14.

Arabic within it. There were of course many possible answers to the challenge of foreign cultures. It could be argued, for instance by conservative groups, that the Qur'an and *Hadith* contained all the wisdom needed for salvation. It could also be argued, for instance by Ibn al-Muqaffa' and his 'school', that ancient cultures had set standards of wisdom which later cultures could never hope to match, thus implicitly consigning Arabic-Islamic culture to a derivative and inferior historical role. In between, many shades of opinion were possible but the controversy itself provoked a great deal of comparative historical research and reflection.

A tale told by Hisham ibn al-Kalbi best captures the international dimensions of the *Shu'ubiyya* controversy. It concerns a trip which the Arab king of Hira, al-Nu'man ibn al-Mundhir, made to the court of his overlord, the Persian king Kisra (Chosroes), where he found assembled delegations from Byzantium, India and China. When the delegations began to speak of their kingdoms and countries, al-Nu'man extolled the Arabs, preferring them to all other nations, not excluding Persia. The Persian king then spoke as follows:

I have thought about the question of Arabs and other nations . . . The Byzantines, I find, are distinguished by their unity, the territorial extent of their kingdom, their many cities and their great monuments. They have a religion which distinguishes the licit from the illicit and punishes the sinner . . . India I likewise found their equal in wisdom and medicine, a country of plentiful rivers and fruit trees, amazing craftsmanship, spices, exact mathematics and great population. The Chinese, too, I found to be distinguished by their unity, their military craftsmanship, iron industries, chivalry, sense of purpose and a kingdom which unites them. Even the Turks and the Khazars, despite their wretched existence . . . have kings who unite their furthest regions . . . But I have seen no marks of virtue among the Arabs in matters of religion or state, no wise policy and no strength. Further proof of their lowly and abject condition is provided by their homeland with its wild beasts and birds of prey. They kill their own children because of poverty and resort to cannibalism when there is need.[47]

The Arab king speaks again, praising his people's courage, genealogies, generosity, poetry and loyalty. He later dispatches a delegation of Arab sages who sing the eloquent praises of their people to Kisra, one of whom predicts the coming victory of Islam.

This tale, belonging as it does to a period of intense *Shu'ubiyya* polemic, is typical of the comparative cultural debates engendered by that clash of spirits. Where historiography is concerned, the earliest debates may well have been sparked off by the contrast between the rediscovery of the *Jahiliyya* on the one hand and the translation of Persian and Indian histories and books of wisdom on the other, two processes that were approximately contemporaneous. The heritage and relevance of foreign cultures

---

[47] Ibn 'Abd Rabbihi, *'Iqd*, 2:2–5.

was ultimately too strong to ignore. Indeed, the Qur'an itself echoed with the traditions of earlier 'nations and eras' but their relationship to Islam, framed in an eternal present tense, needed to be explicated in historical detail. Information had to be gathered on the histories, cultures and national characteristics of foreign nations, ancient and modern, and the value or relevance of all this needed to be spelled out. Early historians like Wahb ibn Munabbih may have satisfied and entertained their Umayyad audiences with their epic tales of Yemeni splendour, but in the Abbasid context the political and scientific heritage of Persia and India could not simply be narrated: it had to be synthesized and assimilated.

Adab, *Hikma* and history: Jahiz

Jahiz (d. 255/868) was a great theorist of *Adab*, a polymath who wrote on a wide variety of subjects and a thinker who made fundamental contributions to the controversies set forth in the section above. He never wrote a work of history but he was very much interested in key aspects of historical understanding and argumentation. But before analysing some passages bearing on history, and in order to avoid the danger of distorting his overall perspective, his intellectual position needs to be briefly examined.

Broadly speaking, two dominant influences may be detected on his thought: *Adab* and Mu'tazilite theology. Jahiz was to advance the theory and practice of *Adab* by employing it as a system for the study of nature and society, a system that eschews narrow specialization in favour of a discursive, multi-faceted approach, willing to investigate all natural and social phenomena in a tolerant and sceptical spirit. Jahizian *Adab* is an *Adab* which believes in the infinitely didactic possibilities of nature, in man's need to investigate this world of reason and harmony which God has placed at his disposal and for his instruction, a world where even the 'wing of a mosquito' is enough for a lifetime of research. For Jahiz, Islam is, intellectually, a beginning and not an end. He believed that Islam had inherited world civilizations and that its true task was to carry through this legacy, to advance it by claiming as its own all the best that had ever been thought or accomplished. Just as Islam was the final and complete religious message, so its culture was to be heir to all earlier cultures. Accordingly, neither the veneration of antiquity or foreign cultures nor a conservative refusal to tolerate foreignness was acceptable but an open-mindedness which sought wisdom in all its manifestations, and whatever its source.

The other influence on Jahiz, the Mu'tazilite movement, will be discussed briefly here, to be more fully discussed in the next chapter. In the days of Jahiz, the movement had already developed its main theological position, often referred to as the 'Five Principles' (*al-Usul al-Khamsa*). Of these, only one will concern us here, the justice (*'Adl*) of God and man's subsequent freedom. The Mu'tazilites argued that the world was created in accordance with divine wisdom and that wisdom is manifested in all God's creation through a moral and natural harmony or reason. Unaided human reason can determine such things as the existence of God, His essence and attributes, as well as the fundamental rules of ethics. In such a world, man could only be held responsible for his acts if he was truly free to pursue a moral choice, since predestination would negate divine wisdom and render the whole scheme of creation haphazard and incomprehensible. The Mu'tazilites, therefore, posited a rational view of the world which excluded an arbitrary, 'magical' or mysterious God.

Adab and Mu'tazilism went hand in hand in Jahiz's exploration of nature and society. By temperament he was a critic and polemicist, and the words 'experience' (*tajriba*), 'test' (*imtihan*) and 'proof' (*burhan*) are found frequently in his scathing comments on the scholars and scholarship of his age and in his own criteria of verifiability. His observations on history are scattered among his many books and epistles but can best be introduced, perhaps, in the following passage which sets forth some of the basic conceptual problems of historiography:

> I shall discuss historical reports (*akhbar*) and describe religious traditions (*athar*). I shall distinguish between the grounds for false proof and the grounds for true, and further distinguish between proof that is considered compelling by the elite and not the commoners, and the kind in which the elite act as proof against the commoners. I shall also explain the areas where a few reports are more convincing as proof than many reports and the reasons why a particular report gains currency although weak in its foundation while another, strongly based, gains no currency. I shall further elucidate the kind of report which may be considered safe from corruption and alteration despite its antiquity and its host of critics, as well as the need to relate traditions and hear historical reports . . . and why nations have achieved consensus over the truth in certain fields and differed in others . . . It is surprising that jurists do not distinguish between traditions and theologians do not bother to rectify historical reports since it is through history that people can tell a true from a false prophet, an honest man from a liar . . . Therefore, having classified and divided historical reports, I shall turn to the proofs of the Prophet . . . then categorize traditions by importance and arrange them in ranks . . . using time-honoured methods and necessary proofs.[48]

Somewhat typically, Jahiz does not actually answer all the questions he has set himself in this particular essay. For his style is restless and to that extent well suited to the *Adab* ideal of moving from subject to subject. But the passage above is probably his longest statement on the nature of history and will be used as epicentre from which to trace his other reflections on this theme. One should add that the general context of these particular observations on historical reports and religious traditions was a surge in debate and polemic in the third/ninth century among the various

---

[48] Jahiz, *Rasa'il*, ed. Sandubi, pp. 117–18.

Muslim sects and between Muslims on the one hand and non-Muslims, especially Christians, on the other. Apart from strictly theological issues, questions such as the truth and falsity of historical reporting, the weight ,of evidence and the proper transmission of sacred texts were all debated with great vigour. Jahiz himself played a prominent role in these sectarian polemics.

Turning first to how historical reports are transmitted, Jahiz offers the following magisterial judgement:

Know that all knowledge of an absent entity, whatever it may be, can be attained in one of three ways . . . As regards things not observed by you but which are perceptible and were in fact perceived by others, the mode of attaining knowledge thereof is through reports of multiple witnesses, carried by friend as well as foe, the pious man as well as the villain. These are so widespread that, for those who hear them, there is no problem in believing them. In this mode of knowledge, the learned and the ignorant are on the same level. But there may be another kind of report, more specific, but known only through inquiry . . . such as a group who transmit a report which you know full well – even if most do not – that a similar group could not have conspired to fabricate, given the differences in their way of life and the unlikelihood that they could have known each other. In such a report, falsehood is impossible. But there may be other reports, even more specific, trans-mitted by one or two men, who may be telling the truth or may be lying. The truth of this report depends at heart on the good opinion you have of the reporter and your confidence in his impartiality. But this kind of report can never attain the same status, in your or anyone else's heart, as the first two kinds of reports.[49]

Concerned that scholars of his age had paid insufficient attention to the principles of historical knowledge, including both secular narrative and prophetic *Hadith*, Jahiz set out to show how one could distinguish truth from falsehood by classifying reports in categories of accreditation. Impli-cit in this classificatory scheme is the establishment of criteria of truth quite different from those prevalent among *Hadith* scholars: reports trans-mitted by only a few can, if they pass the test of rational inquiry, possess the same credibility status as reports of multiple witnesses (*tawatur*). The intellectual elite (*al-khassa*), a word beloved by the *adibs* of the age, demanded standards of truth that were quite distinct from those that satis-fied the commoners (*al-ʿamma*).

When appraising the substance of historical reports, the concepts of the possible (*jaʾiz*) and the impossible (*mumtaniʿ*) occupy a central place. These are initially described as follows:

The truth which God commanded, made desirable and urged us to embrace is that we should reject two kinds of reports: those that are contradictory and implausible and those that are impossible in nature and beyond the capacity of created beings. If a report belongs to neither of these two kinds, and is subject to being judged

---

[49] Jahiz, *Rasaʾil*, ed. Harun, 1:119–20.

possible, one proceeds by seeking confirmation (*tathabbut*). In this matter, truth must be your object and honesty your aim, whatever it may be, and whether you assent to it willingly or unwillingly.[50]

'Seeking confirmation' involves the systematic study of nature and society, a task that Jahiz attempted in his major work, the *Book of Animals* (*Kitab al-Hayawan*) and in numerous smaller works and essays. His aim was to describe, through observation, trustworthy information or literary anecdote, the behaviour and habits of wild and domestic animals but with particular emphasis on reports considered implausible by scholars in his age. In fact Jahiz seems to have delighted in the investigation of the grey area between the natural and the supernatural. According to him, some men will accept as true only what the consensus of their community decrees can happen in the world. Thus they reject a phenomenon like metamorphosis. Others, observing how a particular climate or environment can cause both men and animals to acquire or shed basic characteristics necessary for adaptation, accept the possibility of metamorphosis.[51]

For Jahiz, investigation (*bahth*) and experience (*tajriba*) is an endless process: 'the created mind may be finite but the experiential mind is infinite'. Knowledge progresses from age to age because it occurs, in both men and animals, by repetition of experiences. And yet the mind is a fragile entity which can fall prey to 'diseases' such as blind imitation and the power of natural instincts.[52] From the study of the religious beliefs of civilized nations, Jahiz concludes the following:

Mankind singles out religion for absurdity of error and outrageous statements in a manner in which they single out no other science, opinion, art or craft . . . the evidence for my view is that the nations which may be relied upon for rationality, eloquence, right opinion, literature and diversity of crafts are four in number: the Arabs, Indians, Byzantines and Persians. Once you move them from worldly affairs on to the subject of religion, you would imagine they had become feeble-minded.[53]

It is soon made clear that religion is embraced by people through imitation and that imitation is no more likely to lead to truth than it is to falsehood. Hence, Jahiz can build upon his theories of cognition and of the mind's workings and move, in the best *Adab* tradition, from this to comparative culture and to patterns in the historical reception of religions.

---

[50] Jahiz, *Hayawan*, 3:238–9.
[51] On metamorphosis, see *Hayawan*, 4:68 ff. For instructive parallels and contrasts to these views, see Robert M. Grant, *Miracle and Natural Law in Graeco-Roman and Early Christian Thought* (Amsterdam: North-Holland Publishing Company, 1952).
[52] On the experiential mind, see *Buldan*, p. 465. On cognition, see *Min Kitab al-Masa'il wa'l Jawabat fi'l Ma'rifa*, 325–6. On Jahiz and progress, see T. Khalidi, 'A Mosquito's Wing: Jahiz on the Progress of Knowledge' in R. el-Droubie, ed., *Arabic and Islamic Garland: The Tibawi Festschrift* (London: Islamic Cultural Centre, 1977). On the mind's diseases, see, e.g., *Tarbi'*, paras. 193 and 197, and *Min Kitab al-Masa'il*, 323.
[53] Jahiz, *Al-Akhbar wa kayfa tasuhh*, 91. The Arabs referred to are of course the pre-Islamic.

Where other civilizations are concerned, Jahiz is very much aware of the debt that his own civilization owes them. Indeed, it is probable that it was Jahiz who originated the view that the civilized nations were four in number. But his belief in the progress of knowledge, or at least in the possibility of its infinite increase, meant that he had no excessive admiration for ancient literature:

The books of the Indians, the wisdom of Greece and the literature of the Persians have all been translated. Some have gained in charm while others lost nothing . . . These books were transmitted from nation to nation, from era to era and from language to language until they finally reached us and we were the last to inherit and examine them . . . Our practice with our successors ought to resemble the practice of our predecessors with us. But we have attained greater wisdom than they did and those who follow will attain greater wisdom than we have.[54]

Jahiz was a supreme stylist of the Arabic language, but he always wrote with tongue in cheek, a Socratic 'fly' stinging the Islamic 'horse', a deflator of bubbles. He adopted a style which delighted in opposites, always ready to see, even fabricate, an opponent's point of view but always happy to demolish it with wit and cunning. In his major work on eloquence and style, *Kitab al-Bayan wa'l Tabyin*, and in other epistles, Jahiz argued for a literary taste which appreciated good poetry irrespective of the age to which it belonged and a style which favoured the plain, ready-to-hand phrase and avoided the contrived and uncouth. As with the order and economy of nature, so with language: conciseness was indispensable to eloquence, a quality that Jahiz preferred to illustrate rather than to analyse.[55]

Jahiz left his distinctive mark on so many fields that he came to dominate the *Adab* of his and of later ages, and even to obsess some of its leading figures, like Ibn Qutayba and Tawhidi. His genius was perhaps unmatched but he had shown what could be done if *Adab* is used as a rational method of exploring nature, society and history.

Adab, Hadith and history: Ibn Qutayba

The modern reader will not find Ibn Qutayba (d. 276/889) as nimble, incisive, or as beguiling an intellect as Jahiz. Running through the surprisingly large corpus of his writings which has survived is a pedantic streak which one associates with earnest reformers, with those who bow to the piety of a dominant group, or with the newly converted. And perhaps Ibn Qutayba

[54] Jahiz, *Hayawan*, 1:75, 86. His views on national characteristics are best expounded in *Rasa'il*, ed. Harun, 1:67–73.
[55] See, e.g., *Hayawan*, 2:27, 108; *Rasa'il*, ed. Harun, 2:116; *Hayawan*, 3:130 (on literary taste for 'Ancients' and 'Moderns'). See also *Hayawan*, 3:368 and *Bayan*, 1:75 ff., 144 ff. (issues of style and conciseness). See also the discussion in T. Khalidi, *Islamic Historiography* (Albany: SUNY Press, 1975), pp. 14–27.

was all three of these things. He was an *adib* of very wide accomplishments but one who was intent upon bringing *Adab* into line with the moral expectations of the formidable regiments of *Hadith* scholars of his day. At the same time he was also a *muhaddith* who was out of patience with the obscurantism of many *hadith* scholars. He tapped a wider spectrum of sources and cultural traditions – Indian, Persian, Greek – than the typical *adib* and had a truly impressive command of Arabic poetry and grammar. Nevertheless, the sparks of originality, of free-floating speculation, are few. In the *Shuʿubiyya* controversy, he vigorously defended the Arabs while acknowledging his own Persian origins, and may have seen himself as a latter-day Ibn al-Muqaffaʿ, although he lacked the fiercely independent analytical powers of the master.

And yet Ibn Qutayba's works straddle many disciplines and genres: the principles of *Hadith* and Qurʿanic *Tafsir*, anthologies of *Adab* and of historical reports, polemical essays, the secretarial handbook. In all of these works, his intentions, his authorial presence and his method are all very much in evidence:

Although this book does not deal with the Qu'ran, the Sunna, the religious laws or the science of the licit and illicit, it nevertheless addresses noble themes, counsels honesty and virtue, rebukes debauchery and . . . inspires proper control and correct assessment of affairs . . . There is no one single path to God, nor is virtue summed up in spending nights in prayer, endless fasting and the knowledge of licit and illicit. Rather, the paths to God are many and the gates of virtue are wide open. Religion is set aright when times are set aright, and times are set aright when government is set aright . . . I have composed these *ʿUyun al-Akhbar* [The Most Noteworthy Reports] as an eye-opener to the person ignorant of *Adab*, as a reminder to religious scholars, as a tutor to rulers and ruled, as a relaxation for kings . . . I organized it in chapters (*abwab*), linking each chapter, report and word to its like to facilitate learning, memorization and reference.[56]

His *ʿUyun al-Akhbar* is an anthology of literary reports drawn, he says, from many quarters: old and young, Arab and non-Arab, learned and ignorant, believers and non-believers, 'Ancients' and 'Moderns'.[57] Nevertheless, the division into titled chapters (*kutub*) parallels the divisions of the two renowned and contemporary *Hadith* collections (*Sahihan*) of Bukhari and Muslim. The coexistence of the two spirits, of *Hadith* and *Adab*, in Ibn Qutayba's work is recognized by him as requiring two separate methodologies. The religious and legal sciences demand an imitative relationship (*taqlid*) to a master who is then adopted as a guide or proof (*hujja*) for the pursuit of the pious life. But *Adab*, which for Ibn Qutayba meant exemplary patterns of speech and moral conduct, could be sought in any quarter and from any source. If the 'gates to virtue' are wide open,

---

[56] Ibn Qutayba, *ʿUyun al-Akhbar*, 1: *ya'*, *kaf*.
[57] Ibn Qutayba, *ʿUyun*, 1: *sin*.

and religious reform depends upon the reform of political life, *Adab* was a necessary complement to the good life. At the same time, Ibn Qutayba compared his *'Uyun al-Akhbar* to a table laden with food to satisfy all tastes, 'both those who crave this life as well those who crave the afterlife', the elite as well as the commoners, and was eager to amuse his reader and not to tire or bore him.[58]

But the *'Uyun* is essentially a selection, an anthology of verse and anecdotes, and apart from the author's introduction, lacks any commentary on the reports and sayings so carefully chosen and arranged under appropriate, *Hadith*-like headings. It is a directory of historical information rather than a work of history. In this sense, Jahiz and Ibn Qutayba were at one, since neither felt the need to arrange *akhbar* in chronological order, treating history instead as a collection of individual reports which illustrated or displayed various aspects of the human condition.

His other celebrated work of *Adab*, the *Kitab al-Ma'arif*, is a compendium of 'useful information', addressed to a restricted and more aristocratic readership, and somewhat more chronological in structure:

For there can hardly be any *majlis* devoted to learning, convened in sobriety or conducted with honour in which some aspect or another of knowledge is not discussed, whether it be the mention of a prophet, a king, a scholar, a genealogy, an ancestry, times past or a battle-day of the Arabs. He who attends the *majlis* would then need to know the story itself, the home of the tribe in question, the era of that king, the condition of the man named and the circumstances of the well-known proverb. Many a nobleman have I seen who is ignorant of his ancestry . . . and I have seen sons of Persian kings who knew nothing of the conditions of their parents or times . . . My aim in all the stories I have cited has been conciseness, lightness of touch and the pursuit of celebrated rather than obscure information.[59]

In the *Ma'arif*, Ibn Qutayba chose a broadly chronological framework, beginning with the creation, passing on to the prophets, then Muhammad and the Companions, caliphs and Successors, then the great jurists and scholars of the community. The last part, however, breaks the rough temporal sequence to become a miscellany of scattered knowledge: geographical information, curiosities, sects, proverbs and ancient kings. The *Ma'arif* is a book of useful facts, a 'nobleman's' *vademecum*, a historical compendium of which every *adib* stands in need. But the rough chronology is an organizing structure meant to facilitate reference rather than a method of explanation. No evolutionary patterns are sought and no attempt is made to dissect or analyse *akhbar*. Unlike Jahiz, Ibn Qutayba was distrustful of philosophers and theologians and thus not inclined to examine issues such

---

[58] On separate methodologies and imitation, see *'Uyun*, 1: *sin*, *'ayn*; on the table laden with food and the entertainment of the reader, see *'Uyun*, 1: *lam*.

[59] Ibn Qutayba, *Ma'arif*, pp. 1–2, 6–7.

as the credibility or otherwise of historical reports. He was much taken with what he considered to be the progressive deterioration of knowledge and morality, although his view that 'God did not limit knowledge, poetry and eloquence to one age rather than another' would seem to qualify his 'pessimism'.[60]

Ibn Qutayba's scholarly output belongs to the second half of the third/ninth century. It was approximately in that period that the Abbasids, and after a hundred years or more of dramatic shifts in religious policy, seemed at last to be adopting what was eventually to become Sunni 'orthodoxy'. One manifestation of this crystallization of religious orientation was the emergence in the historiography of the period of a more friendly image of the Umayyads, an open admiration for the political sagacity of some caliphs, e.g. Mu'awiya, 'Abd al-Malik and Hisham, and a more general esteem for Umayyad poets, jurists, ascetics and *Hadith* scholars. Shi'ism too, motivated largely by the desire to demonstrate its historical legitimacy, was beginning to consolidate both its doctrinal and its legal edifice. In the late third/ninth century, two contrasting reconstructions of history were instrumental in demarcating Sunni from Shi'i Islam.

As a result of the rapid increase in the delineation of political and religious positions, there followed what may in intellectual history be called a textbook period, a period rich in textbooks of *Adab, Hadith*, grammar, *Tafsir*. Ibn Qutayba's works, like those of Jahiz, possess a textbook quality and address a cultivated reader. Neither man treated history directly. But as Jahiz had begun to investigate society and nature as well as the instruments involved in their investigation, including historical reports, so Ibn Qutayba was to be important in recreating an image of a past, proudly Arab, proudly Muslim, but also very much aware of the ties that this culture had with immediate as well as distant antecedents.[61]

Intention, space, time and number

Adab had helped to guide history in new directions, some of which have been sketched in outline, above. One must now attempt to show in some detail how *Adabi* historical thought and writing grew to constitute a recognizable genre, and one quite distinct from *Hadith* historiography in sub-

---

[60] For his view that God did not limit knowledge to one age, see *al-Shi'r wa'l Shu'ara'*, pp. 5–6. This is to be contrasted with his strong views about the decline of knowledge and morals as expressed, e.g., in *al-Ikhtilaf fi'l Lafz*, p. 7, or in *Adab al-Katib*, pp. 1–6, 9. His distrust of philosophy and theology is apparent in *Adab al-Katib*, pp. 3–4.

[61] Ibn Qutayba put up a vigorous defence even of *Jahili* Arabs against their detractors and taunted the Shu'ubis for attacking the Arabs 'in their own tongue': see *Kitab al-'Arab* in Kurd 'Ali, *Rasa'il*, pp. 344–77, *passim*. He often quoted Plato and Aristotle and gave highly accurate quotations from the Old and New Testaments, a rare practice among *adibs* and historians – see chapter 2, note 116, above, and G. Lecomte, 'Les citations de l'Ancien et du Nouveau Testament dans l'œuvre d'Ibn Qutayba', *Arabica*, 5 (Jan. 1958), 34–46.

stance and form. New configurations of social class and political power, alluded to in earlier sections and discussed again below, undoubtedly helped to remould the conceptualization of the past. No less important, however, were developments in the understanding of man as a microcosm, that is to say in the understanding of both man's interiority as well as his complementarity with the natural environment.

If any one single train of events is sought to date these conceptual developments in the understanding of man, it may well be that train of events which was set in motion by the Inquisition (*Mihna*) instituted by the Abbasid caliph al-Ma'mun in 218/833.[62] The *Mihna*, quite apart from its momentous political and sectarian implications, was an invasion of privacy and an assertion of the power of the royal will over individual conscience on a massive scale. The *Mihna* forced the religious scholars of the empire to submit to an examination the result of which determined not only their chances of employment as judges and teachers but even their status in society as believing Muslims. The caliph had concluded 'after careful reasoning and reflection' that belief in an uncreated Qur'an was a source of great danger and harm to his subjects. He was therefore convinced that the leaders and scholars of the community, by virtue of the wisdom and knowledge instilled in them by God, were entrusted with the task of guiding men to true belief through 'revealing to them matters hidden or confusing so as to repel doubt and enlighten men with clear proof'.[63]

The subsequent course of this extraordinary episode need not detain us. But one of the effects of this foray by the caliph into the realm of religious knowledge was to highlight the practical effects of belief in certain theological dogmas, so that scholarly issues such as the status of the Qur'an and the responsibility of the individual were matters relevant to everyday living and not solely to salvation. The great public debate initiated by the *Mihna* invited a closer examination of man's inner being: not merely his religious conscience but his reason, will and psyche. The religious scholars were explicitly given the role of guides of the community, leading to a greater sense of their own 'ecclesiastical' importance as arbiters of true belief. After all, the caliph himself had decided to lead them.

Where *Adab* and historical writing are concerned, a number of significant developments can be more or less directly traced to the *Mihna* or its aftermath. The *Mihna* may have been in origin an act of state interference in personal belief. However, over the course of the century or so which followed, one of its more obvious effects was to invite scholars and thinking men to emulate their caliph, to exercise 'careful reasoning and

---

[62] On the *Mihna*, see *EI2*, s. v. (by M. Hinds). My views on the *Mihna* crystallized in conversations with Tamima Beyhum Daou.
[63] Ibn Abi Tahir Tayfur, *Tarikh Baghdad*, pp. 344–5.

reflection' and thus to assert more forcefully than ever before their role as guardians of 'orthodoxy' and guides to salvation. Our attention will now be directed to a few areas in *Adabi* historiography where the intellectual ferment of the post-*Mihna* period left its clearest imprints.

Intention

Histories written under the influence of *Adab* display more clearly than ever the *persona* of their historian-author, his programme and purpose in writing. As we saw above with Jahiz and Ibn Qutayba, these two being very prominent examples of this trend, histories acquire introductions in which intentions, method and organization are spelled out and some indication is offered as to why the work has been produced and to whom it is addressed. This, for instance, is how Hamza al-Isfahani (d. after 350/961) introduces his 'History of the Years of the Kings of the Earth and Its Prophets':

This is a work in which I have included the histories of the years of the kings of the earth and its prophets . . . dividing it into ten chapters (*abwab*) . . . before detailing these histories, I begin with an introduction from which may be inferred the changes in the modes of historical dating and the corruption and confusion therein. In it I also discuss the territorial extension of great nations on the earth's surface and where the small nations fit in between, from which may be seen how some were able to gain mastery over others and how the power of some was absorbed into the power of others, so that these events became the cause for the confusion of historical dates.[64]

The history of Tanukhi (d. 384/994), known best as *Nishwar al-Muhadara*, has a more elaborate introduction, Jahizian in inspiration, and deemed necessary by the author because the historical reports he cites, based on first-hand experiences,

may be thought feeble by a reader if he finds that these experiences do not conform to the common definition of what constitutes history . . . But the reason which led me to write them down is that I used in former days to consort with venerable and virtuous scholars and literati who had come to know about religions . . . kingdoms . . . kings . . . state secretaries and viziers.

There follow two pages of the sources from which these tales were derived, arranged in contrasting pairs (e.g. the high and the mighty, philosophers and sages, labourers and peasants, fools and simpletons) to suggest that these reports of actual experiences cover the whole gamut of society. The tales, says the historian, were related in passing by his scholar friends,

---

[64] Hamza al-Isfahani, *Tarikh*, p. 6; cf. Tha'alibi, *Lata'if*, p. 3, who also divides his work into ten *abwab*.

partly to avoid boring their audience with their pedantry and partly to illustrate their learning with their own lived experiences of the world.

I would immediately note down these reports and make use of them from time to time. But when the years passed and many of the scholars who had supplied these tales had died, and only a few remained who would take these tales with them to the grave if they were unrecorded, I found that the manners and habits of our own rulers and leaders do not allow for the kind of virtue which may be derived from such reports.

His own days, says the historian, are not lacking in men of intellect and wisdom but leaders and rulers no longer patronize learning, with the result that scholars do not bother to produce the kinds of works which record human achievements. Accordingly, he decides to set down as much as he can remember from these old and true stories so that they would act as a substitute for experience,

to the end that the wise and rational man, the clever and educated man, when he hears and digests these tales can benefit therefrom . . . so that he may dispense with direct experience or learning their like from the mouths of men, and become well versed in the ways of this world and the next, fully acquainted with the consequences of virtue and vice . . . thereby not needing to spend his whole lifetime in learning from experience or waiting to see what would result from the passage of years.[65]

This concept of history as lived experience was coupled with a heightened sense of the value of direct testimony and witness and thus greater concern for contemporary history and personal memoirs. Historical reports in the form of true stories recorded by, or directly from those who witnessed them came to be highly prized as illustrations of moral states, consequences of action, or trials of the human soul, precisely because they were truly lived experiences of fully identified, flesh and blood individuals rather than the exploits of distant historical personalities. The unusual memoirs entitled 'Recompense' (*Mukafa'a*) by Ibn al-Daya (d. after 330/ 941) begin with an introduction in which the author states:

I include in this treatise reports about recompense for good or ill which comfort the soul and fulfil the heart's desire. These were stories we heard from persons of older generations or witnessed ourselves in our own days.

Later, he recapitulates and introduces a new theme:

Having fulfilled my promise to you of relating stories about recompense for good or ill, in the hope that this would encourage the continued pursuit of virtue . . . I found it proper to append . . . some well chosen tales of people who were sorely tried but bore their trials with patience. The fruit of this patience was a good outcome. For if the soul is not aided during periods of great distress so that it

---

[65] For the quotations from Tanukhi, see *Nishwar al-Muhadara*, pp. 3–9.

renews its strength, it may succumb to despair and die. Man knows that it is
inevitable for conditions to turn into their opposites . . . Therefore, contemplation
of the stories of this chapter would encourage the soul to persevere patiently . . .
by raising the pious hope that all will be well when the trial is over.[66]

The theme of the soul on trial enhanced the value of personal or recollected history as food for thought and comfort for the distressed. In contrast to public, *isnad*-regimented history, lived history placed a new
emphasis on direct observation of the present, on autobiography and a
more explicit discussion of the strengths and weaknesses of the sources of
information. Historians of their own times like Tanukhi, Ibn al-Daya and
Muhammad ibn Yahya al-Suli (d. 335/946) step into the action, so to
speak, naming facts and figures and specifying times and places. The
author's sensibilities are revealed as when Suli, for instance, wrestles with
the problem of documenting conversations:

What I have already reproduced of his [the caliph al-Radi's] conversation and what
I shall quote below is as I reported it or similar or akin to what he said. For I was
not always able to memorize his very words although I recollect the gist of what
he said.[67]

Meanwhile, systematic or occasional citation of bibliography, with or without critical commentary, spells out more clearly the way that the historian
has decided to proceed and indicates some of his own criteria of accuracy
and reliability.[68]

Space

Ya'qubi (d. *c*. 284/897) was the author of the earliest surviving world history in the Arabic historical tradition. His history was to have several
imitators but it was a work which manifested a number of unusual characteristics such as its accurate citations of ancient sources and its use of
astronomy to establish exactitude of dating. His history and his two other
surviving works, on geography and on the affinity between people and
their age, may be taken as a point of departure for the discussion of certain
questions that had to do with what may broadly be termed the function
of space in *Adabi* historical writing.

As Persian and then other foreign history became known to literate
circles of the late-Umayyad and early-Abbasid empires, the curiosity it

[66] For the two quotations from Ibn al-Daya, see *Mukafa'a*, pp. 3, 160–1.
[67] Suli, *Akhbar al-Radi*, p. 18. Suli reveals more of his sensibility when apologizing for
    troubling the reader with his personal sorrows, as on pp. 212 and 219. This follows the
    very vivid description of the attack on his house, pp. 210 ff. and on his estate, p. 218.
[68] Good examples of citations of bibliography may be found in Hamza al-Isfahani, *Tarikh*,
    p. 9 (Persian history), p. 48 (Greek history), p. 54 (source criticism), p. 55 (Greek history),
    and p. 57 (Israelite history); see also Ya'qubi, *Tarikh*, 2: 5–6.

aroused was, as we saw above, one of the major impulses behind the development of *Adab*. As more and more of this foreign history was incorporated into literary and historical works, it not only forced a constriction of *isnad*, which was no longer available or appropriate, but inclined historians to deal with this material with greater critical freedom than what would normally be displayed towards subjects closer to home:

> The Persians make many claims for their kings which cannot be accepted, for instance exaggerated features such as a person with many mouths and eyes and another said to have a face made of copper . . . and similar claims which are rejected by reason and to be treated as jesting and make-believe. Rational and scholarly Persians and other nobles and aristocrats, royal princes and gentry, as well as historians and *adibs* reject such stories and refrain from relating them . . . There are other well-established tales which we have seen most people to have rejected . . . and have therefore set aside because our principle is to excise offensive reports.[69]

Yemenite history also came in for a lot of criticism from world historians for incredibly long reigns when compared with the small number of kings, as did the Alexander legend propagated by the *qussas*, a group now openly despised by the professional historians.[70] Accordingly, ancient history became, for many historians, a field where they could exercise and sharpen their critical faculties without running the risk of antagonizing the parties and sects of their own days. In consequence, the parts devoted to ancient history in many world histories frequently possess a liveliness of treatment and a critical latitude which is lacking in the Islamic portions of these works.

Ya'qubi was also the author of a work on geography in which he went beyond mere description of the characteristics of countries to suggest the manner in which climate and habitat give shape to the culture of various nations. Jahiz had already discussed the effects of the environment on man and Ya'qubi's geography followed in that tradition:

> I begin with Iraq because it is the centre of the world, the navel of the earth. I describe Baghdad because it is the centre of Iraq, the great city that has no equal . . . in greatness and extent, habitation, abundance of water and salubrity of air, and because it has been inhabited by all sorts of men from all kinds of countries . . . There is no country which does not have a living quarter and a market in it . . . and there is to be found in it what is found in no other city on earth . . . Thus, due to the moderate air, good soil and sweet water, its inhabitants are virtuous, their faces are radiant and their minds are sharp to the point where they

---

[69] Ya'qubi, *Tarikh*, 1:158–9.
[70] On Yemenite history, see Hamza, *Tarikh*, p. 89; on the *qussas* and the Alexander legend, see Hamza, *Tarikh*, p. 30. See also Tha'alibi, *Ghurar*, pp. 10, 35, for severely critical comments on Persian history.

excel all others in learning, understanding and culture . . . as well as in commerce and crafts.[71]

It may well have been geography which encouraged Jahiz and, later on, Ya'qubi to seek to detect patterns in the histories of nations, patterns of social behaviour, rise and fall, expansion and decline. In a short treatise entitled 'The affinity of people with their own times' (*Mushakalat al-nas li zamanihim*), Ya'qubi set out to show, by numerous historical examples arranged chronologically, how people living under succeeding caliphates tend to imitate the behaviour and attitudes of each caliph and to act 'in accordance with what they see of him, adhering closely to his morals, actions and speech'.[72] Then follow the examples: Mu'awiya came to power and built palaces and mansions, hid himself from popular view and interposed guards and chamberlains between himself and his subjects. His family, children and governors followed his example. Later came 'Abd al-Malik, a bloodthirsty and energetic ruler, and his policies were imitated by his governors and officials. And so it goes on for other caliphs, in a pattern which suggests that royalty sets the tone for every age and helps to explain contrasts and reversals of policy.

It was undoubtedly *Adab*-inspired historical writing which first investigated critically the patterns that might be derived from the comparative examination of ancient cultures. This was most often done by designating a certain number of nations, four or seven being the commonest number, who were said to have excelled in certain branches of culture or art.[73] The historical imagination could roam freely here, establishing 'firsts', the first to institute this or that custom or action, and linking these cultures and nations in various ways, one of the more unusual being the geopolitical 'map' of Hamza al-Isfahani:

Know that the inhabited part of the earth's quarter, despite diversity of regions, is divided among seven great nations: China, India, Black Africa (*al-Sudan*), the Berbers, the Byzantines, the Turks and the Aryans. Among them, the Aryans, who are the Persians, are in the midst of these kingdoms, surrounded by these six nations. For the south-east of the earth is held by China, the north-east by the Turks, the mid-south by India and opposite them the Byzantines in the mid-north, the south-west by the *Sudan* and opposite them the Berbers in the north-west . . . The Aryans are in the midst.[74]

---

[71] Ya'qubi, *Buldan*, pp. 233–5.
[72] Ya'qubi, *Mushakala*, p. 9. Tha'alibi, *Lata'if*, pp. 70–1, reports a similar pattern on the authority of al-Haytham ibn 'Adiyy, in illustration of the adage that 'men follow the religion of their kings' and that 'government is a market to which is imported what is consumed therein'.
[73] For ancient nations, see T. Khalidi, *Islamic Historiography*, pp. 81 ff. and A. Shboul, *Al-Mas'udi and His World* (London: Ithaca Press, 1979), pp. 95 ff.
[74] Hamza, *Tarikh*, p. 6.

Hamza proceeds to show how some of them used a lunar, others a solar calendar and how their world histories reveal great discrepancies, while each nation gives an account of the history of its neighbours 'as false as a dream'.

But despite the 'confusions' and 'falsehoods' in the histories of ancient nations, to narrate their history was to pass in review the history of human culture itself. Historians like Ya'qubi and Hamza al-Isfahani would record the achievements of each nation in the arts and sciences, in law and religion, in urbanism and agriculture, philosophy and astronomy and in the craft of government. From this long stream of history it was possible to observe how and why certain beliefs and customs had originated, for instance idolatry and fasting as in the following account:

> In his days there began the worship of idols and graven images. The reason was that some people, distressed at the death of their beloved, carved statues in their likeness so as to comfort themselves by looking at them. Time passed and they were tempted to worship these images under the impression that these idols would mediate between them and God . . . In his days too there began the custom of fasting. This was originated by poor people . . . and the reason was scarcity of food. They agreed to pass the whole day without food and end it by drinking enough water to prevent them from perishing. Having, after a while, grown accustomed to this habit, they came to regard it as a form of religion and of the worship of God.[75]

In the geographical works of this period, most of which surveyed the known world from east to west, it was commonly asserted that the diversity of regions and nations revealed their creator's wisdom since their very diversity insured that they would be interdependent. Each region was granted certain resources denied to others, necessitating commerce, industry, travel and the exchange and enjoyment of each other's goods, and demonstrating the just and proper arrangement of the created world.[76] Culture, likewise, was seen to have passed from nation to nation until the arts and sciences of the nations converged upon 'the centre of the world'.

Time

How old was the world? Could anything be learnt from ancient remains on the one hand and from sciences like astrology on the other? Could any sense or order be inferred from the chronology of ancient nations which would throw light on such problems? How old were cities?

Islamic scholarship had from earliest times manifested a pronounced curiosity regarding the site of events. Much care was taken, for example,

---

[75] Hamza, *Tarikh*, pp. 23–4; cf. a similar passage on the origins of idolatry in Ya'qubi, *Tarikh*, 1:21, which may have been the source of Hamza's account.
[76] See, for instance, Ibn al-Faqih, *Mukhtasar*, p. 251.

to locate sites of religious and historical interest for the life of Muhammad. A historian like Waqidi first acquired his reputation as an expert on the sacred topography of the Hijaz and at one time acted as a guide to the caliph Harun al-Rashid when on a visit to the holy places. This topographical curiosity was soon accompanied by an interest in the history of urban settlements. Jahiz, for example, believed that houses and buildings existed from the beginning of the world, while the geographer Ibn Hawqal (d. c. 362/973) refers to certain cities as 'eternal *a parte ante*' (*azali*). Cities were often said to have been founded by important Biblical or Qur'anic figures and some were said to be older than even the time of king Solomon, a famous city builder of the Arabic-Islamic tradition. In the classical geographers, however, the Persian kings were historically the most vigorous city builders. The Arabs inherited these cities and, according to Abu Hayyan al-Tawhidi (d. after 400/1010), were not found lacking in the trappings of urban culture.[77]

It would appear therefore that it was the intensive urbanism of the first two centuries of the Abbasid empire which inspired speculation, first about the structure and character and later about the age of cities. The geographer Muqaddasi (d. c. 380/990) believed that Islamic cities 'abrogated' (*tansakh*) one another, whereas eastern capitals (*amsar*) were ancient and did not deplete each other.[78] But the concept of a very ancient past tended to focus on one or two literary images:

[When Quraysh wanted to date an event] they would say that it took place the year Hisham died or the year of the coming of the elephant or the days when the Ka'ba was built. The other Arabs would date an event by the days of the *Fithal* or the Year of the *Khinan* or the Year of the *Jihaf* or the days of the inundating flood. If they meant something more ancient they would say that the event occurred when rocks were still wet or when boulders were still as soft and moist as mud.[79]

Abu Hilal al-'Askari (d. after 400/1010), who gave the fullest account of these reports of very ancient days, was himself very sceptical about them. Nor did archaeological remains fare much better, at least not at the hands of *Adabi* historians who tended to note their presence but not to show sustained interest in their chronology.[80] The resulting confusion concerning these 'pre-historic' days was highlighted by Ibn Hazm (d. 456/1064):

[77] For the eternity of cities, see Jahiz, *Buldan*, p. 482; Ibn Hawqal, *Surat al-Ard*, 1:110 and *passim*; Ibn Rusteh, *Al-A'laq al-Nafisa*, p. 25. For cities older than Solomon, see Ibn al-Faqih, *Mukhtasar*, p. 117. For Tawhidi, see *Al-Imta' wa'l Mu'anasa*, 1:85.
[78] Muqaddasi, *Ahsan al-Taqasim*, pp. 270–1.
[79] Hamza, *Tarikh*, p. 95. These same images of the very ancient past occur in Qali, *Amali*, 1:238 and in Abu Hilal al-'Askari, *Awa'il*, 1:81–3: this last contains the fullest account and explains the names of the years cited. The images grew out of a few lines of verse already known to Jahiz.
[80] 'Askari, *Awa'il*, 1:83, ends his account of 'geological' time with tales of snakes which could fly and other marvels which he curtly dismisses. Hamza, *Tarikh*, pp. 23 and 24, refers briefly to archaeological remains as support for evidence.

And he who is ignorant of this must surely know that there exists no historical report anywhere in the world about any king from the kings of the earth or about any past generation that goes back further than the history of the dominion of the Israelites which the commoners possess or else what we possess of the history of the kings of the Greeks and Persians. All this goes no further back than two thousand years. Where then is there any mention of those who inhabited the earth before them? Has this not vanished without a trace and is it not totally forgotten?[81]

The Qur'anic division of time into eschatological and earthly, where one day of the eschaton equals one thousand years of earthly time, was adopted by *Hadith* scholars as a means of calculating the total age of the world. This finds its most detailed form in Tabari who computes the total age of the world at fourteen eschatological days or fourteen thousand earthly years, divided into two equal halves: from the creation to Adam and from Adam to the Coming of the Hour.[82] Even Ya'qubi, who is far from being a *Hadith*-inclined historian, strives to pinpoint the passing of each of these thousand-year periods in the introductory chapters of his history. But the confusion remained. In calculating the 'number of years from the beginning of human generation to the year of the Hijra', the Jews and Christians, calculating from the Bible, gave, according to Hamza al-Isfahani, two entirely different figures: the Jews calculated it at 4240 years, the Christians at 5990.[83]

Spearheading the attack on traditional or scriptural methods of time calculation were the astronomers and astrologers who in the 3rd–4th/9th–10th centuries seemed to have established their usefulness and credibility, first of all to the proper ordering of governmental affairs, and later on to the scholarly community as a whole.[84] A famous *adib*-statesman like al-Sahib ibn 'Abbad (d. 385/995), for example, instructed his agents to pay close heed to the reckoning of land-tax (*kharaji*) months and lunar months so that dates would fall due with regularity and leap years be computed as ordained.[85] Ya'qubi manifested a most unusual interest in astrology, citing for the reign of each caliph the exact position of the planets and stars and thereby fixing both the time of accession as well as – or so it seems – the fortunes of the ruler. It must have been the strong antipathy against astrology which prevented Ya'qubi from spelling out explicitly how the position of the stars determined the fates of his caliphs. Only the reader well versed in astrology would be able to deduce this for himself.

---

[81] Ibn Hazm, *Rasa'il*, 1:408; cf. Jahiz, *Hayawan*, 3:377, where 'thousands upon thousands of years' are said to be 'the least that nations date their histories'.
[82] Tabari, *Tarikh*, 1:54–5.
[83] Hamza, *Tarikh*, p. 11.
[84] The affinities between the natural sciences, including astronomy and astrology, and historical writing will be discussed more fully in Chapter Four.
[85] Al-Sahib ibn 'Abbad, *Rasa'il*, pp. 64–5.

But the distinction between astronomy and astrology was not always a sharp one either in these sciences themselves as they were practised or in their reception by the public. Swings of mood were detectable so that even determined enemies of astrology like the Muʿtazilite theologians could sometimes be found to relent in their opposition.[86] Besides, there was no escaping the fact that, for any historian seriously interested in cosmogeny, the astronomical tradition conflicted starkly with estimates based on sacred scripture. Where Biblical computation of the age of the world and Islamic calculations based thereon spoke of a few thousand years:

The astronomers (*ahl al-nujum*) cite figures that surpass this completely, claiming that the age of the earth from the very first day in which planets were set in motion . . . until the day that the caliph al-Mutawakkil set out for Damascus amount to four thousand thousand thousand, multiplied by three, and three hundred thousand thousand and twenty thousand thousand solar years.[87]

Hamza al-Isfahani offers a rare insight into the influence of astronomy on historical chronology when he relates how, having found great discrepancies in ancient Persian chronologies, he decided to consult with a famous astronomer in Maragha. They sat down together and proceeded to compare the Persian chronology with the era of Alexander which is well established in the astronomical almanacs (*hisab al-munajjimin fi'l zijat*) until they had finally brought order to the chronology of the various Persian dynasties. It appears that Hamza owed his interest in astronomy to the views of the celebrated astronomer Abu Maʿshar al-Balkhi (d. 272/886) who seems to have made one of the earliest attempts to correct chronologies by use of astronomical calculations after having noted that:

most chronologies are interpolated and corrupt. Corruption enters when a nation has lived through a long period of time. Thus, when chronologies are copied from one book to another or one language to another, mistakes occur through addition or subtraction as happened to the Jews regarding the years between Adam and Noah and between other prophets and nations described in history. They differ in this respect and other nations also differ from them. Confusion also afflicts the history of Persian kings, despite a continuous kingdom from the very beginning of time until its final disappearance. There is much muddle and corruption here. The Persians claim for instance that the earth remained often and for long periods of time without having kings from them or any other nation.[88]

The use of astronomy by Yaʿqubi and Hamza is typical of the influence that the climate of *Adab* exercised on historiography in encouraging the investigation of chronography and in transcending the traditional scriptural sources for the inquiry into ancient history. With this went a sharper sense

---

[86] See the charming story of the Muʿtazilite theologian Abu ʿAli al-Jubbaʾi and his student al-Ramhurmuzi in Tanukhi, *Nishwar*, p. 270.
[87] Hamza, *Tarikh*, p. 11.
[88] Hamza, *Tarikh*, p. 10. For the meeting at Maragha, see *Tarikh*, pp. 15–16.

of beginnings, of the origins of things. In such works as the *Ma'arif* of Ibn Qutayba, the *Muhabbar* of Ibn Habib (d. 245/859) and the *A'laq* of the geographer Ibn Rusteh, a chapter or more is devoted to 'firsts': the first to perform, discover or establish some feat, science or custom. To begin with, these lists of firsts appear to fit in well with the anecdotal (*nawadir*; *lata'if*) presentation of history that *Adab* sometimes inspired. They are of course mythic since they celebrate a heroic age but their value as entertainment has been high in all ages and for all cultures.

However, a more extensive investigation of origins yielded a more orderly treatment of 'firsts'. In the *Awa'il* of Abu Hilal al-'Askari, these firsts are no longer lists of curios but systematically arranged historical reports based on the premise that time affects all things except the fame of scholars and that scholarship is most useful when it satisfies what men desire most to know. For 'Askari, the origins of things, a subject about which all men are curious, was to be set forth in a treatise of ten chapters arranged in rough chronological order, where it is not so much the sensationalism of records but the evolution of beliefs and customs which deserves investigation. The beginnings of idol worship in Mecca, for example, lead into the more general theme of idolatry, itself in origin star worship. Idols were first set up by kings because 'kings need religion as much as they need wealth and men' and that is because 'kingship cannot be firmly established except by homage and homage needs an oath and there can be no oath without a religious community'.[89] From the simple nativity of things, history has moved to the more challenging question of the patterns of their continuities.

Number

As we saw earlier, the mirror held up by *Adabi* historians was much closer to contemporaneous reality than the mirror of *Hadith* historiography. The Baghdad of Tayfur, Suli or Tanukhi, for instance, is peopled with vivid characters whose lives the reader is often made to share in all their intimate detail. History-as-personal-experience placed a new emphasis on specificity, on the elaboration of fact and circumstance. The *khabar*, liberated from its cumbersome *isnad*, was free at last to roam the streets, picking up the sights and sounds of strata of society hitherto unrecorded.

The official document, the memoir, the private diary – these can all be detected on or near the surface of contemporary history. Inevitably, perhaps, dates, facts and figures appear to be accurate even if they are not always so in reality simply because someone seems to have taken the trouble of noting them down when first perceived. Thus, the prices of commodities are quoted as illustration of material hardship or ease. The

---

[89] 'Askari, *Awa'il*, 1:75–6.

day of the week and even the time of day is given especially when the historian himself steps into some dramatic segment of the action. Taxation figures for particular regions, even whole budgets, are cited. Some half-hearted guesses are made at population figures.[90]

The state secretarial contribution to this growing sense of the importance of numbers must obviously have been considerable.[91] Two histories devoted to state secretaries and viziers, the *Wuzara'* of Jahshiyari (d. 331/942) and the *Tuhfat al-Umara'* of Hilal al-Sabi (d. 448/1056), have such a dense fiscal texture to them that they could between them provide the skeleton for an economic history of the first four centuries of Arab Islam. Letters and rescripts, promissory notes and lease agreements, in short all the trappings of medieval commercial life are displayed here while the anecdotes, especially in al-Sabi, gain their significance precisely because of the seemingly effortless accuracy of his statistics and figures.

No less important was the contribution of new methods of measurement demanded by the natural sciences, to be investigated in the next chapter. But society itself under the early Abbasids may also have become increasingly conscious of numbers through such factors as the accumulation of vast wealth in a few private hands, the increasing attention that had to be paid to finance by the caliphs and their senior officials, recurrent fiscal crises in the third/ninth century and the creeping feudalization of the military class. All these developments intensified the demand for book-keeping and enhanced the ultimate authority of numbers.

Numbers were of course employed symbolically or as metaphors for magnification or mystery.[92] It is usually not very difficult for a modern reader to detect the symbolic usage of numerals since, to be efficacious as symbols, they need to be limited in number, so that seven, forty, seventy, and a thousand are far and away the most common symbolic numbers. Scholars of *Hadith* and *Tafsir* showed an obvious interest in the symbolic value of these numerals, an interest which was generally inherited by historians who sheltered under their wing. But here too *Adabi* historical writing shows a contrast. The *Hadith* scholars themselves admitted that the *adibs* were generally more critical and discriminating than they were.[93]

---

[90] For day of the week and time of day see, e.g., Suli, *Akhbar al-Radi*, pp. 1, 210 and Hamza, *Tarikh*, pp. 124 ff. For prices, see Tayfur, *Tarikh*, p. 134. For taxation, see Ya'qubi, *Buldan*, pp. 328–9 and Jahshiyari, *Wuzara'*, p. 287. For budget, see Jahshiyari, *Wuzara'*, p. 281 ff. For population figures, see Tanukhi, *Nishwar*, p. 240. It is not suggested, of course, that this sort of information appears in these *Adabi*-minded historians for the first time. The important point, however, is that such information begins to appear regularly and *by design* in historical and geographical works.

[91] See footnote 43, above, where the quotation is attributed by Suli to 'state secretaries'.

[92] See, e.g., the recent discussion of this question by Lawrence Conrad, 'Abraham and Muhammad: Some Observations Apropos of Chronology and Literary *Topoi* in the Early Arabic Historical Tradition', *BSOAS*, 50 (1987).

[93] See footnote 44, above.

In short, closer attention to present realities on the one hand and a sharper sense of the inordinate and the excessive, honed in the process of assimilating the poetry of *jahili* Arabia and the histories of foreign nations, inclined the historian-*adibs* to a less symbolic, more literal use of numbers. Could these ancient kings and patriarchs really have lived for so long? Could all the verses of this poem be genuine? Was it possible to reconcile discrepancies in the figures cited by different accounts? The full implications of these doubts were elaborated by the *Hikma*-oriented historians of the next chapter, but a blanket of scepticism was already being drawn by the historian-*adibs* across the facts and figures of ancient history even as the facts and figures of their own day were being brought into sharper focus.

Three aspects of historical thought: pattern, argument and style

Patterns were more frequently unravelled and articulated as deeper contemplation of the moral of Qur'anic narratives on the one hand and encounter with the history of foreign nations on the other induced a more comparative approach to historical reports. *Adabi*-minded historical argument was embedded across a wide spectrum of interpretation, wide as the interests of *Adab* itself in nature, society and the tests of reason. Style, including mood, was increasingly invaded by canons of literary criticism. But it is not always easy to separate these three aspects of *Adabi* historical thought and writing. The detection of patterns is often the basis of cause and argument while all these together may need to be expressed in a new manner. What a particular textual tradition regards as a legitimate historical cause has an important bearing on the question of the attitude of that tradition to the function of history. That function may in turn dictate the tone and mood in which history is projected.

That particular nations made particular contributions to world culture was an insight first circumstantiated by Ya'qubi. His works on geography and political affinities had already manifested, as was seen above, an awareness of the importance of climate and of the example of the political elite. In his history, Ya'qubi traversed the ancient nations largely in the role of a cultural guide. The ancient Chaldeans invented astronomy, calculated the eclipses of sun and moon and mapped out the constellations. The Babylonians built cities, fortresses and palaces, dug canals and discovered the principles of agriculture. The Indians with their arithmetic, the Greeks with their philosophy and other nations and dynasties with their learning, customs and even intellectual controversies, all were intended by Ya'qubi to acquaint the *adib* with the story of world culture and with the manner in which it finally flowed into Islam.

Within Abbasid history itself, caliphal patterns were detected:

It is said that the Abbasids have a beginning, a middle and an end. The beginning is al-Mansur, the middle is al-Ma'mun and the end is al-Mu'tadid. It also used to be said that the wealth gathered by al-Saffah, al-Mansur, al-Mahdi and al-Rashid was dissipated by al-Amin, and the wealth gathered by al-Ma'mun, al-Mu'tasim and al-Wathiq was dissipated by al-Mutawakkil.[94]

The reign of the caliph al-Ma'mun was seen as a return to the Barmakid period.[95] Within the cities, long observation of urban patterns of life began to yield insights into the causes and consequences of human association. Here, too, Jahiz poses the most frequent and most fertile questions concerning the structure of human societies:

The need of men for each other is an attribute of their very nature . . . This need was made to be of two kinds: a need that has to do with livelihood and sustenance and another to do with pleasure, gratification of desire and the increase of power . . . For deficiency is an attribute of all creation and characterizes all God's servants. God created no one who can satisfy unaided his own needs.[96]

Jahiz noted how certain craftsmen, for instance weavers, slave sellers and fishmongers, were 'in all ages and in all countries' endowed with the same traits of character, namely angry, foolish and unjust. Some of the reasons for enmity among men are, he argues, 'similarity of profession and neighbourly proximity, while close kinship and large numbers are among the causes of enmity in clans and tribes'. He further cites the abiding hostility between rentiers and tenants, rich and poor, the mounted and the pedestrian, the manly and the eunuch.[97] Climatic factors were also seen to have important consequences for a people's level of culture and manners, and cities were commonly thought to have a putrid air and to be unhealthy.[98] Even prophecy, according to Jahiz, seemed to conform to some iron necessity of social origin whereby only city men were chosen by God for this calling but never nomads. Speculating about livelihoods in cities, Jahiz observes certain patterns which seem to be among the earliest instances of economic theorizing in the Arabic–Islamic tradition:

There is no city on earth kinder to its inhabitants than one where coins are not scarce and where all commodities may be bought and sold. In the larger region of al-Sham and in similar regions, the *dinar* and the *dirham* are scarce and commodities are cheap because of the long lines of transportation and the scarcity of buyers.

---

[94] Tha'alibi, *Lata'if*, p. 71.
[95] Ibn al-Daya, *Mukafa'a*, pp. 74–8. The narrator of this story is almost certainly al-Ya'qubi.
[96] Jahiz, *Hayawan*, 1:42–3.
[97] For craftsmen, see *Hayawan*, 2:105; for causes of enmity, see *Hayawan*, 7:96 and compare the remarks on the character of wealthy men in the Islamic heartlands as opposed to Transoxania in Istakhri, *Masalik*, pp. 162–3.
[98] On the influence of climate, see the quotation from Ya'qubi in footnote 71, above. See also Jahiz, *Hayawan*, 1:70–1, echoed in Ibn Rusteh, *A'laq*, p. 59, but also *A'laq*, pp. 101–3, for an extended discussion of climes, cities and levels of culture.

Their lands constantly produce more than they need. In Ahwaz, Baghdad and 'Askar, the *dirham* is plentiful while buying and selling is slow because of the multitudes of people and of *dirhams*. In Basra, prices and expenditures are both reasonable as are products and wages . . . I know of no city anywhere where prices are reasonable and the population is very large except Basra.[99]

As *Adabi*-minded scholars and historians began to pay closer and more consistent attention to their own contemporaneous history, society and environment, to emphasize the importance of experiential knowledge (*tajriba*; *mubasharat al-ahwal*), and to assume a more critical attitude to the histories of foreign nations, it was to be expected that they would concern themselves with the problem of the possible and the impossible in history and nature.[100]

To understand the parameters of this problem, it may be recalled that many *adibs* had begun to feel that the devaluation of the present had gone far enough. The view that good poetry could be found in *any* age was quickly gaining ground, as were sentiments like the following:

There can be no saying more harmful to scholarship and to scholars than the view that the first left nothing for the last.[101]

For some *Adabi* historians it followed that no one age was more 'marvellous' than another, either with respect to wisdom or in the more literal sense of the extraordinary events that could happen in it. Such might *appear* to be the case either because scholars are not patronized by kings and men of wealth and authority, and thus do not produce scholarly works in sufficient quantity and quality, or else contemporary marvels fail to be recorded, are forgotten and are subsequently deemed implausible.[102] In order to preclude that last eventuality, Hamza al-Isfahani devotes a whole section of his *Tarikh* to quoting reports from earlier historians that seem to 'disobey natural custom' (*kharaja 'an al-'ada*) to which he appends a list of eight examples of supernatural events which he himself witnessed or obtained from witnesses, between the years 291 and 344 (903 and 955). As instances of what a scholar of that period regarded as extraordinary events, they are perhaps worth citing in some detail:

1 A grain harvest in full swing suddenly hit by an icy gale and totally destroyed. Only empty husks were harvested. This was an event 'people had never seen before nor even heard of' since it took place at the height of the hot season.

---

[99] Jahiz, *Buldan*, pp. 503–4. For prophets from cities, see Jahiz, *Hayawan*, 4:478.
[100] The contribution of theologians and philosophers to this problem will be discussed in Chapter Four, below.
[101] Ibn 'Abd al-Barr, *Jami'*, 1:99; see also the discussion of the debate between 'Ancients' and 'Moderns', above.
[102] See the arguments in Tanukhi, *Nishwar*, p. 8 and Hamza, *Tarikh*, p. 127.

2 A river, Zarinrudh, overflowed its banks and bridges, isolating the nearby city of Isfahan and rising until it breached its walls. Panic gripped the citizens and messages had to be tied to arrows and shot across the flood.

3 A famine which caused the death of more than two hundred thousand people in Isfahan.

4 An unprecedented snowfall in Isfahan which took place in a summer month.

5 Another unprecedented snowfall in the spring followed by excessively cold weather which destroyed all fruit trees throughout the east.

6 A famine in Baghdad which dispersed its male population and forced its maidens to leave the women's quarters and walk the streets in groups of twenty, arms linked, and crying: hunger, hunger. When one fell down, all twenty would fall down dead. A rich man of Baghdad gathered one thousand maidens in his house and fed them throughout the period of famine, then married them all off, supplying each with her dowry.

7 A blight of lice affected the entire agricultural region (*rustaq*) of al-Taymara al-Kubra and was so severe that people despaired of the harvest and decided to abandon their fields and homes. A species of bird akin to the hawk but the size of a sparrow settled in woodland nearby. A bird would fly to the top of a tree and give an uninterrupted whistle. The birds would then divide into groups and each descend upon a village where they would pick the lice until their craws were filled. Turning to water, the birds would cool themselves, drop off the excrement, and go back to picking lice until sunset. This cycle was repeated exactly as described until all the lice were exterminated. The birds then left the woodland and have not been seen since.

8 An epidemic of blood and bile in Isfahan which would afflict people for between two to ten days. Bloodletting was found to be the best remedy. The epidemic had reached Isfahan from Ahwaz. It had moved from Baghdad to Wasit then to Basra where it combined with a plague to kill 1,000 to 1,200 people every day. From Basra it descended to Ahwaz whence it forked off right to Arrajan and the province of Fars and left to Isfahan, where its consequences were mild.[103]

Before examining Hamza's list, it may be recalled that *Adabi*-minded historians had shown a marked degree of scepticism regarding reports of freaks or monstrosities, especially as encountered in the histories of foreign nations.[104] The issue here, however, is freaks of nature and a different, more cautious approach seems to have prevailed. Behind this approach are a number of suppositions which need to be spelled out.

---

[103] Hamza, *Tarikh*, pp. 124–6. Two more incidents are added, one a terrible storm and the other a chance discovery of a hoard of ancient manuscripts on vellum in an unknown language.

[104] See, e.g., notes 24, 45, 50 and 69, above.

To begin with, the fact that Hamza appends his own list of natural oddities to one he had quoted from Tabari and others implies a continuity as between past and present in the occurrence of prodigies. He may thus intend his reader to infer that freaks of nature such as abnormal epidemics, blights, earthquakes and icy winds happen at *all* times and places. Secondly, one detects in Hamza's treatment an open mind as regards nature's oddities, so that these are not pronounced implausible without further investigation. Thirdly, it is emphasized that these events should be witnessed directly by men with a reputation for honesty and learning so that accounts of them are as accurate as possible. Finally, it is important that these accounts be supplied with exact names and dates so that they are anchored in a verifiable reality and not in hearsay.

Hamza's list of nature's freaks shows *Adab* extending to nature the critical method but also the wide measure of tolerance and comparative practice it had already extended to literature. These strategies may again be detected in the range of argumentation used in the explanation of causes. Much of this range has already been illustrated in the analysis of *Adab*'s wide-flung influence on historical thought. But some additional instances of causation may be singled out. Thus, the causes of human association and of enmity as set forth by Jahiz, above, seem to have originated in a more sustained interest in the cosmopolitan societies of Iraqi cities of the period and in the development of rational systems (of law or theology, for instance) which explored the Qur'anic text in search of corroboration. Jahiz would also argue, as we saw earlier, that religion is perpetuated by imitation and not reason. But since imitation embraces truth no quicker than it does falsehood, this is why flagrant error and shocking opinions attach themselves more tenaciously to religion than to any other system of thought, opinion or art, an argument grounded in the comparative analysis of religions. Then, again, direct evidence from nature provided Jahiz with the means to reject the theory of a shrinking universe: having examined ancient relics, such as old swords or ancient and narrow gateways, could one still maintain that men of the past had bigger bodies than we do? And what about men before and after them?[105] On the other hand, reflection upon comparative political history was behind the view that ancient Persian and Arab histories were intimately connected while a history largely written by religious scholars would naturally be inclined to suggest for the decline of the Abbasid caliphate the following chain of causes:

The first institution of public administration to suffer decline in the days of the Abbasids, and as we ourselves witnessed, was the judiciary. [The vizier] Ibn al-Furat demeaned it and admitted into its ranks people who had bribed their way

[105] Jahiz, *Tarbi'*, paras. 61–2.

into it and had no learning whatever . . . Within a few years, the vizierate itself began to decline and to be held by men unworthy of the office . . . The decline of the vizierate was followed by that of the caliphate until it reached the point we can see today. Thus the decline of the Abbasid state was caused by the decline of the judiciary.[106]

Given such concerns, *Adabi*-minded historical thought was bound to express itself in a new style and mood. Many elements of that new style have already been reviewed, such as the conciseness, simplicity and gradual shedding of *isnad* associated with *Adab* writers. A few remarks need to be added in this regard which would also help to bring this chapter to a conclusion.

The dropping of the *isnad* meant a shift in stylistic form as well as mood. Stylistically, the individual, discrete unit (*khabar*) of historical information beloved by *Hadith*-oriented historiography was yielding to the 'longer narratives' (*al-akhbar al-tiwal*), the precise title of the history of Abu Hanifa al-Dinawari (d. 282/895). In this celebrated example of *Adabi* historical writing, the story teller's art is to the fore, mixing the drama of wars with wisdom, dialogue, speeches, letters and argument: the normal exhibits of the *adib*'s trade. It is as if the animal fables of Ibn al-Muqaffa', *Kalila wa Dimna*, have been translated into the realm of history, or as if the Arab Muslim state is shown to have inherited the long and distinguished history of Persia. So engrossed is the prose of Dinawari in the art of dramatic narrative that even dates are scarce until the very end, when the historian approaches his own days. The same combination of long, *isnad*-shedding, dramatic narrative and didactic intention is followed later in Tha'alibi's *Ghurar Akhbar Muluk al-Furs wa Siyarihim*, a history explicitly modelled on the 'elegant phrases of writers of epistles' and addressed to 'elites and commoners, *jahilis* and Muslims, Arabs and non-Arabs'.[107]

The shift in mood can best be seen perhaps in two respects: first in the self-conscious pursuit of originality and, secondly, in the increasingly comic, even burlesque tone creeping into the *Adabi*-inspired historiography of the period. These two mood shifts were probably connected, such that the new value placed on originality, on 'that which no one has dealt with before', elided with the intention to entertain the reader with 'anecdotes, amusing diversions, witty summaries' (*nawadir, turaf, luma'*). Originality could take the form of bold assertions such as are found in the

---

[106] Tanukhi, *Nishwar*, p. 114. On the connection between Persian and Arab history, see Hamza, *Tarikh*, p. 71.

[107] See, e.g., Tha'alibi, *Ghurar*, p. xlix. The moral lessons of history are scattered all over the text, e.g. pp. 42, 59–60, 234–6. The *other* Tha'alibi, author of the *Lata'if al-Ma'arif*, describes his work (p. 2) as derived from history books 'in accordance with long days' (*'ala al-ayyam al-tiwal*), a phrase which echoes Dinawari's *al-akhbar al-tiwal* and seems also to denote long narrative histories.

celebrated critical work of the poet Ibn al-Muʻtazz who stated categorically
that no one before him had ever collected figures of speech.[108] It could
also take the form of explicitly avoiding what others had dealt with more
thoroughly so that one's own work could be devoted to exploring new
themes.[109]

The comic mood appeared as soon as it became commonly accepted
that it was as legitimate for a *khabar* to amuse or entertain as it was to
edify, guide or inform. This shift of mood, from the solemnity of public
Hadith recitation and its equally solemn methods of transmission, to the
ribaldry and hilarity of the private anecdote, best savoured by the lone
reader or a small circle of cultured friends, was clearly effected by *Adab*.
It would be hazardous to attempt to explain fully the reasons and circumstances of this shift in mood. But it seemed at first to have happened
hesitantly and apologetically and then to have picked up slowly in volume
until the laughter became loud and raucous in the works of Jahiz. What
may perhaps have happened, and what is of clear interest to us here, was
a slow evolution in attitudes to more ancient times and personalities. At
about the time that schools of law and *Hadith* began to sacralize the past,
to establish the *in illo tempore* needed for all myths of foundation, free
and iconoclastic spirits conjured up an alternative image of a past whose
many revered models of piety were seen to have fallen far short of the
ideal. The 'epic' past of *Hadith* pitted against the 'romantic' past of *Adab*:
a contrast shorn of many subtleties but one that could be left to stand as
representing what most distinguished one manner of historical thought
from another.[110]

[108] Ibn al-Muʻtazz, *Badiʻ*, p. 106; see also Qudama ibn Jaʻfar, *Naqd al-Shiʻr*, p. 4, where all
subjects are said to be allowable to the poet.
[109] See, e.g., Tanukhi, *Nishwar*, p. 10; Ibn al-Daya, *Mukafaʼa*, p. 3; Thaʻalibi, *Ghurar*, p.
108; Hamza, *Tarikh*, p. 96; Yaʻqubi, *Tarikh*, 2:5–6.
[110] Once again, the inspiration here has come from M. M. Bakhtin's distinction between
'epic' and 'romantic': see chapter 2 note 78, above.

CHAPTER 4

History and *Hikma*

Hikma, meaning 'sound judgement' or 'wisdom', was a Qur'anic term destined for a long and fecund career in Arabic cultural history. For our present purposes, it suffices to remember that it was the term which the rational sciences, that is to say the sciences which did not descend directly from the Qur'an and *Hadith*, tended most often to adopt as the description of their subject-matter. The third/ninth century probably witnessed the appearance of the first cleavage between the revealed and the rational sciences, between *Shar'* and *Hikma* or their numerous equivalents. *Hikma* grew into a tree of knowledge, shedding some branches and sprouting others over the course of centuries. Its most enduring branches, however, were made up of the natural sciences, i.e. mathematics, astronomy, alchemy and medicine, and of the philosophical sciences, i.e. logic, philosophy and dialectical theology. Under the epistemic umbrella of *Hikma*, the range of issues relating to historical thought reached its widest theoretical extent. Scholars and historians inspired by *Hikma* provide us with the most detailed answers regarding historical knowledge, what it is, how it occurs and what purposes it serves. Perhaps the best way to introduce *Hikma*-inspired historical writing is to examine in some detail the work of one historian, al-Mas'udi (d. 345/956), whose histories reflect a broad spectrum of systematic concern with the theory and practice of history. We will then go on to discuss the origin and development of a number of theoretical questions arising from the work of al-Mas'udi. We end with a discussion of the works of some prominent historians inspired by *Hikma*.

Mas'udi: *Adab, Hikma,* history

It was *Adab* which had, without doubt, set the agenda of *Hikma*-inspired historical thought and writing. Scholars and historians like Jahiz, Ya'qubi and Hamza al-Isfahani had between them, as we saw above, determined the territory of history, its patterns, its social and political relevance and some of the criteria to be used in judging the veracity of historical reports. They had done so largely under the influence of *Adab* and of its invitation to the study of man, society and nature unfettered by any compulsion to work within a formal, rigid, self-authenticating tradition. We also saw how the emergence of sciences like theology in the case of Jahiz and astronomy in the case of Ya'qubi and Hamza expanded the scope of verification and criticism, resulting in histories at once more accurate, less 'sacred', more pragmatic and more obviously directed at a cultured and leisurely *reader*. Traversing these two layers of *Adab* or *Hikma*-inspired historical thought, one concept compels special attention: the concept of *bahth*, of research and inquiry, particularly as it underpins the work of Mas'udi.[1]

To anyone who pays close attention to the surface of Mas'udi's text, the primary impression is likely to be one of a tightly knit and well-documented narrative. Very near the beginning of his major surviving work, *Muruj al-Dhahab*, there is a detailed 'table of contents' where numbered chapters are listed together with their headings. This is followed by an extensive 'critical bibliography' where the works of important predecessors are listed and assessed. As one reads through the text of the *Muruj* or of his other surviving work, *al-Tanbih wa'l Ishraf*, one very frequently encounters what in a modern text might more properly belong to a footnote, e.g. such scholarly comments as: for more information on this or that theme the reader should consult this or that book of ours; this present edition of our work is more complete than the edition of the year such and such; the present work is a sequel to other works treating such and such themes. The ultimate and explicit intention of the author is 'to bequeath to the world . . . a well-ordered science' (*'ilman manzuman*).[2]

How seriously should one take this last phrase? Is it a rhetorical flourish which belongs to the conventions of that day and age or should one take Mas'udi at his word and attempt to investigate what he meant by science? And does this 'well-ordered science' have anything to do with the concept of 'research'? None of these questions are clear-cut for they straddle the territories of history and of *Hikma*, but Mas'udi's reader is quite simply led to ask them because they force themselves so often upon his attention in numerous reflective passages. Added to these theoretical considerations there is the equally compelling issue of the panoramic sweep of his works, the sustained interest in philosophy, theology, geography, medicine, astronomy, meteorology and zoology in addition to his interests in the more traditional Islamic sciences like jurisprudence, *Hadith* and so forth. For the author, however, these scholarly investigations were merely a preamble to

---

[1] Mas'udi has received more critical attention than most Arabic historians, with the exception of Ibn Khaldun; see now the extensive article 'Mas'udi', *EI2* (by Charles Pellat). See also Bernd Radtke, 'Towards a Typology of Abbasid Universal Chronicles', in *Occasional Papers of the School of Abbasid Studies*, University of St Andrews, no. 3 (1990/1991), which raises some interesting questions in relation to Mas'udi, although the term 'salvation history' which Radtke applies to these chronicles says little about them which cannot also be said about many other branches of Islamic culture of the period.

[2] Mas'udi, *Muruj*, section 7.

the study of history. In the course of describing what he regards as the merit and originality of his works, Mas'udi discusses the place of history in relation to his other writings:

Furthermore, we conferred with all manner of kings of diverse morals and ambitions, and from countries far apart, and we investigated every single aspect of their conduct. But the traditions of science are no more . . . fools have increased in number while the wise have become few. You scarcely encounter anyone who is not an ignorant sham . . . content with guesswork and blind to certitude. We therefore did not see fit to engage in this type of science (*'ilm*) and kind of art (*adab*) until we had written our works on the various sorts of dogmas and religions . . . and on the principles of jurisprudence and the foundations of religious judgements . . . as well as all the rest of our books that deal with the exoteric and the esoteric . . . with politics . . . and natural religion . . . with the structure of the universe and the heavenly bodies.[3]

For Mas'udi, history was the culmination of his scholarly output, the final end towards which all his earlier research had pointed. Before we advance very far in Mas'udi we meet a passage that spells out explicitly his views on history, this time not as the culmination but as the fountainhead of all the sciences. Because of its importance, it is cited here at some length:

Were it not that scholars all through the ages recorded their thoughts, the foundations of the sciences would have collapsed and their conclusions would be lost. That is because, for any science to exist, it must be derived from history (*akhbar*). From it all wisdom is deduced, all jurisprudence is elicited, all eloquence is learnt. Those who reason by analogy build upon it. Those who have opinions to expound use it for argument. Popular knowledge is derived from it and the precepts of the wise are found in it. Noble and lofty morality is acquired from it and the rules of royal government and war are sought in it. All manner of strange events are found in it; in it too all kinds of entertaining stories may be enjoyed. It is a science (*'ilm*) which can be appreciated by both the educated and the ignorant, savoured by both fool and sage, a much desired comfort to elites and commoners and practised by Arab and non-Arab alike. It can also supplement any discourse, adorn any rank . . . The superiority of history over all other sciences is obvious. The loftiness of its status is recognized by any person of intelligence. None can master it nor gain certainty as to what it includes nor receive and transmit it except one who has devoted his life to knowledge, grasped its true meaning, tasted its fruits, felt its true dignity and experienced the pleasure it bestows.[4]

The elevated status of history encountered here has no parallel in any work of history before its author's time and scarcely any since. The cadence of Mas'udi's sentences, the parallelisms, the declamatory tone: these belong to the *Adab* tradition of his age. But the intellectual apotheosis of history, remarkable in itself, is even more astonishing when one remembers the

---

[3] Mas'udi, *Muruj*, sections 5–6.
[4] Mas'udi, *Muruj*, section 989.

somewhat low view of history dominant in the Aristotelean tradition, one of the major feeders of Mas'udi's thought. It seems that the importance he assigned to the investigative-experiential method, typified in the word *bahth*, derived from his conception of history as the ultimate origin of all experience, the primary epistemic key. Had we possessed all his works, we might have been able to follow in detail the plan which he pursued in laying out first the building blocks of knowledge and finally the structure into which they fit: history. But even in the two works we do possess, one of which, *al-Tanbih wa'l Ishraf*, is the last in a series of some thirty-six titles, we sense an increasingly abstract historiographic approach where history is introduced through cosmology and geography, and a searching after the broad patterns of historical development, fortified by belief in the progress of knowledge. This belief is evidently connected with the concept of *bahth* and is expressed as follows:

As for us, and although our own age follows upon that of scholars who preceded us and our own days are far removed from theirs, let us hope that we shall not lag behind them in the works we wish to compose or in the ends we aim to accomplish. Although they have the advantage of precedence, we possess the merit of emulation. Ideas and intentions may also be held in common. It may be that the latter is a better scholar and a more accomplished writer by reason of the prudence engendered by experience, the fear of close imitativeness and vigilance against falling into error. Accordingly, the sciences progress without end because the last discovers what the first has missed. This progress continues without any circumscribed or definite end.[5]

This 'prudence engendered by experience' (*hanakat al-tajarib*) is what an investigation of nature (*bahth*) reveals and what history (*khabar*) records. Both the study of nature and the study of history have proofs (*barahin*; *dala'il*) – the proofs of reason in the case of nature and the proofs of authenticity in the case of history. Nature is approached by Mas'udi from a position of consistent adherence to the principle of causality. The external physical universe operates in accordance with causes and effects, itself a demonstration of the wisdom of its Creator.[6] The investigation of nature proceeds through several epistemic channels such as direct observation (*'iyan*), the reliance on the best scientific authorities (*ahl al-bahth wa'l nazar*), and the application of well-known scientific principles to explain certain marvels or oddities. A notable example of this last is his attempt to explain such hybrid creatures as the *nasnas* and the *'anqa'*, creatures that were favourites with story-tellers, mariners' tales and popular histories. According to Mas'udi, such creatures may well have been species of animals which were not well transformed by nature from potentiality to actuality and so remained rare or unique specimens inhabiting the

[5] Mas'udi, *Tanbih*, p. 76.
[6] Mas'udi, *Tanbih*, p. 9.

remotest regions of the earth.[7] In general, Mas'udi believed that the great
merit of his histories was that he had himself travelled over most of the
lands whose histories he records, that he had seen for himself what other
scholars or historians merely wrote about and that his interest in natural
science enabled him to offer plausible explanations of phenomena hitherto
considered miraculous by the gullible or impossible by the sceptics.[8]

As regards historical reports, *Hadith* scholars had already distinguished
between 'widely known' (*mustafid*) reports or those 'narrated by multiple
witnesses' (*mutawatir*) on the one hand and reports 'narrated by a single
authority' (*khabar al-wahid*). The first type were said to have the force of
consensus and to engender both legal duties (*'amal*) and knowledge (*'ilm*).
The second type were reports which could be either accepted or rejected
depending on further evidence of their authenticity and engendered knowledge if acceptable but not legal duties. For a historian like Mas'udi who
dealt with a vast array of reports concerning not only foreign nations but
the world of nature as a whole, the *Hadith* edifice was obviously too limited. What that epistemic field considered to be a criterion of authenticity,
e.g. an uninterrupted chain (*isnad*) of trustworthy Muslim witnesses, was
inapplicable for much of Mas'udi's history of man and nature. Other criteria had to be found to test these reports, many of which fell into the
category of the 'possible' (*ja'iz*). It is precisely here that historical thought
and writing can be seen to have summoned to its aid, and in a systematic
manner, the full resources of the natural and human sciences, to have
become *Hikma*-inspired. Most of Mas'udi's reflections on historical veracity revolve around the concept of possibility, and his preoccupation with
bahth is largely the result of his continuous exploration of the bounds of
that concept.

In sum, the histories of Mas'udi combine what in the Hellenistic tradition would be called *historia naturalis* with the broadly cultural history of
ancient and contemporary nations and ends with Islamic history arranged
by caliphates. The vast range of topics discussed, the arrangement of the
material and even the transitions from one subject to the next often strike
the reader of Mas'udi as lying outside the bounds of what in any cultural
tradition would properly be called history. This is because Mas'udi
demands from his reader not merely a reflective attitude to nature and
history where the first unlocks the secrets of the second but a specific
willingness to see in history the ultimate science. It is for this reason that
his historical works are designed to tie together, to integrate his earlier
and non-historical works and why one so frequently encounters references
to the contents and arguments of these earlier investigations. What

[7] Mas'udi, *Muruj*, sec. 1344. These views seem to echo Aristotle, *Generation of Animals*,
  770b 25–7 and 776a 1–8.
[8] For details, see Khalidi, *Islamic Historiography*, chapter 2.

emerges from this confluence of *historia naturalis* and history properly so
called is first of all the recognition of what Mas'udi often calls a 'wise
system' (*nizam hakim*) or a 'regularity of disposition' (*tartib mu'allaf*) in
nature pointing to the wisdom of their Creator. The four quarters of the
earth, the four seasons of the year, the four humours of the body, the
four stages of a man's life correspond with each other in a perfect rhythm.[9]
Then again the seven geographical climes (*iqlim*) and the seven great
'ancestral races' (*umam*) of antiquity illustrate the effect of geography on
history and human culture. This divinely instilled order and regularity of
nature was reflected in varying degrees by rational laws and social structures which organize human life. The clearest manifestation of social order
is justice. Where justice prevailed, prosperity followed. Where justice was
neglected, kingdoms fell into ruin.[10]

But for a historian who paid such close attention to the cultures of
foreign nations and who prided himself on the investigative originality of
his work, there was one other, more intellectualist reason for the rise and
fall of kingdoms, nations and cultures: the relapse into error and false
opinions through the adoption of blind imitation (*taqlid*) and the forsaking
of research and inquiry.[11] Such perhaps may be considered the outstanding
moral of the cultural history of ancient nations as reviewed by Mas'udi.
In criticizing the 'literalists' (*Hashwiyya*) among *Hadith* scholars on the
one hand and those who forsook astronomy for astrology on the other,
Mas'udi feared that the same obscurantism and the same patterns of
decline and fragmentation might overtake his own Islamic culture.[12]

Accordingly, one might see in Mas'udi's work the conjunction of several
intellectual traditions, foremost among which was the tradition of Hellenistic philosophy and natural science. From within his own Islamic tradition,
he drew heavily upon Shi'ism and Mu'tazilite theology. As a result of
these wide-ranging interests, he was the first Arab Muslim historian to
apply the principles of scientific method and philosophical reasoning to
the study of history, which he regarded as the goal towards which all his
earlier endeavours had been a preparation. In investigating the intellectual
background of his thought and that of other historians and scholars with
similar interests, one obtains a description of the structure of *Hikma*-
inspired historical thought and writing. We begin with the *khabar*, the
basic unit of historical reports. To do so, we need to move back a little in
time.

[9] See, e.g., *Tanbih*, pp. 15–16, 23–5.
[10] Mas'udi, *Tanbih*, pp. 39–40; for details, see Khalidi, *Islamic Historiography*, index, under
justice.
[11] See Khalidi, *Islamic Historiography*, p. 66.
[12] Mas'udi compares his own days to the period of fragmentation between Achaemenids and
Sasanids in *Tanbih*, p. 400. For the *Hashwiyya* and astrology, see *Muruj*, sec. 288 and
Tanbih, pp. 13–14.

The *khabar*: jurists and theologians

The following saying was attributed to the Mu'tazilite theologian Ja'far ibn Harb (d. 236/850):

The believer is like a discriminating and prudent merchant who considers what type of trade is more profitable for him and safer for his merchandise and turns to it, seeking what is religiously permissible for his livelihood. He is a man of great compassion, stands in awe of God and is fearful of sin. He makes a habit of repentance and constantly asks forgiveness for what he knows and what he does not know, from both high and low. Such will be his way of life until God decrees his end.[13]

In the new, vigorous and prosperous cities of Abbasid Iraq of the third/ninth century, the connection between trades and crafts on the one hand and the rise and development of schools of jurists and theologians on the other was often intimate. In one form or another, the connection between the aristocrats of the marketplace (e.g. booksellers and perfumers) and scholarship has persisted until this century in many Islamic cities. Behind the increasing concern with legal system and the concept of justice may be detected a greater interest in contracts and obligations by merchant classes who were then establishing far-flung networks of trade. These networks in turn reinforced the networks of scholarship which gave the Islamic world one of its most distinctive characteristics.[14]

There can be little doubt that the jurist who first postulated a systematic connection between law and reason and sought to demonstrate this in discourse often reminiscent of Platonic dialogue was the celebrated Shafi'i (d. 204/820). In his *Epistle* (*Risala*) on the principles of jurisprudence, Shafi'i argues that the normative practice of Muhammad (*sunna*) is in fact commensurate with wisdom (*hikma*). This allowed him to introduce reason and proof (*'aql, dalil*) as legitimate modes of analogy (*qiyas*) and inference (*istidlal*) and to criticize the imitation of authority (*taqlid*) as conducive to ignorance. Having used reason to harmonize the Qur'an with Muhammadan practice, Shafi'i proceeded to construct a system which he claimed was of manifest clarity (*bayan*) where almost all major aspects of the law can be deduced by the use of reason.

What concerns us most directly in Shafi'i's system is his views on *akhbar* (reports, traditions) which in their totality constitute the *Hadith* of Muhammad. It must be emphasized that for Shafi'i, as for many jurists and theologians, the *akhbar* that they had in mind when they discussed this issue were not historical reports in the general sense of the term but

---

[13] 'Abd al-Jabbar, *Tabaqat al-Mu'tazila* in *Fadl al-I'tizal wa Tabaqat al-Mu'tazila*, pp. 282-3.
[14] Recently and most eloquently described in Albert Hourani, *A History of the Arab Peoples* (London: Faber, 1991). I investigated the connection between scholars, especially the Mu'tazilites, and merchants in my *Dirasat fi Tarikh al-Fikr al-'Arabi al-Islami* (Beirut: Dar al-Tali'a, 1979), chapter 2.

Muhammadan *Hadith*. Accordingly, their discussion of this topic was not
a foray into the realm of historical veracity but an investigation of certain
reports about Muhammad with a view to determining their value as legal
precedent. Nevertheless, such discussions were an essential part of the
context in which truth and falsehood were debated, and hence relevant to
the image of the past and the uses to which it could be put.

Shafi'i distinguished between two kinds of *akhbar*: a *khabar* related by
many (*khabar al-'amma*) and one related by a single authority (*khabar
al-wahid*; *khabar al-khassa*). The first kind had very little theoretical interest for him since it amounted to knowledge so common and prevalent in
the Muslim community and so much beyond dispute that it must by inference be both legally binding and truly transmitted.[15] The second kind was
one to which Shafi'i devoted much thought and argument. There were
many reasons for this. To begin with, very many reports fell into this
category and their status had to be clearly determined. Then again, Shafi'i
was concerned to combat both the sceptics as well as the 'conservatives'
among his opponents. Both these groups, or so it seems from their arguments as preserved or contrived by Shafi'i, had serious objections to
khabar al-wahid, especially since the acceptance of this kind of *khabar*
was in apparent conflict with the normal rules of witness (*shahada*).[16]

Shafi'i was to argue at length for the acceptance of *khabar al-wahid* as
sufficient ground for proof, provided it satisfied certain conditions. These
were that the transmitter should be trustworthy, known to be truthful in
his speech, aware of the import of what he transmits and of how the
meaning of the report could be verbally distorted, a verbatim transmitter,
in agreement with other transmitters and innocent of all defective transmission (*tadlis*), such as relating from someone he met what he did not hear
from him. The same conditions need to apply of course to all the transmitters 'above' and 'below' him in the chain (*isnad*). Shafi'i's interests were
of course primarily legal, that is to say he defended the inclusion of this
kind of *khabar* among the acceptable sources of legal proof. Many of his
arguments in its defence revolved around distinguishing between *khabar
al-wahid* and the testimony of witnesses. But he would also argue that the
veracity of *any* report depended to a large extent upon the veracity of the
reporter:

The truth or falsity of most *Hadith* cannot be inferred except through the truth or
falsity of the narrator, except for a few special instances where truth or falsity may
be inferred if the narrator narrates what cannot possibly be the case or if the item

[15] Shafi'i, *Risala*, pp. 357–9. Examples include the five daily prayers, fasting, the pilgrimage
and so forth.
[16] See, e.g., the exchange between Shafi'i and his opponent in *Risala*, pp. 383 ff. See also
Joseph Schacht, *Origins of Muhammadan Jurisprudence* (Oxford: Clarendon Press, 1950),
chapter 6.

of information is contradicted by another better established or more bolstered with proof of veracity.[17]

Shafi'i was able to show how this principle was practised by referring to numerous historical examples where the Companions of Muhammad acted in immediate obedience of a *khabar al-wahid* when it emanated from someone whose veracity they had no reason to question.[18]

Over the years, the views of Shafi'i were to have a cumulative influence of immense proportions. Thus his view that the truth or falsity of a *khabar* depended upon the credibility of its narrator, a view which he was the first to formulate in a systematic legal context, gained general acceptance and was echoed, as we have seen already, by many prominent *Hadith*-oriented historians of his own and of later generations. But his discussion of *akhbar* was incomplete in one important respect. He never attempted to explain precisely what he meant by the narration of 'what cannot possibly be the case', that is to say impossibilities, nor did he expound fully how one proof could be said to be 'better established' than another by means other than the criterion of narration. These were problems which theologians could be expected to attack.

It was in fact the *enfant terrible* of early-Muslim theology, the Mu'tazilite Nazzam (d. *c.* 225/840), the teacher of Jahiz, who was to question in the most radical fashion the assumptions of jurists and other scholars regarding the truth of history and of narration. The opinions of this iconoclast as reported by both friend and foe and the overall influence he exerted on the works of Jahiz allow for an approximation to what he generally taught on such topics as knowledge through multiple transmission (*tawatur*) and miracles. The more general reason why Nazzam and some other Mu'tazilites took an interest in these topics was their desire to maintain the integrity of their theological doctrines by reinterpreting, or if necessary attacking certain central assumptions of *Hadith* scholars and jurists. Among these was the assumption which Shafi'i, as we saw above, treated as self-evident, namely that the *khabar*, 'transmitted by the multitude from a prior multitude' (*yanquluhu 'awammuhum 'an man mada min 'awammihim*), created a 'common knowledge' (*'ilm 'amm*) not susceptible to error and beyond all dispute.[19]

We do not know the specific reasons which impelled Nazzam to attack *tawatur*. It is possible that a thoroughgoing rationalist like him refused to allow that knowledge transmitted by 'the multitude' was necessarily true. This was especially valid when these 'multitudes' were non-Muslim; for if

[17] Shafi'i, *Risala*, p. 399.
[18] The most famous example was the change of the direction of prayer (*qibla*) from Jerusalem to Mecca: see *Risala*, pp. 407–8.
[19] The term that came to be employed for this mode of transmission, *tawatur*, was known to Shafi'i but not used by him as a technical term: see *Risala*, p. 433.

the principle of *tawatur* was admitted, there was little that one could offer by way of argument against the religious opinions of non-Muslim sects. In any case, later scholars were to pick their way among his reputed sayings and to demolish or uphold his reasoning on *tawatur*, as on other problems, with little to go on beyond a few sentences. But he seems, even by the admission of his enemies, to have generated an enormous storm of controversy which was still raging at least two centuries after his death.[20] We shall first cite how some of his enemies reported and refuted his views on *tawatur*, then turn to a more friendly report by a fellow Mu'tazilite and end with an attempt at a reconstruction.

Two hostile reports come from 'Abd al-Qahir al-Baghdadi (d. 429/ 1037), a theologian who lived some two hundred years after Nazzam:

(1) *Regarding the proof that the report by multiple transmission is an avenue to knowledge.* Our dispute regarding this topic is with . . . the Nazzam faction who maintain that the *umma* may agree upon an error and that reports by multiple transmission carry no conviction because they may occur falsely. In this manner they slandered the Companions of the Prophet and annulled the principle of analogy in law. But even though they dispute regarding the falsity of these reports, they yet must know of their existence and of the existence of their own ridiculous arguments. Their knowledge of all this is necessary (*daruri*) and not open to doubt. There can be no avenue to their knowledge of this except through a report by multiple transmission which could not have been the result of collusion.[21]

(2) *The sixteenth disgraceful thesis* [of Nazzam]. Among his disgraceful theses is his view that the report by multiple transmission, despite the fact that its transmitters are innumerable to him who hears the report and despite differences in their interests and intentions, may in fact be false, while maintaining at the same time that some reports transmitted by single transmitters may engender necessary knowledge.[22]

The more friendly report comes from the Mu'tazilite theologian and jurist Abu al-Husayn al-Basri (d. 436/1044):

Regarding the fact that a report transmitted by one person does not engender knowledge. Most people maintain that this kind of report does not engender knowledge. Others argue that it does and this group differ amongst themselves . . . As to whether this kind of report engenders knowledge, Abu Ishaq al-Nazzam made this conditional upon it being accompanied by evidence (*iqtiran qara'in bihi*), and he is said to have posited the same condition for reports by multiple transmitters. The example he gave was of our being informed, for instance, about the death of X, then we hear the sounds of mourning, then we see the funeral procession

---

[20] Baghdadi, *Farq*, pp. 114–15, who lists the most famous works devoted to the refutation of Nazzam.

[21] Baghdadi, *Usul*, pp. 11–12. See also *Usul*, pp. 16–17, for further arguments against the views ascribed to Nazzam.

[22] Baghdadi, *Farq*, p. 128.

outside his house, all the time knowing that there is no sick person in his house except him . . . Where evidence regarding reports by multiple transmitters is concerned, it may be that Abu Ishaq meant the impossibility of collusion in deceit among the transmitters or that no such collusion had been demonstrated.[23]

Nazzam had evidently conducted a logical probing of the circumstances which accompany the transmission of reports and found that the criteria advanced by Shafi'i and other jurists were not rigorous enough in themselves to guarantee sound transmission. More was needed to establish truth than the truthfulness of the reporter or even of many reporters. But since to doubt *tawatur* was also to doubt consensus (*ijma'*), as implicit in the accusation of slander against the Companions, Nazzam's views were taken to imply an attack on one of the fundamental credal and juristic principles of the faith. In point of fact Nazzam was arguing that evidence was needed in all reports, irrespective of their mode of transmission, and that such evidence would have to come from reason, nature or custom. The example he gives of the report concerning the death of a person and the need for further evidence before knowledge is engendered is significant because it is taken from ordinary life and not Muhammadan *Hadith*. The *khabar* is 'secularized'; it is of interest to a wider group than *Hadith* scholars and of relevance to people from all walks of life who may be concerned with the problem of the authenticity of information.

In sum, Shafi'i and Nazzam represent two approaches to the question of the veracity of the *khabar* which ultimately reflected two divergent preoccupations with its function. The jurist was concerned with the *khabar* as a fitting source of legal judgement. The theologian was more obviously interested in its epistemic status. The first was primarily interested in arriving at the kind of judgement which would help him to make practical, real-life decisions. The second was more concerned with increasing the scope of human knowledge. Between them and their followers, these two thinkers account for a great deal of the speculation and controversy surrounding *akhbar*. Thus, a straight line led from the 'evidence' of Nazzam, via Jahiz, to the 'research' of Mas'udi.

In the 3rd–4th/9th–10th centuries, interest in world religions and cultures, accompanied by increased intimacy with their sacred and literary texts, was combined with a marked expansion of geographical and scientific knowledge. Much of this is reflected in the works of Jahiz and of later thinkers who were stimulated by acquaintance with world literatures to re-examine the status of *akhbar*.[24] But for sheer sophistication in the analysis of *akhbar*, there can be few works from this period which rival the *Risala* entitled *Fi al-Tasdiq* (Concerning the criteria of truth), ascribed to

---

[23] Basri, *Mu'tamad*, 2:566–7.
[24] See especially the pseudo-Qudama ibn Ja'far, *Naqd al-Nathr*, pp. 57–8, where the author discusses the role of *akhbar* in ancient literatures.

an obvious *nom de plume* and dated by its editor to the fourth/tenth century.[25] In it the author attempts to distinguish the various categories of
akhbar transmitted by a multitude (*kathirun*) and to establish sound and
rational criteria of verifiability. From the very outset, it is evident that the
author is concerned with a theoretical and not a juristic problem and his
arguments are drawn from theology and logic rather than Islamic jurisprudence. His examples too are drawn from the opinions and traditions of
non-Muslim communities. In structure, the *Risala* is highly didactic, using
diagrams to illustrate frequent either/or distinctions and the conclusions
appropriate to each. Several arguments are novel e.g. the distinctions
between 'weak' and 'strong' *akhbar* in their origin and in later transmission
and the importance of establishing the 'original intention' (*al-qasd
al-awwal*) of the *khabar* in the determination of its degree of prejudice:

> I argue therefore that a report transmitted by many is divided, in so far as it is or
> is not widespread and well known, into two kinds: (1) it is either widespread
> among many nations of whom it is known that by transmitting it they did not
> originally intend to prove or disprove something; but rather it happens that this
> report proves or disproves something. Every rational man should give credence to
> this kind of report, when it is known that it is of this kind; or, (2) it is not
> widespread among many nations but only among one or two. With the aid of this
> report, this or that nation seeks by virtue of an original intention to prove or
> disprove something, not that this report accidentally proves or disproves some-
> thing. In this case, a man of reason should suspend credence . . . In any case, the
> reason which establishes the credibility of a report is not transmission by a multi-
> tude who cannot be said to have connived in it but that the transmitter, whether
> one or many, should not be suspected of having arbitrarily added to the report.[26]

It is ultimately what the author calls 'rational evidence' (*al-dalil al-'aqli*)
which establishes credibility and not numbers. Just as proof in sciences like
geometry and medicine is derived from the principles of these sciences, so
in *akhbar* the rational man must investigate how they first originated and
developed or test their validity by reference to what is generally accepted
among the most eminent specialists in each science.

The *khabar*: four formulations of the fifth/eleventh century

By the fifth/eleventh century, the Islamic world had spawned three caliphates and several powerful sultanates, many of which had open pan-Islamic
ambitions. Outwardly, that world had lost its unity; in point of fact it
had acquired a cultural diversity born from the centrifugal tendencies of
divergent local cultures and polemics on the one hand and of the centri-

---

[25] Marie Bernand-Baladi, 'Des critères de la certitude: un opuscule de Hasan ibn Sahl sur
la crédibilité de dire transmis par un grand nombre', *Journal Asiatique*, 257 (1969), 95–
138.
[26] 'Des critères', 128–9 (of Arabic text).

petal compromises and accommodations of Islamic sects on the other. Thus, the specific political and geographical circumstances of Muslim Spain, for instance, gave specific colour to its culture, but debates with other Muslims tended towards the creation of uniformity and consensus over the broad issues of law and theology.

Where the theory of *khabar* was concerned, one might single out four major formulations as broadly typical of the currents of thought some two hundred years after Shafi'i and Nazzam. In a very real sense, these formulations were attempts to refine and explicate opinions and arguments first posited by these two figures and by their followers. But despite the often bitter tone of polemic, there is an unmistakable inclination in the direction of compromise and consensus, if only because the technical terms and rules of the polemic seemed to have become widely accepted. A recognized procedure had evolved with which to attack problems like that of the *khabar*, itself a focal point upon which law, theology and epistemology converged.

'Abd al-Jabbar

The first of these four major formulations was by the famous Mu'tazilite theologian al-Qadi 'Abd al-Jabbar ibn Ahmad (d. 415/1024). By his days, an intimate relationship had come to exist between the various forms of *khabar* on the one hand and the branches of knowledge on the other. A brief account of this question would need to make clear at the very outset that one is dealing with two tripartite divisions: three avenues to obtaining knowledge of *akhbar* and, secondly, three categories of *akhbar*. Let us begin with the first division.

'Abd al-Jabbar defines knowledge (*ma'rifa*; *'ilm*) as that which produces in the knower a state of inner tranquillity (*sukun al-nafs*) that what he believes to be so is in fact so.[27] Knowledge may be either necessary (*daruri*) or acquired (*muktasab*). The difference between them is not related to the degree of certainty that either produces in the knower but rather in the manner in which they occur. Necessary knowledge is produced by immediate perception (*idrak*; *mushahada*), acquired knowledge by ratiocination (*nazar*; *istidlal*). Another way in which 'Abd al-Jabbar distinguishes between these two types of knowledge is to argue that necessary knowledge occurs in us (*fina*), i.e. is placed in us by God, whereas acquired knowledge occurs through our own effort (*min qibalina*).[28] Again, unlike acquired knowledge, necessary knowledge requires no proof (*dalil*) to demonstrate its certainty and no doubt (*shakk*; *shubha*) can attach to it.

[27] 'Abd al-Jabbar, *Sharh al-Usul al-Khamsa*, pp. 46–7; cf. *Mughni*, 12:57. The best introduction to 'Abd al-Jabbar's epistemology is George F. Hourani, *Islamic Rationalism: The Ethics of 'Abd al-Jabbar* (Oxford: Clarendon Press, 1971), pp. 17–36.
[28] 'Abd al-Jabbar, *Sharh*, p. 48; cf. *Mughni*, 12:223.

There is also a third type, not strictly speaking, of knowledge but of what may be called belief or strong belief (*zann, ghalib al-zann*). This results when neither necessary nor acquired knowledge takes place and must depend upon an appropriate indicator, sign or pointer (*amara*).[29] Thus belief is liable to increase and decrease in degree of confirmation whereas knowledge is not.

This threefold division is found in matters of both reason (*'aqliyyat*) and revelation (*shar'iyyat*).[30] Certain aspects of revelation for example are known by necessity (e.g. some legal obligations), others by acquisition (e.g. analogy or *qiyas*) and still others are matters of belief (e.g. individual legal reasoning or *ijtihad*). Finally, proof (*dalil; hujja*) may be of two kinds, rational (*'aqli*) or revealed (*sama'i*) and has four sources: reason (*'aql*), the Qur'an, the Sunna and consensus.[31] As reason proves God's existence, unity, justice and so forth so the Qur'an and Sunna become corollary proofs. Reason establishes general principles which revelation later explicates.[32]

The first are the *akhbar* which lead to necessary knowledge. They have two characteristics: (1) their transmitters must report what they have known by necessity and (2) their number must be more than four.[33] It is immaterial whether the transmitters of these *akhbar* are believers or infidels. In fact these *akhbar* need no proof of the way in which they lead to necessary knowledge. Thus, to know that Mecca exists is the same as having been there and perceived it directly. The copula 'is the same as' is what 'Abd al-Jabbar often refers to as custom (*'ada*). Through *'ada* we know that there are in this world countries which we have not seen and that there once lived kings whose *akhbar* have reached us. *'Ada* is what God ordained to be the custom in normal human association and common existence.[34] The number four is of course known by revelation (*sama'*) and connected with testimony (*shahada*) in law. Custom decrees that such a *khabar* becomes more widespread until necessary knowledge is attained. This process is *tawatur* and *tawatur* is itself a custom. In brief, *akhbar* whose truth is known by necessity include reports of 'countries and kings' as well as reports about the Prophet's indisputable practice (e.g. his prayer, fasting and so forth) and information of similar nature. What chiefly distinguishes these *akhbar* is the fact that their first transmitters knew what they reported by necessity.[35]

---

[29] 'Abd al-Jabbar, *Mughni*, 17:362–3 and 15:332.
[30] 'Abd al-Jabbar, *Mughni*, 17:276–7.
[31] 'Abd al-Jabbar, *Sharh*, p. 88.
[32] 'Abd al-Jabbar, *Mughni*, 15:117.
[33] 'Abd al-Jabbar, *Mughni*, 15:333.
[34] 'Abd al-Jabbar, *Mughni*, 15:182 ff., 368 ff.
[35] 'Abd al-Jabbar, *Sharh*, p. 768.

The second type of *khabar* is one whose truth is known by inference (*istidlal*). This is divided into three kinds: (1) a *khabar* transmitted by a source which cannot, and does not choose, to lie, e.g. the *khabar* of the Qur'an and Sunna. This is how we come to know about God's unity and justice, Muhammad's prophethood and similar matters; (2) a *khabar* held to be true (*tasdiq*) by one whom we know to be incapable of falsehood. Thus, even a *khabar* reported by Satan himself would be regarded as true provided God or His Prophet, who are incapable of falsehood, do not condemn it outright as false; (3) a *khabar* whose particular circumstances (*ahwal*) are such that were the *khabar* itself to be false, these circumstances would not have accompanied it. Into this category falls the type of *khabar* which 'Abd al-Jabbar calls *tawatur muktasab*, that is to say a report transmitted by many whose truth may be known by inference and where there is no collusion (*tawatu'*) or mental confusion (*labs*) among its transmitters. Another type of *khabar* which falls here is the one reported by one man through direct perception and conveyed to the many who then raise no objections.[36]

In all three classes of such *akhbar*, rational investigation is required into the circumstances (*ahwal*) of both the report and its reporter. Many reports of religious significance, e.g. the miracles of the Prophet, must be subjected to investigation before their veracity is finally established. Further, such *akhbar* must be transmitted by so many that doubts or mental confusion cannot possibly attach to them. We know by inference that there is no reason for these transmitters to lie and, conversely, that the many might lie if they embrace a doubtful dogma.[37]

There are, finally, the *akhbar* which lead to belief (*zann*). They do not lead to knowledge because they do not occur by way of perception (*idrak*) and are not accompanied by proofs (*dala'il*) but by indicators or pointers (*amarat*). The chief example of such *akhbar* is the report transmitted by an individual (*khabar al-wahid*) which, according to 'Abd al-Jabbar, constitutes the basis for most acts of worship (*'ibadat*).[38] The degree of belief is liable to increase or decrease. To be valid, it must satisfy certain conditions, e.g. that the transmitter must be known to have been free from frivolity and immorality. Accordingly, the character of the first transmitter and the number of later transmitters may vary the force of such belief.[39] These *akhbar* are often accompanied by other indicators which make them obligatory for religious acts though not for knowledge.[40] A judge for example may pass judgement in accordance with the testimony of two

---

[36] 'Abd al-Jabbar, *Mughni*, 15:338–9.
[37] 'Abd al-Jabbar, *Mughni*, 15:339 and 16:18.
[38] 'Abd al-Jabbar, *Sharh*, p. 769.
[39] 'Abd al-Jabbar, *Mughni*, 15:339.
[40] 'Abd al-Jabbar, *Mughni*, 17:88 and 15:396.

witnesses, even though he is acting, not according to knowledge but to strong belief or probability (*ghalib al-zann*).

Where the second tripartite division of *akhbar* is concerned, namely the three categories of *akhbar*, 'Abd al-Jabbar defines a *khabar* as a particular statement (*kalam makhsus*), leading to knowledge, which can be said to be either (1) true or (2) false or (3) neither true nor false.[41] For convenience, one may begin with false *akhbar*:

In the case of a *khabar*, its falsity cannot be known in the same manner as its truth, that is, either by necessity or by inference, since it cannot lead to the knowledge that it is false, for it can only lead to the knowledge that corresponds to it (*al-'ilm al-mutabiq lahu*) and this is not possible in falsehood. Therefore it must be known that the information reported is not as it should be. In some *akhbar*, this is known by necessity, in others by inference, rational or revealed . . . If we know that the Christians intended to report that the one is three, we would know their falsehood by necessity. If we know that the Kullabiyya assert that God knows by a knowledge, we would know their falsehood by inference.[42]

All other *akhbar* are either true or neither true nor false. 'Abd al-Jabbar's discussion of these *akhbar* is theological and juristic in character and *akhbar* are divided and defined in terms of their final end which is their use (*fa'ida*) to those who are responsible under religious law (*mukallafun*). He is only indirectly concerned with what a historian understood to be the use of *akhbar*.

Baghdadi

The second formulation is by the Ash'arite theologian, heresiographer and enemy of the Mu'tazilites, 'Abd al-Qahir al-Baghdadi (d. 429/1037). Here too we begin with a survey of his views on knowledge, which Baghdadi divides into two kinds, necessary and acquired. What distinguishes them is the power of the knower over each: necessary knowledge occurs without inference (*istidlal*) and without the exercise of any power over it whereas acquired knowledge occurs through both the power and the inference of the knower.[43] Necessary knowledge is divided into self-evident (*badihi*) and sensible (*hissi*). Acquired knowledge is divided into four kinds: (1) inferred by the mind, (2) known through experiences (*tajarib*) and customs ('adat), (3) known through revelation (*shar'*) and (4) known through inspiration (*ilham*) in some men. Inference proves among other things the creation of the world and the eternity, unity, justice and wisdom of its Creator. Experiences and customs furnish the type of knowledge gained with practice, e.g. the various crafts. Revelation provides knowledge of

---

[41] 'Abd al-Jabbar, *Mughni*, 15:319 and *Sharh*, p. 768.
[42] 'Abd al-Jabbar, *Mughni*, 16:39–40; cf. *Sharh*, p. 769.
[43] Baghdadi, *Usul*, p. 8.

what is licit (*halal*) and illicit (*haram*) while the truth of revelation is proved by inference from the truth of prophecy, itself also proved by inference. Inspiration furnishes aesthetic knowledge of the kind evident in poetic appreciation.[44] All types of acquired knowledge may be made necessary by God in us through reversal of custom (*qalb al-'ada*). Thus Adam came to know the names of God by necessity and not by inference. On the other hand, what we know by necessity may not be known by inference since the self-evident is the foundation of the inferential (*al-bada'ih muqaddimat al-istidlal*).[45]

In Baghdadi's view, *akhbar* are either true, i.e. those which take place in accordance with their content (*'ala wifqi mukhbarihi*), or false, i.e. those which do not.[46] They are divided into three types: (1) *tawatur*, (2) *ahad* and (3) *mustafid*. The first type is one in which collusion (*tawatu'*) in forging it is impossible and produces necessary knowledge by the truth of its content. The *tawatur* of Christians, for instance, is invalid because suspicion of collusion exists as regards their original accounts of events like the crucifixion.[47] Among other conditions of *tawatur* is that:

Those who transmitted it at its time of origin did so through direct observance or necessary knowledge of what they transmitted such as their transmitting the *akhbar* of countries they themselves had seen or of nations seen by people of the time of origin and from whom they transmitted, or the *akhbar* of earthquakes, hot and cold weather and all other such events in times past . . . However, if *tawatur* occurs in a *khabar* about something whose truth is known by investigation and inference, this does not engender knowledge. This is why the materialists (*Dahriyya*) and all other infidels do not attain knowledge of the truth of the *akhbar* of Muslims regarding the truth of the religion of Islam because the truth of religion is known by investigation and inference, not by necessity.[48]

The second type, the *akhbar al-ahad*, necessitate action (*'amal*) but not knowledge (*'ilm*) and may be compared to legal testimony. They need to satisfy several conditions before they can be acceptable, e.g. their *isnad* must be correct and their content (*matn*) must not be rationally impossible. Examples of this last are the *hadith* related from Abu Hurayra that God made a horse to run in a race and then created another horse from the sweat of the first. On the other hand, other *hadith*s that appear impossible to the mind may nevertheless be capable of interpretation (*ta'wil*) and need not be rejected.[49]

The third type of *khabar*, the *mustafid*, has in common with the first the necessity it creates for both action and knowledge but differs from it in

---

[44] Baghdadi, *Usul*, pp. 14–15.
[45] Baghdadi, *Usul*, p. 16.
[46] Baghdadi, *Usul*, p. 13.
[47] Baghdadi, *Usul*, p. 21.
[48] Baghdadi, *Usul*, pp. 21–2.
[49] Baghdadi, *Usul*, pp. 22–3.

that the knowledge derived therefrom is acquired (*muktasab*) whereas knowledge derived from *tawatur* is necessary. This type is in many parts: (1) the *khabar* of one whose truthfulness is attested to by a miracle, such as the prophets, (2) the *khabar* of one whose truthfulness has been reported by a miracle worker, (3) the *khabar* related at first by trustworthy men (*thiqat*) and then its transmitters spread across the generations until they attain the level of *tawatur*, such as the *akhbar*, mostly having to do with the afterlife, of the Vision, the Pool, the Intercession, the Judgement in the Grave and so forth, (4) a *khabar al-ahad* present in every generation where the community has agreed unanimously to abide by its provisions, e.g. the rule that there can be no will to an heir.[50]

Basri

The third formulation is by the Mu'tazilite theologian and jurist and student of 'Abd al-Jabbar, Abu al-Husayn Muhammad ibn 'Ali ibn al-Tayyib al-Basri (d. 436/1044). Basri follows his master fairly closely in the basic divisions of *akhbar*, adding here and there some refinements such as the importance of investigating, in the case of certain *akhbar*, the circumstances of both the transmitter of a report and the one to whom the report was transmitted.[51] However, the passage that has most epistemic relevance to historical reports is the one where Basri debates with unnamed opponents concerning *khabar al-wahid* and whether such a *khabar* can lead to knowledge:

If they say: We know the truth of some *akhbar al-ahad* but not others, we reply: do you know this by necessity or acquisition (*daruratan aw iktisaban*)? If they say by necessity we reply that this is false since the *khabar* by itself is not sufficient for us to get to know its content without taking other things into account . . . thus requiring that we know it by acquisition. Those other things relate either to the reporter (*mukhbir*) or they do not. An example of the second case would be the conjuncture of the wailing woman and the presence of the funeral procession with the *khabar* about death. An example of the first would be that the reporter has a reason which deters him from lying . . . such as the fact that he is generally averse to lying or that he is a messenger from a ruler ordering the army to proceed to its master, the ruler's punishment being sufficient deterrence against lying, or the case where a man reports the prices of his city and is a man of honour which makes him averse to deceit, or he has no motive to lie. Another example would be for a man to be preoccupied in other affairs and then be asked suddenly about something where he responds at once, it being known that he had no time to devise an answer . . . If they now argue: we know the truth of *khabar al-wahid* by inference (*istidlalan*) as you have just demonstrated, we reply: there is nothing in what we argued that leads to knowledge. For a man might inform us of the death of a sick man, when in fact his family intends, by wailing and preparing the funeral, to

---

[50] Baghdadi, *Usul*, pp. 12–13.
[51] Basri, *Mu'tamad*, 2:546 ff.

deceive the ruler into thinking that he is dead so that he can escape his punishment, or he may have fainted or someone else may have died suddenly. Again, a man may be very much averse to lying in appearance but not in reality . . . Furthermore, a man might pretend to be preoccupied when in fact he is very much interested in the question being put to him . . . In the case of the man who reports the prices of commodities, it may be that he had taken a previous vow to lie about prices or that he wants people to be impressed either by how expensive or by how cheap they are . . . or his motive may be a brisk sale of his or his friend's goods . . . As for the ruler's messenger, he may have received a large bribe to inform the ruler's subjects and army of the order to proceed to their master, or else the ruler himself may have ordered him to lie on purpose, either in mockery or to test the loyalty of his troops. If all these alternative explanations are possible, it cannot be known that the reporter intended only the truth. Hence his truthfulness cannot be known, even if this is probable (*wa in ghalaba al-zann*).[52]

Here, in Basri, the interpretation of ordinary historical evidence is to the fore. The examples chosen for analysis betray a concern with the manner in which many everyday facts are reported and the kinds of criticism to which they are liable.

Ibn Hazm

The final formulation is by the celebrated Andalusian jurist, theologian, heresiographer and man of letters, Abu Muhammad ibn Hazm (d. 456/ 1064). Ibn Hazm was a radical literalist, a thinker who rejected a great deal of the theology of his age in the name of a return to the literal meaning of Qur'an and Sunna, interpreted when really necessary not by allegorization and analogy but by Aristotelean logic. The novelty of the structure of his thought made him a formidable opponent to many dominant intellectual currents of his age by virtue of the fact that his ideas cut across traditional combinations and positions without belonging to any recognized school. He was very much interested in *akhbar*, in their legal as well as epistemic status, in the history of the human sciences and in the value of history for ethics and politics. His formulation was therefore broader in scope than the first three set out above.

From the epistemic point of view, perhaps one of the most original aspects of his discussion of *akhbar* is the manner in which he analyses the problem of collusion (*tawatu'*) in the fabrication of reports. Having first argued that both the one and the many may lie or collude to lie, he proceeds to define a *khabar* that leads to necessary knowledge as follows:

If two or more people come forward, after we have ascertained that they never met or communicated secretly with one other and had no vested interest in, and no fear of what they report and each was then to report separately a long report

[52] Basri, *Mu'tamad*, 2:568–70.

which no two people can possibly concur in the imaginative fabrication thereof, and each was to mention his having witnessed or met a group who witnessed or reported from another group that they had witnessed this report, this would be a true report which anyone who heard it would doubtless be obliged to believe . . . This is known perceptibly (*hissan*) by anyone who ponders and examines the *akhbar* he receives in daily life concerning a death, a birth, a marriage, a dismissal, an appointment, a battle and so forth. If you were to commission one man to fabricate a long and false report, he could do so . . . But if you were to lock up two people in two different houses where they could not meet and asked each one to fabricate a false report, it would be utterly impossible that they would produce a similar report from beginning to end . . . We ourselves witnessed the case of two poets producing an exactly similar half-line of verse, but this happened only twice in our lifetime.[53]

One crucial aspect of this analysis by Ibn Hazm is the question of the *length* of a report. It is this aspect which raises the problem of collusion and illustrates what many historians are often up against, as they wrestle with problems such as facticity in contrast with the genesis and development of specific historical traditions.

The four formulations examined

In analysing the four formulations and attempting to understand the nature and range of the debate about *akhbar*, it is clear to begin with that despite the formal theological differences between, say, the Mu'tazilites and their opponents, a stage has been reached where the basic constituents of a theory of knowledge seem to be held in common. The extremism of Nazzam, for instance, in rejecting *ijma'* and *tawatur* is found objectionable by all. Common to them all too is the distinction between necessary and acquired knowledge and between a *khabar* which engenders legal obligation and one which engenders knowledge. It is equally obvious that much of this debate, though by no means all of it, revolves around Muhammadan *Hadith* and the use to which this may be put in legal judgement, especially as regards the problematic status of *khabar al-ahad*.

One of the more prominent differences among these formulations relates to a type of knowledge derived from a *khabar* which the two Mu'tazilites insist on calling 'belief' (*zann*) but which Baghdadi would label true and classify as *mustafid*. Thus many *akhbar* about the end of the world would certainly be subject to interpretation (*ta'wil*) according to the two Mu'tazilites but would be acceptable as transmitted to Baghdadi. The *isnad* provides another point of contrast. The word itself appears infrequently in the works of 'Abd al-Jabbar and Basri. It may be assumed that what these two call an investigation into the 'circumstances' of the *khabar*

---

[53] Ibn Hazm, *Ihkam*, 1:107–8; cf. *Fisal*, 5:118–19.

and its reporter involves more than the traditional *isnad* criticism of Bagh-dadi.[54] For it implies that this scrutiny of *matn* and *isnad* should reveal no taint of any doctrine that could remotely be labelled 'corrupt' (*fasid*). The rigour of this scrutiny reveals earlier traces of the Mu'tazilite tendency to reject a great many *akhbar* as untrustworthy in the course of defending their own doctrinal position. In addition, the relationship between neces-sary and acquired knowledge has some bearing on this issue. Baghdadi argued that necessary knowledge is the foundation of acquired and that acquired knowledge may be miraculously transmuted into necessary by God. To 'Abd al-Jabbar, rational knowledge (*'aql*; *istidlal*) is a principal basis of religious obligation and this entails the rigorous examination of all types of *akhbar* which are not, strictly speaking, necessary.

In general, rational intention, psychological motivation, possibility and probability, and the manner in which collusion takes place were all found relevant in determining the truth or falsehood of *akhbar*. The embedding of *akhbar* in theories of knowledge was the achievement of the theolo-gians. This had the effect of expanding the prevailing conventions and themes which governed the discussion of these problems. Much of the credit for this expansion in the use of the concept of *khabar* must belong to the Mu'tazilites. They were in fact the first to argue in a systematic manner that the *purpose* for which a *khabar* is intended was crucial to the determination of its truth.[55]

Miracle and custom

The mental world of *hikma*-inspired historical thought and writing was overshadowed by the question of miracles and of what is possible or impossible for God and men. Related to this was the issue of the natural and the supernatural and the proper definition of custom (*'ada*) and the breaking of custom. Some aspects of this question were raised in earlier chapters. It remains important to attempt to delineate the parameters of normalcy for this particular tradition of historical thought in order to round out their notion of what is or is not acceptable in *akhbar*. There is also a more general reason why this attempt should be made. For the definition of the miraculous and the customary is one place where it is possible to close in upon the differences between the medieval and the modern conceptions of admissible knowledge.

The historical context in which the question of miracles was discussed between the 3rd–5th/9th–11th centuries was not of course fixed. In the earlier part of this period the introduction of science and philosophy, Greek and Indian, to an Arab-Islamic imperial society that had already

---

[54] See footnote 39, above.
[55] Most cogently argued in 'Abd al-Jabbar, *Mughni*, 16:18–19.

begun to systematize and rationalize its institutions, its laws, its socioeconomic structures and its basic theological and polemical skills created the atmosphere in which the natural could be compared to the supernatural. It could be argued that in this matter also the controversy about the created Qur'an was a turning point. Was not the view that the Qur'an was created an invitation to speculate on God's relationship to His created world? A created Qur'an was surely created in time and space and therefore belonged to the 'natural' world more than an uncreated Qur'an.

In the latter part of this period, the issue of prophecy was of central importance. Certain Muslim philosophers and mystics on the one hand, and, on the other, the rise of a religious movement with a powerful intellectual and populist appeal, the Isma'ilis, posed a challenge to Sunni and Shi'i theology alike. Such doctrines as the eternity of the world, the denial of prophetic miracles, the possibility of divine incarnation and the denial of the finality of Muhammadan prophecy brought forth a response of sustained energy from theologians who were slowly closing ranks. What was needed was nothing less than the redefinition of prophecy and its rearming with theological 'proofs'.

But the debate may conveniently be said to have begun with the ubiquitous Nazzam, whose unconventional views on *tawatur* were discussed above. It is conceivable that Nazzam's quoted opinions on miracles were inspired by his interest in what may be called the relative autonomy of nature. Nazzam accepted the occurrence of the extraordinary (*burhanat*) and of monstrosities and oddities (*maskh*; *a'ajib*) in nature. Their credibility is enhanced for him if reported by or on behalf of a prophet.[56] Regarding Muhammadan miracles, however, his position was somewhat sceptical and not easily understood. It is fairly certain that he questioned the splitting of the moon, a miracle mentioned in the Qur'an, on the grounds that (1) if it had occurred in a literal sense, it would have been reported by all peoples and (2) it could be a future and not a past event.[57] It is equally certain that he accepted the *possibility* of apologetic miracles. What he probably disliked was the fact that the wholesale acceptance of prophetic miracles would take something away from the rational basis of belief. The miraculous was possible but needed to be corroborated, e.g. by a well-transmitted report.

Other thinkers were more sceptical. It is reported, for instance, that the physician-philosopher Muhammad ibn Zakariyya al-Razi (d. 313/925) was very much interested in the question of miracles. He is said 'to have written

---

[56] Jahiz, *Hayawan*, 4:73.
[57] 'Abd al-Jabbar, *Tathbit*, 1:55. There is an adequate though by no means complete discussion of this problem in H. A. Wolfson, *The Philosophy of the Kalam* (Cambridge, Mass.: Harvard University Press, 1976), pp. 569–70. Little credence can be placed in what Baghdadi reports to be the views of Nazzam on miracles in, e.g., *Farq*, pp. 128, 135.

at length on this topic in the form of question and answer' and 'to have undermined the arguments of those who asserted the truth of prophetic miracles'. It appears that he argued that Muhammad's miracles were reported by one, two or three persons only and that collusion was hence possible in the transmission. He seems also to have cited the tricks of conjurers and magicians and the oracular speech of fortune-tellers as evidence against the acceptance of miracles. The scepticism of Razi, whose roots extended back to the Pre-Socratics, was instrumental in effecting some change in the mainstream patterns of thought on this topic.[58] Theology, which in many cultural traditions gives the appearance of being a rescue operation, had to devise solutions which reconciled divine omnipotence with the workings of nature.

A curious work of history written from a Mu'tazilite viewpoint by al-Mutahhar ibn Tahir al-Maqdisi (wrote 355/966) advanced and expanded the debate on miracles. The crucial passage runs as follows:

> A thing may be a miracle at one time while at another time it is not a miracle. It may be a miracle for one nation but not for another. A thing may in the totality of its parts be a miracle but each individual part by itself might not be a miracle. This is what we maintain about the victory of the Prophet at Badr . . . and about the Qur'an.[59]

A miracle was thus relative to time and circumstance. In general, miracles cannot take place except at the hands of prophets or in their time. In the Qur'anic story of the Sleepers in the Cave, for instance, either a prophet was alive at that time or one or all of the sleepers were prophets.[60] If a miracle has been accurately transmitted but no prophet was known to have been alive at that time, an allegorical interpretation may be necessary.

Where the miracles of Muhammad are concerned, three types may be distinguished. First, the miracle is true if attested in the Qur'an or in a trustworthy report, whether a parallel can be found in nature or not. The Qur'an itself is a miracle because of the unmet challenge to imitate it, its eloquence and its foretelling of events. Secondly, there is a group of miracles reported in the biographies of Muhammad such as a wolf speaking, a branch of a tree yearning for Muhammad and so forth. They include some *akhbar* with defective *isnad* and need not be accepted as true. Thirdly, there are reports that the Prophet cast no shadow, that he had no body odour and so forth. These lack a good *isnad* and have no parallel

---

[58] The views of Razi are cited in Abu Hatim al-Razi, *A'lam al-Nubuwwa*, pp. 191–2. For Pre-Socratic and other antecedents, see Robert M. Grant, *Miracle and Natural Law*, pp. 41–60. For his influence, see footnote 61, below.

[59] Maqdisi, *Bad'*, 4:175–6; on Maqdisi, see T. Khalidi, 'Mu'tazilite Historiography: Maqdisi's *K. al-Bad'* wa'l *Ta'rikh*', *Journal of Near Eastern Studies*, 35/1 (Jan. 1976), 1–12; cf. 'Abd al-Jabbar, *Mughni*, 15:182–4 and Baqillani, *Bayan*, paras. 14–16.

[60] Maqdisi, *Bad'*, 3:129–34.

in nature and must therefore be rejected.[61] As regards the charisms of holy men (*karamat al-awliya'*), the general Mu'tazilite position, as opposed to the Ash'arite, was that they must be rejected.[62]

A later age brought forth new challenges. The discussion of miracles centred no longer on a harmony detected or formulated between the divine and the natural or between theology and science. Rather, and as mentioned above, it was the 'heretics', the Isma'ilis of Egypt, Syria and Arabia on the one hand, and the Sufi 'saints' on the other, who were now the targets of the theological polemic on miracles. The first group announced the coming of a messianic figure, al-Qa'im, as the harbinger of a new historical era miraculously different from all that preceded it; the second were performing 'miracles' of speech and act which impressed themselves indelibly on the imagination of followers. Both groups were in effect preaching the reality of the breaking of natural custom, grown ever more marvellous through propaganda, dramatic victory or arcane science. They were 'the challenge' to the Qur'an and the Prophet which traditional theology had maintained was never met.

Against this background, the title of 'Abd al-Jabbar's major work on prophecy, 'Establishing the Proofs of Prophecy' (*Tathbit Dala'il al-Nubuwwa*), has a defiant ring to it, although the work itself is occasionally melancholic on the subject of contemporary learning and of Islam. 'Abd al-Jabbar sets out to argue that the life of Muhammad was itself the real miracle, a triumphant historical process which raised the prophet, against all odds, all natural custom, from a position of abject weakness to one of great power. His prophecies about the future were amply vindicated so that all his enemies were eventually overthrown and his own plans were realized. As for his Companions, they too, as promised in the Qur'an, turned out to be 'the best *umma* ever brought forth among mankind' (*khayru ummatin ukhrijat li'l-nas*). For is it not the custom (*'ada*) for men when they come to power to abuse that power and behave like tyrants?[63] And yet, miraculously, his rightly guided caliphs all led exemplary lives of simplicity and piety. Even the decline of Islam at the end of time has been predicted by Muhammad.[64]

Compared with this, the historical record of the Isma'ilis, both Fatimids and Qarmatians, is, according to 'Abd al-Jabbar, scandalous. Senseless in their violence and in their doctrine, these heretics could never agree on who or what their Mahdi really was. Again and again, a supernatural reign

---

[61] Maqdisi, *Bad'*, 5:3. Maqdisi expresses approval for the work entitled *Kitab al-Khawass*, by Muhammad ibn Zakariyya al-Razi, in *Bad'*, 4:92 ff. This work, now lost, was almost certainly devoted to an examination of the natural characteristics of external physical bodies. See also Biruni, *Risala fi Fihrist Kutub Muhammad ibn Zakariyya al-Razi*, p. 21, no. 183.

[62] See, e.g., 'Abd al-Jabbar, *Mughni*, 15:226 ff., 241–3.

[63] 'Abd al-Jabbar, *Tathbit*, 1:34.

[64] 'Abd al-Jabbar, *Tathbit*, 2:339–40.

of justice would be promised only to end in ludicrous failure.[65] In point of fact the very comparison between the two historical records is sufficient to convince any rational human being of the truth of Muhammadan prophecy and, one could add, in its Sunni and Mu'tazilite interpretation. For 'Abd al-Jabbar does not spare the Shi'is who maintained that 'Ali had been designated the Imam after Muhammad, even as he extolled 'Ali's special merits.[66] In an age when custom and miracle were being used heavily as weapons of polemic, 'Abd al-Jabbar undertook not only to define the miraculous theoretically but also to review the record of the various factions of the Muslim community in order to demonstrate the historical miraculousness of Muhammadan prophecy.[67]

But what exactly is custom? For 'Abd al-Jabbar, the evidential signs (ayat) which violate custom (naqd al-'ada) are innumerable, as many as the instances where, against all expectation, Muhammad won through or achieved something. Many are echoed or predicted in the Qur'an. There are, for example, cases where to have said something other than what he did say would have 'normally' been more prudent or to have revealed what was revealed to him and not be contradicted would have been impossible. There are cases where his defiance of numerous and powerful enemies were acts that no reasonable ('aqil) man would do were it not that he felt so confident in God's succour. There are others where his followers would certainly have abandoned him had they felt the least suspicion concerning his sincerity, especially as this would have been easy for them to do given the heavy demands he made upon them. Again, there are instances where the Qur'an heaps scorn on Muhammad's contemporaries and challenges them to debate but they, though famous for their towering pride, found no argument against Muhammad and no way to defend their honour.[68]

The breaking of custom is defined as an 'increase in the normal course of things' (ziyada 'ala al-amr al-mu'tad). It is reality exaggerated, as in the example given by the Jubba'i school of the Mu'tazilites and quoted approvingly by 'Abd al-Jabbar:

We do not deny that before Muhammad's prophetic mission began there did occur something like a shower of stars. But we know from the evidence we presented that what occurred at the time of the Prophet's mission was something which violated custom, for the sky was filled with such showers. It is this increase in the

[65] 'Abd al-Jabbar, Tathbit, 2:517.
[66] 'Abd al-Jabbar, Tathbit, 2:510.
[67] The more theoretical discussion of miracles is in Mughni, vol. 15. 'Abd al-Jabbar also devoted many pages of his Tathbit to attacking the historical record of Christianity.
[68] For prudence, see Tathbit, 1:16, 56–7; for God's succour, see Tathbit, 1:41; for abandonment by followers, see Tathbit, 1:67; for challenges to debate, see Tathbit, 2:360–2. In Tathbit, 2:361 'Abd al-Jabbar accuses Christians of unwillingness to use reason and investigation and philosophers of unwillingness to debate with theologians whom they accuse of 'sophistry'.

normal course of things which constitutes proof [i.e. of the prophecy]. This may be compared to the Flood. For the waters before Noah would often rise and increase in a normal and well-known manner. But when Noah came into the world, the waters increased in a manner which violated custom and reached beyond the normal course of things. That increase is itself the evidential sign, the proof.[69]

Accordingly, the accumulation of historical examples by ʿAbd al-Jabbar is designed to prove the truth of Muhammadan prophecy through the sheer weight of evidence in his favour and the evidence against his enemies, rivals and detractors. The miracles and signs which violate custom complement each other such that one may, for example, infer the truth of Muhammad's prophecy from the eloquence of the Qurʾan without knowing about the Qurʾan's foretelling of future events, and vice versa.[70] But the general Muʿtazilite position on miracles was in one sense academic. Believing that miracles were essentially apologetic phenomena designed by God as evidence for the truth of prophecy, and believing of course that prophecy had ended with Muhammad, the Muʿtazilites regarded miracles as phenomena of the past. It was with relief that ʿAbd al-Jabbar contemplated this state of affairs for he argued that the reason why so many Christian philosophers were unbelievers was because their religion tolerated the continual occurrence of miracles and signs.[71]

ʿAbd al-Jabbar dealt even more harshly with astrological predictions, talismans and other supposedly paranormal phenomena. Astrology was a hit-and-miss game, no better than the games of chance played by children and fools. Talismans were peculiarities of geography created by God and for a purpose and benefit (*maslaha*) known only to Him.[72] Their danger, bluntly put, was:

that some historians, with no knowledge of theology, may encounter such reports or works and include them in their histories, where they are read by the ignorant or by those who do not consult scholars about these matters. As a result, they are puzzled and confused.[73]

Despite earlier disagreements on the question of causality and thus of custom and miracle, the theologians of the fifth/eleventh century, both Muʿtazilites and Ashʿarites, held many views in common regarding these issues. The Ashʿarite theologian Abu Bakr al-Baqillani (d. 403/1012), who

---

[69] ʿAbd al-Jabbar, *Tathbit*, 1:69. ʿAbd al-Jabbar also discusses *ʿada* in *Mughni*, 15:182 ff., 366, 376 and 16:337 ff. At *Mughni*, 15:366 and 376, ʿAbd al-Jabbar argues that it is *ʿada* which strengthens the *khabar al-wahid* so that as transmitters increase, belief is transformed into knowledge.

[70] ʿAbd al-Jabbar, *Tathbit*, 2:509 and 1:86.

[71] ʿAbd al-Jabbar, *Tathbit*, 1:175, 208–9.

[72] On the two phenomena, see ʿAbd al-Jabbar, *Tathbit*, 1:176–9. Ibn Hazm argues in *Fisal*, 5:4 that talismans are akin to magnetic forces implanted by God and manipulated by men in earlier ages. Their effects may still be observed but the craft (*sinaʿa*) which produced them has perished.

[73] ʿAbd al-Jabbar, *Tathbit*, 1:75.

wrote an important work on miracles, held a position which differed in detail but not in essence from 'Abd al-Jabbar. He admitted that the miraculous could be regarded as being of two kinds, one of which God alone could be said to have power over, and the other a kind over which men customarily have power but which becomes miraculous in excess. Thus, the raising of the dead, the creation of bodies and so forth belong to the first, exclusively divine miracle. On the other hand, individual words or phrases of the Qur'an are within human power but the orderly perfection of the text as a whole is the miracle.[74]

Sorcery (*sihr*) was of course a reality for all theologians. It was therefore important for them to distinguish a miraculous from a magical act in order to preserve the integrity of prophetic witness. For Baqillani, one kind of sorcery is done through instruments, sleight-of-hand and illusion. The other, attested in the Qur'an and traditions, is a potentially harmful activity punishable by death. The ultimate creator of sorcery is God and for purposes known only to Him. If a sorcerer does claim prophecy by his sorcery, God would nullify his acts by making him forget his sorcery or would cause other sorcerers to imitate his acts and thus void his claims.[75]

As regards custom (*'ada*), Baqillani defined it as a kind of repetition or regularity of knowledge and of the thing known. It cannot be ascribed to God, for whom repetition is impossible, but only to the rational agent who finds that things occur or recur in a regular manner. Customs are of various kinds. Some are common to all men of all times; some are particular to some men but not others; some are relative to time and place; some are customary for men and not *jinn* or angels, and vice versa. A violation of one kind of custom need not be a violation of another. Therefore, a miracle must violate the custom of the whole genus (*qabil*) to which the prophet is sent: of angels if sent to angels, of *jinn* if sent to *jinn* and of men if sent to men.[76]

But there was one important difference between the Mu'tazilites and the Ash'arites in the area of the miraculous. This concerned the charisms of holy men (*karamat*), generally denied by the Mu'tazilites but affirmed by the Ash'arites. In obvious pique, the Ash'arite 'Abd al-Qahir al-Baghdadi argued that the Mu'tazilites rejected the charisms of holy men because they had no holy men of their own to boast of. He defines charisms as being similar to miracles in that both are violations of custom. The major difference between them is that the person for whom a miracle is enacted does not hide it but broadcasts it and challenges his opponents to produce its like, whereas the holy man usually strives to keep the charism a secret and makes no claims or challenges. If God decides to reveal the

---

[74] Baqillani, *Bayan*, paras. 17–28.
[75] Baqillani, *Bayan*, paras. 109–18.
[76] Baqillani, *Bayan*, paras. 57–65. On *'ada* in general theological and philosophical debate, see Wolfson, *The Philosophy of the Kalam*, pp. 544–58.

charism, this is only by way of drawing attention to the piety of the holy man. Another difference is that the man of miracle is incapable of any change in character and is sinless after the miracle has appeared whereas the charism does not engender such change. To the Mu'tazilite objection that charisms denigrate the evidence of prophetic miracles, Baghdadi responds that the evidence of the miracle is not confined to prophecy but is an indicator of the truth, sometimes of prophecy, sometimes of the sincerity and honesty of the holy man.[77]

Herein lies one central point of the theological debate on miracles: Can God control nature and prophecy, and does he actually do so? The first is a question that relates to His omnipotence, and the miracles were seen to be illustrations of that control. On this there was no disagreement. But the second is a historical question and here the Mu'tazilites argued that the miraculous event was essentially apologetic, intended by God to prove the truth of prophecy; but they denied His ceaseless violations of custom in favour of an unending procession of holy men.

Time and the philosophers

Concepts of time so far encountered have been divided and contrasted into time human and time divine. Time has been measured in centuries, in generations, in years, in reigns. It has been brought near for close scrutiny or cut adrift among ancient nations. Its beginning, its end and its form were issues of passionate intensity to a large cross-section of scholars. When the Muslim philosophers turned their attention to these 'intractable problems' (*masa'il 'awisa*), as Ibn Rushd called them,[78] they were forced to tackle a matrix of interrelated questions of direct relevance to both physics and theology. Time, motion and magnitude could not be divorced from the larger issue of God's relationship to the world and so to the question of eternity and origination. To complicate matters, motion, which in almost all philosophical discussion was intimately connected with time, was widely regarded as a sign of life so that the heavens were, in the phrase of Ibn Sina, 'an animal obeying God'.[79]

The philosophers were to adopt a broad spectrum of views on the question of time. Proceeding largely from the Aristotelean notion that 'time is either the same thing as movement or an attribute of movement',[80] one of the earliest of the Muslim philosophers, al-Kindi (d. *c.* 252/866), argued that body, motion and time were isochronic so that none of them could

---

[77] Baghdadi, *Usul*, pp. 174–5.
[78] Ibn Rushd, *Fasl al-Maqal*, p. 21.
[79] Ibn Sina, *Najat*, p. 258; cf. Ibn Tufayl, *Hayy ibn Yaqzan*, p. 54, and S. H. Nasr, *An Introduction to Islamic Cosmological Doctrines* (Cambridge, Mass.: Harvard University Press, 1964), p. 63.
[80] Aristotle, *Metaphysics*, 1071b 8–9.

be said to precede or succeed the others. Since there could be no such thing as an infinite body, infinite time was also impossible. Time was a quantity so there could be no endless time in actuality. The world is a body and must therefore have both a beginning and an end.[81] This was a conclusion which agreed both with the Ash'arite view and with the Mu'tazilite as set forth in Maqdisi's historical work, *al-Bad' wa'l Ta'rikh*, a principal purpose of which was to demonstrate the origination of the world.

But the encounter with Plotinus was to add to the complexity of the discussion of time. For between time finite and time infinite there was injected the concept of effusion or emanation (*fayd*), necessitating a reformulation of time as a process or a state of being and a refinement in the concepts of priority and eternity. A new cosmology, best represented by Farabi (d. 339/950), substituted for the personal creator-God of traditional Islamic theology a hierarchic universe of beings ranked as the First Cause, the Second Causes, the Active Intellect, the Soul, form and matter. The First Cause is the only being that can be described as truly one, self-sufficient, perfect, eternal, absolute. What emanates from the First Cause is not 'after' Him in time but in being, a distinction that became current in most systems of thought influenced by Neo-Platonism.[82] This in turn raised the problem of the world's eternity, the Achilles' heel of the philosophers as they began to face an increasingly hostile and sophisticated scrutiny from the traditional, finite-world theologians.

Perhaps the best-known philosophical discussion of the question of eternity and origination is the one offered by Ibn Rushd (d. 594/1198). In his days, the topic had bloomed into public debate largely through Ghazali's celebrated condemnation of the emanationist philosophers as unbelievers. Ibn Rushd, however, saw no compelling reason to accept either pre-eternity or temporal origination as the only two possible attributes of the universe. For Ibn Rushd, time is a continuum or, as he put it, 'the aggregate of what comes before and what comes after' (*jama'at al-mutaqaddim wa'l muta'akhkhir*).[83] It functions as a divisor of movement by means of endless moments (*anat*), each of which resembles a point on a line separating a past from a future. More particularly, it is a point on a circle and must be considered as 'adjunct to a circular and eternal movement' (*tabi' li haraka azaliyya mustadira*).[84] No part of time can exist in

---

[81] Kindi, *Rasa'il*, 1:116–22, 194–8, 201–7.

[82] Farabi, *al-Siyasa al-Madaniyya*, p. 48: 'Hence the existence of what exists from Him does not in any way come after Him in time but comes after Him in all other senses of the term.' Ibn Sina writes in *Najat*, p. 117: 'Hence time is not originated in a temporal sense (*huduthan zamaniyyan*) but in a creative sense (*huduth ibda'*) and is not preceded by its originator in time and period but in being.' For the views of Ibn Sina and their critique by Ghazali, see Wolfson, *The Philosophy of the Kalam*, pp. 444–55, and Nasr, *An Introduction*, pp. 202–14.

[83] Ibn Rushd, *Rasa'il: K. al-Sama' al-Tabi'i*, p. 50.

[84] Ibn Rushd, *K. al-Sama'*, p. 52.

act and present time is mere convention. Building upon these arguments, Ibn Rushd concludes that the world is neither truly pre-eternal nor truly originated because 'the truly originated is by necessity corruptible and the truly pre-eternal has no cause'.[85]

The denial that time can ever be 'in act' (*bi'l fi'l*), the assertion that only an awareness of the present moment imparts a sense of a before and an after, and the view that priority is not only temporal but ontological were philosophical opinions which helped to spread what may be called a psychic view of time.[86] The discussion of pre-eternity and origination and the growing interest in 'geological' time introduced conceptions of time stretching far beyond those of ordinary historiographic and pietist parameters. Thus, for example, in discussing the transformation of land into sea and vice versa Ibn Rushd introduces a relatively rare analysis of the relationship of the historical record to these aeons of time:

The reason why some parts of the earth become sea after they had been land and land after they had been sea . . . is the obvious corruption of particular components of the elements . . . This is also determined by direct observation of shells and other objects to be found in depressions and glens which are found only in seas . . . The reason why these incidents are not recorded so that they reach us is, as Aristotle says, the span of time and epochs and because this appears only in thousands of years so that languages and scripts change and writing perishes. If it does survive, there may be no one left who can read it, as in the case of the script on the Pyramids of Egypt. It may also be that all who witnessed or were informed of such events have perished either through floods that occur in the world or through pestilential winds or wars.[87]

Inspired partly by the same Aristotelean and Neo-Platonic sources as the philosophers, the Isma'ili movement offered what was probably the most epochal scheme of history ever produced by Arabic-Islamic culture. Central to this scheme was a circular conception of time divided into eras (*adwar*), a correspondence between the macrocosm and the microcosm such that all events are both actual and symbolic and a view of history which contrasted vividly with contemporaneous Islamic conceptions of the past.

A seminal work in the development of Isma'ili doctrine and of the Isma'ili conception of history was the *Kitab Ithbat al-Nubu'at* ('The Vindication of Prophetic Missions') of Abu Ya'qub al-Sijistani (d. *c.* 360/970).

---

[85] Ibn Rushd, *Fasl*, p. 20. See the discussion of this problem and a translation of a treatise of Ibn Rushd on this subject in Barry S. Kogan, 'Eternity and Origination: Averroes' Discourse on the Manner of the World's Existence' in Michael Marmura, ed. *Islamic Theology and Philosophy: Studies in Honor of George F. Hourani* (Albany: SUNY Press, 1984), pp. 203–35.

[86] This is best captured in Ibn Rushd's statement that 'where there is no soul there can be neither time nor motion': see *K. al-Sama'*, p. 51. The Qur'anic Sleepers in the Cave are said to be an illustration of the principle that where there is no awareness there is no time: see *K. al-Sama'*, p. 47.

[87] Ibn Rushd, *Rasa'il: K. al-Athar al-'Ulwiyya*, pp. 31–2.

Divided into seven chapters, itself a reflection of the centrality of numerology in the Isma'ili image of the universe, the work, which lacks its seventh chapter, begins with cosmology, proceeds to prophetology and ended, it seems, with symbolism. It posits a geometrical universe of concentric circles, the centre of which is the Intellect and from which radiate Souls in descending order of reality. A system of spiritual and material correspondences links Intellect and Souls with the sublunary region and Being with history. Messengers (*rusul*) are a manifestation of the concern of the Spiritual World (*al-'Alam al-Ruhani*) for the Corporeal World (*al-'Alam al-Jismani*), the individual mind being the first in the series of Messengers who call upon man to bear witness to the existence of the Creator.

The Messengers, while the best of mankind, nevertheless vary in rank and virtue. The reason advanced for this variation serves to introduce the epochal conception of history:

This manner of dividing the Messengers is due to the fact that nations are superior one to the other across the passage of time. The proverb expresses this idea by saying that people resemble their own times more than they resemble their ancestors. Hence, each period of time by necessity manifests the varying effects of the movements of the heavenly bodies by way of transparency or density, thus varying men's natural dispositions and morals. Therefore, the Messenger sent to them must accord with what each period has received from the transparency of the heavenly bodies through the lower bodies, or from their density.[88]

From this difference in Messengers and epochs proceeds a difference in messages, each of which is specifically addressed to a particular epoch. Messages are revealed such that, within any given epoch, each will attain its ultimate and natural end. This is decreed by the physical nature of the universe itself as arranged by the movements of the heavenly bodies for one has only to observe the various planets revolving in their orbits at various speeds to recognize the wisdom of the Creator in sending messages at different intervals. For Abu Ya'qub, this also implies the necessity for the successive abrogation of religious laws (*naskh al-shara'i'*), the reasons for this, again seven in number, being:

First . . . that after the passage of a long period of time, the religious law becomes unsuitable to the spirit of the following age, especially after man has advanced in knowledge and progress . . . despite the fact that . . . all religious laws are adopted one from the other, all issuing from the same fountain and source. The second reason is that, just as the human body has a limited end which it approaches in stages, so too the religious law which, as it approaches its end, becomes liable to abrogation . . . Thirdly, if mankind were left with only one religious law and they grew accustomed to its usages . . . they will come to take it for granted . . . and it ceases to be a form of divine worship.[89]

---

[88] Sijistani, *Ithbat*, pp. 41–2.
[89] Sijistani, *Ithbat*, pp. 76–8.

Other reasons, not all of them fully clear, have to do with the necessity for the progressive revelation of wisdom hidden in each law, the need for each epoch to enjoy the law and wisdom appropriate to the times, the correspondence between the movements of the seven planets and time in the sublunary region, and the need for men perpetually to investigate the questions of salvation.

The Prophetic Messages are therefore seen as 'the cause of time' (*'illat al-zaman*) for it is the repetitive rituals of religious laws which mark time off in regular intervals whereas time itself has no natural signposts, expanding and contracting without strict regularity.[90] Time has two principal eras, the Era of Concealment (*dawr al-satr*) and the Era of Disclosure (*dawr al-kashf*). The current Era of Concealment began with Adam who was followed by Noah, Abraham, Moses, Jesus and Muhammad. Each was a 'speaker prophet' (*natiq*) and each was accompanied by a 'silent prophet' (*samit*), the first being the promulgator of law and the second the teacher of its hidden wisdom. Each *samit* has seven successors, the seventh of whom advances to become the *natiq* of the next law. The present time for Abu Ya'qub is one which finds the world poised to witness the end of a great Era of Concealment when the seventh and final figure in this cycle, al-Qa'im (the 'Resurrector'), will appear and usher in the Era of Disclosure, at which time the final truths of all religions will be fully revealed.

This Isma'ili vision of time and prophecy bears little resemblance to any Arabic-Islamic conception of time. But it does manifest the effects of certain philosophical notions of time as a measure of psychic activity. It describes a cosmic drama which alternates, seemingly without end, between night and day, the hidden and the revealed, destruction and regeneration, public knowledge and law and private wisdom and gnosis.[91] It is clearly not a narrative of events but more like an epiphany, or perhaps a cyclic succession of epiphanies where time, nature and prophecy obey a rhythm set for them by their wise Maker.

History and the philosophers

Taking its cue perhaps from the famous remarks in the *Poetics* of Aristotle, the Arabic-Islamic philosophical tradition tended to regard history as a subject with little theoretical interest. It will be recalled that Aristotle, in comparing history with poetry, argued that the second was more philosophic and of graver import than the first because the statements of poetry

---

[90] Sijistani, *Ithbat*, p. 106.
[91] The Isma'ili theories of time are discussed with much sensitivity in Henry Corbin, *Cyclical Time and Ismaili Gnosis* (London: Kegan Paul International, 1983): see especially pp. 44 ff. and 176 ff. for a discussion of evolution and history.

are universal whereas those of history are singulars.[92] Scattered here and there in the Arabic philosophical corpus are remarks which suggest that the kind of knowledge imparted by history was of a low order, imparting at best a sort of belief or probability (*zann; ghalib al-zann*). In Farabi's *Ihsa al-'Ulum* ('Enumeration of the Sciences'), history is not mentioned at all but, in a passage we shall return to below in his *Kitab al-Huruf*, it is said to be one of the earliest 'crafts' (*sina'at*) evolved by mankind. The most articulate attack on the epistemic status of history came from Abu al-Barakat al-Baghdadi (d. *c.* 560/1164) who detected an inherent deterioration in its subject-matter:

The principles used in this field of knowledge cannot be demonstrative (*yaqiniyya*) since they are partial and relative to usage and custom, times and rulers, judgement and judges . . . and in accordance with circumstances and kinds of evidence about which there is no consensus among people as regards the manner in which they are perceived or known. Thus, he who personally witnesses and knows a prophet who institutes a religious law . . . cannot be counted as equal in authority to another person who narrates his history. The same holds true for successive narrators later on in various times and countries.[93]

But we ought to distinguish here between the philosophers' attitude to the theoretical value of history and their attitude to the relevance of the past. Here, too, they may have taken their cue from Aristotle whose *De Anima*, for instance, commences with a long review of earlier theories on the subject. Aristotle initially proposes to determine whether any profit may be derived from the views of his predecessors but ends by dismissing them all to make a 'completely fresh start'.[94] But the sense of indebtedness to a specific philosophical heritage was more dense and pervasive among the Arabic-Islamic philosophers. It was Kindi who first formulated the shape and extent of this debt to the Greeks by arguing that one ought to be grateful to earlier scholars, 'our colleagues and partners' in knowledge, for providing the means, unreachable by individual effort alone, whereby further advances in knowledge may be attained. Partly echoing Aristotle, he asserts that he will follow:

in this our present work our habit in all our other works, namely to review fully the opinions of the ancients . . . and to complete what they did not fully consum-

---

[92] Aristotle, *Poetics*, 1451b 39 to 1452a 12. Aristotle explains by saying that poetry deals 'with what such or such a kind of man will probably or necessarily say or do' whereas history deals with what, for example, 'Alcibiades did or had done to him'.

[93] Baghdadi, *Mu'tabar*, 1:274. Baghdadi may have been echoing an earlier and similar view in Ibn Sina, *Mantiq al-Mashriqiyyin*, p. 5, who divides the sciences into those whose principles are valid for all time and those whose principles are relative to time and place. But Ibn Sina does not discuss the relative sciences. A signal exception to this low view of history may be found in Abu al-Hasan al-'Amiri, *al-I'lam bi Manaqib al-Islam*, pp. 111–12, who finds history to be the subject-matter (*madda*) of all sciences, a viewpoint one might be tempted to label historicist. But Ibn Sina savagely repudiated 'Amiri's association with philosophy: see *Najat*, p. 271.

[94] Aristotle, *De Anima*, 403b 20–5 and 412a 1–7.

mate, in accordance with modern linguistic usage and the custom of the age . . .
citing our reasons for this and . . . avoiding the misrepresentation of many so-called
scholars of today.[95]

Ibn Rushd expresses a similar gratitude to philosophical ancestors,
expanding on Kindi's arguments while Farabi states that the only philosophical system worthy of the name is that 'handed down to us by the
Greeks from Plato and Aristotle'. It is possible that Ibn Sina was the
philosopher most willing to advertise his indifference to any divergence
between his views and those of the Peripatetics although he too acknowledges with gratitude the 'superiority of the best of them [Aristotle]'.[96]

Given the general respect in which Greek philosophy was held, the
concern with the history of the sciences seems to have been a very early
activity, as early as the movement of translation itself. The desire to understand the genesis and development of the philosophical tradition and,
more importantly, the ways and means by which it was 'handed down to
us' may have reflected a sense, not so much of confidence by its Islamic
practitioners but of isolation within an often hostile religious community.
These histories of the sciences served to propagate the view that the philosophical sciences had a very ancient lineage, were not foreign to Islam
and to the proper worship of God and should be received as a corpus of
wisdom accumulated and transmitted from nation to nation. One of the
earliest of these histories of the sciences, the 'History of Physicians' by
Ishaq ibn Hunayn (d. 289/910), sets out some of the more important
themes of these works such as the divine inspiration of the medical art,
the controversy as to whether it proceeds by experience (*tajriba*) or by
analogy (*qiyas*), its pre-Galenic phase, Galen as the 'seal of physicians'
(*khatam al-atibba*') and the post-Galenic commentators.[97] This is no doubt
a history meant to evoke certain parallels with the history of religion and
to lend intellectual respectability to its practitioners. In more subtle ways
it suggests a line of descent from ancient Greeks to the author's own days
intended as a legitimizing process for a corps of professionals many of
whom were suspect because they were non-Muslim.

From the fourth/tenth to the seventh/thirteenth centuries in particular,
the mental world of Islamic scholarship became inordinately receptive to
the idea that *Hikma* was a common human pursuit, at least among those
nations whose total natural environment distinguished them from others,
enabling them to devise the principles of the sciences or to practise the

[95] Kindi, *Rasa'il*, 1:102–3.
[96] For Ibn Rushd, see *Fasl*, pp. 9–11; for Farabi, see Muhsin Mahdi, trans. *Alfarabi's Philosophy of Plato and Aristotle* (Ithaca, N. Y.: Cornell University Press, 1969), para. 63; for
Ibn Sina, see *Mantiq al-Mashriqiyyin*, pp. 2–3.
[97] Franz Rosenthal, 'Ishaq b. Hunayn's Tarih al-Atibba'', *Oriens*, 7 (1954), 55–80.

arts and crafts.[98] Many histories of science and philosophy were produced; many discussions of the history and progress of *Hikma* are to be found in philosophical treatises. In most of these accounts, *Hikma* is noted for two things: it migrates from nation to nation and it disappears and reappears due to a complex set of causes. The nations concerned with theoretical learning were commonly said to have been seven or eight in number: the Indians, Persians, Chaldeans, Hebrews, Greeks, Byzantines, Egyptians and Arabs. Others, like the Chinese or Turks, excelled only in practical crafts or pictorial arts.[99]

Given the limited number of nations concerned with the sciences, it followed that the migrations of *Hikma* across time took place within a closed circle: from the Egyptians to the Hebrews to the Greeks; from Chaldeans to Egyptians to Greeks to Arabs; from Hebrews and Egyptians to Greeks; from Greeks and Romans to Arabs; from Persians to Greeks to Indians to Persians.[100] Behind these migrations lay concepts of time stretching ever longer as earth and cosmos became more intimately united in systems of thought and belief. Behind it too lay the attempts to identify the causes of intellectual progress and decline and linked now to several centuries of Arab Islamic history, time enough to provide their own examples of political and military advances and retreats.

Why do the sciences rise and fall? A range of explanations is offered, some having to do with the sciences themselves, some with their environment. Among the first, more proximal or intrinsic causes, Kindi implies that philosophy plays a key role in the progress or decline of the sciences as a whole. Thus, where philosophy declines, astronomy degenerates into astrology and then to idolatry.[101] Biruni (d. 448/1048) offers an Aristotelean model:

Turning once more to those who maintain that the world is pre-eternal, we say: they believe that the sciences and crafts are also pre-eternal and that the world has never been lacking in them. But if one wishes to avoid a rash judgement, one would have to say that they exist at times in potency, at others in act. That is because nations often experience circumstances which resemble annihilation . . . even if they are not totally destroyed. From their remnants rise some whose simple

[98] Most succinctly put in Farabi, *Siyasa Madaniyya*, pp. 70–1, from where Mas'udi derived, almost verbatim, his own ideas on the differences among nations. Miskawayhi, *al-Hikma al-Khalida*, pp. 375–6, is unusual in rejecting intellectual differences among nations and arguing that 'the rational capacity among all nations manifests itself in the same manner and does not differ in accordance with regions or times'.
[99] A typical account of these nations may be found in Sa'id, *Tabaqat al-Umam*, pp. 7–8.
[100] For these and other permutations, see, e.g., Sa'id, *Tabaqat*, p. 22; *Alfarabi's Philosophy*, para. 53; Shahrzuri in Uthman Amin, ed. *Nusus Falsafiyya*, pp. 146, 151–2, 161–3, 167. For suggestive parallels, see the magisterial analysis by Richard Southern, 'Aspects of the European Tradition of Historical Writing 2. Hugh of St Victor and the Idea of Historical Development', *Transactions of the Royal Historical Society*, 21 (1971), 159–79.
[101] Kindi, *Risala*, in Amin ed., *Nusus Falsafiyya*, p. 66.

lifestyle resembles that which obtained at the beginning. As they increase in number and in communal life the crafts begin to appear among them, increasing with the passage of time and becoming more complex until they reach their ends. Beyond all ends there can be nothing but ruin. Events then erupt in such a manner as to transform them once again from act to potency. Whatever the case may be, according to those who believe in pre-eternity, it proceeds in circular eras. But if you set aside plurality and consider only one of these eras you will find that matters run in accordance with those who maintain that the world is originated.[102]

Tawhidi, the 'Boswell' of the philosopher Abu Sulayman al-Mantiqi, quotes an opinion of which the master apparently approved, namely that a particular science may in certain epochs grow in strength and popularity to the point where religion itself commands its teaching and dissemination. Deduction and research (*istinbat wa bahth*) become so common that accuracy (*isaba*) predominates and error disappears. In other epochs the same science could grow weak and full of errors so that religion prohibits its practice. In yet a different epoch matters may be in a state of balance or equilibrium such that error and accuracy are equal.[103]

In all three cases of proximal causation cited above, the sciences are on the whole seen as obeying certain rhythms of growth and decline characteristic of time itself or inherent in the nature of science, as in Kindi's emphasis on the role of philosophy. But other explanations were also suggested which were less proximal and had more to do with the environment in which the sciences grow or decline. Shahrzuri (fl. 7/13), for instance, appears to believe that great royal figures acted historically as revivers of the sciences following periods of decline. Such figures as Hermes, Alexander the Great or the Persian Sasanid Ardashir manage, in the process of restoring political unity to previously fragmented regions, to restore the unity of the sciences also, so that sciences once scattered among many nations are reunited under one sovereign state and can once more flourish.[104] Abu al-Barakat al-Baghdadi linked the history of the sciences with the manner in which they are learnt and transmitted. Earlier scholars had communicated their knowledge orally to select groups of students who in turn purveyed this knowledge to later generations. Corruption set in once the number of teachers and students decreased, for the sciences also decreased and resort was had to books and commentaries. These multiplied so much that it was no longer possible to confine scholarship to genuine scholars.[105] Ibn Hazm divides the sciences into two kinds, those peculiar to a nation and those common to all nations. The first kind are the sciences of religious law, history and language while the second

[102] Biruni, *Risala*, p. 28.
[103] Tawhidi, *Muqabasat*, p. 134.
[104] Shahrzuri in Amin, *Nusus*, pp. 161–2, 167–8.
[105] Baghdadi, *Mu'tabar*, 1:2–3; cf. a similar explanation ascribed to Abu Sahl al-Nawbakhti in Shahrzuri, p. 160.

include astronomy, arithmetic, medicine and philosophy. As these sciences are transmitted some remain while others disappear leaving only traces but no principles, such as the sciences of sorcery or of talismans. For Ibn Hazm, the crucial factor is social need: a science survives as long as a particular nation needs it.[106] Finally, Saʿid (d. 462/1070) stressed the link between knowledge and political power. Speaking, for example, of the reign of the Abbasid caliph al-Maʾmun, he uses the unusual phrase 'the state of wisdom came into being in his days' (qamat dawlat al-hikma fi ʿasrihi) and compares the Abbasid to the Greek state when this latter was at the height of its culture and unity. Beginning, however, with the year 300 of the Hijra, Saʿid notes a decline in royal authority and the predominance of corruption and of the Turkish elements. This led to the neglect of the sciences because of successive civil disorders, to the point where 'the sciences are almost totally absent in our present day and age.' The only exceptions are small groups of scholars, attached to the Abbasids and other Muslim rulers, who still practise the sciences of astronomy, geometry and medicine, 'writing valuable books in which they devise marvellous results'.[107]

In this second series of causes proposed to explain the rise and fall of the sciences, external factors such as state power, societal need and the training of professional scholars are to the fore. But the most profound of all analyses of the rise and progress of the sciences is the one found in Farabi's Kitab al-Huruf. It is a passage of enormous value in intellectual history, without parallel in any ancient literature known to me and comparable in some respects only to Vico. The aim is to establish a universal paradigm of the evolution of the sciences and it proceeds as follows:

It is evident that the commoners and masses precede the elite (khawass) in time and that the body of common knowledge (maʿarif mushtaraka), which constitutes the basis of all popular opinions, precedes in time the practical crafts (sanaʾiʿ ʿamaliyya) and the kinds of knowledge peculiar to each single craft. In their aggregate, these constitute the body of popular knowledge, the first to be produced and attained by mankind . . . at a time when their souls are readied and directed towards certain types of knowledge, opinions and perceptions in limited degrees . . . Then, once words have stabilized in their meaning (istaqarrat al-alfaz ʿala al-maʿani) . . . similes and metaphors emerge . . . Hence the craft of rhetoric is always the first to arise . . . it being the earliest of the analogical crafts (sanaʾiʿ qiyasiyya) . . . At that point in time, the words of that nation become more eloquent than before and their language and speech are perfected . . . The art of writing is then deduced . . . by which they record in books what was difficult for them to preserve in memory . . . Five crafts are then found among them: the craft of rhetoric, the craft of poetry, the ability to preserve their history . . . the craft

---

[106] For the division of the sciences, see Ibn Hazm, Rasaʾil, p. 78; for social need, see Rasaʾil, p. 59.
[107] Saʿid, Tabaqat, pp. 48–51.

of the science of their language and the craft of writing . . . But once the practical
crafts are perfected, the soul longs to know . . . the causes of sensible things . . .
and this leads to the investigation of mathematical matters and of nature . . . After
a lapse of time, they come to discover the dialectical methods and these are then
distinguished from the sophistical, whereupon the methods of mathematics and of
demonstration are investigated . . . Matters then proceed until philosophy arrives
at the point it reached in the days of Plato . . . and is further transmitted until it
settles finally at where it settled in the days of Aristotle. Thereupon, practical
theorizing (*nazar 'amali*) comes to an end, all methods are distinguished, theoretical, popular and universal philosophy is perfected and no room is left in it for any
further investigation. It becomes a mere craft, to be learnt and taught only . . .
But once all this has occurred, the need arises to lay down laws and to educate
the masses . . . whence religion arises, by which the masses are educated and
morals are instilled and by which also they are held responsible for all things
through which they may attain happiness . . . If it happens thereafter that some
men come to contemplate what that religion includes . . . the craft of jurisprudence
emerges . . . to be followed derivatively by the craft of theology . . . Accordingly,
it is in this order that the analogical crafts occur among nations, if these crafts
proceed from their own inspiration and native intelligence.[108]

To complete this model, Farabi argues that the sort of religion which
follows a perfected philosophical edifice is the best. If the philosophical
edifice is incomplete, the religion that follows it is also incomplete. If this
natural order of evolution is disturbed by the transference of a religion
from one nation to another and *then* the arrival of a philosophy, tension
results between religion and philosophy.

In reflecting upon this model for the evolution of the sciences, one notes
to begin with the manner in which the history of the human sciences
recapitulates the evolution of human intelligence. A kind of amorphous
infancy precedes the rise of the individual intellect which itself then passes
from the literal to the metaphorical, from the practical to the theoretical,
from the philosophical to the educational, as if one is passing in review
the career of a philosopher-king, a great teacher or a consummate prophet.
It is a model which lacks historical examples because it is designed not so
much as a picture of a linear historical reality but as an account of a
process which can be, and often is reversed, a pendulum swing which
sometimes completes a circuit. Of great importance in this synoptic paradigm is the role of language, for it is language which through its various
permutations and refinements helps to create the possibility of abstract
thought and thus of the sciences. But mathematics and nature too, as in
Plato, are critically important as avenues to the realm of theory. Aristotle
becomes a resting place, a terminus beyond which philosophy cannot
advance, the end of the theoretical cycle. The philosophical edifice thus

[108] Farabi, *Huruf*, paras. 114–46.

constructed is prior in both time and being to religion whose highest principles are derived from philosophy.[109]

Farabi's model of the evolution of the sciences is paralleled to some
extent by his account of human political associations, but that account is
clearly more prescriptive than descriptive. For Farabi, these associations
are extensions of moral and psychological states of the soul and are not
seen in terms of a diachronic progress or regress but of what are largely
timeless patterns of conduct. A virtuous ruler, king or law-maker is seen
as the agent of the Active Intellect and prime mover of the virtuous city.
It is he who arranges it in ranks of service, educates its citizens and prepares them for true happiness. But the virtuous type of city is rivalled by
other, ignorant or corrupt or errant cities, with their various subdivisions,
arranged in accordance with their mistaken notions of happiness. There
is no hint in Farabi of any sequential process of transformation from one
city type to another and no reference to any historical examples.[110]   .

This problem of the types of cities and of their transformation was taken
up by Ibn Rushd in his commentary on Plato's *Republic*. Ibn Rushd
devoted many pages to a discussion of the degeneration of cities and also
provided examples from Arabic and Islamic history as illustration, going
far beyond Farabi's abstract and timeless theorizing. Following Plato, Ibn
Rushd posits five (or six) principal types of cities organized in accordance
with their guiding principles and their rulers: the virtuous, timocratic, olig-
archic, democratic and despotic. These types are historically mutable and
their mutations tend to follow certain patterns, for they are seen by Ibn
Rushd as lying on a spectrum with the virtuous city opposed to the despotic
and the other cities positioned in order of proximity to each end. The two
most historically frequent patterns of mutation are, first, the virtuous into
the timocratic city and, secondly, the democratic into the despotic. As
examples of the first, Ibn Rushd cites the transformation effected by Muʿawiya as the Umayyad state replaced the Rightly-Guided caliphate, and the
degeneration of the Almoravid dynasty in Andalusia. As examples of the
second he cites the history of his native Cordoba and the despotic rule of
Ibn Ghaniya in the middle of the sixth/twelfth century. In his own day
and age, most cities are said to be democratic, i.e. cities admired by the

---

[109] Farabi, *Milla*, p. 47.
[110] Farabi, *Siyasa Madaniyya*, pp. 69 ff.; Majid Fakhry, 'The Devolution of the Perfect
State: Plato, Ibn Rushd and Ibn Khaldun' in G. N. Atiyeh and I. M. Oweiss eds.,
Arab Civilization, Challenges and Responses: Studies in Honor of Constantine K. Zurayk
(Albany, N.Y.: SUNY Press, 1988), p. 94, argues that the type called the 'necessary city'
is for Farabi 'the primordial form of political organization'. There is no hint of this in
Farabi, at least not in his *Siyasa Madaniyya* where the discussion of the various cities
makes no reference to time or historical permutations. On the views of Plato, see Jacque-
line de Romilly, *The Rise and Fall of States according to Greek Authors* (Ann Arbor:
The University of Michigan Press, 1991), pp. 10–11.

multitude because they are imagined to be free but in fact are little more than a conglomerate of domestic households engaged in the pursuit of private ends. But the timocratic type is also found 'among us', presumably in Andalusia, and the public declaration of al-Mansur ibn Abi 'Amir is held up as typical of the timocratic spirit:

> Let whoever holds himself to be prince of the faithful command me to humble myself before them. By my soul! I shall be honoured by them for he does not honour the soul who does not humble and abase it.[111]

One other permutation is worthy of note, namely that between the so-called necessary city and the democratic. The necessary city is 'by nature' prior, being directed solely at the satisfaction of necessities such as agriculture, hunting or robbery. The democratic city represents an advance on the former as trade and attachment to private property replace the earlier and 'necessary' mode of existence. On the other hand, the democratic city itself can potentially become any other type since, like the fragmented soul, it holds within it the promise of both sickness and health.[112] In point of fact, one may understand Ibn Rushd as arguing that the transformations from one type to another are caused by psychic states operating at the level of society: inattention, greed, love of power, fear, lust and envy. The examples from Arabic-Islamic history and the frequent references to contemporary conditions suggest that Ibn Rushd intended his commentary on the *Republic* to have direct relevance and value in understanding and perhaps even reforming his own political community.

As one surveys the relevance of the past for the Arab Islamic philosophers, one detects a more tolerant attitude than the frequent mingling of history and fable by Plato or the curt dismissal of ancestors by Aristotle. The history of the sciences and the fate of cities held a clear moral for these philosophers. The first helped to situate their own activity within a particular time-frame, to determine the status of philosophy *vis-à-vis* the *shari'a* and to warn against a facile optimism in an endless advance of knowledge. The second helped to explain the genesis and potentialities of human societies and thus to warn against or to encourage the varied signs of disease or of health.

History as administrative experience: Miskawayhi (d. 420/1030)

'We are driven by nature to death, by reason to life': thus Abu Sulayman al-Mantiqi al-Sijistani (d. *c.* 375/985), a philosopher whose 'table-talk' has

---

[111] Ralph Lerner trans., *Averroes on Plato's 'Republic'* (Ithaca: Cornell University Press, 1974), p. 108. For Mu'awiya, see p. 121; for the Almoravids, see p. 125; for Cordoba and Ibn Ghaniya, see pp. 133–4.

[112] For the priority of the necessary city, see Lerner, *Averroes*, pp. 116, 128; for the democratic city and its material advancement over the necessary, see pp. 110–11; for the potentialities of the democratic city, see pp. 110, 128.

been preserved by an admiring disciple.[113] Abu Sulayman was an important member of a group of Muslim philosophers of the 4th/5th–10th/11th centuries who seem to have veered away from the Farabi tradition of metaphysics and political philosophy towards a more sustained concern with practical ethics and conduct, what Miskawayhi would later on call the 'refinement of character'. It would be hazardous to suggest historical reasons for this change in philosophical emphasis. The palpable collapse of the Abbasid caliphate, its replacement by a series of powerful *condottieri* in Iraq and western Persia and the subsequent restoration of relative unity and stability to that region by the Buyid dynasty are merely the historical backdrop to that philosophical shift. Perhaps more to the point is the fact that the very rapid fragmentation of central authority – Miskawayhi places this squarely in the reign of the caliph al-Muqtadir (d. 320/ 932)[114] – led almost at once to the scuttling of political life and the inrush of local power holders, each determined to consolidate or expand his power base. The class to which Miskawayhi belonged, the state secretaries and fiscal experts of the old caliphate, became even more valuable to the often illiterate strong men and in a better position to observe and counsel them. If, in the Greco-Muslim philosophical tradition, politics was ethics writ large, here was a situation which a philosopher could find amply suitable for the formulation of rules of conduct.

However, it is not at all certain that Miskawayhi did in fact subscribe to the view that politics, or political history, was macro ethics. And herein lies the significance of his vision. Miskawayhi was a prolific author, a philosopher of very broad interests, an accomplished poet and *adib*, as well as a universal historian.[115] With thinkers of such breadth, it is almost always tempting to plot their ideas as a refractive system, perhaps under the influence of a popular view of all medieval thought as a sort of ladder of being, a structure of parts and wholes, a complementarity of micro and macro. But this cannot be demonstrated for Miskawayhi. Towards that end, two of his works are singularly relevant, his *Tahdhib al-Akhlaq* ('Refinement of Character') and his *Tajarib al-Umam* ('Experiences of the Nations'). The first is a treatise on individual ethical conduct, the second a most unusual history of kings and notables, a long parable on the art of government. It will be argued that Miskawayhi's originality lies precisely in dissociating the first, or individual ethical realm, from the second or public realm, thus departing from the hitherto dominant Greco-Muslim philosophical pattern.

[113] Tawhidi, *Muqabasat*, p. 243.
[114] Miskawayhi, *Tajarib*, 1: 233–41.
[115] The most accomplished study of his thought is in Mohammed Arkoun, *Contribution à l'étude de l'humanisme Arabe au IVe/Xe siècle: Miskawayh (320/325–421)=(932/936–1030), philosophe et historien* (Paris: J. Vrin, 1970). The present analysis differs in some respects from Arkoun's.

The *Refinement* is a concise essay in six sections whose object, as defined by Miskawayhi,

is to acquire for ourselves such a character that all our actions issuing therefrom may be good and, at the same time, may be performed by us easily . . . This object we intend to achieve according to an art, and in a didactic order. The way to this end is to understand, first of all, our souls: what they are, what kind of thing they are, and for what purpose they have been brought into existence within us . . . what their faculties and aptitudes are, which, if properly used by us, would lead us to that high rank . . . and what it is that keeps our souls pure so that they prosper, as well as what it is that corrupts them so that they fail.[116]

Miskawayhi proceeds, in terse and functional prose so unlike the rhymed prose becoming popular among his contemporaries, to show how man can, by volition and education, train and accustom his soul to practise the virtues which alone can lead to both happiness and everlasting life. If there is one guiding principle in this curriculum it may be argued that it is an elaboration of the precept of Abu Sulayman al-Mantiqi, quoted above. Nature, defined largely as the collective temptations of the senses, is essentially deceptive, causing unhappiness and moral death. Reason, on the other hand, liberates. It brings man closer to the intelligibles and to the spiritual, freeing him from servility to the body and allowing him to pursue those higher ends which alone can truly fulfil him and bring him lasting happiness. Breaking with essentialist psychology, Miskawayhi believed that man was capable of willing his character, a position which may by contrast, and with many reservations, be called existentialist:

Some have expressed the view that he who has a natural character does not lose it. Others have said: No part of character is natural to man, nor is it non-natural. For we are disposed to it, but it also changes as a result of discipline and admonition either rapidly or slowly. This last view is the one we favour because we observe its truth plainly and because the former view leads to the nullification of the faculty of discernment and reason, to the rejection of all forms of guidance, to the surrender of people to savagery and neglect, and to the abandonment of youths and boys to the state in which they happen to be without any direction or instruction. This is manifestly very disgraceful.[117]

The *Refinement* pays little attention to the virtues of rulers or cities. Miskawayhi repeats the conventional wisdom that man needs society to perfect his virtue and that justice leads to the prosperity of cities while injustice destroys them. He also argues that the prudent man would do well to emulate the example of prudent kings: just as they prepare themselves to meet their enemies so too must the prudent man prepare himself against greed, anger and other such 'enemies'. Ideally, rule belongs to the wise

[116] Miskawayhi, *Refinement*, p. 1.
[117] Miskawayhi, *Refinement*, pp. 29–30.

and virtuous, but of greater significance is the view that the life of kings for Miskawayhi is an unhappy one because they seek blessings external to themselves and are not satisfied with what they have. He quotes no less an authority than the first Muslim caliph, Abu Bakr al-Siddiq, who is said to have sermonized that a king,

is indifferent to what he has and desirous of what others have . . . He shortens the term of his life and fills his heart with anxiety. For the king begrudges the little and is embittered by plenty. He is bored by easy life, and splendour ceases to have attraction for him. He does not learn by example nor has he confidence in anybody's trustworthiness . . . And after his soul has passed away . . . then God will call him to account and will be severe in reckoning and sparing in pardon. Indeed, kings are the ones who deserve pity![118]

Miskawayhi adds that his own experiences of the lives of kings bears out fully the sermon of Abu Bakr, even when kings are firmly in power. Their lot is a hard and difficult one, their need for money is constant, their anxieties perpetual, their aspirations unfulfilled.

It is at this point that one must introduce the history of Miskawayhi, entitled *The Experiences of Nations and the Succession of Endeavours*. In conception, it is a universal history, assuming an annalistic form in the Muslim era. In structure, it manifests a number of striking differences from the general historiographic tradition and has had no imitators. Let us begin with its introduction, in which Miskawayhi explains his purpose and plan:

Having examined the histories of nations and lives of kings . . . I found them to contain useful experiences in events which still recur and may be expected to recur in similar ways such as the origins of states and kingdoms, the later incipience of disorder, the measures taken to redress matters . . . or the neglect . . . leading to weakness and destruction. Relevant to all this are the policies followed in bringing prosperity to countries, unity among subjects, goodwill among armies, tricks used in warfare and the machinations of men, both those that were successful against enemies and those that backfired. Mention was also made of the reasons for which some men have advanced in status with kings while others declined.[119]

Warming to his subject, Miskawayhi finds that past parallels could be emulated since worldly affairs are similar. If these experiences are kept in view, they serve to prepare man for the unexpected. But common books of history are generally obscured by fables and entertainments, 'soporifics' without significance or wit. Hence,

I have collected this work, calling it the *Experiences of the Nations*. Those who stand to benefit most from it . . . are those who have achieved most worldly

---

[118] Miskawayhi, *Refinement*, p. 162. For the need for society, see p. 25; for justice and cities, see p. 104; for emulation of kings, see p. 168; for the rule of the wise and virtuous, see p. 105.

[119] Miskawayhi, *Tajarib* (1909), pp. 1–2.

success, such as viziers, army commanders, governors of cities and leaders of the high and the low . . . I begin . . . with the period after the Flood because little trust can be placed in what came before and also because what has been transmitted is of no value to my present purposes in this work. It is precisely for this reason that I have excluded the miracles of prophets and the plans they set accordingly. This is because the people of our own days will find no experiences therein from which they can profit as they strive to solve their problems, with the exception of human undertakings not linked to miracles. I have also made mention of events that happened by accident and luck, even though they contain no experience and are not subject to the will, doing so only in order that one may take them into account . . . even if one cannot avoid their harm except by recourse to God, or hope for success except by His succour.[120]

Here then is a history addressed primarily to the rulers and ruling classes, those who, if we are to believe the *Refinement*, stand most in need of God's mercy, are the most anxious and frustrated of creatures and are least receptive to historical example. In short, they are 'sick' and the *Tajarib* is designed primarily, not to educate them in virtue nor to bring them 'closer to the intelligibles' but to offer them practical examples of successful government. This is the novelty of Miskawayhi's intention and not his alleged attempt to turn history into a screen upon which are projected the virtues and vices of mankind.[121]

The *Tajarib* unfold according to a strict plan. Indeed, the plan is so strict that it is uncertain whether one can really call it a history in the normal sense. There is hardly any mention of sources. There is a conscious attempt not to be comprehensive. Within each year, there are very few dates by month or day. All history is subjected to his iron rule of utility: if an event yields no practicable lesson, it is quite simply, and very often explicitly, excluded. The *maghazi* of Muhammad and the early Arab conquests are prominent examples. Being in his opinion superhuman events in the sense that God Himself took a hand in the proceedings, they are of no earthly use.[122] What remains is a narrative made up of carefully selected stories, an anthology of historical events placed in chronological sequence but consisting entirely of 'experiences'.

It is in the details that one gains most insight into Miskawayhi's purpose and method. For the *Tajarib* are divided not only by years but also by sections, each carrying a title and normally one illustrative story. The most common titles are the following: an act of deception (*khud'a*), an act of cunning (*daha'*), a good counsel (*ra'y sadid*), an act of discretion (*hazm*), a trick (*hila*), a stroke of good luck (*ittifaq hasan*), a ruse (*makr*), a plot (*makida*). Between one power holder and another a *wahsha* (tension or

---

[120] Miskawayhi, *Tajarib* (1909), pp. 4–6.
[121] It will be noted that the analysis here differs from the otherwise admirable interpretation of Arkoun as set forth in his *Contribution*, p. 336 and *passim*.
[122] Miskawayhi, *Tajarib* (1909), p. 307.

crisis) often arises, to be resolved by a *siyasa* (stratagem). But underpinning them all is the axial concept of *tadbir*, the proper management or direction of public affairs, the ability to anticipate events, control their course and prepare the necessary resources to meet all eventualities:

> If *tadbir* is built upon perverse foundations, this will in time become apparent, even if it is at first imperceptible. It is analogous to a man who diverges slightly from the main road but this cannot at first be detected. Having walked a long distance, he leaves the road behind, and the more he plunges on, the more distant he is from the road and the more obvious his error and his divergence.[123]

Tadbir involves, to begin with, the ability to manage public finances. Much of Miskawayhi's history of his own times is devoted to a detailed narration of examples of financial mismanagement and subsequent collapse. This reaches a high point with the caliph al-Muqtadir, a spectacular squanderer of money to whom Miskawayhi devotes many pages and whose fiscal record he examines with the meticulous expertise of an accountant. He calculates that more money was squandered in this single reign than was ever *gathered* in the reign of Harun al-Rashid and concludes that the collapse of the caliphate was thereafter inevitable.[124]

The second aspect of *tadbir* is the military art. Here, too, the *Tajarib* record innumerable instances of military skill or the lack thereof, the tricks used in warfare, the importance of military preparedness and the value of a good spy system. Here, cunning (*daha'*) is of the greatest advantage, the ability to outwit the enemy, distract his attention or feign attacks and retreats calculated to deceive him. With this must go the patience and diplomatic skill necessary to carry through such military plans; otherwise, cunning is useless, as in the following example:

> When Bakhtiyar left Baghdad to fight 'Imran, he made it appear that he was out hunting . . . in an attempt to deceive 'Imran and in the hope that he would snare him into lack of caution and preparedness. And kings do indeed act thus, but with it must go perseverance and the patience necessary to exhaust the enemy with ruses that resemble what Bakhtiyar began by doing, not that such a policy (*tadbir*) would begin well . . . and proceed to jesting and frivolity, to the point where military power is neglected, the army is left unattended, gravity and dignity are abandoned and the enemy comes to know that the army is mutinous . . . and that this was why Bakhtiyar was forced to sue for peace.[125]

Story after story drives in the moral: that a strong treasury is indispensable for war and diplomacy. But government for Miskawayhi is also a skill requiring 'day-by-day and moment-by-moment' attention and supervision. To that end, any amount of money spent by rulers on accurate information

---

[123] Miskawayhi, *Tajarib*, 2:96–7.
[124] Miskawayhi, *Tajarib*, 1:238.
[125] Miskawayhi, *Tajarib*, 2:295–6. See a similar ruse that backfired in 1:282–3.

and reliable informers is well spent, in view of the enormous benefits derived. With government agents, a ruler should avoid antagonism and deal kindly with those who deserve it but should not hesitate to exercise utmost harshness with those incapable of reform.[126] Miskawayhi admired the resourceful ruler who can turn the tables on his enemies or reverse his fortunes with a clever *coup*.

In dealing with a thinker so deeply interested in ethics and justice, one must obviously ask whether the *Tajarib* are in any sense concerned with moral conduct. Miskawayhi was at pains to show, especially in the early portions of the *Tajarib*, that religion was essential to kingship. In the later part of his history, he frequently alludes to the way in which fortune, always understood as a divine agency, intervenes to rescue or frustrate the designs of men. And yet, one is driven to conclude from this strange historical anthology that government is not an activity that takes place on the moral plane, and that history can only be of value if it is abridged into a manual on the use and abuse of power.[127]

History and natural science: Biruni

Where Arabic philosophers, especially of the Aristotelean mould, tended to adopt a cyclical view of history and to believe that the arts and sciences also follow a cyclical path of evolution, each cycle ending with what Farabi called the 'perfection' of philosophy, the natural scientists tended to believe in the endless progress of knowledge.[128] The reasons for such optimism are fairly obvious: their sense of belonging to a tightly knit community of like-minded colleagues engaged in a common pursuit based on the continuous examination of nature and re-examination of each other's results united them in the belief that science was open-ended, that the shortcomings of one generation of scientists could be made good by the next.

It is this belief in the progress of scientific knowledge which may serve as an appropriate introduction to the work of Biruni. A scholar of immense learning, Biruni excelled as an astronomer, mineralogist, physicist and mathematician. Even more startling was his knowledge of non-Muslim religions and cultures: Judaism, Christianity and Manichaeanism. To all this he added a portrait of the Indian culture of his age unique in its

---

[126] Miskawayhi, *Tajarib*, 2:36–7.

[127] A very telling 'experience' in this regard is cited in *Tajarib*, 2:392–5, involving Miskawayhi and the Buyid ruler 'Adud al-Dawla. At issue is sparing the life of a personally virtuous rebel but Miskawayhi, who defends the rebel's cause to 'Adud al-Dawla, is finally forced to admit that good *siyasa* does indeed require his surrender to his former master, where certain death awaits him.

[128] For Farabi, see footnote 108, above. For the concept of progress in medieval Arabic Islamic culture, see my 'The Concept of Progress in Classical Islam', *Journal of Near Eastern Studies*, 40/4 (Oct. 1981).

accuracy because it was based upon first-hand knowledge of the sources acquired through learning Sanskrit. Fond of controversy, he was nevertheless intellectually tolerant and always ready to distinguish between the ignorant and vulgar defenders of a religion or cultural tradition on the one hand and the views of its scholarly community on the other. There was no doubt in his mind that the intellectual tradition to which he belonged was superior to all others, past as well as present, and that it occupied among them the position of an arbiter. But he was also of the view that these other cultures had something to teach his own, if only about the transmission of learning from one nation to the next or about cultures at comparative stages of development.

Shortly before he died, Biruni wrote a brief work entitled *Epistle regarding the list of books written by Muhammad ibn Zakariyya al-Razi*. The first half is a cautious defence of Razi, a very controversial scientific figure, and the second is taken up with sundry reflections on the history of science and a list of his own works. In his remarks on the origin of the sciences, Biruni sets forth two common explanations: the first asserts that the sciences were divinely inspired, each science having first been revealed by a prophet, while the second claims that man came to a knowledge of the sciences by his own deductive reasoning. Biruni clearly prefers the second explanation and argues that, given man's ability to reason by analogy, the merest hint of divine inspiration such as may be found in certain verses of the Qur'an would suffice to complete his education. He continues:

Once a beginning has been made, analogy is a continuous process while experience and reflection produce results and fill in the details. Time has a span traversed by succeeding generations where the achievements of ancestors are transmitted to posterity until such achievements accumulate and multiply. This is indeed true transmigration and not what is commonly referred to as such . . . for it involves the transmission of the sciences from those who have departed to those who follow, just as new books are copied from old . . . Given length of time and breadth of space, the principles of knowledge and action are thus accumulated by man.[129]

Biruni wrote two major works which may be said to have a direct relevance to historical thought, *al-Athar al-Baqiya 'An al-Qurun al-Khaliya*, commonly referred to as 'The Chronology of Ancient Nations', and *Tahqiq ma li'l Hind min Maqula, Maqbulatin fi'l 'Aql aw Mardhula*, commonly 'Alberuni's India'. Neither work is in any sense a popular treatise, nor were they intended as such. A reader who is not well versed in medieval astronomy would find large sections of these two works incomprehensible as Biruni fills page after page with complex calculations, calendars, tables and diagrams, since 'he who examines this work must necessarily be more advanced in mathematics than the stage of beginners'.[130]

[129] Biruni, *Risala*, pp. 22–3.
[130] Biruni, *Athar*, pp. 135–6.

The genesis of Biruni's 'Chronology' may be sought in the attempts made by Arabic-Islamic scientists and historians to bring some order into the chronology of ancient nations. In Chapter Three above, we discussed one prominent example of that endeavour, the work of Hamza al-Isfahani, to which Biruni himself often refers. In the two centuries or so preceding Biruni, spectacular advances had been made in astronomy and several astronomical almanacs (*zij*) had been drawn up which were regarded by their authors as clearly superior to anything that any previous nation had produced. This tended to fortify an already strong sense of cultural leadership, derived from a host of factors such as military strength, a favourable geographical location at the very centre of the known world and a feeling that Islam had consummated not only the world's religions but its arts and sciences as well. In terms of revelation, the most manifest debt was owed to the Judaeo-Christian tradition. Biruni's attempts to bring order and method into the chronology of that tradition were in line with earlier and similar attempts by writers like Hamza and Tabari. However, Biruni brought to this task the rigour and detachment of a professional scientist determined to examine the internal consistency of these chronologies rather than to synchronize them, as was most often the case, with Persian chronology. His intention, clearly stated, was the 'scientific determination of dates and not the criticism of historical reports' (*tahsil al-tawarikh la intiqad al-akhbar*).[131]

Biruni begins his 'Chronology' with an introduction in which he asserts that he is writing in response to the request of an *adib* who asked him about the chronologies used by diverse nations and the differences that arise among them. In reply, Biruni says,

The simplest method in responding to this request is to acquire a knowledge of the history of ancient nations . . . most of which consists of historical reports about them and vestiges of their culture and customs. But there can be no way to arrive at this through inference from intelligibles or analogy from perceptible sense-data. One can only adopt what authors of books and men of religion . . . have themselves used in this regard, and assume this as a base to be built upon later, then compare their statements and views . . . one to the other, after having rid the soul of diseases that prove fatal in most men . . . such as familiarity of habit, prejudice, feelings of superiority, surrender to caprice, vying for supremacy and the like . . . But the principle I have adopted . . . is no easy matter. Rather, its complexity and difficulty makes it almost unattainable in view of the great quantity of falsehood which has crept into historical reports . . . Nor can all such reports be judged implausible . . . In fact, if any of them fall within the realm of possibility, they are to be treated as true, provided other testimony does not controvert it. Indeed, certain natural occurrences may be, and have in fact been witnessed, the like of which, if reported from an age long before our own, we would judge implausible. A whole lifetime would not suffice to gain accurate knowledge of one nation's

---

[131] Biruni, *Athar*, p. 100.

history. How then can one aspire to know the history of all nations? . . . This being so, our task is to adopt the most readily available and most famous reports, taking them from their own authors, and to correct what we can correct but leave the rest as they are so that a seeker after truth and a lover of wisdom may be helped in dealing with similar reports and in attaining what we ourselves could not attain.[132]

The novelty here lies in Biruni's reliance on what the historians and scholars of various nations have to say about their own chronologies and his endeavour to bring order and coherence into them *on their own terms*. He soon demonstrates that the common chronologies of Jews, Christians, Magians and Manichaeans are internally inconsistent. Adopting only what he considers reliable eras such as those of Alexander, Yazdgird, Augustus, Diocletian and so forth, he devises a method by which one era can be converted into another.[133] Confusion is created when ignorant and zealous followers of a religion take it upon themselves to compute dates with the help of arbitrary and symbolic systems of calculation (*hisab al-jummal*) which can be manipulated to produce almost any result desired.[134]

But there is much more to Biruni's 'Chronology' than the mere tabulation of comparative dating. His purpose was not solely to bring scientific order into ancient chronology or to demonstrate the superiority of contemporary astronomy. He also intended to reform the chronometry of his own historiographic tradition and to show how it could serve as a standard for all others. But the careful examination of so many ancient histories led him also to distance himself from the extreme scepticism of many scientists of his age as regards reports of natural oddities. He refused to dismiss reports of longevity, gigantism or the jinn. Even more telling is his defence, formulated through reading the primary sources, of certain religious sects falsely accused by his own community of repulsive or immoral teachings.[135]

Biruni was thus by temperament and training particularly suited to examine the civilization of India. His portrait of that civilization, entitled *An Examination of Indian Doctrines, Rational and Irrational*, is an extraordinary monument of pre-modern scholarship, remarkable both for its anthropological detachment and for its first-hand grasp of the written sources. It is not strictly speaking a work of history, although it is deeply aware of historical parallels in the realm of culture. Above all else, Biruni seeks the truth 'for just as a virtuous character is found satisfying and desirable for its own sake, so also is truth'. To tell the truth requires a 'superior kind of courage, not the sort of courage that commoners think

---

[132] Biruni, *Athar*, pp. 4–5.
[133] Biruni, *Athar*, pp. 140–3.
[134] Biruni, *Athar*, p. 17.
[135] On oddities of nature, longevity and gigantism, see *Athar*, pp. 77–84; on the jinn, see *Athar*, p. 237; on his defence of certain religious sects, see *Athar*, p. 208.

is such when they witness bravery on a battlefield . . . but an indifference to death, whether in speech or act'. Where India was concerned, most books that deal with the opinions of religions and sects were either falsely ascribed to the Indians or copied uncritically from each other without reference to their true doctrines. At the request of a scholar who sought the 'plain truth, without prejudice or favouritism', Biruni is asked to

set down what I came to learn about them . . . And I did so, seeking neither to slander my opponents nor to be constrained in reporting their doctrines, even when they were false or reprehensible, for it is their belief and they are more discerning about it. Nor is the present work a work of polemics and debate where I marshal the arguments of opponents and refute those who veer from the truth. Rather, it is an account (*hikaya*) in which I reproduce Indian doctrines *verbatim* ('*ala wajhihi*), and to which I append similar doctrines of the Greeks in order to draw a parallel between them for, while their philosophers sought the truth, the commoners among them were bound by religious symbols and legal conventions. Nor do I report the doctrines of any other group along with theirs, except for the ideas of certain Sufis and Christians, there being much in common among them all in questions such as incarnation and union with God.[136]

Biruni then proceeds to explain the difficulties of his subject, beginning with the disparities of language, religion and customs. Comparison with Greek, Sufi, Christian and Arabian *jahili* beliefs and customs are frequent. The Indian caste system is identified as the single most important difference between Indian culture and Islam. But the overall impression created by Biruni's text is one of demystification: there is scarcely any area of Indian civilization which is treated as though it were exotic, outlandish or unfathomable. At times he seems to go out of his way to emphasize the familiarity of certain Indian customs as when, for example, he treats the question of idol-worship:

It is well-known that the character of common people inclines towards sensibles and shuns intelligibles, which are intellected only by scholars who in every time and place are few in number. Finding comfort in similitudes, many religions have resorted to image-making in books or temples, as the Jews, the Christians and especially the Manichaeans have done. Let the following example suffice. If you were to show a picture of the Prophet Muhammad or of Mecca and the Ka'ba to a commoner or a woman, such would be their joy . . . as if they had seen the actual object depicted . . . This is in fact the reason which lies behind the idols named after great prophets, wise men or angels, for they act as reminders of them when they disappear or die . . . But as the centuries pass, their original purpose is forgotten and they become a ritual and a custom. When religious lawyers entered the scene, it was through idol-worship, this being the most impressive aspect of religion. So the lawyers made idol-worship obligatory. This is also how history reports the ante-diluvian era . . . for it is said that mankind were united in idol-worship before the era of prophets began . . . Hence, as we proceed to report the

[136] Biruni, *Hind*, p. 4.

situation in India, we shall report their myths in this regard, having made clear that this is characteristic only of their commoners. As for those among them who seek salvation or are acquainted with the methods of disputation and theology and pursue true inquiry . . . they would not deign to worship anything other than God the Exalted, let alone His graven image.[137]

The distinction drawn between commoners and scholars is maintained throughout the treatise and is clearly designed to dispel any vulgar or crude notions current in his own culture as regards the true character of Indian civilization. However, as Biruni passes in review in section after section the various branches of Indian learning such as their theology, literature, geography, and law, the bulk of the work is given over to their astronomy and astrology and, here, Biruni was both admiring and critical. If there is one single overriding criticism of Indian science, it has to do, in his view, with the manner in which science and the religious law are intermingled to the detriment of the former.[138] In view of Biruni's own views on the genesis and progress of science cited above, it would be tempting to argue that he was indirectly addressing a problem which plagued his own scientific tradition.

In sum, and just as Tabari may be regarded as typifying *Hadith*-inspired historiography, one could claim that Biruni typified many of the salient features of *Hikma*-inspired historical writing that have been the subject of this chapter. True, he was not strictly speaking a historian but he was committed to sharpening the tools of the historical craft: through exact calculation in his 'Chronology' and by means of detachment and the comparative study of cultures substantiated from their original sources in his 'India'. Wherever history was touched by *Hikma*, it was left a more accurate, more law-like, more practicable and more comparative discipline.

---

[137] Biruni, *Hind*, pp. 53–4.
[138] See, e.g., Biruni, *Hind*, pp. 136, 196.

CHAPTER 5

History and *Siyasa*

The temporal boundaries of the present chapter lie roughly between the eleventh and fifteenth centuries. These are centuries immensely rich in primary sources, a fact which is itself a reflection of times considered stirring and even unparalleled by contemporaries. This sense of the uncommonness of the hour will be our starting point, for it serves to demarcate a new attitude to history among its practitioners. Whereas earlier historiography was largely an interpretation of a momentous past, the new historiography boldly projected its own present as being of equal if not greater significance. This tone is well captured in the history of the reconquest of Jerusalem written by Saladin's secretary of state, 'Imad al-Din al-Katib al-Isfahani (d. 597/1201):

I began this historical record at the beginning of the year 583 [1187] because histories usually begin either with the creation of mankind or with the succession of states . . . Were it not for history, the endeavours of men of sound policies (*siyasat fadila*) would all be in vain and praise or blame would not be the criterion by which to judge them . . . I, on the other hand, chose to date my history from a second *Hijra* . . . this *Hijra* being the *Hijra* of Islam to Jerusalem, undertaken by the Sultan Salah al-Din . . . History would do well to be dated from this year . . . Indeed this *Hijra* is of more lasting significance (*abqa*) than the first . . . My testimony is based entirely on what I witnessed . . . and I have been concerned to record only what I myself experienced.[1]

The background

One must explore, beneath the audacity of these words, the texture of events and mentalities which made them possible. For they clearly do not emanate naturally from earlier conceptions of the past and of its relationship to the present. In point of fact, they explicitly controvert the dominant scheme of Islamic dating and suggest the need for a new calendar, a new beginning said to be more important than the first. As is shown below,

[1] 'Imad al-Din, *Fath*, pp. 2, 5, 10.

this acute sense of the arrival of a new era was widely shared by historians who followed 'Imad al-Din. Their views will be explored as we attempt to reveal the period's own conception of its place in history. But first, what were the contours of this new age?

The arrival in the heart of the Arab East of military–feudal dynasties of Persian and Turkish origins, a process which began in the tenth century and continued in some sense right up to the twentieth, had far-reaching effects on the structure of power and social relations, and on the theory and practice of politics.[2] Then, between the eleventh and thirteenth centuries, came the terrifying onslaughts of Crusaders and Mongols, the memory of which continues to pulsate in modern Arab historical sensibility. Most of this chapter will deal with the repercussions of these fateful events as recorded by contemporaries. In broad terms, however, the increasing militarization of Arab-Islamic society, a process which antedated the Crusader-Mongol onslaughts, brought about stricter control over the lives of individuals as the total resources of communities became mobilized. The ruling military elites, having monopolized political power, constantly interfered in the economic, social and religious life of their subjects. A high degree of bureaucratization and hierarchization of society as a whole became visible, largely in order to facilitate such control. In turn, society itself began to show greater differentiation in rank and status among the various political actors: the feudal army, the judges and scholars, the state secretaries, the merchants, the urban gangs, the mob – and even the mob had classes.

At the top of the military–political pyramid stood the sultanate, an office which grew into maturity in the heyday of Seljuq power in the eleventh century. The sultanate coexisted with the earlier but now much reduced caliphate, intertwining loyalties and forcing a reassessment of the purpose and structure of political power. Where earlier scholars had debated the qualifications and legitimacy of the caliphate, later theory was more concerned with the efficiency of government. The ruler is perceived not so much as a repository of justice but as an instrument of public order. The consolidation of the sultanate brought into currency the term *siyasa*, meaning rule or governance, soon to be contrasted with *shar‘*, or religious law. In the discordance between these two terms lay the tension between the secular and the sacred, a tension more palpable than ever before.[3]

It is the argument of this chapter that a new historiography came into being under the umbrella of *siyasa*, most typically represented in what may be called the imperial bureaucratic chronicle. These chronicles were

---

[2] The best modern European introduction to this subject is still Claude Cahen, 'The Turkish Invasion: the Seljuqids' in K. M. Setton, ed., *A History of the Crusades*, vol. 1 (Philadelphia: University of Pennsylvania Press, 1955), pp. 513–27.
[3] There is a brief analysis of this literature in my *Classical Arab Islam* (Princeton: Darwin Press, 1985), pp. 103–15.

often voluminous, reflecting the historians' encyclopaedic attitude towards the subject-matter of history. The Mamluk chronicles, in my opinion the climax of this *siyasa*-oriented historiography, broadened to include the alpha and the omega, the *bidaya* and the *nihaya* of history.[4] In another direction, history became micro-history, regularly including economic and social data hitherto considered beneath the dignity of history. When one reads these chronicles one is often reminded of a feudal survey or land assessment (*'ard*; *rawk*) undertaken within a tight annalistic or dynastic framework. Archival and diplomatic material is more consistently quoted, lending these histories a documentary authority derived in a great many instances from direct experience of government among the historians themselves. These documents, with their epistemic finality, seem to compensate for the *relative* lack of interest in theoretical questions such as the veracity of historical knowledge. To these historians, historical knowledge is all knowledge that bears a direct or indirect relationship to the governance of *mamalik*, or feudal principalities. At the same time, biography interpenetrated history to the point where terms like *tarajim* and *siyar* became synonymous with *tarikh*. The vast Mamluk biographical dictionaries were built upon, among other things, the desire to 'survey' an entire cross-section or group of the community.

In sum, the connection between power and knowledge in this kind of history was pronounced. To survey, to comprehend, to control, to consummate: these are the verbs embedded in the titles of many works of history of that period.

Images of a new age

The intensely dramatic events associated with Crusaders and Mongols impelled historians and scholars to seek parallels which they often found in the equally dramatic events of early-Islamic history or else to judge their own times as unprecedented. In either case, this 'then-and-now' motif was a fertile source of historiographical speculation, re-exciting memories, demanding comparisons, relativizing moral and political values and instituting a quest for patterns of private or public conduct by which the community could be morally and politically re-armed to face the dangers of the hour.

There were, to begin with, scholars and historians who viewed their own times as utterly unlike anything that the world had ever witnessed before, a conclusion stated in its strongest terms by the geographer Yaqut al-Hamawi (d. 626/1229), normally a model of sobriety:

[4] Mamluk historiography has been the subject of two fairly recent studies: Ulrich Haarmann, *Quellenstudien zur fruhen Mamlukenzeit* (Freiburg i. Br.: D. Robischon, 1969) and D. P. Little, *An Introduction to Mamluk Historiography* (Wiesbaden: Otto Harrassowitz, 1970). Both are source-critical in approach.

In the year 616 [1219/20] there occurred events the like of which have not happened since the creation of the heavens and the earth. I refer to the arrival of the Mongols, may God forsake them, from the land of China.[5]

In a well-known passage, the historian Ibn al-Athir (d. 630/1232) wrestled with his own emotions as he attempted to express what was for him the most important event of world history:

I remained for a number of years reluctant to mention this incident, being in awe of it and loath to discuss it, putting one foot forward and retracting the other. For where is the man who can find it easy to announce the death of Islam and Muslims? . . . I wish I had never been born or had died before this time, forgetting and forgotten. However, while I hesitated, some friends had urged me to write it down. Eventually I realized that to abandon this task would be futile. To proceed, this section comprises an account of the most important event, the most terrible catastrophe, the like of which the stream of days and nights has never brought forth. It afflicted the world of creation in general, the Muslims in particular. If someone were to maintain that the world, ever since the Almighty created Adam and until the present time, has never been blighted by anything similar, he would be right, for there is nothing in the historical record that comes anywhere near it. Among the great events mentioned in history is the massacre of the Israelites by Nebuchadnezzar and his destruction of Jerusalem. But what was Jerusalem in comparison to the destruction wrought upon entire countries by the execrable Mongols, any city of which is many times the size of Jerusalem? And what were the Israelites in proportion to those who were killed? The massacred inhabitants of a single city outnumber the Israelites. Mankind may never witness a similar event until the world becomes corrupt and the earth passes away . . . Even the Anti-Christ spares the lives of his followers and kills only those who oppose him. But the Mongols spared no one. They massacred men, women and children. They cut open the bellies of pregnant women and killed the very embryos . . . Neither ancient history nor modern records any event similar to what happened with these Mongols, namely that a group of people would emerge from the frontiers of China and within one year would reach Armenia from one direction and approach Iraq from another. I doubt not but that those who come after us, following a long lapse of time and seeing this event recorded, would reject it and judge it improbable. And they would be right. Let them consider, however, that I and every other historian of my generation recorded this event at a time when everyone was familiar with it. So celebrated was it that the ignorant and the learned were at one in knowing about it.[6]

These were images of catastrophe. Not long before, however, and as we saw above with 'Imad al-Din, the mood had been celebratory, resulting in an alternation not unlike the one that obtained during the first Islamic century, its uplifting victories blending with the terrors of civil war. In the process, the historians were treated to a spectacle rich in relativism. One

[5] Yaqut, *Mu'jam*, 1:250.
[6] Ibn al-Athir, *Kamil*, 12:233–4, 245.

fairly common perspective adopted was to express thankfulness for having lived in an age where one could look back upon so much achievement, as occurs for instance in Abu Shama (d. 665/1267), historian of the Zengid and Ayyubid dynasties (twelfth to thirteenth centuries):

It was the Almighty's will that we should be the last of the nations. He made us familiar with the history of those who came before us so that we can draw the moral from the events of centuries gone by . . . and follow the example set by prophets and pious rulers. If it is God's pleasure, we hope to meet those among them who enter paradise and discuss with them the historical reports transmitted to us about them.[7]

Here, too, one meets an audacity, an omniscience which drove the historian to link past with future and to prolong his function as judge beyond the grave, and which must have derived from an acute awareness of the importance of his own days. It is as if the historians had come to play the role of the masters whose achievements they so minutely recorded, for they too had come to feel themselves masters, not solely of the past but of destiny.

The past often recalled for purposes of contrast by these historians was the period of the Rashidun caliphs and of the early Arab conquests. It may be convenient to call it the 'not-since' motif: not since the conquests of Khalid or Saʿd have such glorious victories been recorded. This is corroborated by frequent citations from Qur'an and *Hadith*, meta-historical vindications for such comparisons and intended to suggest that time has turned back upon itself to reveal, once again, a pattern of salvation. Thus, the conquering Mamluk sultans are said to have re-enacted both a splendid, divinely ordained history and a series of 'marvellous coincidences' (*'aja'ib al-ittifaq*), this latter being a frequent device to underline the uncommonness of the hour.[8] This was an age which, as ʿImad al-Din expressed it in his biographies of contemporary poets, needed to be rescued from the ravages of time so that it could be immortalized.[9]

There were other voices, no less impressed by the times but more concerned with the peculiarities of historical disparity. The celebrated poet Abu'l ʿAla' al-Maʿarri (d. 449/1058) had once pronounced all ages equally

---

[7] Abu Shama, *Rawdatayn*, 1/1:4. These sentiments were echoed some two centuries later in Ibn Taghribirdi, *Nujum*, 1:1–2. See also Ibn Khaldun's defence of the Idrisids: 'I have argued in their defence in this life hoping they would argue in my defence in the afterlife', *Muqaddima*, p. 25.

[8] For *'aja'ib al-ittifaq*, see, e.g., Ibn ʿAbd al-Zahir, *Rawd*, p. 474 and *passim*. This biography of the Mamluk sultan Baybars is full of allusions to the early Arab conquests. For comparisons with the Rashidun caliphs, see, e.g., Ibn al-Athir, *Bahir*, p. 163, and Abu Shama, *Rawdatayn*, 1/1:5. For comparisons with *all* earlier rulers and states, see Ibn Wasil, *Mufarrij*, 1:1, Ibn ʿAbd al-Zahir, *Rawd*, p. 45 and Ibn al-Tiqtaqa, *Fakhri*, p. 19. For the pattern of salvation, see Ibn ʿAbd al-Zahir, *Tashrif*, pp. 57–8, where the sultan Qalawun is said to be a chosen instrument of divine mercy and power.

[9] ʿImad al-Din, *Kharida*, 1:3–7.

myth-ridden: 'In every age there are myths (*abatil*) in which men believe. Has any age ever monopolized the truth?' No historian seems to have taken up the theological challenge thrown down by Abu'l 'Ala', for it was the political realm which was selected to display the nuances of difference. For the pro-Shi'i, pro-Mongol bureaucrat, Ibn al-Tiqtaqa (wrote 701/ 1302), the contrast between historical periods is seen most clearly in the political norms appropriate to each:

I argue that this speech [by the Umayyad caliph Yazid III] was suitable for that age and for the conventions current among its people. For these were the conditions considered by them as qualifying a person to rule. As for our own age, if some king were to boast that he will not dig a canal or build one stone upon another or charge his people to choose another ruler in his place, he would be considered foolish and they would concur that he be replaced.[10]

But for stern moralists like Ibn Taymiyya (d. 728/1328) and Taj al-Din al-Subki (d. 771/1369), their own age was one teeming with heresies and innovations (*bida'*) in thought and manners. Ibn Taymiyya wrote and acted as if a new *Jahiliyya* had overtaken the community, a resurgent idol-worship (*wathaniyya*) threatening to subvert Islam and the Muslims and driving them to imitate the beliefs and practices of Christians. His adopted motto for reform was trans-historical: the present community will not be rectified except by that which rectified it when it first began. To recapture the purity of origins has always implied, for Ibn Taymiyya as for like-minded reformers before and since, a willingness to throw out the 'baby' of the present with the 'bathwater' of tradition. In Ibn Taymiyya's view, *all* religious communities are prone to a decrease in adherence to the basic teachings of their prophets and to a subsequent weakness of faith. They are 'compensated' for this with innovations, heresies and polytheism.[11]

Subki, no less stern, did not, however, possess the radical creativity of Ibn Taymiyya. But in a curious, quasi-autobiographical work entitled *Mu'id al-Ni'am wa Mubid al-Niqam* (Restorer of Blessings and Extirpator of Misfortunes), Subki looked carefully at his own age and did not like what he saw. Neither the Mamluk military elite nor the scholars and professionals of his age seemed to be doing their duty. Much of the work was then devoted to a detailed, manual-like series of instructions, arranged in chapters each devoted to a profession, where ideal conduct was set forth. Only such conduct can restore the blessings of God and avert His displeasure. But Subki was also writing within a well-known literary genre which one may call books of comfort, works designed to reassure the disconsolate

---

[10] Ibn al-Tiqtaqa, *Fakhri*, pp. 98–9. The verse of Abu al-'Ala' is in *Luzumiyyat*, 2:177.
[11] For Ibn Taymiyya's views on the heresies of his age, see his *Iqtida'*, *passim*. For his 'motto', a saying of the celebrated Imam Malik, and the decrease of faith among religious communities, see *Iqtida'*, p. 367.

that God has not forsaken them and liberally illustrated with historical examples. Here the image of the age hovers between an ideal past which, although unmatchable, must yet be recalled, and a model of future salvation extrapolated from that ideal.[12]

Images of a new society

Orders and ranks are the dominant images in the historiographical constructs of this period. Each rank is carefully defined and distinguished from the others. This is not only how things are but how things should be: without strict social differentiation, political as well as moral chaos would ensue and the vicious would come to rule over the virtuous. To keep this structure in place, new emphasis is put by the historians on the value of loyalty and of keeping faith with lords and masters. It is an age of castle and siege, of principalities large and small constantly sparring for power, of scholars gaining in self-esteem as they approach closer to men of power or use the appeal of the sermon to sway the sentiments of the believers. We see the age, of course, largely through the eyes of the turbaned and industrious '*ulama*' but have little or no opportunity to see it through the eyes either of the military class or the immensely popular Sufi orders. It might be useful, therefore, to begin with a chronicle which is one of the very few that reflect the military elite's point of view.

The chronicle of Ibn al-Dawadari (wrote 736/1335) stands apart from other histories of the period in its lack of literary ostentation, its spontaneous, often comic, narrative tone, its relish for prodigies, dreams, omens and 'marvellous coincidences', its almost colloquial style and its unaffected reflections on history and the exercise of power. Where other '*ulama*'-produced annals end each year with obituaries of men of their own kind in most cases, Ibn al-Dawadari is oddly silent on the lives of scholars. Instead, we are in the company of the Mamluk military elite, as they march to battle or converse amongst themselves. This is anti-history, one of the earliest in a genre of popular historiography which in later centuries saw chronicles produced by barbers, farmers, minor state officials and other 'outsiders' to a discipline normally seen to be the preserve of cultivated scholars.[13]

It is primarily the portraiture of Ibn al-Dawadari, innocently capturing 'the king without his clothes', which arrays the age in a new light. Of all his portraits, that of the dreaded Mongol conqueror Hulagu is perhaps the most startling. We see him with his wife, smacking each other in jest as

---

[12] To the books of comfort genre belong such works as Tanukhi, *al-Faraj ba'd al-Shidda* and Ibn al-Abbar, *I'tab al-Kuttab*. For the unmatchable past, see Subki, *Mu'id*, pp. 20, 40–2.

[13] A study of the genre of 'popular' historiography would be a welcome addition to our knowledge. It might include the works of such people as the eighteenth-century Damascene barber al-Budayri or the eighteenth-century South Lebanon farmer al-Rukayni.

he catches her eyeing a group of handsome prisoners. This *tableau* of a domestic scene so unlike the terrifying images of the man in other historians, or else the story of Baybars lost and fleeing across the desert and coming to a wondrous 'green city', transport the reader to a different plane of reality unfiltered by intellectual prejudice or high ethical purpose.[14] For men of power, Ibn al-Dawadari displays a touching weakness:

The hearts of kings are sensitive to public affairs and the events of time, and this is why God has placed them in charge of men's lives. For they see the events of their age from behind a thinly transparent veil and gain God's approval by following rightly guided policies.[15]

The lessons of history for Ibn al-Dawadari are straightforward: kings who apply their energies to destruction last only a short time while those who build last long. This is because it is in the nature of life to build and of death to destroy. For usurpers of power he reserves an ironic tone:

Meanwhile, Time (*dahr*) itself was laughing at his arrogance and secretly devising for him something far different from what he envisaged, as if to say to him: Abandon those impossible dreams to which your soul has tempted you! The affairs of government have their own proper guardians and keepers and it is they who are entrusted with the management of states.[16]

Ibn al-Dawadari provides us with valuable clues to the importance that the period placed on the maintenance of rank and order. Perhaps most revealing in this regard is his description of a formal assembly called together by the sultan Baybars:

And there came into his presence the judges, lawyers and Sufi shaykhs, and they all sat in their proper ranks, *as was the custom with Seljuq kings* [my emphasis].[17]

The institution of rank

From the political counsels of Turtushi (d. 520/1126) to the cryptic pronouncements of the great Sufi master Ibn 'Arabi (d. 638/1240) on the stages of the soul's ascent to God, the scholarship of the period seems to be preoccupied with the significance of station and rank. Turtushi believed that it was a mark of sound policy for a ruler to maintain each person in the station proper to him and each leader in his customary position. In this manner, the ruler would gain their support for, without their leaders, the commoners are 'headless corpses'.[18] Ibn Fadlallah al-Umari

---

[14] On Hulagu and his wife, see Ibn al-Dawadari, *Kanz*, 8:53–6. On the 'green city', see *Kanz*, 8:26–8.
[15] Ibn al-Dawadari, *Kanz*, 8:344.
[16] Ibn al-Dawadari, *Kanz*, 8:357.
[17] Ibn al-Dawadari, *Kanz*, 8:201.
[18] Turtushi, *Siraj*, p. 338. Abu Nu'aym al-Isfahani (d. 430/1039) states in the introduction to his biographies of Sufi 'saints' that his intention is to distinguish genuine Sufis from false pretenders: see *Hilyat*, 1:3–4.

(d. 749/1349), author of a celebrated manual of administration, begins his work by praising God:

For having distinguished ranks and legislated laws . . . We praise Him for having created distinctions which increased the merits of the sciences and made known the differences among the ranks of pious men (*awliya*') who say: There is not one of us but has a well-known rank (*maqam ma'lum*). We confess that our lord Muhammad, God's servant and prophet, attained the nearest rank to his lord.[19]

Thereafter, 'Umari cites specimens of diplomatic correspondence with caliphs, sultans, emirs, and rulers of various specified countries. For each king and ruler, a particular mode of address is appropriate, including even the kings of Christian states with whom war was at all times possible.[20] The historian of Aleppo, Ibn al-'Adim (d. 660/1262), suggests that it was a sign of a ruler's consolidation of office that his titles would become fixed.[21]

With this emphasis on rank, the virtue of loyalty to lord and master acquired new prominence, wedded as it now became to what, for lack of a more accurate term, one would call a feudal structure of society. This structure, briefly, assumed one of its many shapes first under the Buyid dynasty in tenth- and eleventh-century Iraq and western Iran. The Buyids increasingly granted to their powerful military followers fiefs of revenue which these followers tended to abuse or even destroy to gain more lucrative grants as central power declined. When the Seljuqs in the eleventh century replaced the Buyids as paramount rulers, great Seljuq viziers like Nizam al-Mulk were fully aware of this danger and strove to implement a policy of stricter control over the granting of fiefs. The early Seljuq sultans made their grants conditional upon military service, attempted to disperse the fiefs in order to prevent territorial aggrandizement and enforced sovereign state rights such as the collection of government revenue. The decline of the Seljuqs and the rise of what Ibn Khaldun called 'branch states' (*furu'*; *'amalat*; *tawa'if*) such as the Zengids and Ayyubids was often accompanied by a revival of strict feudal land grant policies. Thus, Nur al-Din Zengi is credited by his admirer Ibn al-Athir with having inscribed the names of the soldiers of each emir in a register, together with their arms and riding animals, to prevent the emirs from reducing their number out of greed. His father, 'Imad al-Din, is said to have forbidden his emirs from acquiring private property, insisting that fiefs made it possible for them to dispense with such property and holding that this would protect the subjects from their violence and injustice.[22]

[19] 'Umari, *Ta'rif*, p. 2. For *maqam ma'lum*, see *Qur'an*, 37:164.
[20] 'Umari, *Ta'rif*, p. 64, citing the proper formula for addressing King Alfonso of Toledo.
[21] Ibn al-'Adim, *Zubdat*, 2:9.
[22] The literature on Arab-Islamic *Iqta'*, or 'feudalism', is extensive and there is a debate proceeding which questions the legitimacy of the use of the term feudalism in the Arabic-Islamic context. In Arabic, the works of 'Abd al-'Aziz al-Duri are fundamental. For

The chronicles of the period make it plain that warfare was largely an affair of sieges and fortresses, the major ones being entrusted only to the most faithful of military followers. The prestige conferred upon a castellan or *sahib al-qal'a* is captured in the story of a local strong man who was forced to abandon his fortress by Nur al-Din but was compensated with a lucrative fief. Asked later which of his two holdings was more to his liking, the man allegedly replied: 'This one brings in more money. As for glory, that we abandoned at the fortress.'[23]

The scholarship of the period, and more particularly the moralizing of its historians, reflected the gravity attached to feudal allegiance as war against the Crusaders tightened the grip of military elites. Thus, Ibn al-Athir lauds the behaviour of an *atabeg* (guardian of a young prince) for having faithfully discharged his duties of guardianship, contrasting the conduct of 'this solitary alien' with the injustice of many legitimate dynasts and their offspring. Regarding the founder of the Zengid line, Qasim al-Dawla Aqsunqur, Ibn al-Athir's verdict on his character is summarized in the phrase: 'As for his loyalty and good faith, it was honour enough for him to have died defending the interests of his lord and benefactor.' The historian of the Ayyubid house, Ibn Wasil (d. 697/1298), reports approvingly how certain Ayyubid princes resisted the temptation to rebel against relatives 'under whose shadow they sheltered', asserting that they themselves would be the first to suffer if they broke their covenant. Under the Mamluks, loyalty to comrades in arms, the *khushdashiyya*, was widely reported and praised, at least by pro-Mamluk chroniclers.[24]

Sultans and 'ulama'

The mirror of scholarship seems more closely to reflect the power politics of its age than was the case with earlier periods. The *'ulama'* had undoubtedly drawn closer to the sovereign. They had now become regular members of courtly circles, frequently employed on diplomatic missions and other state business. In times of chaos one occasionally finds them assuming a direct political role as leaders of the masses or even temporary rulers of cities. Finally, the vast financial investment in pious endowments

---

western scholarship, the article 'Iqta'' in *EI2* is the starting point as are the studies of Claude Cahen, traceable through the *Index Islamicus* and other works of reference such as Sauvaget-Cahen, *Introduction to the History of the Muslim East* (Berkeley: University of California Press, 1965). There is a clear analysis of the Seljuq feudal system in Carla L. Klausner, *The Seljuk Vezirate; A Study of Civil Administration, 1055–1194* (Cambridge, Mass.: Harvard University Press, 1973). For Nur al-Din, see Ibn al-Athir, *Bahir*, p. 169. For 'Imad al-Din, see Sibt ibn al-Jawzi, *Mir'at*, 8:190.

[23] Ibn al-Athir, *Bahir*, pp. 136–7, echoed in Ibn al-'Adim, *Zubdat*, 2:325.

[24] For the *atabeg*, see Ibn al-Athir, *Kamil*, 12:204–5; for Aqsunqur, see Ibn al-Athir, *Bahir*, p. 15; for Ibn Wasil, see *Mufarrij*, 1:18 and 5:73; for the Mamluks, see, e.g., Ibn 'Abd al-Zahir, *Rawd*, pp. 73–4.

by the Seljuqs and their successor states provided livelihood and power to thousands of scholars and students, thus entrenching religious knowledge as a career, a well-marked ladder of advancement involving teaching, preaching and the judiciary.

For their part, the sultans seem to have recognized the importance of the alliance with the *'ulama'* as they struggled against foreign enemies, internal heretics or domestic rivals. They tended to deploy their patronage in two main directions: towards the legal scholars of the four principal Sunni schools and towards the more devotional, activist and popular Sufi orders. From the legal scholars they hoped to derive the support of *shari'a* as they attempted to bring order and discipline to government and to project an image of justice. From the Sufis, they hoped to derive a type of fervent piety which would help them to mobilize the masses for the war against the infidel.

From both political theory and historiography one gains a more intimate and sustained look at the actual workings of government. Broadly speaking, and before the fifth/eleventh century, Sunni political theory had been expressed in two main moods or currents: a Hanbalite mood generally advocating obedience to the powers that be and idealizing the early-Islamic caliphate, and a Shafi'i mood with a more pronounced interest in the qualifications and conditions of just government. But beginning approximately in the fifth/eleventh century, the two currents drew closer to each other as both strove to accommodate the contemporary Abbasid caliphs within traditional theory, making room for caliphs with less than perfect credentials as well as for caliphs who could legitimately delegate part or most of their secular authority to deputies or helpers, such as the sultans. Historical writing, on the other hand, seems to have focused in ever-narrowing circles on the holders of power and in several notable instances to have functioned quite blatantly as an apologia for one dynasty or another.

The Seljuq state was probably the first systematic patron of the *'ulama'*. Later generations looked back with obvious longing on an age when,

From southernmost Syria, namely Jerusalem . . . and all the way to Samarqand, a distance of almost one hundred days of travel, there was not a single scholar, student, hermit or ascetic in his retreat but received the abundant bounty and largesse [of the Seljuq vizier Nizam al-Mulk].[25]

In return for such largesse, the Seljuqs attempted to impose a certain measure of doctrinal uniformity upon the Sunni schools of law, either through formulas of reconciliation announced as public policy or through the establishment of multi-legal colleges of law, *madaris*, where legal

---

[25] Turtushi, *Siraj*, p. 379. The number of beneficiaries is specified as twelve thousand in Ibn al-Qalanisi, *Dhayl*, p. 121.

scholars could hopefully meet and close ranks against the Shi'i 'heretics'.[26]

But the imposition of the will of the state in matters of doctrine and the often openly expressed favouritism shown to one particular legal school in preference to another created or reinforced tensions among sects, groups and ideologies. In the sectarian sphere, Baghdadi Hanbalism was probably the most vociferous between the eleventh and thirteenth centuries. The chronicle of Ibn al-Jawzi (d. 597/1201), himself a leading Hanbalite scholar and preacher, records a rising tide of sectarian violence which pitted Sunnis against Shi'is and Hanbalites against everyone else. The most palpable group tension was between '*ulama*' and Sufis and, to a somewhat lesser extent, between the '*ulama*' and the military class.[27] Many of these tensions, as we shall see below, resulted in a more aggressive historiographic tone. But the tension which concerns us most directly is the ideological: that between *siyasa* and *shari'a*, between *raison d'état* and canon law. It is this more than any other tension which, in this period, seems to have cast the longest shadow of all on the writing and conception of history.

Siyasa and *shari'a*

One of the clearest statements of the problematic relationship between *siyasa* and *shari'a* is in Turtushi's *Siraj al-Muluk*, a work curiously at variance with other writings on political thought and one of the earliest and most influential in a genre often called the 'Mirror of Princes'. History and *adab* rather than law and theology are its main sources of inspiration. Turtushi's introduction goes right to the heart of a dichotomy perceived by him to have existed among the earliest nations:

When I examined the histories of ancient nations . . . and the policies (*siyasat*) they instituted for governing states as well as the laws they adhered to for the protection of their religions, I found these to be of two kinds: legal ordinances (*ahkam*) and state policies. The ordinances, which included what they took to be licit and illicit and the laws governing such things as commerce, marriage, divorce and so forth . . . were all such as they had agreed upon by convention or mentality,

---

[26] For formulas of reconciliation, see, e.g., Sibt ibn al-Jawzi, *Mir'at*, 8:183, on the arrival of Nisaburi in the company of sultan Mas'ud; cf. Ibn al-Jawzi, *Muntazam*, 10:106. The sources provide abundant information on the founding of multi-legal *madaris*.

[27] The Hanbalite Ibn 'Aqil (d. 513/1119) argues that a legal *madhhab* should seek support, not from a state but from rational proof: see his *Kitab al-Funun*, 1:237. For intersectarian tension, see, e.g., Ibn al-Jawzi, *Muntazam*, especially vols. 9 and 10, *passim*, and Ibn Khaldun, *Tarikh*, 3:477 and 536. For tension between '*ulama*' and Sufis, see, e.g., Yunini, *Dhayl*, 4:318; Sibt ibn al-Jawzi, *Mir'at*, 8:24–5 and 61, and Ibn al-Jawzi, *Muntazam*, 9:168, where he criticises Ghazali for having abandoned jurisprudence for Sufism. Ibn Khaldun, *Muqaddima*, p. 441, says that the jurists of his day were divided in their attitudes, with some accepting Sufi claims and others rejecting them. But the *locus classicus* for this tension is Ibn al-Jawzi, *Talbis Iblis*, a work largely devoted to an attack on Sufism. For the tension between the '*ulama*' and the military class, see, e.g., Subki, *Mu'id*, p. 49.

there being no rational proof for any of them nor any commandment about them from God . . . nor were these nations following any prophet. The ordinances had simply been issued by the priests of fire-temples and guardians of idols . . . It would therefore not be impossible for anyone to enact such ordinances on his own initiative . . . But as regards the policies they instituted to uphold and defend these ordinances . . . here they followed the path of justice, sound policy, consensus and equity in obedience to these ordinances, as also in their conduct of war, protection of highways and preservation of wealth . . . In all these matters, they pursued a laudable path, none of which was contrary to reason if only the principles and basics had been sound or compelling. In their admirable pursuit of means to protect their corrupt principles they may be compared to one who embellishes a latrine . . . Hence, I collected together what is of value in their histories.[28]

Turtushi proceeds to make further distinctions, the most central to his argument being the one between divine or prophetic (*ilahi*; *nabawi*) justice and conventional (*istilahi*) justice. The first is the sum total of prophetic teachings; the second approximates to conventional policy (*siyasa istilahiyya*). No religion can exist without a state and no state can exist without some sort of justice. The first type of justice is ideally represented in a ruler gathering around him religious scholars, described by Turtushi as the 'proofs of God', without whose counsel the ruler should not act in any matter. As regards conventional policy, the arrival of Muhammadan *shariʿa* confirmed certain policies and cancelled others. Nevertheless, and in the final resort, what is most important for Turtushi is not the character of the ruler but the good of the community:

It may therefore be said that an infidel ruler who complies with the requirements of conventional policy lasts longer and is stronger than a believing ruler who in his own person is just and obedient to a prophetic policy of justice . . . for you ought to know that a single *dirham*, taken from the subjects in a negligent and foolish manner, even though justly, corrupts their hearts more than ten *dirhams* taken from them in accordance with a policy seen to be well regulated and of a familiar pattern, even though unjustly.[29]

Turtushi had seen in history vindication for the view that what ultimately mattered in the preservation of states was not the pursuit of an ideal justice but order and discipline based on equity. The gradual disintegration of his own native Andalusia may have been uppermost in his thoughts as the sad spectacle of internal dissension, even more than its Christian enemies, had come to seal its fate:

If you were to place in the scales a whole year of injustice from a ruler . . . as against a single hour of sedition, mischief and civil turmoil among his subjects . . . civil turmoil would outweigh the ruler's injustice and be more grievous.[30]

---

[28] Turtushi, *Siraj*, pp. 50–1.
[29] Turtushi, *Siraj*, p. 174. For religion and state, see *Siraj*, p. 188; for the two types of justice, see *Siraj*, pp. 170–3.
[30] Turtushi, *Siraj*, p. 157.

With a wealth of historical examples, Turtushi had stated in clear terms the case for a secular state, one based upon an orderly routine of government and working to maintain public peace and stability. A state well ordained and firmly ruled, no matter what the religion of its ruler, was infinitely preferable to one ruled piously but incompetently. In adopting this approach, Turtushi was bypassing a long tradition of political thought represented by thinkers like al-Mawardi (d. 450/1058) and Abu Yaʿla (d. 457/1065). These thinkers had, with consummate juristic skill, defined the qualifications of the caliphate and debated at length such issues as the degree of obedience owed to unjust caliphs, the status of usurpers and the conditions under which a caliph could be said to have legitimately assumed his office.[31] Where these thinkers were striving to construct a caliphate sanctioned by *shariʿa*, Turtushi was more concerned with *siyasa*, the skills needed to preserve and strengthen a state.

The debate between these two currents of thought was to continue in the following centuries. In broad and simple terms, the case for *shariʿa* was most strongly stated by scholars and historians like Sibt ibn al-Jawzi (d. 654/1256), Subki and Ibn ʿAbd al-Zahir (692/1292). The case for *siyasa* was stated, in very varied terms, by Idrisi (d. *c.* 560/1165), Ibn al-ʿIbri (d. 1286), Ibn al-Athir, Ibn al-Tiqtaqa, Ibn al-Fuwati (d. 723/1323) and Ibn Khaldun (d. 808/1406). In the course of that debate, history became an important battleground for it was to history that many of these thinkers turned for example and corroboration.

To capture the complexion of this debate, it may be instructive to begin with an anecdote related by Sibt ibn al-Jawzi. The scene is Aleppo in the year 613/1216. The ruler is al-Zahir Ghazi, son of Saladin:

On Thursday, we assembled in his presence, in the Hall of Justice (*Dar al-ʿAdl*). A woman was brought in who had falsely accused someone and had subsequently confessed her lie. Turning to the Qadi Ibn Shaddad, al-Zahir asked what her punishment should be. The Qadi replied that she was liable to disciplinary punishment (*taʾdib*) and added: she should be beaten with the whip in accordance with the *shariʿa* and her tongue cut off in accordance with *siyasa*. At which point I intervened and said: the *shariʿa* is *siyasa* perfected. To punish her above and beyond the *shariʿa* would be to do her a violent injustice. Al-Zahir bowed his head in thought. The woman received disciplinary punishment but her tongue was saved from cutting.[32]

The formula that the *shariʿa* was perfected *siyasa* (*al-shariʿa hiya al-siyasa al-kamila*) was one to which Sibt ibn al-Jawzi was often to return in order

---

[31] For the Mawardi-Abu Yaʿla tradition, see footnote 3, above. In calling Turtushi's thought 'secular', I must emphasize that he was writing very much within the Islamic tradition, especially the *Adab*-history tradition. Nevertheless, the Qurʾan was for him 'the mine of siyasat' (*Siraj*, p. 51) while the ethics he advocated, largely of Sufi inspiration, e.g. mercy in the ruler and patience in the subjects, all presume total obedience to the ruler, just or unjust (*Siraj*, p. 188). Uppermost in his mind is state preservation and not the integrity of the ruler nor his relationship to *shariʿa*, as in political thought of the *sharʿi* tradition.

[32] Sibt ibn al-Jawzi, *Mirʾat*, 8:580.

to express the view that state policy in his days was dangerously close to supplanting sacred law.[33] It was particularly galling for him that, to please their political masters, certain self-serving *'ulama'* would countenance such a flagrant violation of the law. For Sibt ibn al-Jawzi, there was no need to look any further than the *shari'a* for the conduct of government and the establishment of justice. To exercise *siyasa* was to admit that the *shari'a* was inadequate.

A century later Subki picked up the thread of these arguments and amplified them. In discussing the Mamluk office of chamberlain (*hajib*), Subki asserted that this office had once been military in nature but now carried judicial responsibilities. He admonished the chamberlain to refer all cases to *shari'a* because '*siyasa* is useless and, indeed, does harm to the land and people, causing chaos and civil unrest'. Warming to his subject, and claiming to have examined the historical record, Subki argued that the *shari'a* was the only salvation from the troubles of this world for sultans and emirs. The histories of *shari'a*-abiding kings and princes with their long periods of peace should be contrasted with the evil ends met by rulers who in their conceit imagined that they could reform the world by use of their own reason and *siyasa*. Returning to the chamberlain, Subki concludes: 'Now if this hapless ass were to say, how can I know any of this, being a simple Turk who knows neither Qur'an nor prophetic sunna? We reply: this will not excuse you before God . . . and if you do not know, you should consult religious scholars.'[34]

For both Sibt ibn al-Jawzi and Subki what was being undermined was not solely the *shari'a* but also the professional status of its upholders. Additionally, Subki was to make the startling claim that the sultan *is* the Great Imam (*al-Imam al-A'zam*), a title traditionally reserved for the caliph – startling because it is found nowhere else in political thought of any hue, but meant perhaps to bring back to the spotlight the old notion that the ideal caliph was in fact a kind of scholar. If the sultan could not be a scholar, he should at least operate under the aegis of scholars rather than throw them and their professional discipline into the shade in his arbitrary pursuit of *siyasa*.[35]

---

[33] See, e.g., Sibt ibn al-Jawzi, *Jalis*, p. 55: 'What many rulers neglect to observe is that they order what the *shari'a* does not permit such as the execution of one who should not be executed or the cutting off of the limbs of another who should not be so punished, calling this *siyasa*. But this is the height of error. For in saying that this is *siyasa* they are in effect asserting that the *shari'a* is incomplete and needs to be supplemented with our own opinion . . . The *shari'a* is perfect *siyasa*.' See also *Mir'at*, 8:195, where he praises the sultan 'Abd al-Mu'min of the Muwahhidun dynasty for having instituted in his realm both perfect *shari'a and* perfect *siyasa*.

[34] Subki, *Mu'id*, pp. 40–2. See also Ibn 'Abd al-Zahir, *Rawd*, p. 86, who praises the sultan Baybars for having himself submitted to the *shari'a* and thus encouraged all his subjects to do so: an excellent *siyasa*!

[35] For Subki's assertion that the sultan is the Great Imam, see *Mu'id*, p. 16. The view that the caliph should possess the attributes of a *'alim* is common in *shar'i* political thought,

By other scholars and historians, the term *siyasa* was used in three primary senses: to denote effective (or ineffective) state policy, to describe acts of government lying outside the *shari'a* or, in a more nuanced sense, to denote an independent art whose object is the preservation of the state. It is perhaps noteworthy that four of these scholars and historians who used the term *siyasa* in any of its senses were writing for or under non-Muslim kings or were themselves non-Muslim: Idrisi, Ibn al-Fuwati, Ibn al-Tiqtaqa and Ibn al-'Ibri. Idrisi lavished praise upon his patron Roger of Sicily 'in whom all *siyasat* reach their ultimate end'. A little later, and describing the abysmal ignorance of the inhabitants of the first region (*iqlim*) of the earth, Idrisi states that their kings 'acquire *siyasa* and justice through instruction received from people who reach them from the third or fourth regions and such as have read the histories and stories of kings'. Ibn al-Fuwati, writing in early Mongol Iraq and in an obituary notice on Hulagu, describes him as a man 'of high ambition and renowned *siyasa*, one who knew the intimate affairs of government and was unsurpassed in perspicacity, greatness of courage and unconquerable *siyasa*'. In fact, *siyasa* is a term he uses regularly to denote either extra-*shari'a* acts by the state or public policy in a general sense.[36]

All these scholars and historians used *siyasa* in its first two senses, namely to signify state policy or acts lying outside the scope of *shari'a*. But Ibn al-Tiqtaqa and Ibn Khaldun deserve separate consideration for their view of *siyasa* as a distinct art of government. Writing for a high Mongol functionary, Ibn al-Tiqtaqa claims that his work aims to expound those '*siyasa* and modes of conduct (*adab*) which are of use in dealing with great events . . . with governing subjects, protecting the realm and reforming character'. More significantly, he argues that the Mongols were specialists in the science of *siyasa*:

Regarding the kings of the Persians, their sciences consisted of wisdom literature, political counsel, ethics, history, geometry and similar subjects. As for the sciences of the kings of Islam, these were the sciences of language such as grammar, philology, poetry and history . . . But in the Mongol state all these sciences were shunned and other sciences found a ready market, namely the science (*'ilm*) of *siyasa* and of arithmetic to regulate the finances of the state and control income and expenditure, and the science of medicine to preserve bodily health.[37]

Siyasa is described as the 'capital' (*ra's mal*) of kingship: essential in preventing bloodshed, protecting wealth and chastity, suppressing crime and

---

especially of the Shafiite tradition as in, e.g., Mawardi and Ghazali. For an echo of this among historians, see Ibn al-Athir, *Bahir*, p. 165, praising Nur al-Din.

[36] For Idrisi on Roger and on the first region, see *Nuzhat*, pp. 4 and 98, respectively. For Ibn al-Fuwati on Hulagu, see *Hawadith*, p. 353. For *siyasa* as public policy and as extra-*shari'a* acts, see *Hawadith*, pp. 485 and 217–18, respectively. For other uses of *siyasa*, see Ibn al-'Ibri, *Tarikh*, p. 359 (the good *siyasa* of 'Imad al-Din Zengi bringing prosperity to Mosul) and Ibn al-Athir, *Kamil*, 11:65 (bad *siyasa* to destroy the city of Edessa).

[37] Ibn al-Tiqtaqa, *Fakhri*, p. 12. For his purpose in writing, see *Fakhri*, p. 11.

preventing the injustices which lead to civil unrest and social turmoil.[38] The *shariʿa* is conspicuously absent from his analysis of government, though not the general ethical principles which the *shariʿa* teaches in common with the ethical wisdom of other nations. But it is clear that for Ibn al-Tiqtaqa, *siyasa* is an independent 'science' of government with its own rules of procedure which need to be adapted, unlike the broad egalitarianism of *shariʿa* justice, to the circumstances of class and rank:

For every class of subjects there is a special mode of *siyasa*. The nobles are ruled (*yusasun*) with noble conduct and kind counsel. The middle classes are ruled with a mixture of blandishment (*raghba*) and intimidation (*rahba*). The commoners are ruled with intimidation . . . The king in relation to his subjects is like a doctor and his patient.[39]

In his history, Ibn Khaldun faces the problem of *shariʿa* and *siyasa* when he arrives in his narrative at the end of the period of the Rashidun caliphs and the beginning of Umayyad rule. Here was a dilemma which many historians and political thinkers had faced before him: in what sense was Muʿawiya, the first of the line, a continuator of the earlier caliphate of the Rashidun? How legitimate was his caliphate when compared to theirs? Shiʿi historians like Yaʿqubi and Masʿudi had dismissed Muʿawiya's rule as *mulk*, kingship, a term which carried distinct connotations of wilfulness and usurpation. Even early pious Sunni circles in Medina and elsewhere were unwilling to regard Umayyad rule as being on the same level of legitimacy as the earlier, increasingly idealized caliphate, as witnessed by its title of 'rightly-guided' (*rashida*; *rashidun*). The wide circulation of a prophetic *hadith* to the effect that the caliphate would last for only thirty years after which there would be *mulk* was obviously designed to coincide with the coming to power of Muʿawiya and to exclude him and his dynasty from the legitimate caliphate. Muʿawiya was therefore a yardstick against which historians and others came to define their standpoint as regards the course of Islamic history and the question of legitimate government. This in brief is the background to the following discussion of the issue by Ibn Khaldun, one which will be cited at some length because of its central importance with respect to the tension between *siyasa* and *shariʿa* and the effect of that tension on historical writing:

This brings to an end our discussion of the Islamic caliphate with its Wars of Apostasy, conquests and other wars as well as the agreement and reunification of the community . . . I ought to have appended Muʿawiya's state and history to the state and history of the [Rashidun] caliphs, for he comes next to them in virtue, justice and companionship of the Prophet. And in this regard, no consideration

[38] Ibn al-Tiqtaqa, *Fakhri*, p. 16.
[39] Ibn al-Tiqtaqa, *Fakhri*, p. 29. For a typical critique of a common saying about the interconnection between *siyasat*, see *Fakhri*, p. 36.

should be given to the *hadith* that 'the caliphate after me will last thirty years', for it is not a sound *hadith*. In truth, Mu'awiya belongs among those caliphs but historians of that period have placed him in a later age for two reasons: first, the caliphate of Mu'awiya's time was one of a struggle for power (*mughalaba*) issuing from the partisanship (*'asabiyya*) which occurred in his days whereas before then the caliphate was a matter of choice and consensus. Historians thus distinguished between the two cases, Mu'awiya being the first to arrive at the caliphate through the struggle for power and partisanship. These caliphs are called 'kings' by Muslim sectarians . . . God forbid that Mu'awiya should be compared to anyone who followed him for he is one of the Rashidun caliphs. Whoever came next to him in piety and virtue from among the Marwanid caliphs is to be judged in similar fashion [i.e. as a legitimate caliph] as also the later caliphs of the Abbasid line. It must not be said: kingship (*mulk*) is lower in rank than the caliphate so how can a caliph be king? You must realize that the type of kingship which opposes, even negates, the caliphate is tyranny (*jabarutiyya*), also called *kisrawiyya* [Kisra = the Persian Chosroes], such as the caliph 'Umar found objectionable when he saw its symptoms appearing in Mu'awiya. As for kingship which is [the result of] the struggle for power and victory achieved through partisanship and sheer force, this is not the antithesis, either of the caliphate or of prophethood. Indeed, Solomon and his father, David, were . . . both prophets and kings . . . Mu'awiya did not seek kingship or its splendour from motives of worldly greed but was driven to it by the very nature of partisanship when the Muslims had conquered all states and he was their caliph. He merely summoned his people to that which all kings summon their peoples whenever partisanship becomes intense and creates the natural need for kingship, as was also the case with later and pious caliphs . . . The law here is to compare their acts with sound historical reports . . . If these acts conform to such reports, then the person is a successor (*khalifa*) of the Prophet in rule over the Muslims. If they do not, then he is a worldly king and called a caliph only metaphorically. The second reason for listing Mu'awiya with the Umayyad caliphs rather than with the first four is that the Umayyads constitute one line, Mu'awiya being its senior member, so he was placed with his line . . . So the caliphate did not pass to another person nor did he have a rival. Thus, his power and authority were firmly established . . . and he remained in power and in his caliphate for twenty years, spending from the merchandise (*bida'a*) of *siyasa*, and no potential contender for the caliphate . . . would have achieved more success at this than he did.[40]

Reflecting upon these passages by Ibn al-Tiqtaqa and Ibn Khaldun, one would register the importance that the question of *siyasa* had come to hold in historical judgement and perspective. If a special skill was in fact needed to govern states, a skill which was parallel to, but not necessarily identical with either the *shari'a* or accepted ethical-prophetic principles, and this could be demonstrated by historical examples, a new set of criteria to revise and understand the past would need to be employed. Power was of

---

[40] Ibn Khaldun, *Tarikh*, 2/2:187–8, 3:4.

the very nature of kingship and was not in and of itself either good or evil. Only the motives of its holder and the manner in which it functioned could be questioned on ethical grounds.

First Ibn al-Tiqtaqa and then Ibn Khaldun had turned the arts and sciences loose in the market-place. Among these sciences, *siyasa* had by now reached maturity. It was a commodity much in demand. Historians who knew or thought they knew something about the affairs of state were more willing than ever to hawk their merchandise and dispense words of counsel.

History and self-consciousness

But who *were* the historians of this period? Unsurprisingly, the histories and other works of scholarship contain a larger body of autobiographical material than ever before. The explanation lies in the changing role of the '*ulama*' in society, alluded to above, and its effect on historical writing and perceptions. As in earlier ages the historians were in their majority drawn from the ranks of religious scholars and the senior bureaucracy. Nor was there anything new in the self-importance felt by the '*ulama*' or their elevated opinion of their role in history.[41] What was new was the high profile that these classes had acquired or been given: as propagandists for the state, as regular recipients of state largesse or beneficiaries of private endowments, as frequent employees on state business, as public preachers. One detects in these historians a greater measure of self-consciousness, with their own contribution to history considered worthy of mention alongside the exploits of lords and masters. But there is also a deliberate distance that they put between themselves and their subject, a pose of objectivity and authority derived from the 'I saw' or 'I witnessed' or 'I was told by the sultan' which often upheld their narrative. They were now more likely to fancy themselves as actors on a stage which they once had only observed.

But let us first note the creeping intrusion of autobiography. Typical in this sphere are the histories of Ibn al-Jawzi and Abu'l Fida (d. 732/1331), Prince of Hama. The specifics recorded include such things as their dates of birth, details of their early and adult lives and extended comments on contemporary figures encountered, in censure or esteem. All of these are displayed as historical episodes, worthy of mention as features of 'events' reported under the years of their annals. Ibn al-Jawzi chronicles his rise to public prominence with the passage of years until, at the acme of fame, he notes how countless thousands attended his sermons, how 'more than

---

[41] See, e.g., Tanukhi, *Nishwar*, p. 114, quoting the view that the decline of the Abbasids was precipitated by the collapse of the judiciary, and Suli, *Akhbar al-Radi*, p. 212, defending the inclusion of obituary notices of '*ulama*' in his history.

a hundred thousand people repented at my hands . . . and no other preacher had ever collected such crowds'. Regarding one of his enemies called Murjan, recently deceased, he reports how a friend, hastening to add 'a pious man', had told him that he saw Murjan in a dream being led away by two people. Asked where they were leading him, the two men replied: 'To hell because he hated Ibn al-Jawzi.' The universal history of the Ayyubid prince Abu'l Fida grows more autobiographical as he approaches his own days. The greatest ambition of his life was the recovery of his ancestral principality of Hama and he records in minute detail the frustrations encountered at every turn from the Mamluks. When he finally achieves his life-long objective, he launches into an aside on the history of Hama and its governors, from Biblical times until the days of 'this humble servant'.[42]

There are other signs of the historian's ego underpinning the narrative. The use of 'I say' (*qultu*) to interrupt the narrative and introduce the historian's personal comments or opinions on people and events becomes frequent enough to be noticeable. From this there flowed the temptation, to which several historians succumbed, of being wise after the event. This took the form of speculation about what might have happened 'if only' (*law*) this or that sultan or ruler had taken this or that action, the implication being that, as guardians of the past, historians should be more frequently consulted on its lessons.[43]

Of all men, sultans are most in need of homily (*maw'iza*) because:

with splendour, authority, joy, wealth, and enforcement of all orders and prohibitions, the soul comes to suffer from a condition akin to inebriation. The need then arises for an antidote in the form of admonition and fright so that the cure can be effective, just as a patient suffering from chill needs to be treated with heat in order to counterbalance his condition.[44]

As the homily reached new levels of public prominence, so the scholars and historians who practised it came to feel that they were specially privileged to admonish rulers and to play a leading role in mobilizing public opinion. One detects traces of this self-assurance in the harsh comments that some historians direct against the conduct of Muslim rulers. Ibn al-Athir is a particularly notable example of this harshness, but other historians also adopted a deploring or condescending tone as they assessed the performance of contemporary rulers:

---

[42] See Ibn al-Jawzi, *Muntazam*, 10:284, on his sermons; on Murjan, see *Muntazam*, 10:213. For further examples, see *Muntazam*, 9:252 and 10:47. For Abu'l Fida, see *Mukhtasar*, 4:8, 21, 24, 49–50, 57, 60–2, 68, 70, 87 and *passim*. See also Sibt ibn al-Jawzi, *Mir'at*, 8:464, 580, 604, 619, 656, 662 and *passim*.

[43] The interruptive *qultu* is particularly noticeable in Sibt ibn al-Jawzi and Ibn Taghribirdi. For 'if only', see, e.g., Ibn al-Athir, *Kamil*, 11:282–3; Ibn Wasil, *Mufarrij*, 5:297; Yunini, *Dhayl*, 1:143.

[44] Sibt ibn al-Jawzi, *Jalis*, p. 39.

In reporting the histories of the sultans of the past and of the present, I deliberately omitted to mention their regnal titles and appellations in order to avoid repeating them all and thus padding my history. No past work of history or of scholarship was ever wont to cite these titles. In the past, the rule was to discard all such titles, and scholars considered them objectionable.[45]

In the opinion of Ibn al-Qalanisi, it was the Buyids and the Seljuqs who popularized the use of such lengthy titles. He proceeds to cite ludicrous examples of rulers whose power bore no relationship to the magnificence of their titles.[46]

The public career of Ibn Taymiyya, his fervent belief in a 'pious remnant' appointed to guide the community from one generation to the next, and his constant interference and participation in political and military affairs, illustrates the extent to which scholars had become conscious of their power and public responsibility. Some historians cast envious eyes at North African dynasties where the *'ulama'* were said to have been put in charge of armies. The North African Ibn Tumart (d. 524/1130), founder of the Muwahhidun dynasty, is reported to have consulted the celebrated Ghazali before he set out on his mission of reform and, ultimately, of state-building. A scholarly vizier like Ibn al-'Amid is said to have taught *siyasa* to his Buyid master, 'Adud al-Dawla, while the Fatimids, alarmed at the growing power of the *'ulama'* among the people, are reported to have banished all *'ulama'* from their domains.[47]

But the closer awareness of their own societal role and of their impact on public affairs also brought about a greater measure of division and mutual stricture among the historians themselves. Sibt ibn al-Jawzi speaks of two antagonistic 'schools' of historians, the Baghdadis and the Shamis, with Ibn al-Qalanisi seemingly the leader of the latter. Ibn al-Athir

---

[45] Ibn al-Qalanisi, *Dhayl*, p. 283. See also Ibn al-Athir, *Kamil*, 12:324–5 (the conduct of Muslim kings is more alarming than the enemy); Ibn 'Idhari, *Bayan*, 1:4 (asking God's forgiveness for Muslim kings fighting amongst themselves). For the sultan's need for preachers to mobilize public opinion, see Sibt ibn al-Jawzi, *Mir'at*, 8:604.

[46] Ibn al-Qalanisi, *Dhayl*, p. 284.

[47] For Ibn Taymiyya's views on the 'pious remnant', see his *K. al-Nubuwwat*, pp. 91–2. His belief in *ijtihad* (independent legal reasoning) was the most important of his legal views. It is remarkable that Ibn Taymiyya was not interested in preserving the caliphate even as a symbol of unity but rather in the unity of the community. The attitude of the *'ulama'* is to aid the ruler in power until he is overthrown, a widespread view in the Mamluk period: see his *Minhaj al-Sunna*, written in response to the Shi'i Hilli's *Minhaj al-Karama*. Typical of his active interest in political and strategic affairs is his *Risala ila al-Sultan al-Malik al-Nasir fi sha'n al-Tatar*, where he advises the sultan to go on the offensive against the Mongols since the enemy should not, according to the *shari'a*, be allowed to cross into Muslim territory. For envy of North African dynasties, see Sibt ibn al-Jawzi, *Mir'at*, 8:749. For Ibn Tumart and Ghazali, see Ibn Khaldun, *Tarikh*, 6:226. For Ibn al-'Amid, see Ibn Khaldun, *Tarikh*, 4:446. For Fatimids and *'ulama'*, see Ibn al-Jawzi, *Muntazam*, 9:16. Perhaps sensing the growing ambitions of the *'ulama'*, Ghazali argued that *'ulama'* have degrees of happiness and rank which they must not overreach: see *Mi'yar*, pp. 66–7.

attacked Ibn al-Jawzi for his Hanbalite prejudice and al-'Imad al-Isfahani for his exaggeration. Ibn Khaldun asserted that many historians were guilty of calumny against the Companions of the Prophet. Ibn Taghribirdi ascribed Maqrizi's hostility to the Mamluks to his fall from their favour. In general, it became quite common for historians to regard themselves as champions of various causes:

I copied the following anecdote from the writing of Ibn 'Aqil: We once attended the council of a notable who asked, has any historian been left in Baghdad after the death of al-Sabi [reputedly a Shi'i]? The people answered, No. There is no power or strength save in God, the notable said. Can this great city really be without a Hanbalite historian? – Ibn 'Aqil of course meant himself – In any case, this is something to thank God for since, when the city was full of pious and distinguished men, God decreed that there be historians to record their achievements. When such men no longer existed, and there remained only the pernicious and blameworthy, God caused historians to disappear so as to hide the shame.[48]

The historians had therefore come to be increasingly conscious of the pitfalls of their discipline, especially of the possible errors of judgement in the assessment of character and motive. Subki warned his colleagues that 'they teetered on the brink of an abyss' because they presumed to judge what men held most sacred. Neither friendship nor enmity should be allowed to distort historical verdicts, now most often taken to refer not to events but to individuals. In illustration, Subki refers to his father's 'rule' (qa'ida) for historians which runs as follows:

Herewith is a most useful rule for historians. It may happen that historians disparage some people and elevate others for reasons of prejudice, ignorance or simply through reliance on untrustworthy transmitters and so forth. Ignorance among historians is greater than it is among the Hadith scholars who practise jarh and ta'dil [disparagement and positive reappraisal of Hadith transmitters]. The same applies to prejudice, for I have rarely seen a history to be free from it. Consider the history of our teacher, Dhahabi, may God forgive him. Despite its merit and scope, it is charged with excessive prejudice . . . He often slanders men of religion, that is the fuqara' [i.e. Sufis], who are the cream of God's creation, and wags his tongue against many leading Shafi'is and Hanafites. He is excessively prejudiced against the Ash'arites and excessively laudatory towards the mujassima ['corporealists', i.e. Hanbalites]. Being the great scholar that he is, what can one expect

[48] Ibn al-Jawzi, Muntazam, 9:42. For the two schools of historians, see Sibt ibn al-Jawzi, Mir'at, 8:135; for Ibn al-Athir's attacks, see Kamil, 11:219, 284; for Ibn Khaldun's accusation of calumny, see Tarikh, 2/2:187–8; for Ibn Taghribirdi on Maqrizi, see Nujum, 15:89. See also Ibn al-Jawzi, Muntazam, 10:108, on one of his Hadith teachers: 'I benefited more from his tears than from his teaching.' For a revealing comment on the quarrels among the 'ulama' of the period, see Ibn Kathir, Bidaya, 14:317, where an amused Mamluk governor addresses a group of quarrelling 'ulama' as follows: 'Time was when we, the Turks, and others, would summon the 'ulama' to patch up our quarrels and disputes. But now that the 'ulama' have started to quarrel amongst themselves, who, I wonder, can patch up their disputes?' A case of Quis pacificat pacificatores!

from ordinary historians? . . . The first condition for a historian is truthfulness. Second, if he copies from another, he should copy the very words and not the gist. Third, what is copied should not be retained at first in the memory and transcribed later on. Fourth, he should name his source. These are four conditions of transmission. Furthermore, it is a condition that any biographical notice he writes on his own authority, whether long or short, should be based on personal acquaintance with the subject's level of scholarship, religious faith and other attributes. This can very rarely be done. The historian must also possess a good turn of phrase and be conversant with lexical meaning. He should possess a wide imagination (*tasawwur hasan*), so that, as he writes his biography, he can imagine the total circumstances of his subject and express these in terms which are neither excessive nor fall short of the mark. He should not be overcome by *parti pris*, and thus be tempted to overesteem someone he likes or underrate another. In point of fact he should either be totally free from *parti pris*, which is very rare, or be sufficiently fair-minded to overcome his prejudices, following the path of equity. So these are four more conditions. You may wish to add a fifth if you like. Wide imagination and knowledge may not be ready to hand at the moment of writing. So the presence of the imagination may be counted as a condition, in addition to good imagination and knowledge. Here, then, are nine conditions for the historian. The most difficult of them all is cognizance of a person's degree of scholarship since this presupposes the ability to share his knowledge and be near to him in order to ascertain his level of attainment.[49]

This passage is probably the most extensive treatment of the skills and attitudes, mental and moral, needed by the historian before Ibn Khaldun. Setting aside its specific injunctions, which are self-explanatory, the most remarkable aspect of these observations on historical writing is the almost total identification of history with biography. This is corroborated in other historians, where the word *siyar* is frequently used as a synonym for *tarikh*. There are grounds for arguing that *siyasa*-oriented historiography had drifted a long way towards treating history largely as the political record of men driven to and from power through correct or incorrect calculation of opportunities and motives. Or else it is the record of men of scholarship whose genuine achievements must be assessed against a backdrop of intense sectarian polemics. To gain a fuller understanding of this question one has to turn to the biographical dictionaries, a genre which may be said to have blossomed in this period.

Biographical dictionaries

Biographical notices of prominent men and women began at a very early period in Arabic historiography and were regularly appended to annals by

---

[49] Subki, *Tabaqat*, 2:22–3. For historians on the brink of an abyss, see *Mu'id*, p. 74. See also Ibn Shaddad, *A'laq*, 1/1:4, who says he wrote 'in the certainty that historiography is liable to be accepted as true or rejected as false and that the historian lays himself open to censure and reproof'.

the fourth/tenth century. Many strands of interest came together to produce the biographical literature known as the books of *tabaqat, tarajim, rijal* or *siyar*. The origins of this genre as exemplified in the *Tabaqat* of Ibn Sa'd have already been discussed in Chapter Two. In brief recapitulation, one might argue that biography was a genre which attracted diverse interests and traditions, some of which go back to pre-Islamic times. Thus, genealogy and the chain of poetic transmission (*riwaya*) were both well-established pre-Islamic cultural interests. Short biographies of the Prophet's Companions were intended to authenticate the history of the early community as these Companions carried with them the guarantee of truth into the far corners of the empire. This was carried over into biographies of *'ulama'* who were increasingly thought of, by members of their own class, as the true guardians of religion. Again, early bureaucratic practice, e.g. the establishment of the *diwan*, or register of tribal warriors, formally inscribed the warrior class in the service of the state. Early literary interests, such as the interest in lists of 'firsts', discussed in Chapter Three, must also have encouraged the desire to collect and classify biographies of prominent figures in various fields of religious or political endeavour. Last, and by no means least, the gradual development of the theory and practice of the *isnad* created the need for lists of transmitters who could be assessed as regards their veracity and sectarian or theological standpoints.[50]

As biographical literature developed, whether in the form of short biographical notices arranged by generation, rank or locality, or in larger scope as in biographies of the Prophet or of prominent Muslims of later ages, it underwent the methodological influence of *Hadith*, *Adab* and historical writing as well as a shift in perspective due to the changing position of the *'ulama'*. Furthermore, the genre witnessed ages of intensity followed by others when it fell into relative neglect. With *siyasa*-oriented historiography, especially under the Mamluks, a new age of intensity was reached. Greater tensions among legal schools and the vacuum created by the eclipse of the caliphate now increasingly filled by a growing sense of mission among the scholarly class were among the more visible causes of a resurgence in biographical literature. Where a sense of mission was concerned, the Sufi input was important, and will be discussed at greater

[50] On *Tabaqat*, see Ibrahim Hafsi, 'Recherches sur le genre *Tabaqat* dans la littérature arabe', *Arabica*, 23 (1976), 227–65; 24 (1977), 1–41, 150–86. Hafsi adopts a narrow definition of the term *tabaqat*, ignoring, e.g., the centennial dictionaries, and links their origins almost exclusively to *Hadith*. His interpretations are in many cases doubtful, e.g., his highlighting of 'Persian' influences and his liberal use of judgements like 'originality' and 'critical spirit' without adequate definition. It is informative and useful for bibliographical purposes. See also my 'Islamic Biographical Dictionaries: a Preliminary Assessment', *Muslim World*, 63 (1973), 53–65. For a general bibliographical guide to the literature, see Paul Auchterlonie, *Arabic Biographical Dictionaries: A Summary Guide and Bibliography* (Durham: Middle East Libraries Committee, 1987).

length below. But the Sufi belief in an uninterrupted 'chain' (*silsila*) of saintly witnesses to the truth, enshrined from the seventh/thirteenth century onwards in Sufi brotherhoods, was undoubtedly a powerful incentive in the search for the origins and continuity of authentic instruction. Under the Mamluks, biographical dictionaries either chronologically or alphabetically arranged proliferated and covered a very large spectrum of legal schools, sects, cities, specializations, professions and so forth. Many were doubtless inspired by the same urge to survey or record the men and women of an entire age or class as was evident in straightforward works of history, discussed above. As sources for the history of their times these works are often of very great importance. But for their conception of history and their organizing principles, one needs to examine their often lengthy introductions or occasional asides as we saw above, for instance, with Subki.

One of the earliest examples of the resurgent biographical genre is the celebrated dictionary of Sufis, *Tabaqat al-Sufiyya*, by Sulami (d. 412/1021), intended to commemorate a line of pious and ascetic *awliya*', saints who in all ages were the true successors of the prophets and guardians of prophetic truth. Sulami was specifically interested in the biographies of the *awliya*' of later days, partly, no doubt, to counteract the view common among some Traditionist circles that true piety had ended with the Companions of Muhammad but mostly to underline the continuity of the Sufi 'chain'. Yaqut's dictionary of men of *Adab* was a comprehensive collection of scholars in disciplines like philology and historiography, a collection which he felt he needed to defend against the charge of superfluousness by insisting on the importance of the linguistic and historical sciences for a better understanding of the faith as for a more efficient government. The same need for justification arose for Ibn Abi Usaybi'a (d. 668/1270) in his dictionary of medical doctors. Medicine, he asserted, has been praised in revealed books to the point where 'the science of the body is akin to the science of religion'. The present age owes the doctors of old a great debt of gratitude for having laid down the principles of this science, 'the kind of debt owed by a pupil to his master'.

In several of these dictionaries devoted to the professions, there was evident concern to demonstrate that their study would have a direct bearing on religion or on orderly government. The 'dignity' (*sharaf*) of a particular science had to be defended in an age which, as it was seriously engaged in holy war against 'Greeks' and Franks, was less tolerant of foreignness on the one hand, and levity on the other. But with Ibn Khallikan (d. 681/1282) and his dictionary of notables in all fields and ages, *Tabaqat al-A'yan*, a distinctive new note is struck. The novelty lay not only in its comprehensive coverage but in a curious introduction which makes no reference to religion and identifies biography with history:

This is a concise treatise (*mukhtasar*) in the science of history (*'ilm al-tarikh*). I was motivated to collect it by my own fondness to acquaint myself with reports relating to prominent figures of the past, their dates of death and birth, and what each age brought forth of their number. Having gathered some information in this field, I was led to seek more and to investigate thoroughly such information. So I read the books devoted to this art and received further information directly from prominent scholars in this area when I could not find it in a book . . . In each case, I mentioned such laudable qualities as befitted the person concerned, whether it be a noble deed, a curious anecdote, a verse of poetry or an epistle, for the amusement of careful readers . . . I was not easy-going in transmitting from unreliable sources but exerted my utmost in determining the truth.[51]

The identification of history with biography had already been made by al-Khatib al-Baghdadi (d. 463/1071) and his imitator Ibn 'Asakir (d. 571/ 1175) in their 'histories' of Baghdad and Damascus, respectively, works which were in very large measure biographical dictionaries, alphabetically arranged, of prominent figures of these two cities. With Ibn Khallikan, the identification is total and explicit, a measure of the extent to which the age had moved in regarding history as the sum total of the lives of the notables, mostly *'ulama'*, who graced its pages.

The influence of Ibn Khallikan was widespread and clearly detectable, for instance, in Subki's *Tabaqat al-Shafi'iyya*:

I was one who seized upon the enchanting speech of men of the past, collecting their scattered pearls, until I had gathered it together in the best possible arrangement. I was also one who, if he heard something virtuous, would spread it about and if he saw something that aroused suspicion would consign it to oblivion . . . So I arranged the Shafi'is in groups . . . assigning a century to each group and collecting them like the stars, all of them being signposts to right conduct . . . This is a work of *Hadith*, jurisprudence, history and *Adab* . . . in which I cite the biography of a person, treated exhaustively in the manner of the Traditionists and Belles-lettrists . . . so that this collection has come to include poetry, anecdotes, sermons, debates, proofs, deductions and edifying stories.[52]

Two other biographers of the same generation as Subki go even further in identifying history with biography. Kutubi (d. 766/1363), the continuator of Ibn Khallikan, affirms that the 'science of history is a mirror of the times' through which one can become acquainted with the 'experiences of the nations'. The phrase 'a mirror of the times' appears to have enjoyed a measure of popularity. A hundred years earlier it had cropped up in the

[51] Ibn Khallikan, *Wafayat*, 1:19–20. On Ibn Khallikan, see Helmut E. Fahndrich, 'The Wafayat al-A'yan of Ibn Khallikan: A New Approach', *Journal of the American Oriental Society*, 93/4 (1973), 432–45. The 'new approach' is content-literary analysis which classifies Ibn Khallikan among "*adab*-writers'. For Sulami, see *Tabaqat*, pp. 3–6. For a typical *hadith* that the best generation is the Prophet's, see, e.g., Ibn Hanbal, *Musnad*, 5:357. For Yaqut, see *Irshad*, 1:52–3. For Ibn Abi Usaybi'a, see *'Uyun*, 1:2–3.
[52] Subki, *Tabaqat*, 1:206–8.

title of Sibt ibn al-Jawzi's chronicle, while the 'experiences of the nations' is a clear echo of Miskawayhi. Both phrases underline Kutubi's concern with the pragmatic rather than the religious value of history-as-biography. The other biographer, Safadi (d. 766/1363), whose massive dictionary is still being edited, begins by praising the study of past generations where 'our understanding roams in the mirror of the inner meaning of the past'. He takes up the phrase 'a mirror of the times' and explains how the study of history enables one to become a contemporary of men of the past, 'sitting with them on the cushions of their thrones . . . seeing clearly their shining faces . . . watching them in battle unsheath their decorative swords'. The soul would derive comfort from this study and be uplifted and diverted from its troubles, for human nature does not vary. History may also instil firmness and determination (*hazman wa 'azman*) in the face of the enemy and the emulation of worthy men is of value as an incentive to greater effort.[53]

Where assessment of character is concerned, many of these biographical dictionaries were directly or indirectly influenced by the critical method practised in *Hadith* and known as *al-jarh wa'l ta'dil*, which, as we saw above, had to do with classifying *Hadith* transmitters on a scale of reliability according to what was known of their character and scholarly attainments. At the same time, a character assessment of this type, thoroughly carried out, was often seen as being at variance with the deeply ingrained ethical principle of shunning *ghiba*, slander or backbiting, i.e. the revelation of a person's secret vices. How, then, was one to reconcile the duty of accurately assessing the reliability of *Hadith* transmitters, a problem of grave religious import, with the duty to avoid exposing men's vices?

One important statement of this question is in *Mizan al-I'tidal*, a dictionary of *Hadith* transmitters by Dhahabi (d. 748/1348). In his introduction, Dhahabi claims that his work includes all varieties of transmitters, from the most reliable to the deliberate forger. He lists in detail the degrees of *jarh* and *ta'dil* but argues that the burden of proof always falls on the one who expresses *jarh* concerning another, thus giving transmitters the benefit of the doubt where no trustworthy *jarh* can be substantiated about them.[54] In another short epistle, Dhahabi takes Ibn Taymiyya to task for his severity in the asssessment of character:

Blessed is he whose vices keep him preoccupied from following the vices of others . . . Until when will you praise yourself and your silly prattle . . . while censuring scholars and tracking down people's vices, knowing full well that the Prophet forbade this practice? Yes, I know that in self-defence you will claim that disparaging those who know nothing of Islam or of what the Prophet brought forth is a *jihad*. No, by God! They did indeed know a lot of virtue . . . and were ignorant

---

[53] For Kutubi, see *Fawat*, 1:1; for Safadi, see *Wafi*, 1:4–5.
[54] Dhahabi, *Mizan*, 1:1–4.

of much that is of no concern to them. It is a virtue for a Muslim to forsake what does not concern him . . . Divine mercy descends when mention is made of the pious, and they should not be insulted and cursed . . . If this is my opinion of you, and I am one who is concerned, affectionate and friendly towards you, how do you imagine your enemies' opinion of you to be?[55]

The controversy over *jarh* and *ta'dil* was never to be fully resolved where biographical dictionaries were concerned. It was by its very nature a moral dilemma which pitted private scruple against public responsibility. Nor were the biographers entirely consistent. Many a 'philanthrope' would proclaim in his introduction his intention to mention nothing but what is good and laudable about his entries only to disparage and calumniate some who for one reason or another did not gain his favour – and the same holds true for 'misanthropes'.

What principles determined the inclusion of an entry in a biographical dictionary? Sulami, as we saw above, intended to commemorate a particular line of succession, the 'saints' who in every generation carry forward the true spirit of Islam and are thus the true successors of the prophets. Ibn Abi Usaybi'a is concerned with the prominent men of the profession only (*mutamayyizun*). Ibn Khallikan, too, states that he recorded only the lives of men of intelligence and general excellence. But the later *Tabaqat* seem to have cast their net wider. Thus, Subki says that he included both the famous as well as those who did not produce much (*muqillun*). Safadi states that he will include the most perfect of the *umma*, the most intelligent, the heroes, the most prominent Companions, kings, princes, judges, governors, viziers, traditionists, jurists, the pious, *awliya'*, men of letters, poets – in short, the most prominent in every art or field of action. But he also says that he has 'summoned the commoners' (*jafala*) to his pages. A cross-section of the whole community, representing both *din* and *dunya*, are to be found in his dictionary.

There was often a disparity between what the biographers said they would include in their dictionaries and what they did in fact include. One encounters nonentities even in the most professedly 'exclusive' works, entries with only two or three lines who cannot possibly be considered distinguished by the standards set down by their biographer. But the gradual development from specialized to more general dictionaries is typified in the rise of centennial dictionaries which, from about the eighth/fourteenth century, constituted a series grouping entries in centuries. These may well be seen, in addition to their commemorative purpose of extolling the virtues of the *'ulama'*, as a 'summoning of the commoners', an indication of

---

[55] Dhahabi, *Bayan*, pp. 32–4. The epistle is entitled the 'Golden Counsel' (*al-nasiha al-dhahabiyya*, a pun on Dhahabi's name). Dhahabi himself was attacked for his severity against the Ash'arites: see Subki, *Mu'id*, p. 74. For later developments in this controversy, see my 'Islamic Biographical Dictionaries', 59–60.

the power of the Mamluk empire and its institutions – military, political, religious – to survey, record and assess the lives of its citizens. By far the most common *hadith*s cited by the biographers were: 'Give to each man what is his by right' and 'Place men in their proper ranks'.

Safadi gave one standard plan of presentation of the biographical entry which was widely accepted by later biographers. One begins with the name and surname, then *kunya*, then connection to a town, then descent, then school of law, then the person's particular knowledge, craft, power, position or principality. The teachers of a person are well to the fore. Scholars are described either as *'allama* or else as *hafiz, imam, shaykh, faqih* and then *usuli, nahwi, mantiqi* and so forth, where applicable. The date of birth, or more commonly of death, is given and the general character estimate comes at the end. With particularly important entries, the biographers often devoted a final section to an assessment of the personality as seen by other biographers, by themselves if they possessed first-hand information or by collating several authoritative opinions. Information in a 'typical' entry included, in addition to the standard data, a résumé of a person's career, a few anecdotes to illustrate virtues or skills and often a personal touch, e.g. 'he kept himself aloof from others', 'he was much given to laughter', 'he was miserly', and so forth. These touches illuminate a character, especially when the information is first-hand.

The biographical dictionaries had thus become integral to the writing and conception of history in the Mamluk period – so much so, in fact, that biography *was* history in the view of many of its practitioners.[56] As several biographers cited above insisted, biography should not only judge character, thus invoking criteria inspired by *Hadith*, but should also imaginatively evoke a personality, thus invoking criteria inspired by *Adab*. But above and beyond questions of style and judgement was the visible desire to select or include a cross-section of the community deemed worthy of enumeration and arrangement in ranks. In a *siyasa*-oriented environment, only a hierarchy of rank and merit gave meaning to the lives whose sum total constituted the history of the *umma*.

Bezels of wisdom, glimpses of the Unseen

Neither past nor present held much interest for the Sufi movement as it prepared to take its place alongside other, well-established systems of

---

[56] One important exception to this is Safadi, *Wafi*, 1:47, who quotes Subki's *qa'ida* (see footnote 49, above) and adds, 'These conditions bind someone who writes history in accordance with biographical entries (*tarajim*). But he who writes history in accordance with events (*hawadith*) cannot be bound by such conditions because he records the events which happen to occur. Hence, he is bound to be accurate in what he records, knowledgeable in the meanings of terms, fertile in imagination (*hasan al-tasawwur*) and eloquent in his phrasing'.

action and belief. Past and present were states of mind, symbolic realities, shadows without substance. The intellect, whose main function was to understand the then-and-now, was to the Sufis defective by its very nature. Beyond the intellect (*'aql*), and schematically similar to Plato's 'divided line', lay gnosis (*ma'rifa*), the experiential knowledge of the divine which, once 'tasted' – a favourite Sufi term – brought about a radical change of personality and direction. In a reversal of the Adamic fall, caused by tasting the fruit of a forbidden tree, the Sufi recovered the original Adamic state by tasting the fruit of gnosis and thus realigned his soul with God.

To most Sufis, the Qur'an exhibited a pattern of meanings, hidden or visible, the constant contemplation of which ultimately delivered the key to a ladder of spiritual ascent. As Sufism developed, so the steps of that ladder became more carefully distinguished and delineated. The entire ascent was often described as a process of unveiling progressively more profound and meaningful stages of reality and experience, a series of epiphanies each of which brought the Sufi closer to the Absolute Reality. These epiphanies were sometimes expressed in language of great power and beauty, terse, oracular pronouncements, mystifying to the non-initiate, seemingly contradictory in their embrace of opposites, para-Qur'anic in style and energy.

But Sufism must not be seen in this period as a monolithic movement. For present purposes, one could speak of two broad tendencies, a 'high' Sufism represented by the great system-builders, thinkers like Ghazali or Ibn 'Arabi, and a 'low' Sufism represented by popular brotherhoods, itinerant miracle workers, militant preachers and 'holy men' who, somewhat like the contemporary friars of western Europe, managed to transmit their message of rededication and moral reform to the urban masses. It was this 'low' Sufism which appealed to Seljuqs, Zengids, Ayyubids and Mamluks. If one were called upon to explain the secret of their attraction to these military–feudal dynasties who spent so much of their time and energies warring or preparing for war, one might argue that it was the power of prayer. The burgeoning popularity of *ribats* and *zawiyas*, Sufi hostels or retreats endowed by sultans and other public or private figures, was in large measure due to the conditions of the original endowment deeds which specified that prayers would be offered in perpetuity for the soul of the founder and his progeny. The power of prayer can be illustrated by the numerous instances recorded in contemporary chronicles in which holy men succeeded in attaching themselves to rulers and powerful magnates who became convinced of their spiritual efficacy to turn defeat into victory through devotion and supplication. Typical of this is the remark attributed to Nur al-Din Zengi, when his followers urged him, following his defeat in a battle against the Crusaders, to stop his largesse to Sufis and scholars and channel this money into the war effort. In great anger, he replied:

By God, my only hope for victory lies in these people. Your very livelihood and your victories are only possible because of the weak among you. How can I stop my largesse to people who fight on my behalf as I lie on my bed asleep with arrows that do not miss their mark, and divert this largesse instead to others who do not fight for me unless they see me in person, and with arrows that may hit or miss?[57]

These 'arrows' of prayer were the most potent weapons in the Sufi arsenal. It is this perhaps more than any other single factor which impelled the Seljuqs and their successors to create for Sufism a status in society along-side the *'ulama'*, a development accompanied by a great deal of tension and mutual hostility.[58] What concerns us more directly here is the effect of this tension on historical writing, a complex issue which needs to be addressed at several levels simultaneously.

Faith in the effectiveness of prayer permeates many of the chronicles of the period. Prophecies which come true, portents and omens, dreams and extraordinary coincidences: these are a regular feature of Arabic historical writing from its earliest beginnings. But they seem to acquire a new significance in an age perceived by its historians to have witnessed events totally unprecedented in the magnitude of their ferocity. As was shown earlier in Chapter Four, the debate about the miracles and charisms (*karamat*) of prophets and holy men had involved a fairly wide spectrum of theological and philosophical analysis. But the impact of Crusaders and Mongols on the one hand, and the growing influence and social acceptability of the Sufi movement on the other, created a new and *political* sphere of operation for glimpses of the Unseen, portents of triumph or doom, spiritual energies channelled in the cause of war against infidels.

On the face of things, the *'ulama'* did not take kindly to these develop-ments. The Hanbalites in particular seem to have viewed the resurgence of Sufism, in both its 'high' and 'low' varieties, with a great deal of suspi-cion. Ibn al-Jawzi argued that the hallmark of Sufism was excess: among earlier Sufis it was excess of asceticism, among contemporaries it was excess of greed and gluttony. Ibn Taymiyya directed his considerable polemical skills against the all-pervasive influence of the 'high' Sufism of Ibn 'Arabi, detecting in his thought a dangerous confusion between the Creator and His creation.[59] Nevertheless, the struggle between *'ulama'* and Sufis resulted in a seepage of ideas and moods between the two realms of thought, made inevitable by the forced proximity imposed upon them by the state. Where one would expect Ibn al-Jawzi to be hard-headed about reporting oddities, omens, *karamat* and other marvels associated with 'low' Sufism, his chronicle is in fact full of them. Furthermore, it is difficult to see how his own life of preaching to the masses, the 'miraculous'

---

[57] Ibn al-Athir, *Bahir*, p. 118.
[58] For references, see footnote 27, above.
[59] For Ibn al-Jawzi, see *Talbis*, pp. 220–1; for Ibn Taymiyya, see *Iqtida'*, p. 463.

acts of repentance he effected and his role in public affairs differed in its outward aspect from the career of any prominent Sufi figure of his generation.

Charisms, omens, wondrous coincidences, and prophecies come true are a visible part of the fabric of the historical narrative. At times, in fact, they seem to constitute an important element in scholarly strategies of comprehension and interpretation. To include these wonders is of course to emphasize God's total control over nature.[60] But these marvels also help to explain how, against all odds, a victory was won, an escape was effected, a ruler came to power and so forth:

Among these wonders is that I was in the habit of spending three months in the Great Mosque of Damascus. It was a Saturday . . . the same day that Khwarizmi was enveloped in the fog and it happened to be my last day of preaching . . . attended by al-Salih. It was suggested that I pray for victory for the sultan . . . so I prayed, and as I did so, a great fog descended upon the assembly and they all passed out, as I did. When I regained consciousness, I said, al-Ashraf has today been granted victory. The crowd marvelled at this. Ten days later, news of the battle arrived . . . and it was reported that the fog that enveloped us had also enveloped them and that they had won victory in the very hour that we prayed for it.[61]

A great Sufi master of that period, Abu'l 'Abbas al-Mursi (d. 686/1287), had allegedly complained: 'We have partaken of the knowledge of jurists but they have not partaken of ours.' But the above *karama*, attributed by a historian to *himself*, indicates the extent to which the *'ulama'* were prepared to go to meet the Sufi challenge and yet to control these *karamat* so that they could be applied in the best of causes, the war against non-Muslims. In point of fact, a noticeable development of this period is the manner in which marvels and wonders were increasingly the subject, not only of scientific speculation but of juristic supervision. A creature born with two heads or a woman who becomes a man would have obvious juristic implications and scientific interest. But of equal significance is the desire to witness and record such events so as not to encourage the superstitions of the mob. If the *'ulama'* needed to tackle the problem of wonders and marvels, made more palpable by the growing popularity of 'low' Sufism, they did so on their own terms and in a manner which ensured that such phenomena would be properly attested, witnessed and controlled.[62]

---

[60] The most comprehensive treatment of this issue in this period is Qazwini, *'Aja'ib*, pp. 3–13. Qazwini relies heavily on Biruni and Ibn Sina.

[61] Sibt ibn al-Jawzi, *Mir'at*, 8:662; see also *Mir'at*, 8:24–5, where he distinguishes between *sihr* and *karamat*. For more prominent examples of marvels and the attitudes towards them, see the chronicles of Ibn al-Dawadari, Yunini, Ibn al-'Ibri and Ibn 'Abd al-Zahir. This last makes frequent references to marvellous coincidences to accentuate the wondrous rise to power of the sultans: see, e.g., *Rawd*, p. 474.

[62] For the remark of Abu'l 'Abbas al-Mursi, see Yunini, *Dhayl*, 4:318. For examples of marvels attested and controlled, see Ibn Kathir, *Bidaya*, 14:206–7, 248, 279–80. The atti-

There is little doubt that the Seljuqs and their successors were on the whole less sympathetic to the philosophical sciences than, say, the Buyids or Fatimids. The great dialectical theologian Imam al-Haramayn al-Juwaini (d. 488/1095) is said to have 'repented' at the end of his life, declaring:

I sailed the great ocean and dived to the depths forbidden to the Muslims, and all of this in quest of the truth. In olden days I used to shun the emulation of religious authority (*taqlid*). But now I have abandoned all this and returned to the word of truth: Follow the religion of old women.[63]

This sentiment has its parallel in the celebrated literary *tour de force* of the age, the *Maqamat* of Hariri (d. 516/1122), where the hero, Abu Zayd al-Saruji, in reality an anti-hero, deceiver, consummate actor, 'hunter' of the simple-minded, master of the burlesque, clown and mocker of religious sciences, is likewise said to have 'repented' at the end of his adventures and to have become an ascetic Sufi.[64] Truth or fiction, such acts of repentance tally with the mood of the ruling elites. The Ayyubids, for example, are said to have hated the philosopher Amidi (d. 631/1233) because of his preoccupation with logic and the 'sciences of the ancients'. Dhahabi accuses Ibn Taymiyya of being 'poisoned' by philosophy, even though it was Ibn Taymiyya who mounted the most impressive attack of the age on the rational sciences.[65]

It was, however, 'high' Sufism which left a vivid imprint on historiography. To detect that imprint, one needs first to recall the distinction that Sufi theorists persisted in making between the veil and the reality, the eye and the heart, intellection and spiritual vision. The technical vocabulary of the Sufi literary tradition was rich in imagery of unveiling, illumination and theophany. The Sufis, by denying that the present was fully real or intelligible and emphasizing transcendence, helped to diffuse the contrast between appearance and reality in an age when many historians could barely contain their amazement at the speed and scale of events and the ambiguity of their significance. To illustrate, one might turn first to Ibn al-Athir where two passages of lamentation are here conflated:

Glory to Him whose reign does not pass away and no time can change! Woe to this wretched world which does these things to its children! We pray to God the

---

tude to astrology was ambiguous: see, e.g., Ibn al-Athir, *Kamil*, 11:348 (hostile); Sibt ibn al-Jawzi, *Mir'at*, 8:426 (hostile); Ibn Taghribirdi, *Nujum*, 6:102 (hostile, suggesting that astrology is a Sufi practice) and 6:308–9; Ibn al-Qalanisi, *Dhayl*, p. 133 (seemingly more receptive); Qazwini, *Athar*, p. 227 (on Tabriz, seemingly more receptive). Basim Musallam helped to clarify my ideas on many of these issues.

[63] Ibn al-Jawzi, *Muntazam*, 9:19.

[64] Hariri, *Maqamat*, pp. 571 ff.

[65] For Amidi and the Ayyubids, see Ibn Taghribirdi, *Nujum*, 6:249 and cf. Ibn Khallikan, *Wafayat*, 6:343. Saladin's execution of the Sufi philosopher Suhrawardi was an event of considerable public importance. For Dhahabi's charge, see *Bayan*, p. 33. For Ibn Tay-

Almighty that He unveil (*yakshuf 'an*) our hearts so that we can come to see the world with the eye of truth . . . Their dynasty [the Fatimids] from the moment that al-Mahdi appeared in Sijilmasa in the month of Dhu'l Hijja, the year 299, and until the death of the caliph al-'Adid lasted two hundred and seventy-two years and approximately one month. This is the way of the world. It gives with one hand and takes with the other. No sooner is it sweet than it becomes bitter, no sooner pure than it becomes polluted . . . We pray that God accept our hearts as they turn towards Him, that He show us the world in its true reality, make us renounce it and make the afterlife the object of our desire.[66]

What is at issue is not Ibn al-Athir's attitude to Sufism but the manner in which technical Sufi terms had come to infiltrate the historical discourse on the contrast between seeing and knowing, the spurious and the genuine. With Ibn Khaldun the relationship between Sufism and history is more complex. He of course wrote a work on Sufism and one might legitimately examine how this interest in Sufism helped to sharpen the distinction he drew between the outward drama of historical events and their inward meaning. Here, again, are conflated passages:

Hence, knowledge of God is inevitably the most pleasurable of all. For there is nothing in existence that is more sublime, more honourable or more perfect than the Creator of all things . . . It follows that to gain access to the secrets of the divinity and to know, by intuition, inspiration and unveiling, how the divinity arranges and encompasses all existents is the highest type of knowledge, the most perfect, the clearest and the most pleasurable . . . Some of that pleasure may also be felt by students of the acquired sciences when problems, which they have for long pursued and longed to solve, are finally unveiled to them . . . In my work of history, I lifted the veil from the circumstances attending the rise of the generations of men . . . so that this work of mine has come to be unique of its kind in the unusual sciences it treats and in the pieces of wisdom it contains, both veiled and near to hand . . . It is through divine inspiration that I came to discover this science.[67]

Sufism provided the vocabulary that historians would sometimes employ to describe the manner in which they tried to arrive at the inner certainty of things and to relate the fleeting phenomena of history to a higher reality which alone could endow them with ultimate meaning.

Patterns of change

The scholars and historians who presumed to judge the conduct of rulers tended also to take a sombre view of the function and value of their own

miyya's attack on the rational sciences, see especially *Dar'*, 1:177, 183. This work, recently edited, will undoubtedly become a philosophical classic.

[66] Ibn al-Athir, *Kamil*, 11:112, 243.

[67] Ibn Khaldun, *Shifa'*, p. 28 and *Muqaddima*, pp. 9, 10, 37. See also, e.g., Qazwini, *'Aja'ib*, p. 4, quoting the Prophet's *hadith*: 'O God, show me things as they truly are', and Turtushi, *Siraj*, where there are lengthy passages on asceticism of clear Sufi inspiration.

discipline. If some people still believed that history was also meant to entertain, the historians of this age were quick to disabuse them of any such illusion or frivolity. For Ibn al-Athir, history had both a religious and a mundane value. It could be used to reform kingdoms, enrich the mind with experiences and teach the value of asceticism to the truly percipient. Most of his colleagues took an equally lofty view of their subject. For Nuwayri (d. 732/1332) it was a subject of special importance to kings, viziers, governors and state secretaries, from which they could learn the proper conduct of government and war. Then again both rich and poor would gain from it, the rich in knowledge that their wealth cannot last, the poor in asceticism. As for the rest, they could listen to it at social evenings, motivated by the desire to learn about the histories of the nations. For Abu Shama, ignorance of history renders a person confused and blinded, unable to differentiate a caliph from an emir, a sultan from a vizier, a Shafi'i from a Malikite, a Companion (*sahabi*) from a Follower (*tabi'i*), the implication being that the social order itself would be the victim of such ignorance. For Ibn al-Khatib (d. 776/1374), history helps to unite people by acquainting them with their ancestry, to enrich them with experience and to enlighten them regarding what time (*dahr*) may or may not bring forth. The rational man learns to see how divine omnipotence arranges the world in a manner that would fortify his faith. The stories of the Qur'an would then be seen to complement and complete the record of history. For Safadi, history, in addition to its high moral and political purpose alluded to above, can help to uncover fraud, whether in *Hadith* or in official documents.[68]

Such sentiments are broadly typical of the age. Far less is heard of history as entertainment (*tasliya*); far more is heard of history as a moral sermon (*wa'z*) addressed primarily to statesmen and meant to unite and edify society and the state. Thus, Nuwayri proclaims his intention to organize his history in accordance with states rather than annals:

Having observed that most of those who wrote the history of the Muslim community did so according to serial annals and not to states in their proper order and expanse, I realized that this may interrupt the reader's interest in a particular event or concern for a particular issue. The year would pass without full coverage of all its details . . . and with the coming of a new year, the historian would pass on from these particular events . . . moving from east to west, from peace to war, from south to north, from sunrise to sunset . . . The reader would therefore be unable to pick up the thread of his interest except after much difficulty . . . I thus chose to organize history by states and not to turn away from any state until I had covered its history from beginning to end.[69]

---

[68] For Ibn al-Athir, see *Kamil*, 1:7; for Nuwayri, see *Nihaya*, 13:1; for Abu Shama, see *Rawdatayn*, 1/1:4; for Ibn al-Khatib, see *Ihata*, 1:80–1; for Safadi, see *Wafi*, 1:44.
[69] Nuwayri, *Nihaya*, 13:2–3.

Given this tone, reflections on historical change are by and large focused on how states are maintained and how they decline. There is little on how they rise. One presumes that the Qur'an, *shar'i* political theory and the historians' own experiences had instilled the view that the rise of states and dynasties, whether by consent or by force, was a mark of divine favour bestowed for reasons known only to God. On the whole it is only when a state or dynasty is entrenched that the historians begin to take interest in its policies, patterns of succession and the causes of its decline.

In a notable passage on how power tends to circulate within dynasties, Ibn al-Athir records the following pattern:

Having examined many reliable works on Islamic history, I deduced from them that, in many cases, power passes from the immediate family of a state founder to his relatives and kinsmen. In early Islam, power passed from Mu'awiya's immediate family, he being the first of the line, to their cousins the Marwanids. Later, power passed from the family of al-Saffah, the first of the Abbasid line, to his brother al-Mansur. In the case of the Samanids, the first to reign supreme was Nasr ibn Ahmad. Power later passed to his brother Isma'il and his progeny. So too with Ya'qub the Saffarid when power passed to his brother 'Amr and his issue . . . And here we find Shirkuh, his power passing to his brother Ayyub and his line. And then there is Saladin. After he had set up his state and made it great, as if he were the first of his line, power passed to the progeny of his brother al-'Adil . . . For fear of prolixity, I would have cited many more instances. The reason for this is, I think, that the first of a line must commit many acts of murder and violence in order to entrench himself in power. When he finally captures power, the hearts and energies of his immediate family are totally preoccupied with him. This is why God denies power to his issue, for the sake of whom he committed these acts, as a form of punishment.[70]

This was a typical *'ibra*, or historical moral, intended to edify but also to warn. Behind it lies a belief in balance and retribution, often expressed in the view that history was itself well arranged by God and that the historian needed to reflect such symmetry in his work. A very similar *'ibra* was arrived at by Ibn al-Tiqtaqa when he concluded that founders of states do not normally enjoy them:

Induction (*istiqra'*) demonstrates that he who founds or creates a state does not in most cases enjoy it. The Prophet, upon whom blessings, said: Do not desire states lest you be deprived of them. The likelihood is that he who founds a state has in his character such boldness and love of power as is found hard to bear by other proud kings. The more his love of power grows, the more resentful they become until they devise his fall.[71]

---

[70] Ibn al-Athir, *Kamil*, 11:227–8. The last sentence or two of this important passage are unfortunately corrupt. Yunini, who copies the passage in his *Dhayl*, 1:466, was used to amend and supplement the reading. The exact reading of these sentences remains somewhat unclear although the general drift seems plain enough. This passage, which appears to have been widely known, was criticized by Ibn Taghribirdi, *Nujum*, 6:19.

[71] Ibn al-Tiqtaqa, *Fakhri*, pp. 125–6.

To arrive at such 'induction', Ibn al-Tiqtaqa claimed to have 'removed' himself from all considerations of 'origin and culture' and to have assumed 'the posture of an alien and a stranger' so as to have 'no other loyalty but to the truth'.[72]

There is much speculation on the causes of decline in states and this is sometimes expressed in terms borrowed from medicine. Ibn al-Athir, for instance, argues that nothing is more important for a state than continuity of government. Hence, an abrupt change of viziers is as undesirable as an abrupt change of doctors in mid-treatment. Ibn al-Tiqtaqa also compared a ruler and his subjects to a doctor and his patient. Turtushi, of whom Ibn Khaldun would later assert that he 'circled around' the true principles of history without actually hitting upon them, employed similar imagery when he compared the sultan and his subjects to the soul and the body. For Turtushi, seclusion of the ruler is the trait that causes the quickest decline and fall of states. If a ruler secludes himself, it is as if he has died, since seclusion is virtual death.

Thereafter, his courtiers begin to wreak havoc with the lives and wealth of the subjects:

Based on what I myself witnessed during my lifetime and what I heard about former days regarding the onset of corruption among kings, the cause of decline stems from their secluding themselves from direct management of affairs of state. The subjects have a single ruler as long as they have access to him. If he secludes himself, many rulers come into being.[73]

The sultan and his *siyasa* were thus the primary factor in the strength or weakness of states. This holds true for both the admiring biographies of an Ibn 'Abd al-Zahir as well as the more critical verdicts of a Subki. All other factors were in a sense derivative. Without effective government, a society would rapidly 'sicken'. Historians and other scholars occasionally singled out other symptoms of decline such as tensions between various ethnic or sectarian groups, power rivalries, the hoarding of wealth and even the collapse of an efficient and benign military feudal system.[74] But

[72] Ibn al-Tiqtaqa, *Fakhri*, p. 9; cf. Sibt ibn al-Jawzi, *Jalis*, p. 281, who says that learned historians consider it ill-omened to write biographies of living sultans. Presumably, dead sultans facilitate a balanced judgement.

[73] Turtushi, *Siraj*, p. 182; for soul and body, see *Siraj*, p. 162. For Ibn al-Athir, see *Bahir*, p. 184. For Ibn al-Tiqtaqa, see *Fakhri*, p. 29. For Ibn Khaldun on Turtushi, see *Muqaddima*, p. 37.

[74] For Ibn 'Abd al-Zahir, see *Rawd*, p. 46 and *Tashrif*, pp. 57–8 (the wisdom and bravery of the sultan as the most important causes of victory); Subki, *Mu'id*, pp. 16–17 (on the duties and failings of the sultan); Ibn al-'Adim, *Zubdat*, 2:220 (the frivolity of a ruler of Aleppo and its dire consequences). For other symptoms of decline, see Ibn 'Idhari, *Bayan*, 1:123 (ethnic tensions and the collapse of the Aghlabids); Yaqut, *Mu'jam*, 1:297 (intersectarian violence and the decline of Isfahan); Ibn al-Athir, *Kamil*, 11:348 (power rivalries among the Crusaders and subsequent weakness); Turtushi, *Siraj*, p. 373 (hoarding of wealth) and p. 370 (collapse of benign military feudal system in Andalusia).

the intimacy which many historians enjoyed with men of authority caused, on the whole, a concentration of focus on the holder of power and his handling of the state. To explain prosperity or decline it was, once again, *siyasa* and *shariʿa* or *siyasa* versus *shariʿa* which laid down the parameters of interpretation and judgement.

The sense of place

To see for oneself, to witness, to be told by a sultan or a potentate: these were proudly displayed by many historians as distinguishing features of their works. To reinforce their claim of intimate acquaintance with events, the historians of the age cited at length the texts of diplomatic treaties, proclamations, official correspondence, decrees of various kinds: the *ipsissima verba* of the historical drama. When Subki urged historians to name their sources he was preaching to the converted. Many historians not only named their written sources as a kind of bibliographical preface to their work but also took the trouble to explain that their oral information came from specifically named and reliable classes of informants.[75]

With this attention to direct witness went an attention to place. Large segments of geographical lore had been included in works of history as early as the ninth and tenth centuries by historians like Yaʿqubi and Masʿudi. Geographers too would often bind their works together with threads of history and *Adab*. But in this age of imperial bureaucratic chronicles, geography became lexical or administrative in one direction, sacrosanct and a locus of pilgrimage in another. It is not difficult to see why this was so. The vast, still not completely edited geo-administrative encyclopaedia of Ibn Fadlallah al-ʿUmari, *Masalik al-Absar*, is in conception a survey of all kingdoms and principalities known to the author, either directly or from reliable sources. Holding it together is a massively learned bureaucrat's attention to detail and the desire to produce a comprehensive report to his superiors which would constitute the basis for political decision or action. On the other hand, territorial sanctity, issuing from an older concern with the sites of major events, acquired in this age an added urgency because of the creeping territorial losses suffered by Muslims in both east and west. As regions like Andalusia, Palestine, Iraq and Iran fell under non-Muslim rule, the sanctity of territory and the memories of times and places became ever more vivid. Sufism added its own dimension:

[75] For examples of direct witness, proudly displayed, see, e.g., Sibt ibn al-Jawzi, *Mir'at*, 8:464 (most of his informants are said to have been princes, governors and 'ulama'); Ibn al-Qalanisi, *Dhayl*, p. 291 (his informants were merchants, jurists and correspondents); Ibn 'Abd al-Zahir, *Rawd*, p. 46 (direct witness (*mushahada*), not report (*khabar*) distinguishes his history), and also pp. 51 and 76; Ibn Wasil, *Mufarrij*, 5:52, 73; Ibn al-Jawzi, *Muntazam*, 5/2:117. Examples of official documents are far too numerous to cite. For typical bibliographical prefaces, see, e.g., Abu'l Fida, *Mukhtasar*, 1:2–3 and Ibn 'Idhari, *Bayan*, 1:2–3.

the sanctity conferred upon land through tombs of holy men, little islands of peace upon which no act of violence could be tolerated. During the Crusades, Palestine acquired special significance, as seen, for example, in the letter addressed by Saladin to Richard the Lionheart:

> Jerusalem is as much ours as it is yours. In fact, it is of greater significance to us than it is to you because it is the site of our prophet's ascension to heaven and the place where angels assemble. Do not imagine that we can ever surrender it nor will the Muslims stand for this. The land also has been ours from the beginning. Your occupation of it was an accident, occasioned by the weakness of its Muslim inhabitants at that moment in time. God will not permit you to build one stone in this land as long as the war lasts.[76]

In certain works of history, topography, for methodological, administrative and even sentimental reasons, is woven into the historical narrative so as to regulate it (*yandabit*). In his history of Andalusia and North Africa, Ibn 'Idhari found it necessary to break the flow of his narrative whenever he felt that the history of a particular city or region would shed light on events. Similarly, Ibn Shaddad (d. 684/1285) in his history of the princes of al-Sham and al-Jazira wove topography into the fabric of his history, celebrating in this case the modern reconquest of territories by outlining their history since their first conquest by the armies of Islam. Ibn al-'Adim (d. 660/1262) and Ibn al-Khatib (d. 776/1374) were perhaps more sentimental. Both spent many years in exile from their native cities, Aleppo and Granada respectively. Both their works were labours of love, historical topographies born from disasters inflicted directly or indirectly by non-Muslims.

Yaqut and Qazwini (d. 682/1283) use the dictionary form to 'collect', 'arrange' and 'systematize' the topography of the world known to them. The lexical arrangement had been employed before their time but they claimed for their format a degree of exactitude and comprehensiveness unknown to predecessors. Yaqut intended his geographical dictionary to be fully up to date. The great majority of his entries are therefore described as they were known to him in his own days and as they had been in earlier times. Hence, there are many and lengthy passages in Yaqut of comparative history occasioned by his broad topographical interests. The following is a typical reflection on Alexander the Great and the Mongols:

> If it is true that Alexander lived only till the age of thirty-two, it would be a marvel and a breaking of custom. In my view, it is his reign . . . which lasted that long . . . When armies march across the earth, they have to keep a slow pace because at every station they need food . . . The siege of fortresses needs patience and time above and beyond what is required for the march. It is impossible that he

could have had the resolution needed to fight great kings when he had not yet reached the age of twenty. For him to have arranged the affairs of his kingdom, gathered the armies necessary, established his aura of authority among his followers, acquired the skills of leadership, the experience and the reason required for wisdom, all of which are ascribed to him, he would have needed another long span of time. When could he have found the time to march through the earth . . . and establish all these cities? . . . And yet, in our own days . . . and in the years 617 and 618 . . . there occurred such events, associated with the Mongols who came from China, as, had they continued to unfold, would have led to their occupation of the whole earth in a few years . . . In less than two years, they came to rule and ruin vast tracts of Muslim territory . . . Now this may support the claims made for Alexander, although when Alexander conquered a land he built it up . . . and this needs more time than to ruin it.[77]

Qazwini wrote two complementary works, the first (*'Aja'ib al-Makhluqat*) dealing with the cosmos and descending to the mineral, vegetable and animal worlds, and the second (*Athar al-Bilad*) a geographical dictionary tabulated by the seven regions of the earth (*aqalim*). The lexical arrangement is adopted in both works. The premise of the first work is that what may appear wondrous is often simply unfamiliar. The second work is premised upon the view that the great diversity of human societies is intended by their Maker to emphasize their interdependence. Neither premise was entirely original: much is taken from *Adab*, geography and science, although always scrupulously acknowledged. But the broad historical sweep of the second work, with the history of each city or region, as in Yaqut, updated to the author's own days, produced a number of observations on such matters as urban and nomadic existence, the salient characteristics of Muslim cities and the comparative disposition of Christian and Muslim states in his days. A lengthy quotation from Badi' al-Zaman al-Hamadhani (d. 398/1008) appears to capture well the comparative outlook common to both Yaqut and Qazwini:

It is related that a friend wrote to him complaining of the rottenness of the age. Badi' al-Zaman answered: You complain that this is a rotten age? Pray tell me, when was it ever righteous? Was it in the days of the Abbasid state whose end we have witnessed and whose beginnings we have heard narrated? Or was it in the days of the Marwanids, whose history contains enough dust of battle to floor the most nimble of wits? Or was it in the days of the Harbids when swords were sheathed in blood and spears fixed in kidneys? Or was it in the days of the Hashims when 'Ali would say, For every ten of you I wish I had one person from the clan of Firas ibn Ghanm? Or was it in the days of 'Uthman when the whole of Hijaz was in uproar . . . or in the days of 'Umar when 'Umar himself would say, Following decline, there is more decline to come? or the days of Abu Bakr . . . or of the Prophet . . . or of the *Jahiliyya* . . . or the days before . . . or the age of Adam

---

[77] Yaqut, *Mu'jam*, 1:254–5. Yaqut claimed that all histories of ancient nations were riddled with custom-breaking reports: *Mu'jam*, 1:450.

. . . or even the days before Adam was created? No. The age has not become rotten but the analogy has carried us away.[78]

The heightened and comparative sense of historical topography was coeval with an age of elaborate feudal surveys of land, of records centrally maintained which specified details of all feudal land grants and of greater exactitude in the description of all endowment deeds, most of which involved land.

Ibn Khaldun

For our present purposes, no attempt will be made to add to the enormous literature of interpretation on Ibn Khaldun by offering yet another résumé of his thought. It will suffice to try to show that (1) Ibn Khaldun owed much to *siyasa*-oriented historical writing and thought and (2) that his *History*, considered by many modern scholars to be an unworthy sequel of his celebrated *Muqaddima*, or Prolegomenon, was in fact intended to be a precise and carefully constructed demonstration of the principles of historical change outlined in the *Muqaddima*.

It will be recalled that in a lengthy passage from his *History*, cited above, on the relationship between *shariʿa* and *siyasa*, Ibn Khaldun highlighted a dominant concern of the age: the relationship between power and virtue as exemplified in the reign of Muʿawiya. He argued that power was necessary, that it was in itself neither good nor bad but a special kind of skill to be used badly or well in the maintenance of states. Seen in their historical context, these views seem to emanate from reflections on government and justice adumbrated in the thought and writing of Ibn al-Athir, Turtushi and Ibn al-Tiqtaqa. But Ibn Khaldun startles by both the consistency and the expansion of the vision. The consistency lies in the employment of a language whose metaphors are meant to invite the reader to think of power as a 'commodity', while the expansion of the vision challenges the reader to recognize that power permeates societies and the labour of human hands and thought as well as states. For every kind of activity there is an appropriate sense of power and a level of power diffusion. The universe of Ibn Khaldun is a structured whole, with its gradations of reality and meaning. History is the record of this structure and it too reflects the many permutations of *siyasa*, the manner in which the levels interact and develop. The *Muqaddima* sets out the broad outlines of this scheme, the *History* demonstrates how that scheme operated in time. Neither can be fully understood without the other and this relationship between them is frequently underlined by Ibn Khaldun himself.

[78] Qazwini, *Athar*, pp. 326–7. For urban and nomadic existence, see *Athar*, p. 82 (all Islamic cities have a tribal encampment nearby, suggesting a close link with nomadic life); p. 5 (characteristics of cities); p. 338 (comparison between two beleaguered communities, the Muslims of Spain and the Crusaders of the Near East).

To reiterate. Because most modern scholarship has taken relatively little interest in the *History*, tending in fact to dismiss it as an incongruous appendage to the *Muqaddima* or as no better or even worse than many typical histories of that age, it serves our interests well here to show not only that this was not the case, but that Ibn Khaldun's *History* was a rigorous and precisely constructed account, arranged by states, of world history as it needs to be understood and rewritten when the principles of the *Muqaddima* are kept in view. In passage after passage of commentary, criticism and explication, Ibn Khaldun's *History* brings events into line with their context of possibility, explains how and why power was acquired or lost in particular cases, shows how the bond of power (*'asabiyya*) operated in specific situations, details the 'diseases' which afflicted some of the great Islamic cities and states of his age, corrects the genealogies of dynasties by explaining the relationship of genealogy to power and, in general, encourages his readers to 'restore' every historical report (*khabar*) to its appropriate 'locus'.

In many ways the *History* of Ibn Khaldun resembles a Mamluk architectural monument. The powerful scale of the exterior merges slowly into the delicacy of interior detail, just as the grand panorama of great contemporaneous states is worked out on a smaller scale by their numerous offshoots and branches. This image, however, is static whereas the *History* of Ibn Khaldun pans over a wide landscape in motion, where nations are swallowed up in the 'shadows' of cities and cultures, and states succumb to the 'senility' of old age, while other 'younger' and more vigorous nations prepare to assume the power which their vitality has put within their grasp. But as he often enjoins his reader to remember that 'people resemble their own age more than they resemble their ancestors', one must attempt to 'restore' Ibn Khaldun himself to his appropriate context and to show how the building blocks of the *Muqaddima* in general and his *History* in particular were found ready to hand in the historiography of his age. We could therefore begin with a general question: Is there any reason why Ibn Khaldun belongs more appropriately to the *siyasa*-oriented tradition than he does to the *Hikma* tradition? Does he belong to *any* tradition of Islamic historiography?

There is a sense in which one might maintain that Arabic historical thought culminates in Ibn Khaldun. His work seems demonstrably to have synthesized a body of historical reflections which the present work has attempted to assemble under successive 'epistemic umbrellas'. Obvious affinities exist between him and Mas'udi, for instance, while his debt to Islamic philosophy and natural science, studied in detail by modern scholars, would make him at least a fellow traveller with figures like Jahiz, Farabi or Biruni. Therefore one arresting and widespread image of him as a 'comet' streaking through the night sky should certainly be questioned as a depiction of his place in the overall historiographic tradition. That he *belonged* somewhere is a proposition which must be asserted even at the cost of banality and despite the fact that, like literary classics of all cultures, his work invites removal from its context because of its perennial freshness. If the phrase 'a historian's historian' has any meaning, it may fruitfully be applied to Ibn Khaldun to suggest his pedagogic centrality in the historical curriculum of his own as well as other cultures.

Partly in order to explain his centrality, an attempt is made to see him as a Mamluk historian, or more broadly, to see his *History* as a salient exemplar of the *siyasa*-oriented historical writing and criticism which this chapter has tried to outline. Like Nuwayri or Ibn al-'Ibri, for example, he decided to arrange his *History* by states. Like Ibn al-Athir, he drew the sharpest of distinctions between appearance and reality. Like Ibn Wasil, he was always at pains to arrange and control his materials in order to minimize repetition. Like Turtushi, he tried to demonstrate in the *History* the workings of *siyasa*, its functions and limits. If the *Muqaddima* with its philosophical edifice has the science of human culture (*'ilm al-'umran al-bashari*) as its main theme, a demonstrative science in the *Hikma* tradition, the *History* was intended to display and correct the past in the light of that science.

A reader of Ibn Khaldun's *History* would at once note one feature far more densely evident in it than in other contemporary works of history: the ubiquitous correctives. Whenever he corrects historical reports, the tone is decisive, almost dismissive:

[On deliberate alteration of scriptures] Ibn 'Abbas said: God forbid that any nation would turn to its revealed book and set about altering it. Ibn 'Abbas meant that they could only have altered or perverted its interpretation . . . Now it may happen that certain words are altered through oversight . . . and custom would permit this to happen especially when their kingdom has ended and they have been dispersed all over the world so that the careful scholar among them cannot be distinguished from the careless . . . and there is no authority to restrain them from such error once power has departed with the kingdom. Accordingly some alteration or accidental error may have crept into certain pages of the Torah at the hands of their scholars . . . In any case, one can find out what the correct text is if one inquires diligently enough about it.

[On the winter and summer journeys of Quraysh] It is claimed that Hashim ibn 'Abd Manaf was the man who first instituted for the Arabs the two journeys of winter and summer. This is reported by Ibn Ishaq and is incorrect. That is because the two journeys have been Arab customs in every age and undertaken in order to pasture their camels and care for them since their livelihood depends on this practice. This in fact is the true meaning of Arab existence . . . shaping their very character. They are forced to undertake these journeys, whether they are nomadic or settled. This is the very meaning and hallmark of Arabism.

[On the Fatimid caliph al-Hakim] As regards the accusations levelled against him, of being an unbeliever or of having issued decrees cancelling the religious obligation of prayer, these are incorrect and no rational person could make these claims. Had al-Hakim really been guilty of such things, he would have been killed instantly . . . He was a ruler who veered between justice and injustice, terrifying his subjects at one time, reassuring them at another.

[On the Galicians] Ibn Hayyan claims that they were descended from the Goths. This, in my view, is incorrect. The Goths are a nation who withered and died out. Rarely does a kingdom revive once it has passed away. This is a case of a new kingdom and of another nation.

[On Buyid genealogy and descent from Yazdgird] In point of fact, this genealogy has been fabricated by someone who wishes to curry favour with them and knows nothing about the real nature of genealogies. Had their genealogy among the Daylam been faulty the Buyids would never have acquired mastery over them. Although genealogies change, disappear and move from people to people, nation to nation, this happens only over long spans of time and change in generations . . . But between the Buyids and Yazdgird there was only a period of three hundred years, that is, seven or eight generations . . . If one argues that their descent from the Persians was obvious, this would have prevented them from gaining mastery over the Daylam . . . As regards their rise to power, they were pure Daylam in descent and status.[79]

In very many instances the boldness of the criticism is accentuated by the sensitive nature of the opinions expressed. Ibn Khaldun was not only correcting historical reports but also challenging the majority view of theologians, jurists and historians on a large number of controversial issues. In rewriting history, he knew full well that ancient opinions would need to be questioned, prejudices cast away, fabrications exposed.

But perhaps the most striking contrast with other historians is Ibn Khaldun's theory of power and its consequences. Where other historians of the age tended on the whole to ascribe to the ruler most of the credit or blame for the course of events, Ibn Khaldun was aware of larger and more impersonal forces shaping the historical process. To that end, he marshalled a whole range of concepts which in their totality constitute his new science, the science of human culture. The aim of that science was, in his words, the correction of historical reports. Clearly, however, any attempt to explain the current in terms of the recurrent would have implications far beyond what is strictly historical, as this was understood and practised in his own age.

How power is acquired, how it is maintained and how it is lost would bring us close to the heart of Ibn Khaldun's *History* as it was deployed in illustration of the science which forms the subject of the *Muqaddima*. The organization by states, while not original with him, served his purposes

---

[79] For alteration of scriptures, see *Tarikh*, 2/1:6; for winter and summer journeys, see *Tarikh*, 2/1:336; for al-Hakim, see *Tarikh*, 4:60; for the Galicians, see *Tarikh*, 4:179–80; for the Buyids, see *Tarikh*, 4:426.

well because it allowed him to show how power operated in particular cases and with what results. It also allowed him to demonstrate through specific historical examples and temporal succession the various interconnected factors, societal, climatic, religious, occupational and mental, which go into the make-up of power. Here, too, where contemporaneous historians tended to see power largely in terms of powerful individuals leading powerful armies and only rarely to speculate about other constituents of power, Ibn Khaldun painted his picture on a larger screen. Hence, when states rose or fell much more was involved than the rise or fall of rulers or dynasties. Certain things change rapidly; others change very little and can be measured only in generations or centuries. To write history as if the only change worth recording is the rapid and dramatic is to miss the 'laws' which ultimately determine the distribution of power and the fate of states.

A fruitful insight may initially be gained into this issue if one examines Ibn Khaldun's treatment of one of early Islam's most momentous events: the murder of the third caliph 'Uthman in the year 36/656. That murder triggered a chain of events which plunged the community into civil war and created schisms that still plague Muslims to the present day. From the time of Tabari at least, if not before, the Sunni historiographic tradition drew a blanket of exoneration over the whole sorry affair.[80] It was decided, often against weighty evidence, that no Companion of the Prophet directly or indirectly involved in the murder and its terrible consequences could be judged guilty of sinful behaviour. Even Shi'i historians like Ya'qubi or Mas'udi had to express their anti-'Uthmanic sentiments with a great deal of circumspection. To take obvious sides in this divisive episode would be to put at risk the very fabric of the social order. Conspiratorial explanations were acceptable, provided they were related to shadowy figures like 'Abdullah ibn Saba' who was accused of plotting to undermine the unity of the community. But once the unity of the community was accepted as the highest politico-juristic value and took shape in the theory of consensus it was not possible for historians to pass explicit moral judgement on the murder of the caliph without also threatening the basis of that consensus. Ibn Khaldun saw that episode in a totally different light:

When the conquests had reached their limit and the Muslim religion had acquired a fully fledged state (*istukmila li'l milla al-mulk*), and the Arabs had settled down in the camp cities of Basra, Kufa, al-Sham and Egypt, keeping themselves apart from other communities, those privileged with having been Companions of the Prophet and who emulated his example . . . were the Meccan Emigrants and Medinese Ansar from Quraysh and Hijaz, and others equally fortunate in having gained a similar status. The rest of the Arabs, such as the tribes of Bakr ibn Wa'il and 'Abd al-Qays, as well as Rabi'a, the Azd, Tamim, Kinda, Quda'a and others,

---

[80] See chapter 2, footnotes 130 and 131, above.

shared this status in only a few cases. On the other hand, they had played a very prominent role in the conquests and they viewed these conquests as their own achievement. Meanwhile, the virtuous among them believed in giving precedence to those Companions who had attained seniority in Islam (*ahl al-sabiqa*) and in recognizing their merits. They were still dazed and amazed by prophecy, the frequency of divine revelations and angels descending and ascending. When the mist lifted and the earlier state of affairs was somewhat forgotten, the enemy had been crushed and government had become thoroughly repressive (*istafhala al-mulk*), the veins of the *jahiliyya* began to throb once more. They discovered that the Emigrants and Ansar from Quraysh and others had come to lord it over them. Their spirits were too proud to accept this state of affairs and this happened to coincide with the caliphate of 'Uthman. So they began to calumniate his governors in the various camp cities, to take them to task in their every glance or step and to be slow to obey their orders.[81]

Ibn Khaldun acknowledges that his account of early-Islamic history was drawn from Tabari. Like Tabari, he is also determined not to record any historical judgements which involve moral condemnation of the Prophet's Companions and other virtuous Muslims of that period 'such as is most often to be found among sectarian writers'.[82] From this point, however, the two historians diverge. Where Tabari accumulates *akhbar*, layer upon layer of transmission which the reader is left to judge for himself with only minimal hints from the author, Ibn Khaldun projects the events surrounding the murder onto a far larger tableau where the nature and appeal of power and religion to differently ordained segments of a given society must be taken into account in any attempt to understand the significance of events.

Ibn Khaldun repeatedly enjoins his reader to remember that the cause of events is proportionate to their size, that the greater the event, the more complex its causes. Thus, in the example cited above of the winter and summer journeys which almost all historians regularly and piously ascribed to Hashim, the great grandfather of the Prophet, Ibn Khaldun saw these journeys as a defining feature of a particular way of life and therefore not a habit or tradition that could ever have been started by one individual, irrespective of the halo of devotion surrounding him. In this same vein is his view that buildings of monumental dimensions normally take generations to complete and hence cannot be said to be the work of one builder, or the view that all mankind spoke the same language and then woke up one morning to find their languages had become diverse must be judged so 'far out of the ordinary' as to be acceptable only as an instance of a prophetic miracle.[83]

---

[81] Ibn Khaldun, *Tarikh*, 2/2:138. In a well known article, H. A. R. Gibb seems to have drawn heavily upon Ibn Khaldun's analysis: see 'An Interpretation of Islamic History', *Journal of World History*, 1, 1 (1953).

[82] Ibn Khaldun, *Tarikh*, 2/2:187–8.

[83] On monumental buildings, see *Tarikh*, 2/1:50; on languages, see *Tarikh*, 2/1:68.

In the major conflicts of history, Ibn Khaldun frequently resorts to the notion of *'asabiyya*, by far the most familiar Ibn Khaldunian technical term. In the *History*, the student of Ibn Khaldun finds many examples of its diverse functions. At the most basic level, there is what Ibn Khaldun calls 'natural' (*tabi'iyya*) *'asabiyya*:

> This is never absent. It manifests itself in one man asserting dominion (*'izza*) over brother or neighbour by killing him or committing aggression against him. Nothing can ever efface it completely. Nor indeed is it forbidden (*mahzura*). Rather, it is a quality that is wanted and useful in holy war or in summoning people to a religion.[84]

Natural *'asabiyya* is therefore what one might term the aggressive instinct, that which drives one man to gain mastery over another. At certain times, as for instance in the example cited above of 'Uthman's murder, religion may temporarily moderate its effects or divert its selfish energies into worthy causes. But it will reassert itself and adopt different forms whenever the circumstances are ripe. However, that same aggressive instinct is also a bonding agent, that which unites diverse groups together to make them act under one particular banner or cause or self-interest or way of life or occupation or locale: in other words, a channelling of selfishness determined by particular ideologies or attachments. Accordingly, there are as many kinds of *'asabiyyat* as there are men united in groups of common interest. Some are strong and active, some weak and passive. In great military and political conflicts, two *'asabiyya*s should always be seen to be contending. In general, victory goes to the stronger of any two *'asabiyya*s, a proposition which may appear tautologous but in fact encourages the student of history to analyse the components of power on each side of a conflict:

> The soldiers of 'Ali were more numerous because of the status and prestige of the caliphate but they came from diverse tribes . . . whereas the armies of Mu'awiya were made up of the standing army (*jund*) of Syria from Quraysh, and from the most powerful tribes of Mudar. These had settled in the frontier posts of Syria ever since the conquests. Hence the *'asabiyya* of Mu'awiya was stronger and more energetic . . . The community had agreed to pay allegiance to Mu'awiya . . . when men had forgotten the era of prophecy and miracles, reverting to *'asabiyya* and love of power. The Umayyads were thus chosen to lead Mudar and the other Arabs.[85]

From Ibn Khaldun's *History* one grasps the diachronic sweep, the spectacle of states rising and falling in a seriality otherwise lacking in his *Muqaddima* with its achronic, largely philosophical reflections. Of special significance is the question of the rise of states, a topic which, as we saw

---

[84] Ibn Khaldun, *Tarikh*, 3:3.
[85] Ibn Khaldun, *Tarikh*, 3:4.

above, was relatively neglected by historians intent upon understanding the causes of decline in order that they might discover the moral behind it. The kind of power needed for the rise of states was for Ibn Khaldun the fulfilment of a particular type of group *'asabiyya*, the type for instance which might lead a primitive, nomadic or religious group with a strong *'asabiyya* to attack a state whose own *'asabiyya* has been whittled away by the luxury of urban living. In pursuit of such phenomena, Ibn Khaldun marshals a host of factors to explain why primitive *'asabiyya* is generally more disciplined and unquestioning than urban *'asabiyya* and the stages by which urban *'asabiyya* itself reaches a point of weakness and 'old age'. From the examination of young and old states may be deduced a number of indicators (*dala'il*), which one is tempted to call symptoms, in line with Ibn Khaldun's own imagery of the youth, health and decrepitude of states. Thus, a caliph found to be spending his time breeding pigeons or cavorting in the uniform of *futuwwa* 'indicates' a senescent state while states may also be said to contract 'diseases' from which they occasionally 'recover'.[86] Historical reports must therefore be checked against the particular stage at which a state or a people happens to find itself: what may appropriately be done by a 'young' state cannot be ascribed to an 'old', and *vice versa*.[87]

But it is in the history of entire nations or peoples that Ibn Khaldun demonstrates the full range of his analysis, as when he surveys the history of Arabs or Turks:

This particular branch of the Arab nation, the nomadic tent-dwellers . . . have always been among the earth's greatest and most populous peoples. Occasionally they attain dominion and victory through sheer numbers, winning kingdoms, conquering regions and cities, then falling prey to luxury and softness of living, conquest by others and death. They return once more to their deserts, having lost, by dint of luxury, the leaders among them who are fit to rule . . . Because of the Arab Islamic state, they are now a spent force (*anfaqathum al-dawla al-islamiyya al-'arabiyya*) . . . and are swallowed up by far-flung regions . . . Others have come forward to shoulder the burdens of religion and state. The merchandise of arts and crafts has been carried to markets other than their own . . . Their remainder have again taken to the desert . . . as was the case with their ancestors in the *jahiliyya*, Rabi'a, Mudar and Kahlan . . . Thus Arab Islamic kingship has passed away, overtaken, as is customary, by old age.[88]

[86] Ibn Khaldun, *Tarikh*, 3:535 and 7:292.
[87] See, e.g., *Tarikh*, 2/1:20, on Hud and Ya'rub. Compare a revealing passage from Michel de Certeau, *The Writing of History* (New York: Columbia University Press, 1988), pp. 61–2: 'The same movement organizes society and the "ideas" that circulate within it. It is parcelled into orders of manifestation (economic, social, scientific, and so forth) which make up overlapping but differential functions, in which none can be either the reality or the cause of another. Thus, socioeconomic and symbolic systems combine without being identified or ranked in hierarchies. In this way a social change can be compared to a biological change in the human body: like the biological change, the social change forms a language which is proportioned to other types of language, such as the verbal.'
[88] Two passages are conflated here: *Tarikh*, 2/1:236–7 and 6:3.

As the Arabs are seen exiting from the stage, the Turks are described as entering it. The scale is equally panoramic:

The Arabs were not at first in the habit of enlisting the aid of their slaves in any aspect of their public affairs . . . If any slave embraced Islam, they would let him go his own way . . . the reason being that the *'asabiyya* of the Arabs was then at its strongest and their political dominance was clear . . . and they all took an active part, along with their ruler, in public affairs . . . In sum, they were as equal and united as the teeth of a comb, because of closely-knit genealogies and a religion that was still young. But when kingship sharpened its edges and tended to become repressive and the ruler, in order to rule, needed to assert his power against rivals from among his own people by the use of an *'asabiyya* that would protect him against them . . . the Abbasids, from the time of al-Mahdi . . . began to employ palace guards made up of Turkish and Greek clients. These groups then created various Islamic states which in most cases issued from groups possessed of strong *'asabiyya* and solid genealogy as were, for example, the states of the Samanids . . . the Subuktekins . . . or the Tulunids. When the state had become thoroughly engrossed in civilization and luxury and was clad in the attire of misfortune and incapacity, suffering the onslaught of the pagan Mongols, God in His mercy came to the rescue of the faith by reviving its failing spirits and ordained its protection by uniting the Muslims of Egypt . . . sending protecting military commanders from among this Turkish nation . . . who are imported as slaves from the territory of war . . . but a slavery such as conceals within it God's merciful purposes . . . They then embrace the religion with strength of faith and nomadic morality not sullied by malice nor defiled by carnal pleasures nor tainted by the habits of civilization nor enfeebled by the superabundance of luxury . . . They outbid each other in buying them . . . not in order to enslave them but to strengthen *'asabiyya* and reinforce power . . . Thereafter, whoever among them is found fitting comes to occupy the position of sultan . . . In this manner, one new group comes to succeed another, one generation follows the next. Islam rejoices with the power it has gained and the branches of the state sway with the vigour of youth.[89]

As a portrait of the contemporary Mamluk sultanate which in Ibn Khaldun's days was almost a hundred and fifty years old, it is distinguished by the attempt to place it in a much larger historical context and then to detect in it a built-in principle of self-renewal which seemingly transcends the iron rule of the rise, decline and fall of state *'asabiyya*. Is Ibn Khaldun merely pandering to his masters? This is possible, but it detracts little from the breadth of the analysis which brings into play the conjunction of religion and power, the debilitating effects of civilization and the illustrative function of *'asabiyya* as this latter holds together or dissipates the power of states.

In Ibn Khaldun, the fate of cities often parallels that of states and elicits some of his most profound reflections on the nature of change. In cities man is found asserting authority, building monuments, prospering and

---

[89] Ibn Khaldun, *Tarikh*, 5:369–70.

cultivating the arts and sciences. But slowly the arteries of city life begin to constrict, a metaphor not very foreign to Ibn Khaldun's own. Rulers gradually lose the support of the group which brought their fathers to power. They then need a standing army, to maintain which they begin to overtax their subjects. Commerce is suffocated as rulers are increasingly drawn into monopolizing basic foodstuffs and commodities and the state grows weaker and ripe for conquest. As states decline, so do their cities and when they finally wither away or are swept away by a more vigorous 'asabiyya, the cities suffer the same fate; although some cities might once more rise in the bosom of new dynasties. Like states, the arts and sciences might also disappear for ever, 'for where are the sciences of the Persians . . . Chaldeans, Assyrians, Babylonians . . . and Copts? The sciences of only one nation have reached us, the Greeks, simply because the caliph al-Ma'mun was overly fond of translating them and was able to do so because he had many translators at his disposal.'[90]

That Ibn Khaldun sought to pass beyond the particular and the individual and to survey history as it unfolded over generations and as it was made by large forces or groups was due at least in part to his time and place in the tradition of *siyasa*: the geographical sweep of Yaqut and Qazwini, the historical range of Ibn al-Athir and Abu'l Fida, the topographical interests of Ibn al-'Adim and Ibn al-Khatib, the reflections on power and law of Ibn al-Tiqtaqa and Tùrtushi.

[90] Ibn Khaldun, *Muqaddima*, pp. 35–6.

Conclusion

In a striking passage, Paul Veyne commends the following methodology to a historian of historiography:

> So a history of historiography that wanted to get to the heart of the subject would be less concerned with the facile study of the ideas of each historian and more with an inventory of his palette. (*Writing History*, p. 215)

One might wonder to begin with why an inventory of a palette is a task more difficult to accomplish than a report of a processional of great minds. But I suspect that Paul Veyne does not really mean an inventory; rather, a stock-taking of a particular intellectual environment. This has in fact been the central concern of my study of Arabic historical thought. This study was premised on the view that the effect of Islamic revelation on historical thought was preponderant, that the Arabs acquired, with Islam, a new historiography as well as a new religion. It goes on to argue that historical writing began soon after the early conquests, probably in response to the drama of events, but no doubt also in response to early state-formation and the need for a legitimating, precedent-creating past. It further assumes that historical writing in all cultures and times has been peculiarly susceptible to surrounding climates of ideas and beliefs. It postulates that Arabic historical thought and writing gradually underwent the influence of four dominant epistemic 'domes': (1) *Hadith* or the sacred 'traditions', (2) *Adab*, or Belles-Lettres, (3) *Hikma* or the natural and social sciences and (4) *Siyasa*, or political theory and practice. This was also very roughly the chronological order of their appearance. There were of course overlaps: in a science as cobwebby as history, one cannot expect strict categorization.

In broad terms, my argument has been that history was looked upon from four major points of view. History as *Hadith* meant the preservation of the sacred and secular past of the community with the emphasis falling upon the modes of transmission of historical reports rather than on their intrinsic probability. History as *Adab* meant history as a narrative record of human civilization where patterns may be detected as guides to political and ethical conduct. History as *Hikma* meant a more rigorous attention to the workings of nature and rationality in the acceptance of historical reports, largely perhaps in order to prune religion of legend. History as *Siyasa* meant history as an imperial bureaucratic chronicle, authoritative, comprehensive, and designed primarily for administrative use.

This study culminates in Ibn Khaldun and may in one sense be said to constitute an attempt to describe the tradition which made his work possible. On the other hand, and in doing so, it seeks to explore a field which he has for so long overshadowed, both retroactively and prospectively. For it may be argued that the four major 'domes' continued in one sense or another to shelter and to spawn historical works of enormous merit until the eighteenth century. In Ibn Khaldun's own century, major historians like Maqrizi and Sakhawi, and in the following century Ibn Tulun, have still not received the attention they so obviously deserve. It may be that History as *Hadith* fell by the wayside while History as *Hikma* did not advance far beyond Biruni. But History as *Adab* and as *Siyasa* continued to appear, as did the biographical dictionaries. And from the sixteenth century onwards, a totally new genre of historiography made its appearance: histories written by 'commoners' such as barbers, farmers, minor state officials, obscure military commanders. These constitute a small but distinct group whose *mentalités* still await scrutiny by modern anthropologists and historians of ideas. Often written in a clumsy and apologetic style, these 'diaries' and chronicles are nevertheless of surpassing value as a record of the encounter between an oral and popular culture on the one hand and a high literary tradition on the other.

A reader who has come thus far might be curious to know something about the contemporary situation in Arabic historiography. I cannot claim to offer anything other than stray reflections for I am far less familiar with modern than with pre-modern Arabic culture. In the twentieth century, the spectrum of historiography narrowed considerably. Pre-modern historiography was brought into being by a specialized, often hereditary class of scholars, the *'ulama'*, most of whom were polymaths and not exclusively historians. In fact, many of them came to history *after* a long career in scholarship or state service and their works frequently reflected a maturity of judgement and a wide outlook on worldly affairs. Many were supported by charitable institutions, e.g. as teachers in *madaris* or higher colleges, or received regular state salaries. When this social order began to collapse in the nineteenth century, largely under European pressure, the *'ulama'* class collapsed with it. To fill the historiographic vacuum, writers of early European-style textbooks, travellers, journalists, retired doctors or lawyers or dilettantes gradually became the new historians. These happened also to be the classes most materially and spiritually affected by the West. The history they produced was first in awe of the West (including Japan, Asia's great exemplar), and then in awe of their own history. This led to an obsession with the past, a problem nowadays referred to as the problem of *turath*, or heritage. What guidance can the *turath* provide in solving current crises? The *turath* problem has been debated vigorously for about a century but its parameters have not expanded much. Simplistic formulae such as the need to adopt the 'rationality' of the *turath* and to forsake its 'mystification' are as popular today as they were in nineteenth-century journals. Only a few attempts have been made to see the *turath* in its own historical context, while among those attempting it there is, curiously, a preponderance of North African Arabs.

Thus, if the pre-modern spectrum is compared with the modern, one would have to admit that the modern is narrower in scope, more explicitly apologetic in spirit and largely Belles-Lettrist in style. Biography is of course the quintessential product of Belles-Lettrist historiography and under the authoritarian regimes ruling much of the Arab world today, many mythical biographies of leaders, heroes and great minds of past and present are produced. In certain Arab societies where communal consensus is a matter of immediate political urgency, much of the historiography is either bland or tendentious. Furthermore, most Arab historiography is regional in focus: Syrians write on Syria, Egyptians on Egypt and so forth. There is little interest in world history or even in Asian history. In non-Arab history, works on Europe predominate, as they have done since the early decades of this century, but the number of Arab students studying western history in western universities is minuscule. When one contemplates, first, the astonishing tolerance of pre-modern Arab societies and, secondly, their unparalleled curiosity and information about other nations and creeds, matched by no other civilization prior to modern Europe, one might be tempted to feel regret at the present state of affairs. And yet, there is no doubt that late-twentieth-century Arabic historiography is qualitatively superior to that produced earlier this century. As one example, no serious Arabist can any longer ignore modern Arabic historiography as she or he used to do even twenty or thirty years ago. Scientific editions of classical historical texts are produced in bulk each year, bringing the contours of the tradition into ever sharper focus. Works of the first importance on Arab history and culture written in Arabic appear regularly; the same might be said for the quality of many articles in several Arabic historical journals.

What has been the impact of a Western education on recent generations of Arab historians? I doubt whether Arab historians have actually learned anything new about historiography from the West but they have almost certainly needed the West to *remind* them of certain pre-modern principles of historiography, primarily demythologization and documentation. The West has often been the place where Arab students encounter in depth, not so much the *Mu'amalat* ('civics') and *'Ibadat* ('dogmatics') of Islamic culture but its *Adabiyyat*, its humanistic tradition, to which Christians and Jews made such brilliant contributions. One's hope is that *Adabiyyat* will come to constitute the 'dome' of contemporary Arabic historiography.

Bibliography of primary Arabic sources

'Abd al-Jabbar b. Ahmad, al-Qadi (d. 415/1024):
   Tabaqat al-Mu'tazila in *Fadl al-I'tizal wa Tabaqat al-Mu'tazila*. Ed. F. al-Sayyid. Tunis, 1974.
   Sharh al-Usul al-Khamsa, Ed. 'A. K. 'Uthman. Cairo, 1965.
   Al-Mughni fi Abwab al-Tawhid wa'l 'Adl. Vol. 12, ed. I. Madkur, Cairo, n. d.; vol. 15, ed. M. al-Khudayri, Cairo, 1965; vol. 16, ed. A. al-Khuli, Cairo, 1960; vol. 17, ed. A. al-Khuli, Cairo, 1963.
   Tathbit Dala'il al-Nubuwwa. Ed. 'A. K. 'Uthman. Cairo, 1966.
Abu al-'Ala' al-Ma'arri (d. 449/1058):
   Al-Luzumiyyat. Ed. 'A. Zand. Cairo, 1891, 1895.
Abu'l Fida, Isma'il b. 'Ali (d. 732/1331):
   Al-Mukhtasar fi Akhbar al-Bashar. Cairo, 1907.
Abu Nu'aym al-Isfahani (d. 430/1039):
   Hilyat al-Awliya'. Cairo, 1932.
Abu Rifa'a 'Umara b. Wathima al-Farisi (d. 289/902):
   Bad' al-Khalq wa Qisas al-Anbiya'. Ed. R. G. Khoury. Wiesbaden, 1978.
Abu Shama, Shihab al-Din Abu'l Qasim (d. 665/1267):
   Al-Rawdatayn fi Akhbar al-Dawlatayn. Vol. 1/1. ed. M.H.M. Ahmad. Cairo, 1956.
Abu 'Ubayd al-Qasim b. Sallam (d. 224/838):
   Kitab al-Amwal. 'A. M. 'Amir. Cairo, 1970.
Abu Yusuf, Ya'qub b. Ibrahim (d. 182/798):
   Kitab al-Kharaj. Cairo, 1933.
Abu Zayd al-Qurashi, Muhammad b. Abi'l Khattab (d. early fourth/tenth century):
   Jamharat Ash'ar al-'Arab. Beirut, 1963.
Abu Zur'a al-Dimashqi, 'Abd al-Rahman b. 'Amr (d. 281/894):
   Tarikh. Ed. S. Qawajani. Damascus, 1980.
Amin, 'Uthman (ed.):
   Nusus Falsafiyya muhdat ila al-Duktur Ibrahim Madkur. Cairo, 1976.
Al-'Amiri, Abu'l Hasan Muhammad (d. 381/992):
   Al-I'lam bi Manaqib al-Islam. Ed. A. 'A. H. Ghurab. Cairo, 1967.
Al-'Askari, Abu Ahmad al-Hasan b. 'Abdullah (d. 382/993):
   Al-Masun fi'l Adab. Ed. 'A. S. M. Harun. Kuwait, 1960.
Al-'Askari, Abu Hilal al-Hasan b. 'Abdullah (d. after 400/1010):

Al-Sina'atayn. Cairo, 1952.

Al-Awa'il. Ed. M. al-Masri and W. Qassab. Damascus, 1975.

Al-Asma'i, 'Abd al-Malik b. Qurayb (d. 213/828):
  Tarikh al-'Arab qabl al-Islam. Ed. M. H. Al Yasin. Baghdad, 1959.

Al-Azdi, Muhammad b. 'Abdullah (d. third/ninth century):
  Futuh al-Sham. Ed. 'A. M. 'Amir. Cairo, 1970.

Al-Baghdadi, 'Abd al-Qahir (d. 429/1037):
  Al-Farq bayn al-Firaq. Ed. M. M. 'Abd al-Hamid. Cairo, n. d.
  Usul al-Din. Istanbul, 1928.

Al-Baghdadi, Ahmad b. 'Ali (d. 463/1071):
  Taqyid al-'Ilm. Ed. Y. al-'Ishsh. Damascus, 1949.
  Al-Kifaya fi 'Ilm al-Riwaya. Haidarabad, 1938.
  Tarikh Baghdad. Cairo, 1931.

Al-Baghdadi, Abu'l Barakat (d. *c.* 560/1165):
  Al-Mu'tabar fi'l Hikma. Vol. 1. Haidarabad, 1938.

Al-Baladhuri, Ahmad b. Yahya (d. *c.* 279/892):
  Ansab al-Ashraf. Vol. 1, ed. M. Hamidullah, Cairo, 1959; vol. 3, ed. 'A. 'A.
    Duri, Wiesbaden, 1978; vol. 4/1, ed. I. 'Abbas, Wiesbaden, 1979; vol. 4/2,
    ed. M. Schloessinger, Jerusalem, 1938; vol. 5, ed. S. D. Goitein, Jerusalem,
    1936.
  Futuh al-Buldan. Ed. M. J. de Goeje. Leiden, 1866.

Al-Baqillani, Abu Bakr (d. 403/1012):
  Al-Bayan 'an al-Farq bayn al-Mu'jizat wa'l Karamat. Ed. R. J. McCarthy.
    Beirut, 1958.

Al-Basri, Abu'l Husayn Muhammad b. 'Ali (d. 436/1044):
  Al-Mu'tamad fi Usul al-Fiqh. Ed. M. Hamidullah. Damascus, 1965.

Al-Biruni, Abu'l Rayhan (d. 448/1048):
  Risala fi Fihrist Kutub Muhammad b. Zakariyya al-Razi. Ed. P. Kraus. Paris,
    1936.
  Al-Athar al-Baqiya 'an al-Qurun al-Khaliya. Ed. E. Sachau. Leipzig, 1878, 1923.
  Tahqiq ma li'l Hind min Maqula, maqbulatin fi'l 'Aql aw mardhula. Ed. E.
    Sachau. London, 1887.

Al-Dabbi, al-Mufaddal b. Muhammad (d. 164 or 170/780 or 786):
  Al-Mufaddaliyyat. Ed. C. J. Lyall. Oxford, 1921.

Al-Dhahabi, Muhammad b. Ahmad (d. 748/1347):
  Tarajim Rijal rawa 'anhum Muhammad b. Ishaq. Ed. A. Fischer. Leiden, 1890.
  Mizan al-I'tidal fi Naqd al-Rijal. Ed. A. M. al-Bajawi. Cairo, 1963.
  *Bayan Zaghal al-'Ilm wa'l Talab wa yalihi al-Nasiha al-Dhahabiyya li Ibn Tay-
    miyya.* Damascus, 1928-9.
  Tarikh al-Islam wa Tabaqat al-Mashahir wa'l A'lam. Cairo, 1948.

Al-Dinawari, Abu Hanifa Ahmad (d. 282/895):
  Al-Akhbar al-Tiwal. Ed. 'A. M. 'Amir. Cairo, 1960.

Al-Farabi, Abu Nasr Muhammad b. Muhammad (d. 339/950):
  Al-Siyasa al-Madaniyya. Ed. F. M. Najjar. Beirut, 1964.
  Kitab al-Huruf. Ed. M. Mahdi. Beirut, 1970.
  Kitab al-Milla. Ed. M. Mahdi. Beirut, 1968.

Al-Ghazali, Abu Hamid Muhammad b. Muhammad (d. 505/1111):
  Mi'yar al-'Ilm. Ed. S. Dunya. Cairo, 1961.

Hamza b. al-Hasan al-Isfahani (d. after 350/961):
Tarikh Siniyy Muluk al-Ard wa'l Anbiya'. Berlin, 1922.
Al-Hariri, Abu Muhammad al-Qasim b. 'Ali (d. 516/1122):
Maqamat. Cairo, 1908.
Ibn 'Abbad al-Rundi, Abu 'Abdullah Muhammad (d. 792/1390):
Al-Rasa'il al-Sughra. Ed. P. Nuwiyya. Beirut, 1957.
Ibn al-Abbar, Abu 'Abdullah Muhammad (d. 658/1260):
I'tab al-Kuttab. Ed. S. al-Ashtar. Damascus, 1961.
Ibn 'Abd al-Barr, Yusuf b. 'Abdullah (d. 463/1070):
Jami' Bayan al-'Ilm wa Fadlihi. Beirut, 1978.
Ibn 'Abd al-Hakam, Abu Muhammad 'Abdullah (d. 257/870):
Futuh Misr wa Akhbariha. Ed. C. C. Torrey. New Haven, 1922.
Ibn 'Abd Rabbihi, Ahmad b. Muhammad (d. 328/940):
Al-'Iqd al-Farid. Ed. A. Amin *et al*. Cairo, 1940–53.
Ibn 'Abd al-Zahir, Muhyi'l Din Abu'l Fadl 'Abdullah (d. 692/1292):
Tashrif al-Ayyam wa'l 'Usur fi Sirat al-Malik al-Mansur. Ed. M. Kamil. Cairo,
1961.
Al-Rawd al-Zahir fi Sirat al-Malik al-Zahir. Ed. A. A. Khuwaytir. Riyad, 1976.
Ibn Abi Hatim al-Razi, Muhammad b. 'Abd al-Rahman (d. 327/939):
Al-Jarh wa'l Ta'dil. Haidarabad, 1952.
Taqdimat al-Ma'rifa. Haidarabad, 1952.
Ibn Abi Tahir Tayfur, Ahmad (d. 280/893):
Tarikh Baghdad. Ed. H. Keller. Leipzig, 1908.
Ibn Abi Usaybi'a, Ahmad b. al-Qasim (d. 668/1270):
'Uyun al-Anba' fi Tabaqat al-Atibba'. Ed. A. Muller. Cairo/Koenigsberg,
1882–4.
Ibn al-'Adim, Kamal al-Din Abu'l Qasim 'Umar (d. 660/1262):
Zubdat al-Halab fi Tarikh Halab. Vols. 1 and 2, ed. S. al-Dahhan. Damascus,
1951, 1968.
Ibn al-Anbari, 'Abd al-Rahman b. Muhammad (d. 577/1181):
Nuzhat al-Alibba'. Ed. I. al-Samarra'i. Baghdad, 1959.
Ibn 'Aqil, Abu'l Wafa' 'Ali (d. 513/1119):
Kitab al-Funun. Vol. 1, ed. G. al-Maqdisi. Beirut, 1970.
Ibn 'Asakir, 'Ali b.al-Hasan (d. 571/1175):
Tarikh Madinat Dimashq. Vol. 1, ed. S. al-Munajjid. Damascus, 1951.
Ibn al-Athir, Abu'l Hasan 'Izz al-Din (d. 630/1232):
Al-Kamil fi'l Tarikh. Ed. C. J. Tornberg. Leiden, 1851–76.
Al-Tarikh al-Bahir fi al-Dawla al-Atabikiyya. Ed. 'A. Q. A. Tulaymat. Cairo,
1963.
Ibn al-Dawadari, Abu Bakr 'Abdullah b. Aybak (wrote 736/1335):
Kanz al-Durar wa Jami' al-Ghurar. Vol. 8. Ed. U. Haarmann. Cairo, 1971.
Ibn al-Daya, Abu Ja'far Ahmad b. Yusuf (d. after 330/941):
Al-Mukafa'a. Ed. A. Amin and A. al-Jarim. Cairo, 1941.
Ibn al-Faqih al-Hamadani (wrote *c*. 290/903):
Mukhtasar Kitab al-Buldan. Ed. M. J. de Goeje. Leiden, 1885.
Ibn Faris, Abu'l Husayn Ahmad (d. 395/1004):
Al-Sahibi fi Fiqh al-Lugha. Cairo, 1910.
Ibn al-Fuwati, Kamal al-Din 'Abd al-Razzaq (d. 723/1323):

238   Bibliography

Al-Hawadith al-Jami'a wa'l Tajarib al-Nafi'a fi al-Ma'a al-Sabi'a. Baghdad, 1932.
Ibn Habib, Muhammad (d. 245/859):
    Kitab al-Muhabbar. Ed. I. Lichtenstadter. Haidarabad, 1942.
Ibn Hanbal, Ahmad (d. 241/855):
    Musnad. Beirut, 1969.
Ibn Hawqal, Abu'l Qasim b. 'Ali (d. c. 362/973):
    Surat al-Ard. Ed. J. H. Kramers. Leiden, 1938-9.
Ibn Hazm, Abu Muhammad 'Ali b. Sa'id (d. 456/1064):
    Rasa'il. Vol. 1. Ed. I. 'Abbas. Beirut, 1980.
    Al-Ihkam fi Usul al-Ahkam. Cairo, 1927.
    Al-Fisal fi'l Milal wa'l Ahwa' wa'l Nihal. Cairo, 1903.
Ibn Hisham, Abu Muhammad 'Abd al-Malik (d. 218/833):
    Kitab al-Tijan fi Muluk Himyar. Ed. F. Krenkow. Haidarabad, 1928.
Ibn al-'Ibri, Abu'l Faraj (d. 685/1286):
    Tarikh Mukhtasar al-Duwal. Ed. A. Salihani. Beirut, 1890.
Ibn 'Idhari al-Marrakushi, Abu'l 'Abbas Ahmad (wrote 706/1306):
    Al-Bayan al-Mughrib fi Akhbar al-Andalus wa'l Maghrib. Vol. 1, ed. G. S. Colin
    and E. Lévi-Provençale. Leiden, 1948.
Ibn Ishaq, Muhammad (d. 151/761):
    Sira. Ed. M. Hamidullah. Rabat, 1976.
Ibn al-Jarrah, Muhammad b. Dawud (d. 296/908):
    Kitab al-Waraqa. 2nd ed. Ed. 'A. W. 'Azzam and 'A. S. Farraj. Cairo, n. d.
Ibn al-Jawzi, Abu al-Faraj 'Abd al-Rahman (d. 597/1201):
    Al-Muntazam. Vols. 9 and 10. Haidarabad, 1938.
    Talbis Iblis. Cairo, 1928.
Ibn al-Kalbi, Hisham b. Muhammad (d. 204 or 206/819 or 821):
    Jamharat al-Nasab. Ed. N. Hasan. Beirut, 1986.
Ibn Kathir, Isma'il b. 'Umar (d. 774/1373):
    Al-Bidaya wa'l Nihaya. Cairo, 1932-9.
Ibn Khaldun, 'Abd al-Rahman (d. 808/1406):
    Tarikh. Ed. N. al-Hurini. Cairo, 1868.
    Muqaddima. Cairo, n. d.
    Shifa' al-Sa'il li Tahdhib al-Masa'il. Ed. I. A. Khalifah. Beirut, 1959.
Ibn Khallikan, Ahmad b. Muhammad (d. 681/1282):
    Wafayat al-A'yan. Ed. I. 'Abbas. Beirut, 1968-72.
Ibn al-Khatib, Lisan al-Din (d. 776/1374):
    Al-Ihata fi Akhbar Gharnata. Vol. 1, ed. M. A. 'Inan. Cairo, 1973.
Ibn al-Mu'tazz, 'Abdullah (d. 296/909):
    Kitab al-Badi'. Ed. M. al-Khaffaji. Cairo, 1945.
Ibn al-Qalanisi, Abu Ya'la Hamza (d. c. 555/1160):
    Dhayl Tarikh Dimashq. Ed. H. F. Amedroz. Leiden, 1908.
Ibn Qutayba, 'Abdullah b. Muslim (d. 276/889):
    Kitab al-Ma'arif. Ed. T. 'Ukasha. Cairo, 1960.
    'Uyun al-Akhbar. Cairo, 1925-30.
    Ta'wil Mukhtalif al-Hadith. Ed. F. Z. al-Kurdi et al. Cairo, 1908.
    Adab al-Katib. Ed. M. Grunert. Leiden, 1900.
    Al-Shi'r wa'l Shu'ara'. Ed. M. J. de Goeje. Leiden, 1902.
    Al-Ikhtilaf fi'l Lafz wa'l Radd 'ala al-Jahmiyya wa'l Mushabbiha. Ed. M. Z.
    Kawthari. Cairo, 1930.

Ibn Rashiq, Abu ʿAli al-Hasan (d. 463/1071):
  Al-ʿUmda. Ed. M. M. ʿAbd al-Hamid. Cairo, 1934.
Ibn Rushd, Abu'l Walid Muhammad b. Ahmad (d. 594/1198):
  Fasl al-Maqal. Ed. G. F. Hourani. Leiden, 1959.
  Rasaʾil. Haidarabad, 1947.
Ibn Rusteh, Abu ʿAli Ahmad b. ʿUmar (d. early fourth/tenth century):
  Al-Aʿlaq al-Nafisa. Ed. M. J. de Goeje. Leiden, 1892.
Ibn Saʿd, Muhammad (d. 230/845):
  Kitab al-Tabaqat. Beirut, 1958.
Ibn Shaddad, ʿIzz al-Din Abu ʿAbdullah Muhammad (d. 684/1285):
  Al-Aʿlaq al-Khatira. Vol. 1/1, ed. D. Sourdel. Damascus, 1953.
  Tarikh Madinat Dimashq, ed. S. al-Dahhan. Damascus, 1956.
Ibn Shaddad, Bahaʾ al-Din Abu'l Mahasin Yusuf (d. 632/1235):
  Al-Nawadir al-Sultaniyya wa'l Mahasin al-Yusufiyya. Ed. M. ʿA. Sabih. Cairo,
  1927–8.
Ibn Sina, Abu ʿAli al-Husayn (d. 428/1037):
  Al-Najat. Cairo, 1938.
  Mantiq al-Mashriqiyyin. Cairo, 1910.
Ibn Taghribirdi, Abu'l Mahasin Yusuf (d. 874/1469):
  Al-Nujum al-Zahira fi Akhbar Misr wa'l Qahira. Cairo, 1929–72.
Ibn Taymiyya, Ahmad b. ʿAbd al-Halim (d. 728/1328):
  Iqtidaʾ al-Surat al-Mustaqim mukhalafat Ashab al-Jahim. Ed. M. H. Faqi. Cairo,
  1950.
  Kitab al-Nubuwwat. Cairo, 1966.
  Minhaj al-Sunna al-Nabawiyya. Ed. M. R. Salim. Cairo, 1962.
  Risala ila al-Sultan al-Malik al-Nasir fi Shaʾn al-Tatar. Ed. S. al-Munajjid. Beirut,
  1976.
  Darʾ Taʿarud al-ʿAql wa'l Naql. Vol. 1, ed. M. R. Salim. Cairo, 1971.
Ibn al-Tiqtaqa, Safiyy al-Din Muhammad (wrote 701/1302):
  Al-Fakhri fi'l Adab al-Sultaniyya. Cairo, 1929.
Ibn Tufayl, Abu Bakr Muhammad (d. 581/1185):
  Hayy b. Yaqzan. Ed. J. Saliba and K. ʿAyyad. Damascus, 1962.
Ibn Wasil, Jamal al-Din (d. 697/1298):
  Mufarrij al-Kurub fi Akhbar Bani Ayyub. Vol. 1, ed. J. al-Shayyal, Cairo, 1953;
  vol. 4, ed. H. M. Rabiʿ, Cairo, 1972; vol. 5, ed. H. M. Rabiʿ, Cairo, 1977.
Al-Idrisi, al-Sharif (d. c. 560/1165):
  Nuzhat al-Mushtaq fi Ikhtiraq al-Afaq. Ed. E. Cerulli et al. Naples/Rome,
  1970–84.
ʿImad al-Din al-Katib al-Isfahani (d. 597/1201):
  Al-Fath al-Qussi fi al-Fath al-Qudsi. Cairo, 1904.
  Kharidat al-Qasr wa Jaridat al-ʿAsr. Vol. 1. Ed. M. B. al-Athari and J. Saʿid.
  Baghdad, 1955.
Al-Isfahani, Abu'l Faraj ʿAli b. al-Husayn (d. 356/967):
  Al-Aghani. Ed. M. A. F. Ibrahim et al. Cairo, 1970–
Al-Istakhri, Abu Ishaq Ibrahim (d. mid-fourth/mid-tenth century):
  Al-Masalik wa'l Mamalik. Ed. M. al-Hini. Cairo, 1961.
Al-Jahiz, ʿAmr b. Bahr (d. 255/868):
  Min Kitab al-Masaʾil wa'l Jawabat fi'l Maʿrifa. Ed. C. Pellat in *Al-Mashriq*, 63/
  3 (May–June, 1969), 315–26.

240   Bibliography

Al-Bayan wa'l Tabyin. Ed. 'A. S. M. Harun. Cairo, 1948–50.
Rasa'il. Ed. 'A. S. M. Harun. Cairo, 1965.
Rasa'il. Ed. H. al-Sandubi. Cairo, 1933.
Kitab al-Hayawan. 2nd edn Ed. 'A. S. M. Harun. Cairo, 1965–9.
Kitab al-Buldan. Ed. S. A. al-'Ali. Baghdad, 1970.
Min Kitab al-Akhbar wa kayfa tasuhh. Ed. C. Pellat in *Journal Asiatique*, 255 (1967), 65–105.
Kitab al-Tarbi' wa'l Tadwir. Ed. C. Pellat. Damascus, 1955.
Al-Jahshiyari, Muhammad b. 'Abdus (d. 331/942):
  Al-Wuzara' wa'l Kuttab. Ed. M. al-Saqqa et al. Cairo, 1938.
Al-Jumahi, Muhammad b. Sallam (d. 231/845):
  Tabaqat al-Shu'ara'. Ed. J. Hell. Leiden, 1913.
Al-Kindi, Abu Yusuf Ya'qub b. Ishaq (d. c. 252/866):
  Rasa'il al-Kindi al-Falsafiyya. Ed. M. 'A. H. Abu Rida. Cairo, 1950–3.
  Risala. Ed. M. Mahdi in 'Uthman Amin, *Nusus Falsafiyya*.
Kurd 'Ali, Muhammad (ed.):
  Rasa'il al-Bulagha'. 3rd edn Cairo, 1946.
Al-Kutubi, Muhammad b. Shakir (d. 766/1363):
  Fawat al-Wafayat. Ed. M. M. 'Abd al-Hamid. Cairo, 1951.
Al-Maqdisi, al-Mutahhar b. Tahir (wrote 355/966):
  Al-Bad' wa'l Ta'rikh. Ed. C. Huart. Paris, 1899–1919.
Al-Marzubani, Abu 'Ubaydullah Muhammad (d. 384/994):
  Al-Muwashshah. Cairo, 1924.
Al-Mas'udi, 'Ali b. al-Husayn (d. 345/956):
  Muruj al-Dhahab wa Ma'adin al-Jawhar. Ed. C. Pellat. Beirut, 1966–79.
  Al-Tanbih wa'l Ishraf. Ed. M. J. de Goeje. Leiden, 1894.
Miskawayhi, Ahmad b. Muhammad (d. 420/1030):
  Tajarib al-Umam. Leiden, 1909.
  Tajarib al-Umam. Ed. H. F. Amedroz. Oxford, 1920.
  Al-Hikma al-Khalida. 2nd edn Ed. 'A. R. Badawi. Beirut, 1980.
  The Refinement of Character. Trans. C. K. Zurayk. Beirut, 1968.
Al-Mu'arrij b. 'Amr al-Sadusi (d. 195/811):
  Hadhf min Nasab Quraysh. Ed. S. al-Munajjid. Beirut, 1976.
Al-Mubarrad, Muhammad b. Yazid (d. 285/898):
  Al-Kamil. Ed. Z. Mubarak. Cairo, 1936.
Al-Muqaddasi, Muhammad b. Ahmad (d. 390/1000):
  Ahsan al-Taqasim fi Ma'rifat al-Aqalim. Ed. M. J. de Goeje. Leiden, 1906.
Mus'ab b. 'Abdullah al-Zubayri (d. 236/851):
  Nasab Quraysh. Ed. E. Lévi-Provençale. Cairo, 1953.
Muslim b. al-Hajjaj al-Qushayri (d. 261/875):
  Sahih. Beirut, 1972.
Al-Nuwayri, Shihab al-Din (d. 732/1332):
  Nihayat al-Arab fi Funun al-Adab. Cairo, 1923–85.
Al-Qali, Abu 'Ali Isma'il b. al-Qasim (d. 356/967):
  Al-Amali. Cairo, 1906.
Al-Qazwini, Zakariyya b. Muhammad (d. 682/1283):
  'Aja'ib al-Makhluqat wa Ghara'ib al-Mawjudat. Ed. F. Wustenfeld. Göttingen, 1848–9.

Athar al-Bilad wa Akhbar al-'Ibad. (printed with above)
Qudama b. Ja'far al-Katib, Abu'l Faraj (d. *c.* 328/939):
  Naqd al-Shi'r. Ed. S. A. Bonebakker. Leiden, 1956.
  Naqd al-Nathr. (attrib.) Ed. T. Husayn and 'A. H. 'Abbadi. Cairo, 1933.
Al-Razi, Abu Hatim Ahmad b. Hamdan (d. *c.* 322/933):
  A'lam al-Nubuwwa. Ed. S. al-Sawi. Tehran, 1977.
Al-Sabi, Hilal b. al-Muhassin (d. 448/1056):
  Tuhfat al-Umara' fi Tarikh al-Wuzara'. Ed. 'A. S. Farraj. Cairo, 1958.
Al-Safadi, Khalil b. Aybak (d. 766/1363):
  Al-Wafi bi'l Wafayat. Ed. H. Ritter *et al.* Istanbul, 1931–
  Nusrat al-Tha'ir 'ala al-Mathal al-Sa'ir. Ed. M. 'A. Sultani. Damascus, 1971.
Al-Sahib b. 'Abbad, Abu'l Qasim Isma'il (d. 385/995):
  Rasa'il. Cairo, 1947.
Sa'id b. Ahmad b. 'Abd al-Rahman al-Andalusi (d. 462/1070):
  Tabaqat al-Umam. Ed. L. Cheikho. Beirut, 1912.
Al-San'ani, Abu Bakr 'Abd al-Razzaq (d. 211/826):
  Al-Musannaf. Ed. H. R. al-A'zami. Beirut, 1970–2.
Sayf b. 'Umar al-Dabbi (d. 180/796):
  Al-Fitnah wa Waq'at al-Jamal. Ed. A. R. 'Armush. Beirut, 1980.
Al-Shafi'i, Muhammad b. Idris (d. 204/820):
  Risala. Ed. A. M. Shakir. Cairo, 1940.
Al-Shahrzuri (wrote seventh/thirteenth century)
  See 'Uthman Amin, *Nusus Falsafiyya.*
Sibt b. al-Jawzi, Shams al-Din Yusuf (d. 654/1256):
  Mir'at al-Zaman. Vol. 8. Haidarabad, 1951.
  Al-Jalis al-Salih wa'l Anis al-Nasih. Ed. F. Fawwaz. London, 1989.
Al-Sijistani, Abu Hatim Sahl b. Muhammad (d. 255/869):
  Al-Mu'ammarin wa'l Wasaya. Ed. 'A. M. 'Amir. Cairo, 1961.
Al-Sijistani, Abu Ya'qub (d. *c.* 360/970):
  Kitab Ithbat al-Nubu'at. Ed. 'A. Tamir. Beirut, 1966.
Al-Sirafi, Abu Sa'id al-Hasan b. 'Abdullah (d. 368/979):
  Akhbar al-Nahwiyyin al-Basriyyin. Ed. F. Krenkow. Paris/Beirut, 1936.
Al-Subki, Taj al-Din 'Abd al-Wahhab b. 'Ali (d. 771/1369):
  Tabaqat al-Shafi'iyya al-Kubra. Ed. M. M. al-Tinahi *et al.* Cairo, 1964.
  Mu'id al-Ni'am wa Mubid al-Niqam. Ed. M. 'A. al-Najjar *et al.* Cairo, 1948.
Al-Sulami, Muhammad b. al-Husayn (d. 412/1021):
  Tabaqat al-Sufiyya. Ed. J. Pedersen. Paris, 1938.
Al-Suli, Muhammad b. Yahya (d. 335/946):
  Akhbar Abi Tammam. Ed. K. M. 'Asakir *et al.* Cairo, 1937.
  Adab al-Kuttab. Ed. M. B. al-Athari. Cairo, 1922.
  Akhbar al-Radi Billah wa'l Muttaqi Lillah. Ed. J. Heyworth-Dunne. London, 1935.
Al-Tabari, Muhammad b. Jarir (d. 310/923):
  Ta'rikh al-Rusul wa'l Muluk. Ed. M. J. de Goeje *et al.* Leiden, 1879–1901.
  Tafsir. Cairo, 1905.
Al-Tanukhi, Abu 'Ali al-Muhassin (d. 384/994):
  Nishwar al-Muhadara. Ed. D. S. Margoliouth. London, 1921.
  Al-Faraj ba'd al-Shidda. Cairo, 1955.

Al-Tawhidi, Abu Hayyan (d. after 400/1010):
  Al-Imta' wa'l Mu'anasa. Ed. A. Amin and A. al-Zayn. Cairo, 1939.
  Al-Muqabasat. Ed. H. al-Sandubi. Cairo, 1929.
Al-Tha'alibi, Abu Mansur 'Abd al-Malik b. Muhammad (d. 429/1038):
  Lata'if al-Ma'arif. Ed. P. de Jong. Leiden, 1867.
Al-Tha'alibi, Abu Mansur al-Mirghani (d. after 412/1021):
  Ghurar Akhbar Muluk al-Furs wa Siyarihim. Ed. H. Zotenberg. Paris, 1890.
Al-Turtushi, Abu Bakr Muhammad b. al-Walid (d. 520/1126):
  Siraj al-Muluk. Ed. J. al-Bayati. London, 1990.
Al-'Umari, Ahmad b. Yahya b. Fadlallah (d. 749/1349):
  Al-Ta'rif bi'l Mustalah al-Sharif. Cairo, 1894.
Al-Waqidi, Muhammad b. 'Umar (d. 207/823):
  Al-Maghazi. Ed. J. Marsden Jones. London, 1966.
Al-Ya'qubi, Ahmad b. Abi Ya'qub b. Wadih (d. c.284/897):
  Tarikh. Beirut, 1960.
  Al-Buldan. Ed. M. J. de Goeje. Leiden, 1892.
  Mushakalat al-Nas li Zamanihim. Ed. W. Millward. Beirut, 1962.
Yaqut al-Hamawi, Abu 'Abdullah (d. 626/1229):
  Irshad al-Arib ila Ma'rifat al-Adib. Ed. A. F. al-Rifa'i. Cairo, 1936.
  Mu'jam al-Buldan. Ed. F. Wustenfeld. Leipzig, 1866.
Al-Yunini, Qutb al-Din (d. 726/1326):
  Dhayl Mir'at al-Zaman. Haidarabad, 1954.
Al-Zajjaji, Abu'l Qasim 'Abd al-Rahman (d. 340/951):
  Majalis al-'Ulama'. Ed. A. S. M. Harun. Kuwait, 1962.
Al-Zubayr b. Bakkar (d. 256/870):
  Jamharat Nasab Quraysh wa Akhbariha. Vol. 1. Ed. M. M. Shakir. Cairo, 1962.

Index

Arabia (*cont.*)
  antiquities of, in *Adab*, 84, 86, 89
  Arabism of, in Ibn Khaldun, 224
  jahili, 1, 6–7
  northern civilization of, 1, 2
  southern civilization of, 2
Aristotle, 134, 149, 160, 163–5, 168, 170
  concept of time in, and Islamic
    philosophy, 158
  Poetics of, and history, 162–3
asatir, 8
Ash'arites, 154, 156, 157, 159, 203
al-'Askari, Abu Hilal, 119
  on ancient history, 119
  on 'firsts', 122
al-Asma'i, 'Abd al-Malik, 6, 88, 101
astrology, 120, 136, 165
  'Abd al-Jabbar on, 156
  and astronomy, 121
  Indian, 181
  and the Mu'tazilites, 121
  and traditional dating, 120
astronomy, 120, 136, 165, 178
  and the age of the world, 121
  and astrology, 121
  Indian, 181
  and traditional dating, 120
awa'il, 33, 58, 122, 205
  in Hisham al-Kalbi, 53
  in Wahb b. Munabbih, 71
'Awana b. al-Hakam, 52, 76
al-Awza'i, 'Abd al-Rahman, 24
Ayyam al-'Arab, 6, 30
  and *Adab*, 84, 87, 91
  echoed in the Qur'an, 12
  and *futuh* historiography, 63, 67
al-Azdi, Muhammad b. 'Abdullah, 67

Badi' al-Zaman al-Hamadhani, 221–2
al-Baghdadi, 'Abd al-Qahir, 140, 146–8
  on *akhbar*, 147–8, 150
  on charisms, 157
  on knowledge, 146
  on *tawatur*, 140
al-Baghdadi, Abu'l Barakat, 163
  critique of history by, 163
  on the history of science, 166
al-Baghdadi, al-Khatib, 207
bahth, 132, 134, 141, 166
  concept of, in Jahiz, 107
  concept of, in Mas'udi, 135
al-Baladhuri, Ahmad b. Yahya, 58–61, 67–8
  Ansab of, 58–61
  Futuh of, 67–8
  contrasted with Sayf, 68
  critical tools of, 60–1, 68
  and Tabari, 73

al-Baqillani, Abu Bakr, 156
  on custom, 157
  on miracles, 157
Basra, 15, 85
  as home of specialists, 101
al-Basri, Abu'l Husayn, 140, 148–9, 150
  on *akhbar*, 140–1, 148–9
Bible, 1, 68, 69
  age of world in, 120–1
Biblical historical materials, 37, 43, 70, 78
  and Christian historiography, 1
  figures of, as city founders, 119
  in Tabari, 78
biographical dictionaries, 184, 204–10
  and *Adab*, 205–7, 210
  centennial, 209
  and *Hadith*, 208–10
  identified with history, 207, 210
  influence of *Hadith* and *Adab* on, 205
  of professional classes, 206
  selection of entries in, 209
  see also tabaqa
al-Biruni, Abu'l Rayhan, 176–81, 223
  on chronology, 177–9
  and foreign cultures, 177
  on the history of science, 165–6, 177
  on natural oddities, 179
  on possibility, 178
  on scientific progress, 177
al-Bukhari, Muhammad b. Isma'il, 59
Byzantium, 14, 103, 107, 117, 165
  bureaucracy of, 15, 90

causation, 128–9, 156
  in Hamza al-Isfahani, 128
  in Ibn Khaldun, 227
  of intellectual progress and decline, 165–8
  in Jahiz, 128
  in Mas'udi, 134
China, 103, 117, 185
  arts and crafts of, 165
  bureaucracy of, 90
Christianity, 2, 69, 176, 180, 187, 190
  chronologies of, 179
  missionary activity of, 2
  philosophers of, 156
  polemics of Muslims against, 106, 146
  relations of, with early Muslim societies, 69
  tawatur of, 147
consensus, 45, 135
  as confirming truth, 57
  and early jurists, 45
  and genealogy, 57
  genesis of, 45 and n. 47
  and ruling circles, 45
  and *tawatur*, 141

tafsir, 31
time scale in, 9
view of history in, 7, 8, 13, 35, 78
and writing, 6
Quraysh, 30, 55–9, 224, 228
and dating of events, 119

rawiya, 5–6, 205
jahili, 5, 23
and *khabar*, 5
and the Muslim historian, 5
al-Razi, Muhammad b. Zakariyya, 152
in Biruni, 177
on miracles, 152–3

al-Sabi, Hilal, 123, 203
sabiqa, 23, 49
al-Safadi, Khalil b. Aybak, 208–9
on biographical entries, 210
on the value of history, 216
Sa'id al-Andalusi, 167
Sayf b. 'Umar, 63–4, 76, 80
contrasted with Baladhuri, 68
as historian of civil war, 64
as historian of conquests, 63
Seljuqs, 183, 190, 202, 212, 214
as patrons of *'ulama'*, 192
and Sufi brotherhoods, 211–12
and Sunni law schools, 192–3
al-Shafi'i, Muhammad b. Idris, 88, 141, 143, 203, 207
on *akhbar*, 137–9
political theory of school of, 192
on reason and proof, 137
on *sunna*, 137
shari'a, 17, 183
contrasted with *siyasa*, 193–200, 219
Shi'a, Shi'i, 40, 42, 50, 152, 193
and early historiography, 40
historiographic demarcation of, from Sunnism, 111
in Mas'udi, 136, 198, 226
in Muslim's *Sahih*, 42
Shu'ubiyya controversy, 102–3
Ibn Qutayba on, 109
Sibt ibn al-Jawzi, Shams al-Din, 195, 208, 213 and n. 61
on schools of historians, 202
on *shari'a* and *siyasa*, 195–6
al-Sijistani, Abu Ya'qub, 160–2
on prophecy, 161–2
on religious law, 161
on time, 162
sira, 28–9, 30, 35, 51, 86
synonymous with history, 184, 204
in Tabari, 73, 79
siyasa, 182–231
contrasted with *shari'a*, 183, 193–200

primary definitions of, 197
and the sultanate, 183
al-Subki, Taj al-Din, 187, 195, 203, 206, 209
on citing sources, 219
on Ibn Khallikan, 207
and the Mamluks, 187, 196
on rules for historians, 203–4
on *shari'a* and *siyasa*, 196
on the sultanate, 196, 218
Sufis, 154, 180, 189, 192, 203, 205
biographical dictionaries of, 206
and chain of witnesses, 206
'high' and 'low', 211
and historiography, 210–15
and miracles, 154, 212–13
and sanctity of land, 220
al-Sulami, Muhammad b. al-Husayn, 206, 209
al-Suli, Muhammad b. Yahya, 99–101, 115, 122
sultanate, 183, 201–2
as the great imamate, 196
and *siyasa*, 183
and the *'ulama'*, 191–3
sunna, 28, 42, 144
Sunni, 111, 155, 193, 198
Hadith establishment, 50
historiographic tradition, 226
political theory, 192
schools of law, 192
Syria, 1, 14–15, 33, 46, 65, 67, 89, 192

tabaqa, 46–8
and biographical dictionaries, 205
in Ibn Sa'd, 46
and *nasab*, 49, 55
as a time division, 46
al-Tabari, Muhammad b. Jarir, 45, 53, 63, 73–82, 128, 178, 181, 226–7
Adam and Satan in, 79–80
annalistic structure in, 79–80
attitude of, to experts, 77–8
on civil war, 80–1
consensus in, 74
contrast between *History* and *Commentary* of, 76
and earlier historians, 73, 75–6, 80
and historical eras, 120
History of, 75–82
and Ibn al-Kalbi, 77
inference in, 75
intention of, 79
isnad in, 74, 77
and knowledge of the past, 73–4, 80
poetry in, 74
possibility in, 76–7
qiyas in, 74, 75

al-Tabari (*cont.*)
  Qur'anic *Commentary* of, 74–5, 80–1
  and struggle of prophets and kings, 79
al-Tanukhi, Abu 'Ali, 113–14, 115, 122
tawatur, 106, 135
  'Abd al-Jabbar on, 144
  Baghdadi on, 140, 147–8
  of Christians, 147
  and consensus, 141
  Nazzam on, 139–40
  see also khabar
al-Tawhidi, Abu Hayyan, 108, 119
  on the history of science, 166
al-Tha'alibi, Abu Mansur, 129
time, 3–4, 7, 9, 12, 158–62, 186, 189
  and being, 159
  Biruni on, 177
  as circular, 159, 176
  concept of, in Islamic philosophy, 158–62
  as a continuum, 159
  geological, 160
  infinite, 159
  in the Isma'ili view, 161–2
  as psychic, 160
  and the world, 159, 160
Turks, 117, 165, 183
  in Ibn Khaldun, 229–30
al-Turtushi, Abu Bakr Muhammad, 189,
    222, 224, 231
  on injustice of the ruler, 194
  on ruler and subjects, 218
  on *siyasa* and *shari'a*, 193–4, 195
  on social rank, 189
  on the state, 195

'ulama', 86, 188, 191–3, 196, 202, 212
  biographies of, 205, 207, 209
  and historians, 200
  and Sufis, 212–13
  and sultans, 191–3
'Umar b. 'Abd al-'Aziz, 45
'Umara b. Wathima, 71
Umayyads, 27, 30–1, 34–5, 40, 55
  and *Adab*, 84–5
  in Ibn Khaldun, 198–9
  image of, in Abbasid period, 111
  state secretaries of, and *Adab*, 89–96
  and uniformity in law, 45

and written traditions, 27
'Urwa b. al-Zubayr, 30–2, 34, 36, 44
  and official 'orthodoxy', 35
  use of *isnad* by, 31
  and Zubayrid school of jurists, 30

Vico, Giambattista, 167

Wahb b. Munabbih, 7, 36, 70–1, 104
  and tales of prophets, 69
  and Yemeni antiquities, 7
al-Waqidi, Muhammad b. 'Umar, 44–8,
    51–3, 59, 68, 76, 119
  critical attitude of, 47
  dating in, 45–6
  historical method of, 47–8
  and Ibn Ishaq, 48
  life of Muhammad in, 48
  tabaqat of, 46
  and Tabari, 73, 77, 80–1
  'updating' in, 46–7
  use of consensus by, 45, 73
  use of *isnad* by, 48

al-Ya'qubi, Ahmad b. Abi Ya'qub, 2, 115–
    18, 120–1, 131–2, 226
  astrology in, 120
  astronomy in, 121
  geography in works of, 116–17, 124, 219
  historical patterns in, 117, 124–5
  on the Umayyads, 198
Yaqut al-Hamawi, 184, 231
  biographical dictionary of, 206
  on his own times, 184–5
  on topography, 220
Yemenite, Yemen, 7, 37
  historical materials, 7, 37, 71
  in Tabari, 78

al-Zubayr b. Bakkar, 56–8
  and the Zubayrid literary tradition, 56–7
al-Zuhri, Muhammad b. Muslim, 21, 30,
    32–4, 36, 39, 44, 66
  and official 'orthodoxy', 35
  and the Umayyad court, 33
  use of *isnad* by, 33
  on writing, 21